JONATHAN SWIFT

JOURNAL

TO

STELLA

JONATHAN SWIFT
From the portrait by Charles Jervas in the National Portrait Gallery, London

JONATHAN SWIFT

JOURNAL
TO
STELLA

Edited by HAROLD WILLIAMS

VOLUME II

OXFORD
AT THE CLARENDON PRESS

Oxford University Press, Amen House, London E.C.4

GLASGOW NEW YORK TORONTO MELBOURNE WELLINGTON
BOMBAY CALCUTTA MADRAS KARACHI LAHORE DACCA
CAPE TOWN SALISBURY NAIROBI IBADAN ACCRA
KUALA LUMPUR HONG KONG

FIRST PUBLISHED 1948
REPRINTED LITHOGRAPHICALLY IN GREAT BRITAIN
AT THE UNIVERSITY PRESS, OXFORD
FROM SHEETS OF THE FIRST IMPRESSION
1963

CONTENTS

VOLUME II

LIST OF PLATES

VOLUME II

LETTER XXXI

London, Sept. 25, 1711.

I DINED in the city to-day, and at my return I put my 30th into the post-office; and when I got home I found for me one of the noblest letters I ever read; it was from ——, three sides and a half in folio on a large sheet of paper; the two first pages made up of satire upon London, and crowds and hurry, stolen from some of his own schoolboy's exercises: the side and a half remaining is spent in desiring me to recommend Mrs. South, your commissioner's[1] widow, to my lord treasurer for a pension. He is the prettiest, discreetest fellow that ever my eyes beheld, or that ever dipt pen into ink. I know not what to say to him. A pox on him, I have too many such customers on this side already. I think I will send him word that I never saw my lord treasurer in my life: I am sure I industriously avoided the name of any great person when I saw him, for fear of his reporting it in Ireland. And this recommendation must be a secret too, for fear the duke of Bolton[2] should know it, and think it was too mean. I never read so d——d a letter in my life: a little would make me send it over to you.—I must send you a pattern, the first place I cast my eyes on, I will not pick and chuse. [In this place (meaning the Exchange in London) which is the compendium of old Troynovant, as that is of the whole busy world, I got such a surfeit, that I grew sick of mankind, and resolved, for ever after, to bury myself in the

---

1 Cf. p. 116 n.41 Her husband, a Commissioner of the Revenue in Ireland, had died recently. Two years later Swift was still soliciting assistance for her (*Corresp.* ii. 73, 95). Her petitioner was Archdeacon Walls, as appears later (pp. 425, 486). In July he had gone back to Ireland (pp. 318-9) and recorded his experience of London in the letter Swift ridicules.

2 Charles Paulet, or Powlett, 1661-1722, second Duke of Bolton and seventh Marquis of Winchester. He held minor offices during the reigns of William III and Anne. From 1717 to 1719 he was Lord Lieutenant of Ireland. Swift characterized him as 'a great Booby' (*Prose Works*, x. 274).

shady retreat of ———.][3] You must know that London has been called by some Troynovant, or New Troy.— Will you have any more? Yes, one little bit for Stella, because she'll be fond of it. [This wondrous Theatre (meaning London) was no more to me than a desert, and I should less complain of solitude in a Connaught shipwreck, or even the great Bog of Allen.] A little scrap for Mrs. Marget,[4] and then I have done. [Their royal *Fanum*, wherein the Idol *Pecunia* is daily worshipped, seemed to me to be just like a hive of bees working and labouring under huge weights of cares.] *Fanum* is a temple, but he means the Exchange; and *Pecunia* is money: so now Mrs. Marget will understand her part. One more paragraph, and I—Well, come don't be in such a rage, you shall have no more. Pray, Stella, be satisfied; 'tis very pretty; and that I must be acquainted with such a dog as this!——— Our Peace goes on fast. Prior was with the secretary two hours this morning: I was there a little after he went away, and was told it. I believe he will soon be dispatched again to France; and I will put somebody to write an account of his second journey: I hope you have seen the other. This letter[5] has taken up my time with storming at it.

26. Bernage has been with me these two days; yesterday I sent for him to let him know, that Dr. Arbuthnott is putting in strongly to have his brother[6] made a captain over Bernage's head. Arbuthnott's brother is but an

[3] The brackets, used by Deane Swift, represent quotation marks.

[4] p. 276 n.[24]

[5] Deane Swift, followed by subsequent editors, except Scott, reads 'latter'. But this is clearly a printer's error.

[6] George Arbuthnot was born in 1688. On 27 Sept. 1711 he was gazetted Lieutenant in a regiment of foot raised for Col. Kilner Brasier. On 10 Sept. 1712 he became a Captain in the Earl of Orrery's regiment of foot, and, 26 Apr. 1714, Captain in Maj.-Gen. Wetham's regiment of foot (Dalton's *Army Lists*, vi. 164–5, 234, 253; *George the First's Army*, i. 164; Aitken, *Life and Works of Arbuthnot*, p. 40 n.[3]). He appears to have taken part in the rising of 1715. The date of his death is uncertain (Aitken, op. cit., pp. 84, 159 n.[2]). For Bernage see p. 141 n.[12]

ensign; but the doctor has great power with the queen: yet he told me, he would not do any thing hard to a gentleman who is my friend; and I have engaged the secretary and his colonel[7] for him. To-day he told me very melancholy, that the other had written from Windsor (where he went to solicit) that he has got the company; and Bernage is full of the spleen. I made the secretary write yesterday a letter to the colonel in Bernage's behalf. I hope it will do yet; and I have written to Dr. Arbuthnott to Windsor, not to insist on doing such a hardship. I dined in the city at Pontack's with Stratford; it cost me seven shillings: he would have treated; but I did not let him. I have removed my money from the bank to another fund. I desire Parvisol may speak to Hawkshaw to pay in my money when he can; for I will put it in the funds; and in the mean time borrow so much of Mr. secretary, who offers to lend it me. Go to the dean's, sirrahs.

27. Bernage was with me again to-day, and is in great fear, and so was I; but this afternoon at lord treasurer's, where I dined, my brother George Granville, secretary at war, after keeping me a while in suspence, told me, that Dr. Arbuthnott had waved the business, because he would not wrong a friend of mine; that his brother is to be a lieutenant, and Bernage is made a captain. I called at his lodging, and the soldier's Coffee-house, to put him out of pain, but cannot find him; so I have left word, and shall see him to-morrow morning, I suppose. Bernage is now easy; he has ten shillings a day, beside lawful cheating. However, he gives a private sum to his colonel; but it is very cheap: his colonel loves him well, but is surprized to see him have so many friends. So he is now quite off my hands.—I left the company early to-night at lord treasurer's; but the secretary followed me, to desire I would go with him to W—. Mr. Lewis's man came in before I could finish that word beginning with a W, which ought to be Windsor, and brought me a very handsome

7 Col. Edmund Fielding (p. 196 n.[26]).

rallying letter from Dr. Arbuthnott, to tell me, he had, in compliance to me, given up his brother's pretensions in favour of Bernage this very morning; that the queen had spoken to Mr. Granville to make the company easy in the other's having the captainship. Whether they have done it to oblige me or no, I must own it so. He says, he this very morning begged her majesty to give Mr. Bernage the company. I am mightily well pleased to have succeeded so well; but you will think me tedious, although you like the man, as I think.

Windsor, 28. I came here a day sooner than ordinary, at Mr. secretary's desire, and supped with him and Prior, and two private ministers from France, and a French priest.[8] I know not the two ministers names; but they are come about the Peace. The names the secretary called them, I suppose, were feigned; they were good rational men. We have already settled all things with France, and very much to the honour and advantage of England; and the queen is in mighty good humour. All this news is a mighty secret; the people in general know that a Peace is forwarding. The earl of Strafford is to go soon to Holland and let them know what we have been doing: and then there will be the devil and all to pay; but we'll make them swallow it with a pox. The French ministers staid with us till one, and the secretary and I sat up talking till two; so you will own 'tis late, sirrahs, and time for your little saucy Presto to go to bed and sleep adazy; and God bless poor little MD: I hope they are now fast asleep and dreaming of Presto.

[8] Cf. pp. 339, 349, and notes. The secret envoys were Mesnager and the Abbé Du Bois; the priest was the Abbé Gaultier. Cf. the account of this meeting which Swift sent to Archbishop King (*Corresp.* i. 290). On the previous day, 27 Sept., Mesnager had signed preliminary articles of peace on behalf of Louis XIV, and St. John and Dartmouth on behalf of Anne. On the 29th Mesnager and Gaultier were admitted to a secret audience with the Queen. According to Sheridan, *Life*, 1784, p. 429, Swift was present, acting as interpreter, at one of the private conferences between the Ministry and the French envoys. But the story is questionable.

29. Lord treasurer came to-night, as usual, at half an hour after eight, as dark as pitch. I am weary of chiding him; so I commended him for observing his friends advice, and coming so early, &c. I was two hours with lady Oglethorp[9] to-night, and then supped with lord treasurer, after dining at the green-cloth: I stayed till two; this is the effect of lord treasurer's being here; I must sup with him, and he keeps cursed hours. Lord keeper and the secretary were absent; they cannot sit up with him. This long sitting up makes the periods in my letters so short. I design to stay here all the next week, to be at leisure by myself, to finish something of weight I have upon my hands, and which must soon be done.[10] I shall then think of returning to Ireland, if these people will let me; and I know nothing else they have for me to do. I gave Dr. Arbuthnott my thanks for his kindness to Bernage, whose commission is now signed. Methinks I long to know something of Stella's health, how it continues after Wexford waters.

30. The queen was not at chapel to-day, and all for the better, for we had a dunce to preach: she has a little of the gout. I dined with my brother Masham and a moderate company, and would not go to lord treasurer's till after supper at eleven o'clock, and pretended I had mistaken the hour; so I ate nothing: and a little after twelve the company broke up, the keeper and secretary refusing to stay; so I saved this night's debauch. Prior went away yesterday with his Frenchmen, and a thousand reports are raised in this town. Some said, they knew one to be the Abbé de Polignac:[11] others swore it was the Abbé du

9 Sir Theophilus Oglethorpe, 1650–1702, Brigadier-General, married Eleanor, daughter of Richard Wall of Rogane, Tipperary. She bore him seven children and died in 1732. One of her children was James Edward Oglethorpe, the colonist of Georgia and friend of Dr. Johnson.

10 *The Conduct of the Allies.*

11 Melchior de Polignac, 1661–1741, the brilliant diplomat and politician, a representative of France at the conferences of Gertruydenberg and Utrecht. He became a cardinal in 1713.

Bois.[12] The Whigs are in a rage about the Peace; but we'll wherret[13] them, I warrant, boys. Go, go, go to the dean's, and don't mind politicks, young women, they are not good after the waters; they are stark naught; they strike up into the head. Go, get two black aces, and fish for a manilio.[14]

Oct. 1.[15] Sir John Walters,[16] an honest drunken fellow, is now in waiting, and invited me to the green-cloth to-day, that he might not be behind hand with colonel Godfrey, who is a Whig. I was engaged to the Mayor's feast with Mr. Masham; but waiting to take leave of lord treasurer, I came too late, and so returned sneaking to the green-cloth, and did not see my lord treasurer neither; but was resolved not to lose two dinners for him. I took leave to-day of my friend and solicitor lord Rivers, who is commanded by the queen to set out for Hanover on Thursday. The secretary does not go to town till to-morrow: he and I and two friends more drank a sober bottle of wine here at home, and parted at twelve; he goes by seven to-morrow morning, so I shall not see him. I have power over his cellar in his absence, and make little use of it. Lord Dartmouth and my friend Lewis stay here this week; but I can never work out a dinner from Dart-mouth. Masham has promised to provide for me: I squired his lady out of her chaise to-day, and must visit her in a day or two. So you have had a long fit of the finest weather in the world; but I am every day in pain that it will go off. I have done no business to-day: I am very idle.

[12] Guillaume Dubois, 1656–1723, Abbé, later Archbishop of Cambrai and cardinal, who took a prominent part in the negotiations for the Triple Alliance in 1717.   [13] Worry, tease.   [14] p. 43 n.35

[15] On this day Swift sent a long letter of news to King, closing with a reply to advice received from the Archbishop (*Corresp.* i. 288).

[16] Sir John Walter, third baronet of Sardsen, Oxfordshire, who was born about 1673, succeeded to the baronetcy in 1694. He was twice M.P. for Appleby; and M.P. for Oxford in six Parliaments from 1706 to his death in 1722. He was, with Colonel Godfrey (p. 363 n.18), a Clerk Comptroller of the Green Cloth.

2. My friend Lewis and I, to avoid overmuch eating, and great tables, dined with honest Jemmy Eckershall, clerk of the kitchen, now in waiting; and I bespoke my dinner: but the cur had your acquaintance Lovet, the gentleman porter, to be our company: Lovet, towards the end of dinner, after twenty wrigglings, said he had the honour to see me formerly at Moor-park, and thought he remembered my face; I said, I thought I remembered him, and was glad to see him, &c. and I escaped for that much, for he was very pert. It has rained all this day, and I doubt our good weather is gone. I have been very idle this afternoon, playing at twelve-penny picquet with Lewis; I won seven shillings, which is the only money I won this year; I have not played above four times, and I think always at Windsor: cards are very dear, there is a duty on them of sixpence a pack,[17] which spoils small gamesters.

3. Mr. Masham sent this morning to desire I would ride out with him, the weather growing again very fine: I was very busy, and sent my excuses; but desired he would provide me a dinner: I dined with him, his lady, and her sister, Mrs. Hill, who invites us to-morrow to dine with her, and we are to ride out in the morning. I sat with lady Oglethorp till eight this evening, then was going home to write; looked about for the woman that keeps the key of the house; she told me Patrick had it. I cooled my heels in the cloisters till nine, then went in to the musick-meeting, where I had been often desired to go; but was weary in half an hour of their fine stuff,[18] and stole out so privately that every body saw me; and cooled my heels in the cloisters again till after ten: then came in

17 See p. 622 n.[10]

18 '*Swift*, like some others, rather hated than loved musick.'—Deane Swift. For Swift's attitude towards music see *A Tale of a Tub*, ed. Guthkelch and Nichol Smith, pp. 280–1; his satire on the mathematical and musical pursuits of the Laputans in *Gulliver's Travels*; *Poems*, pp. 521–2, 955; and R. W. Jackson, *Jonathan Swift Dean and Pastor*, pp. 142–59.

Patrick. I went up, shut the chamber-door, and gave him two or three swinging cuffs on the ear, and I have strained the thumb of my left hand with pulling him, which I did not feel until he was gone. He was plaguily afraid and humbled.

4. It was the finest day in the world, and we got out before eleven, a noble caravan of us. The duchess of Shrewsbury in her own chaise with one horse, and Miss Touchet[19] with her; Mrs. Masham and Mrs. Scarborow, one of the dressers, in one of the queen's chaises; Miss Forester and Miss Scarborow,[20] two maids of honour, and Mrs. Hill on horseback. The duke of Shrewsbury, Mr. Masham, George Fielding,[21] Arbuthnott and I on horseback too. Mrs. Hill's horse was hired for Miss Scarborow, but she took it in civility, her own horse was galled and could not be rid, but kicked and winced: the hired horse was not worth eighteen pence. I borrowed coat, boots and horse, and in short we had all the difficulties, and more than we used to have in making a party from Trim to Longfield's.[22] My coat was light camblet, faced with red velvet, and silver buttons. We rode in the great park and the forest about a dozen miles, and the duchess and I had much conversation; we got home by two, and Mr. Masham, his lady, Arbuthnott and I dined with Mrs. Hill.

[19] Possibly, as Aitken conjectures, a daughter of Mervyn Tuchet, fourth Earl of Castlehaven. He had three daughters. Eleanor, the eldest, married Sir Henry Wingfield, Bart., of Easton, co. Suffolk. The second and third daughters, Mary and Anne, died unmarried.

[20] Henrietta Maria, daughter of Charles Scarborow (p. 327 n.[29]), who married, 4 Feb. 1711–12, Sir Robert Jenkinson, 1685–1717, third baronet of Walcot and Charlbury (*Wentworth Papers*, pp. 244, 262).

[21] An equerry of the Queen. In July 1712 George Fielding and Conyers Darcy were empowered by commission to execute the office of Master of the Horse.

[22] 'Mr. *Longfield* lived at *Killbride*, about four miles from *Trim*.'— Deane Swift. Robert Longfield, born at Denbigh, Wales, in 1652, obtained extensive grants of lands in cos. Westmeath, Meath, and Clare. He resided at Kilbride, and died in 1710 (Burke's *Landed Gentry of Ireland*).

Arbuthnott made us all melancholy, by some symptoms of bloody ur—e: he expects a cruel fit of the stone in twelve hours; he says he is never mistaken, and he appeared like a man that was to be racked to-morrow. I cannot but hope it will not be so bad; he is a perfectly honest man, and one I have much obligation to. It rained a little this afternoon, and grew fair again. Lady Oglethorp sent to speak to me, and it was to let me know that lady Rochester[23] desires she and I may be better acquainted. 'Tis a little too late; for I am not now in love with lady Rochester: they shame me out of her, because she is old. Arbuthnott says he hopes my strained thumb is not the gout; for he has often found people so mistaken. I do not remember the particular thing that gave it me, only I had it just after beating Patrick, and now it is better; so I believe he is mistaken.

5. The duchess of Shrewsbury sent to invite me to dinner; but I was abroad last night when her servant came, and this morning I sent my excuses, because I was engaged, which I was sorry for. Mrs. Forester taxed me yesterday about the history of the maids of honour; but I told her fairly it was no jest of mine; for I found they did not relish it altogether well: and I have enough already of a quarrel with that brute Sir John Walters, who has been railing at me in all companies ever since I dined with him; that I abused the queen's meat and drink, and said, nothing at the table was good, and all a d—— lie; for, after dinner, commending the wine, I said, I thought it was something small. You would wonder how all my friends laugh at this quarrel. It will be such a jest for the keeper, treasurer, and secretary.——I dined with honest colonel Godfrey, took a good walk of an hour on the terrass, and then came up to study; but it grows bloody cold, and I have no waistcoat here.

6. I never dined with the chaplains till to-day; but my

23 Wife of the Lord Hyde, mentioned 1 Oct. 1710, who succeeded his father as second Earl of Rochester, 2 May 1711 (p. 37 n.[13]).

friend Gastrel and the dean of Rochester had often invited me, and I happened to be disengaged: it is the worst provided table at court. We ate on pewter: every chaplain, when he is made a dean, gives a piece of plate, and so they have got a little, some of it very old. One who was made dean of Peterborow (a small deanry) said, he would give no plate; he was only dean of *Pewterborow*. The news of Mr. Hill's miscarriage in his expedition came to-day,[24] and I went to visit Mrs. Masham and Mrs. Hill, his two sisters, to condole with them. I advised them by all means to go to the musick-meeting to-night, to shew they were not cast down, &c. and they thought my advice was right, and went. I doubt Mr. Hill and his admiral made wrong steps; however, we lay it all to a storm, &c. I sat with the secretary at supper; then we both went to lord treasurer's supper, and sat till twelve. The secretary is much mortified about Hill; because this expedition was of his contriving, and he counted much upon it; but lord treasurer was just as merry as usual, and old[25] laughing at Sir John Walters and me falling out. I said, Nothing grieved me, but that they would take example, and perhaps presume upon it, and get out of my government; but that I thought I was not obliged to govern bears, though I governed men. They promise to be as obedient as ever, and so we laughed; —and so I go to bed; for it is colder still, and you have a fire now, and are at cards at home.

7. Lord Harley and I dined privately to-day with Mrs. Masham and Mrs. Hill, and my brother Masham. I saw lord Hallifax at Court, and we joined and talked, and the duchess of Shrewsbury came up and reproached me for not dining with her: I said, That was not so soon done; for I expected more advances from ladies, especially duchesses: she promised to comply with any demands I pleased; and I agreed to dine with her to-morrow, if I did not go to London too soon, as I believe I shall before dinner. Lady Oglethorp brought me and the duchess of Hamilton to-

[24] See p. 257 n.³   [25] See p. 100 n.³⁵

gether to-day in the drawing-room, and I have given her some encouragement, but not much. Every body has been teazing Walters. He told lord treasurer, that he took his company from him that were to dine with him; my lord said, I will send you Dr. Swift: lord keeper bid him take care what he did; For, said he, Dr. Swift is not only all our favourite, but our governor. The old company supped with lord treasurer, and got away by twelve.

London, 8. I believe I shall go no more to Windsor; for we expect the queen will come in ten days to Hampton-Court. It was frost last night, and cruel cold to-day. I could not dine with the duchess; for I left Windsor half an hour after one with lord treasurer, and we called at Kensington, where Mrs. Masham was got to see her children for two days. I dined, or rather supped with lord treasurer, and staid till after ten. Tisdall[26] and his family are gone from hence, upon some wrangle with the family. Yesterday I had two letters brought me to Mr. Masham's; one from Ford, and t'other from our little MD, N. 21. I would not tell you till to-day, because I would not. I won't answer it till the next, because I slipt two days by being at Windsor, which I must recover here. Well, sirrahs, I must go to sleep. The roads were as dry as at Midsummer to-day. This letter shall go to-morrow.

9. Morning. It rains hard this morning; I suppose our fair weather is now at an end. I think I'll put on my waist-coat to-day: shall I? Well, I will then, to please MD. I think of dining at home to-day upon a chop and a pot. The town continues yet very thin. Lord Strafford is gone to Holland to tell them what we have done here towards a Peace. We shall soon hear what the Dutch say, and how they take it. My humble service to Mrs. Walls, Mrs. Stoyte and Catherine.—Morrow, dearest sirrahs, and farewell; and God Almighty bless MD, poor, little, dear MD, for so I mean, and Presto too. I'll write to

[26] See p. 310 n.[15]

you again to-night, that is, I'll begin my next letter. Farewel, &c.

This little bit belongs to MD; we must always write on the margin:[27] you are saucy rogues.

LETTER XXXII

[TUESDAY]   London, October 9, 1711.

I WAS forced to lie down at twelve to-day, and mend my night's sleep: I slept till after two, and then sent for a bit of mutton and pot of ale from the next cook's shop, and had no stomach. I went out at four, and called to see Biddy Floyd, which I had not done these three months: she is something marked, but has recovered her complexion quite, and looks very well. Then I sat the evening with Mrs. Vanhomrigh, and drank coffee, and ate an egg. I likewise took a new lodging to-day, not liking a ground floor, nor the ill smell, and other circumstances. I lodge, or shall lodge, by Leicester-Fields,[1] and pay ten shillings a week; that won't hold out long, faith. I shall lie here but one night more. It rained terribly till one o'clock to-day. I lie, for I shall lie here two nights, till Thursday, and then remove. Did I tell you that my friend Mrs. Barton has a brother drowned,[2] that went on the expedition with Jack Hill? He was a lieutenant-colonel, and a coxcomb; and she keeps her chamber in form, and the servants say, she receives no messages.—Answer MD's letter, Presto, d'ye hear? No, says Presto, I won't yet, I'm busy: you're a saucy rogue. Who talks?

[27] 'This happens to be the only single line written upon the margin of any of his journals. By some accident there was a margin about as broad as the back of a razor, and therefore he made this use of it.'—Deane Swift.

[1] For Swift's changes of lodging see p. 142 n.[16]

[2] Probably identical with the Robert Barton, who, 24 June 1706, was appointed by Marlborough a Captain in Lieut.-General Meredyth's regiment of foot. At the time of his death, 22 Aug. 1711, he was Lieut.-Colonel of Colonel Kane's regiment of foot (Dalton's *Army Lists*, vi. 347–8).

10. It cost me two shillings in coach-hire to dine in the city with a printer. I have sent, and caused to be sent, three pamphlets out in a fortnight.[3] I will ply the rogues warm, and whenever any thing of theirs makes a noise, it shall have an answer. I have instructed an under-spur-leather to write so, that it is taken for mine. A rogue that writes a news-paper called *The Protestant Post-boy*,[4] has reflected on me in one of his papers; but the secretary has taken him up, and he shall have a squeeze extraordinary. He says, that an ambitious Tantivy,[5] missing of his towering hopes of preferment in Ireland, is come over to vent his spleen on the late ministry, &c. I'll *Tantivy* him with a vengeance. I sat the evening at home, and am very busy, and can hardly find time to write, unless it were to MD. I am in furious haste.

11. I dined to-day with lord treasurer. Thursdays are now his days when his choice company comes, but we are too much multiplied. George Granville sent his excuses upon being ill; I hear he apprehends the apoplexy, which would grieve me much. Lord treasurer calls Prior nothing but *Monsieur Baudrier*, which was the feigned name of the Frenchman that writ his journey to Paris. They pretend to suspect me; so I talk freely of it, and put them out of their play. Lord treasurer calls me now Dr. Martin, because *Martin*[6] is a sort of swallow, and so is a *Swift*.

³ Swift's statements of time and date are not always careful; nor is it clear whether 'sent . . . out' refers to publication or dispatch to the printer. But the pamphlets he had in mind must be (1) *A New Journey to Paris*, first edition 11 Sept., second edition 20 Sept.; (2) *The Duke of M[arlboroug]h's Vindication*, advertised in *The Spectator*, 26 Sept., *The Daily Courant*, 1 Oct.; (3) *A Learned Comment upon Dr. Hare's Excellent Sermon*, advertised in *The Post Boy*, 2–4 Oct. The *Vindication* was by Mrs. Manley (*post*, p. 390). Swift's part in *A Learned Comment* seems to have been larger than he was prepared to admit (*post*, p. 402; and *Prose Works*, v. 171–2).

⁴ The first number of this publication appeared on 4 Sept. 1711.

⁵ A post-Restoration nickname for High Churchmen and Tories. The attack appeared in *The Protestant Post-Boy* of 25 Sept. 1711.

⁶ 'From this pleasantry of my Lord *Oxford*, the appellative *Martinus*

When he and I came last Monday from Windsor, we were reading all the signs[7] on the road. He is a pure trifler; tell the bishop of Clogher so. I made him make two lines in verse for the *Bell and Dragon*, and they were rare bad ones. I suppose Dilly is with you by this time: what could his reason be of leaving London, and not owning it? 'Twas plaguy silly. I believe his natural inconstancy made him weary; I think he is the king of inconstancy. I stayed with lord treasurer till ten; we had five lords and three commoners. Go to ombre, sirrahs.

12. Mrs. Vanhomrigh has changed her lodging as well as I. She found she had got with a bawd, and removed:[8] I dined with her to-day; for though she boards, her land-lady does not dine with her. I am grown a mighty lover of herrings; but they are much smaller here than with you. In the afternoon I visited an old major-general, and eat six oysters; then sat an hour with Mrs. Colledge, the joiner's daughter that was hanged; it was the joiner was hanged, and not his daughter; with Thompson's wife, a magistrate. There was the famous Mrs. Floyd of Chester, who, I think, is the handsomest woman (except MD) that ever I saw. She told me, that twenty people had sent her the verses upon *Biddy*,[9] as meant to her: and indeed, in point of handsomeness, she deserves them much better. I will

Scriblerus took its rise.'—Deane Swift. In the winter of 1713–14 the Scriblerus Club was formed by Pope, Swift, Arbuthnot, and Gay, with Parnell as an occasional visitor. From this association sprang the *Memoirs of Scriblerus*, not published till 1741, and in some degree *Gulliver's Travels*. See *Poems*, pp. 184–8; and R. J. Allen's *Clubs of Augustan London*, pp. 260–83.

[7] In his *Imitation of the Sixth Satire of the Second Book of Horace*, 1714, Swift describes how he and Oxford, in their drives together on the Windsor road, would

> gravely try to read the Lines
> Writ underneath the Country Signs.

Poems, p. 201.

[8] See p. 360. On 11 Oct. Swift moved to St. Martin's Street, Leicester Fields (p. 142 n.[16]).

[9] Written in 1709. See p. 217 n.[8]; and *Poems*, p. 117.

not go to Windsor to-morrow, and so I told the secretary to-day. I hate the thoughts of Saturday and Sunday suppers with lord treasurer. Jack Hill is come home from his unfortunate expedition, and is, I think, now at Windsor: I have not yet seen him. He is privately blamed by his own friends for want of conduct. He called a council of war, and therein it was determined to come back. But they say, a general should not do that, because the officers will always give their opinion for returning, since the blame will not lie upon them, but the general: I pity him heartily. Bernage received his commission to-day.

13. I dined to-day with colonel Crowe, late governor of Barbadoes; he is a great acquaintance of your friend Sterne, to whom I trusted the box. Lord treasurer has refused Sterne's business; and I doubt he is a rake; Jemmy Leigh stays for him, and nobody knows where to find him. I am so busy now,[10] I have hardly time to spare to write to our little MD; but in a fortnight I hope it will be over. I am going now to be busy, &c.

14. I was going to dine with Dr. Cockburn, but Sir Andrew Fountain met me, and carried me to Mrs. Van's, where I drank the last bottle of Raymond's wine, admirable good, better than any I get among the ministry. I must pick up time to answer this letter of MD's, I'll do it in a day or two for certain.——I am glad I am not at Windsor, for it is very cold, and I won't have a fire till November. I am contriving how to stop up my grate with bricks. Patrick was drunk last night; but did not come to me, else I should have given him t'other cuff. I sat this evening with Mrs. Barton, it is the first day of her seeing company; but I made her merry enough, and we were three hours disputing upon Whig and Tory. She grieved for her brother only for form, and he was a sad dog. Is Stella well enough to go to church, pray? no nummings[11] left? no

---

10 With writing *The Conduct of the Allies.*

11 Numbings, either due to an illness or a physical tendency natural to Stella. Cf. p. 354.

darkness in your eyes? do you walk and exercise? Your exercise is ombre.——People are coming up to town; the queen will be at Hampton-court in a week. Lady Betty Germain, I hear, is come, and lord Pembroke is coming: his new wife[12] is as big with child as she can tumble.

15. I sat at home till four this afternoon to-day writing, and ate a roll and butter; then visited Will Congreve an hour or two, and supped with lord treasurer, who came from Windsor to-day, and brought Prior with him. The queen has thanked Prior for his good service in France, and promised to make him a commissioner of the customs. Several of that commission are to be out; among the rest, my friend Sir Matthew Dudley; I can do nothing for him, he is so hated by the ministry. Lord treasurer kept me till twelve, so I need not tell you it is now late.

16. I dined to-day with Mr. secretary at Dr. Cotesworth's,[13] where he now lodges till his house be got ready in Golden-Square. One Boyer, a French dog, has abused me in a pamphlet,[14] and I have got him up in a messenger's hands: the secretary promises me to swinge him. Lord treasurer told me last night that he had the honour to be

[12] Lord Pembroke (p. 75 n.[39]) married 21 Sept. 1708, as his second wife, Barbara, Dowager Baroness Arundell of Trerice, widow of Sir Richard Mauleverer, and daughter of Sir Thomas Slingsby, second Baronet of Scriven, co. York. She died in 1722. Cf. p. 443 n.[13]

[13] Caleb Coatesworth, who was created a doctor of medicine by Tillotson, Archbishop of Canterbury, 3 Mar. 1692. Admitted a Fellow of the Royal Society in 1718, he was Physician to St. Thomas's Hospital. He amassed a fortune of between one and two hundred thousand pounds; and died 2 May 1741. See Munk, *Roll of the Royal College of Physicians*, i. 478–9; *Gentleman's Magazine*, xi. 277.

[14] Abel Boyer, 1667–1729, who was of French origin, came to England in 1689, taught French, and became an active miscellaneous writer in the Whig interest. His best known publication is the monthly *Political State of Great Britain*, which he conducted from 1711 till his death. The pamphlet to which Swift here refers was *An Account of the State and Progress of the Present Negotiations for Peace* (*Political State*, ii. 390). Boyer was taken up, but discharged, he says, through the intervention of Lord Oxford (*Annals of Queen Anne*, 1711, pp. 264–5).

abused with me in a pamphlet. I must make that rogue an example for warning to others. I was to see Jack Hill this morning, who made that unfortunate expedition; and there is still more misfortune; for that ship, which was admiral of his fleet, is blown up in the Thames,[15] by an accident and carelessness of some rogue, who was going, as they think, to steal some gun-powder: five hundred men are lost; we don't yet know the particulars. I am got home by seven, and am going to be busy, and you are going to play and supper; you live ten times happier than I: but I should live ten times happier than you, if I were with MD. I saw Jemmy Leigh to-day in the street, who tells me that Sterne has not lain above once these three weeks in his lodgings, and he doubts he takes ill courses; he stays only till he can find Sterne to go along with him, and he cannot hear of him. I begged him to enquire about the box when he comes to Chester, which he promises.

17. The secretary and I dined to-day with Brigadier Britton,[16] a great friend of his. The lady of the house is very galante, about thirty-five; she is said to have a great deal of wit; but I see nothing among any of them that equals MD by a bar's length, as hope saved. My lord treasurer is much out of order; he has a sore throat, and the gravel, and a pain in his breast where the wound was: pray God preserve him. The queen comes to Hampton-Court on Tuesday next; people are coming fast to town, and I must answer MD's letter, which I can hardly find time to do, though I am at home the greatest part of the day. Lady Betty Germain and I were disputing Whig and

---

15 The *Edgar* of 70 guns, with a crew of between four and five hundred, was blown up at Spithead on 15 Oct. Sir Hovenden Walker was ashore at the time (W. L. Clowes, *The Royal Navy*, ii. 529).

16 William Breton, or Britton, became a Lieut.-Colonel in 1702, Colonel of a new Regiment of Foot in 1705, and a Brigadier-General, 1 Jan. 1710 (Dalton's *Army Lists*, iii. 228). In Dec. 1711 he was appointed Envoy Extraordinary to the King of Prussia. He died Dec. 1714 or Jan. 1715. See *Wentworth Papers*, pp. 203–4, 217–18, for town scandal about St. John and Mrs. Breton.

Tory to death this morning. She is grown very fat, and looks mighty well. Biddy Floyd was there, and she is, I think, very much spoiled with the small-pox.

18. Lord treasurer is still out of order, and that breaks our method of dining there to-day. He is often subject to a sore throat, and some time or other it will kill him, unless he takes more care than he is apt to do. It was said about the town, that poor lord Peterborow was dead at Frankfort; but he is something better, and the queen is sending him to Italy,[17] where I hope the warm climate will recover him; he has abundance of excellent qualities, and we love one another mightily. I was this afternoon in the city, eat a bit of meat, and settled some things with a printer.[18] I will answer your letter on Saturday, if possible, and then send away this; so to fetch up the odd days I lost at Windsor, and keep constant to my fortnight. Ombre time is now coming on, and we shall have nothing but Manley, and Walls, and Stoytes, and the dean. Have you got no new acquaintance? Poor girls; no body knows MD's good qualities. 'Tis very cold; but I will not have a fire till November, that's pozz.—Well, but coming home to-night, I found on my table a letter from MD; faith I was angry, that is with myself; and I was afraid too to see MD's hand so soon, for fear of something, I don't know what: at last I opened it, and it was over well, and a bill for the two hundred guineas![19] However, 'tis a sad thing that this letter is not gone, nor your twenty-first answered yet.

19. I was invited to-day to dine with Mrs. Van, with some company who did not come; but I ate nothing but

[17] Peterborough busied himself at Frankfort with matters outside his instructions, and was sent to Italy on a nominal mission to keep him out of the way.

[18] Probably with Morphew, who published *The Conduct of the Allies*.

[19] Possibly a remittance of Swift's own money from Ireland with which to repay Francis Stratford for the advance for investment in Bank Stock. See pp. 74, 87, 94. Or it may have been connected with Rebecca Dingley's exchequer business mentioned two days later. See pp. 226, 387, 449. Swift also speaks of a repayment of £100 due to Mrs. Walls (p. 411).

herrings: you must know I hardly ever eat of above one thing, and that the plainest ordinary meat at table; I love it best, and believe it wholesomest. You love rarities; yes you do; I wish you had all that I ever see where I go. I was coming home early, and met the secretary in his chair, who persuaded me to go with him to Britton's; for he said, he had been all day at business, and had eaten nothing. So I went, and the time past so, that we staid till two, so you may believe 'tis late enough.

20. This day has gone all wrong, by sitting up so late last night. Lord treasurer is not yet well, and can't go to Windsor. I dined with Sir Matthew Dudley, and took occasion to hint to him that he would lose his employment, for which I am very sorry. Lord Pembroke and his family[20] are all come to town. I was kept so long at a friend's this evening, that I cannot send this to-night. When I knocked at my lodgings, a fellow asked me where lodged Dr. Swift? I told him I was the person: he gave me a letter he brought from the secretary's office, and I gave him a shilling: when I came up, I saw Dingley's hand: faith I was afraid, I do not know what. At last it was a formal letter from Dingley about her exchequer business.[21] Well, I'll do it on Monday, and settle it with Tooke. And now, boys, for your letter, I mean the first, N. 21. Let's see; come out, little letter.—I never had the letter from the bishop that Raymond mentions; but I have written to Ned Southwel, to desire the duke of Ormond to speak to his reverence that he may leave off his impertinence. What a pox can they think I am doing for the archbishop here? You have a pretty notion of me in Ireland, to make me an agent for the archbishop of Dublin.——Why; do you think I value your people's ingratitude about my part in serving them? I remit them their First-Fruits of Ingratitude, as freely as

[20] Lord Pembroke (pp. 75, 384, and notes) had a large family, seven sons and five daughters, by his first wife, Margaret, only daughter and heir to Sir Robert Sawyer of High Cleer, Kt. She died 17 Nov. 1706.
[21] For Rebecca Dingley's exchequer business see pp. 226, 391.

I got the other remitted to them. This lord treasurer defers writing his letter to them, or else they would be plaguily confounded by this time. For, he designs to give the merit of it wholly to the queen and me, and to let them know it was done before the duke of Ormond was lord lieutenant. You visit, you dine abroad, you see friends; you pilgarlick;[22] you walk from Finglass, you a cat's foot. O Lord—lady Gore[23] hung her child by the waist; what is that *waist*,[24] I don't understand that word; he must hang on till you explain or spell it.—I don't believe he was pretty, that's a liiii.—Pish; burn your First-Fruits; again at it. Stella has made twenty false spellings in her writing; I'll send them to you all back again on the other side of this letter, to mend them; I won't miss one. Why; I think there were seventeen bishops names to the letter lord Oxford received.—I will send you some pamphlets by Leigh: put me in mind of it on Monday, for I shall go then to the printer; yes, and the *Miscellany*.[25] I am mightily obliged to Walls, but I don't deserve it by any usage of him here, having seen him but twice, and once *en passant*. Mrs. Manley[26] forsworn ombre! What; and no blazing star appear? no monsters born? no whale thrown up? Have you not found out some evasion for her? She had no such regard to oaths in her younger days. I got the books for nothing, madam Dingley; but the wine I got not;[27] it was but a promise.—Yes, my head is pretty well in the main, only now and then a little threatening or so. ——You talk of my reconciling some great folks. I tell you what. The secretary told me last night, that he had found the reason why the queen was cold to him for some

[22] See p. 285 n.[18]

[23] It is not possible to say which Lady Gore, of several then living, is here referred to.

[24] 'Modern usage has sanctioned Stella's spelling' as Scott observes. Swift's spelling was 'wast', and 'tast' for 'taste'.

[25] *Miscellanies in Prose and Verse*; see p. 62 n.[52]

[26] Mrs. Isaac Manley.

[27] See p. 312.

months past; that a friend had told it him yesterday; and it was, that they suspected he was at the bottom with the duke of Marlborough. Then he said, he had reflected upon all I had spoken to him long ago; but he thought it had been only my suspicion, and my zeal and kindness for him. I said I had reason to take that very ill, to imagine I knew so little of the world as to talk at a venture to a great minister; that I had gone between him and lord treasurer often, and told each of them what I had said to the other, and that I had informed him so before: he said all that you may imagine to excuse himself, and approve my conduct. I told him, I knew all along, that this proceeding of mine was the surest way to send me back to my willows in Ireland, but that I regarded it not, provided I could do the kingdom service in keeping them well together. I minded him how often I had told lord treasurer, lord keeper, and him together, that all things depended on their union, and that my comfort was to see them love one another; and I had told them all singly, that I had not said this by chance, &c. He was in a rage to be thus suspected; swears he will be upon a better foot, or none at all: and I do not see, how they can well want[28] him in this juncture. I hope to find a way of settling this matter. I act an honest part; that will bring me neither profit nor praise. MD must think the better of me for it: nobody else shall ever know it.[29] Here's politicks enough for once; but madam D. D. gave me occasion for it.   I think I told you I have got into lodgings that don't smell ill—O Lord! the spectacles: well I'll do that on Monday too; although it goes against me to be employed for folks that neither you nor I care a groat for. Is the eight pounds from Hawkshaw included in the thirty-nine pounds five shillings and two-pence? How do I know by this how my account stands? Can't you write five or six lines to

[28] 'To be without'. The verb is used in its older sense.
[29] Deane Swift reads 'know it'; Sheridan, Nichols, Scott, Ryland, Aitken, 'know of it'.

cast it up? Mine is forty-four pounds *per annum*, and eight pounds from Hawkshaw makes fifty-two pounds. Pray set it right, and let me know; you had best.—And so now I have answered N. 21, and 'tis late, and I will answer N. 22 in my next: this cannot go to-night, but shall on Tuesday: and so go to your play, and lose your money, with your two eggs a penny; silly jade: you witty? very pretty.

21. Mrs. Van would have me dine with her again to-day, and so I did, though lady Mountjoy had sent two or three times to have me see and dine with her, and she is a little body I love very well. My head has ached a little in the evenings these three or four days, but it is not of the giddy sort, so I do not much value it. I was to see lord Harley to-day, but lord treasurer took physick, and I could not see him. He has voided much gravel, and is better, but not well; he talks of going on Tuesday to see the queen at Hampton-Court; I wish he may be able. I never saw so fine a summer day as this was; how is it with you pray? and can't you remember, naughty packs. I han't seen lord Pembroke yet. He will be sorry to miss Dilly: I wonder you say nothing of Dilly's being got to Ireland; if he be not there soon, I shall have some certain odd thoughts; guess them if you can.

22. I dined in the city to-day with Dr. Freind, at one of my printers;[30] I enquired for Leigh, but could not find him: I have forgot what sort of apron you want. I must rout among your letters, a needle in a bottle of hay. I gave Sterne directions, but where to find him Lord knows. I have bespoken the spectacles; got a set of *Examiners*, and five pamphlets, which I have either written or contributed to, except the best, which is the *Vindication of the duke of Marlborough*;[31] and is entirely of the author of the

[30] Probably Barber.
[31] p. 381 n.[3] Reprinted in Nichols's *Supplement to Swift's Works*, 1779; in his edition of Swift's *Works*, 1801, xviii. 63; and by Scott, 1814, vi. 129.

Atalantis. I have settled Dingley's affair[32] with Tooke, who has undertaken it, and understands it. I have bespoken a *Miscellany*: what would you have me do more? It cost me a shilling coming home; it rains terribly, and did so in the morning. Lord treasurer has had an ill day, in much pain. He writes and does business in his chamber now he is ill: the man is bewitched; he desires to see me, and I'll maul him, but he will not value it a rush.——I am half weary of them all. I often burst out into these thoughts, and will certainly steal away as soon as I decently can. I have many friends, and many enemies; and the last are more constant in their nature. I have no shuddering at all to think of retiring to my old circumstances, if you can be easy; but I will always live in Ireland as I did the last time; I will not hunt for dinners there; nor converse with more than a very few.

23. Morning. This goes to-day, and shall be sealed by and bye. Lord treasurer takes physick again to-day: I believe I shall dine with lord Dupplin. Mr Tooke brought me a letter directed for me at Morphew's the bookseller. I suppose, by the postage, it came from Ireland; it is a woman's hand, and seems false spelt on purpose;[33] it is in such sort of verse as Harris's petition;[34] rallies me for writing merry things, and not upon divinity; and is like the subject of the archbishop's last letter,[35] as I told you. Can you guess whom it came from? it is not ill written; pray find it out; there is a Latin verse at the end of it all rightly spelt; yet the English, as I think, affectedly wrong in many places.——My plaguing time is coming. A young fellow brought me a letter from judge Coote,[36] with recom-

---

[32] p. 387 n.[21]

[33] A letter from Stella.

[34] *Mrs. Harris's Petition*, written by Swift in 1701; *Poems*, p. 68.

[35] p. 359 n.[7]

[36] The Hon. Thomas Coote, third son of Lord Coote of Coloony, entered the Middle Temple in 1683. Recorder of Dublin, 1690, and M.P. for that city in 1692. He was appointed a Justice of the King's Bench in 1693, but was superseded after the accession of George I. Ball,

mendation to be lieutenant of a man of war. He is the son of one Echlin,[37] who was minister of Belfast before Tisdall, and I have got some other new customers; but I shall trouble my friends as little as possible. Saucy Stella used to jeer me for meddling with other folks affairs: but now I am punished for it.—Patrick has brought the candle, and I have no more room. Farewel, &c. &c.

Here is a full and true account of Stella's new spelling.

> Plaguely,—Plaguily.[38]
> Dineing,—Dining.
> Straingers,—Strangers.
> Chais,—Chase.[39]
> Waist,—Wast.
> Houer,—Hour.
> Immagin,—Imagine.
> A bout,—About.
> Intellegence,—Intelligence.
> Aboundance,—Abundance.
> Merrit,—Merit.
> Secreet,—Secret.
> Phamphlets,—Pamphlets.
> Bussiness,—Business.

Tell me truly, sirrah, how many of these are mistakes of the pen, and how many are you to answer for as real ill spelling? There are but fourteen; I said twenty by guess.

Judges in Ireland, ii. 60–2; Lodge's *Peerage of Ireland*, iii. 215; Dunton, *Life and Errors*, 1818, p. 521.

[37] There seems to be some mistake. William Tisdall (p. 66 n.⁹) held the living of Drumcree with that of Belfast, 1711–36. The nearest official connexion with a member of the Echlin family appears to be that on 2 Jan. 1703 Tisdall was collated to the rectory of Loughgilly, was resident in that year, but was succeeded by James Echlin, who was collated to Loughgilly 15 Mar. 1703. Echlin died in 1704. See J. B. Leslie, *Armagh Clergy*, pp. 263, 353; and the Rev. John Echlin's *Genealogical Memoirs of the Echlin Family*.

[38] 'This column of words, as they are corrected, is in *Stella*'s hand.'— Deane Swift.

[39] 'Yet here is one word still false spelt.'—Deane Swift.

You must not be angry, for I will have you spell right, let the world go how it will. Though after all, there is but a mistake of one letter in any of these words. I allow you henceforth but six false spellings in every letter you send me.

LETTER XXXIII

[TUESDAY]　　　　　　　London, Oct. 23, 1711.

I DINED with lord Dupplin, as I told you I would, and put my thirty-second into the post-office my own self; and I believe there has not been one moment since we parted, wherein a letter was not upon the road going or coming to or from PMD.[1] If the queen knew it, she would give us a pension; for it is we bring good luck to their post-boys and their pacquets: else they would break their necks and sink. But, an old saying and a true one; Be it snow or storm or hail, PMD's letters never fail: Cross winds may sometimes make them tarry; But PMD's letters can't miscarry.——Terrible rain to-day, but it cleared up at night enough to save my twelve-pence coming home. Lord treasurer is much better this evening. I hate to have him ill, he is so confoundedly careless. I won't answer your letter yet, so be satisfied.

24. I called at lord treasurer's to-day at noon; he was eating some broth in his bed-chamber, undressed, with a thousand papers about him. He has a little fever upon him, and his eye terribly blood-shot; yet he dressed himself, and went out to the treasury. He told me, he had a letter from a lady with a complaint against me, it was from Mrs. Cutts, a sister of lord Cutts,[2] who writ to him, that

---

1 'That is, *Presto* and *MD*.'—Deane Swift.

. 2 John Cutts, 1661–1707, was a brave and distinguished soldier, who fought at the Boyne; and, at the siege of Namur in 1695, he won the name of 'Salamander' for his fearlessness under fire. In 1690 he was created Baron Cutts of Gowran. Swift's abusive verses, 'The Description of a Salamander' (*Poems*, p. 82), composed in 1705, and first printed in the

I had abused her brother: you remember the *Salamander*; it is printed in the *Miscellany*. I told my lord, that I would never regard complaints, and that I expected whenever he received any against me, he would immediately put them into the fire, and forget them, else I should have no quiet. ——I had a little turn in my head this morning; which, though it did not last above a moment, yet being of the true sort, has made me as weak as a dog all this day. 'Tis the first I have had this half year. I shall take my pills if I hear of it again. I dined at lady Mountjoy's with Harry Coote, and went to see lord Pembroke upon his coming to town.——The Whig party are furious against a Peace, and every day some ballad comes out reflecting on the ministry on that account. The secretary St. John has seized on a dozen booksellers and publishers, into his messengers hands.[3] Some of the foreign ministers have published the Preliminaries agreed on here between France and England; and people rail at them as insufficient to treat a Peace upon; but the secret is, that the French have agreed to articles much more important, which our ministers have not communicated, and the people, who think they know all, are discontented that there is no more. This was an inconvenience I foretold to the secretary; but we could contrive no way to fence against it.——So there's politicks for you.

25. The queen is at Hampton-Court; she went on Tuesday in that terrible rain. I dined with Lewis at his lodgings, to dispatch some business we had. I sent this morning and evening to lord treasurer, and he is much worse by going out; I am in pain about evening. He has

Miscellanies, 1711, cannot be excused. Joanna Cutts, the youngest of three sisters to Lord Cutts, died unmarried.

[3] On 23 Oct., the first day of Term, fourteen booksellers, printers, and publishers, who had been taken into custody on warrants issued by St. John, appeared before the bar of the Court of the Queen's Bench. They were remanded on their own recognizances till the last day of Term (Boyer's *Political State*, ii. 389; cf. Bolingbroke's *Letters*, i. 255).

sent for Dr. Radcliffe; pray God preserve him. The chancellor of the exchequer[4] shewed me to-day a ballad in manuscript against lord treasurer and his South-Sea project;[5] it is very sharply written: if it be not printed, I will send it you.   If it be, it shall go in your pacquet of pamphlets.—I found out your letter about directions for the apron, and have ordered to be bought a cheap, green silk work apron; I have it by heart; I sat this evening with Mrs. Barton, who is my near neighbour. It was a delicious day, and I got my walk, and was thinking whether MD was walking too just at that time that Presto was.——This paper does not cost me a farthing, I have it from the secretary's office. I long till to-morrow to know how my lord treasurer sleeps this night, and to hear he mends: we are all undone without him; so pray for him, sirrahs, and don't stay too late at the dean's.

26. I dined with Mrs. Van; for the weather is so bad, and I am so busy, that I can't dine with great folks; and besides I dare eat but little, to keep my head in order, which is better. Lord treasurer is very ill, but I hope in no danger. We have no quiet with the Whigs, they are so violent against a Peace; but I'll cool them, with a vengeance, very soon. I have not heard from the bishop of Clogher, whether he has got his statues.[6] I writ to him six weeks ago; he's so busy with his parliament. I won't answer your letter yet, say what you will, saucy girls.

27. I forgot to go about some business[7] this morning, which cost me double the time; and I was forced to be at the secretary's office till four, and lose my dinner; so I went to Mrs. Van's, and made them get me three herrings, which I am very fond of, and they are a light vittals:

---

[4] Robert Benson, p. 60 n.[44]

[5] Scott, *Works*, 1814, ii. 388–9, prints the words of a ballad, 'The South-Sea Whim', which he assumes to be the lampoon referred to by Swift.   [6] Cf. pp. 250, 414.

[7] The business was probably in connexion with the composition of *The Conduct of the Allies*.

besides, I was to have supped at lady Ashburnham's; but the drab did not call for us in her coach, as she promised, but sent for us, and so I sent my excuses. It has been a terrible rainy day, but so flattering in the morning, that I would needs go out in my new hat. I met Leigh and Sterne as I was going into the Park. Leigh says he will go to Ireland in ten days, if he can get Sterne to go with him; so I will send him the things for MD, and I have desired him to enquire about the box. I hate that Sterne for his carelessness about it; but it was my fault.

29. I was all this terible rainy day with my friend Lewis upon business of importance;[8] and I dined with him, and came home about seven, and thought I would amuse myself a little after the pains I had taken. I saw a volume of Congreve's Plays in my room, that Patrick had taken to read; and I looked into it, and in mere loitering read in it till twelve, like an owl and a fool: if ever I do so again; never saw the like.[9] Count Gallas, the emperor's envoy, you will hear is in disgrace with us: the queen has ordered her ministers to have no more commerce with him;[10] the reason is the fool writ a rude letter to lord Dartmouth, secretary of state, complaining of our proceedings about a Peace; and he is always in close confidence with lord

[8] Hints for *The Conduct of the Allies*.

[9] In Dec. 1710 Tonson published the first collected edition of Congreve's *Works* in three octavo volumes. Elwin, Pope's *Works*, vii. 141 n.3, interprets Swift to be writing in disparagement of Congreve, whereas Swift means that he could not stop reading for five hours, despite poor candlelight which made him 'like an owl and a fool'.

[10] Count de Gallas, the Imperial Minister in London, openly associated himself with the Whigs in opposition to the peace. St. John sent him as a private paper a copy of the document which had been transmitted to Holland. De Gallas sent it to *The Daily Courant*, in which paper it appeared on the 13th of October. Reprinted in *The Flying-Post*, 16 Oct. On Sunday, 28 Oct., he was forbidden the Court in Her Majesty's name, and told that the Queen no longer looked upon him as a public Minister. At the same time a message was directed to the Emperor announcing that Her Majesty desired to receive another Austrian Minister (Bolingbroke's *Letters*, i. 253, 278, 293, 295; *Wentworth Papers*, pp. 205, 207).

Wharton, and Sunderland, and others of the late ministry. I believe you begin to think there will be no Peace; the Whigs here are sure it cannot be, and stocks are fallen again. But I am confident there will, unless France plays us tricks; and you may venture a wager with any of your Whig acquaintance that we shall not have another campaign. You will get more by it than by ombre, sirrah.— I let slip telling you yesterday's journal, which I thought to have done this morning, but blundered. I dined yesterday at Harry Coote's with lord Hatton,[11] Mr. Finch, a son of lord Nottingham,[12] and Sir Andrew Fountain. I left them soon; but hear they staid till two in the morning, and were all drunk; and so good night for last night, and good night for to-night. You blundering goosecap, an't you ashamed to blunder to young ladies? I shall have a fire in three or four days, now, oh ho.

30. I was to-day in the city concerting some things with a printer, and am to be to-morrow all day busy with Mr. secretary about the same.[13] I won't tell you now; but the ministers reckon it will do abundance of good, and open the eyes of the nation, who are half bewitched against a Peace. Few of this generation can remember any thing but war and taxes, and they think it is as it should be: whereas 'tis certain we are the most undone people in Europe, as I am afraid I shall make appear beyond all contradiction. But I forgot; I won't tell you what I will do, nor what I will not do: so let me alone, and go to Stoyte, and give goody Stoyte and Catherine my humble service; I love goody Stoyte better than goody Walls. Who'll pay me for this green apron? I will have the

[11] William, 1690?–1760, second Viscount Hatton. His half-sister, Anne, married in 1685, as his second wife, Daniel Finch, second Earl of Nottingham.

[12] Probably the Right Hon. William Finch, the Earl's second son (Collins, *Peerage of England*, 1812, iii. 402). By his first wife Nottingham had only one child, a daughter; by his second wife thirty children, according to Collins, of whom ten died young, and seven were stillborn.

[13] *The Conduct of the Allies.*

money; it cost ten shillings and six pence. I think it plaguy dear for a cheap thing; but they said, that English silk would cockle,[14] and I know not what. You have the making into the bargain. 'Tis right Italian: I have sent it and the pamphlets to Leigh, and will send the *Miscellanies* and spectacles in a day or two. I would send more; but faith I'm plaguy poor at present.

31.[15] The Devil's in this secretary; when I went this morning he had people with him; but says he, We are to dine with Prior to-day, and then will do all our business in the afternoon; at two Prior sends word, he is otherwise engaged; then the secretary and I go and dine with brigadier Britton, sit till eight, grow merry, no business done; he is in haste to see lady Jersey,[16] we part, and appoint no time to meet again. This is the fault of all the present ministers, teazing me to death for my assistance, laying the whole weight of their affairs upon it, yet slipping opportunities. Lord treasurer mends every day, though slowly: I hope he will take care of himself. Pray, will you send to Parvisol to send me a bill of twenty pounds as soon as he can, for I want money. I must have money; I will have money, sirrahs.

Nov. 1. I went to-day into the city to settle some business with Stratford, and to dine with him; but he was engaged, and I was so angry I would not dine with any other merchant, but went to my printer, and ate a bit, and did business of mischief with him, and I shall have the spectacles and *Miscellany* to-morrow, and leave them with Leigh. A fine day always makes me go into the city, if I can spare time, because it is exercise; and that does

14 To pucker, to crease.

15 Deane Swift, *Essay*, p. 331, quotes part of this day's entry with some variant readings.

16 Lord Jersey married, in 1705, Judith, only daughter of Frederick Herne, a city merchant. His reputation was bad, and she was a subject of scandal. 'The world says Lady Har. Rialton has lately been in Pickell for her sins, and Lady Jersey in the same way; if they are as bad as the town says they are, I wonder they are ever out of it' (*Wentworth Papers*, p. 214).

me more good than any thing. I have heard nothing since of my head, but a little, I don't know how, sometimes: but I am very temperate, especially now the treasurer is ill, and the ministers often at Hampton-Court, and the secretary not yet fixed in his house, and I hate dining with many of my old acquaintance. Here has been a fellow discovered going out of the East-India house with sixteen thousand pounds in money and bills; he would have escaped, if he had not been so uneasy with thirst, that he stole out before his time, and was caught. But what is that to MD? I wish we had the money, provided the East-India Company was never the worse; you know we must not covet, &c. Our weather, for this fortnight past, is checquered, a fair and a rainy day; this was very fine, and I have walked four miles, wish MD would do so, lazy sluttikins.

2. It has rained all day with a *continuendo*, and I went in a chair to dine with Mrs. Van; always there in a very rainy day. But I made a shift to come back afoot. I live a very retired life, pay very few visits, and keep but very little company; I read no news-papers. I am sorry I sent you the *Examiner*; for the printer is going to print them in a small volume: it seems the author is too proud to have them printed by subscription, though his friends offered, they say, to make it worth five hundred pounds to him. The *Spectators*[17] are likewise printing in a larger and a smaller volume: so I believe they are going to leave them off, and indeed people grow weary of them, though they are often prettily written. We have had no news for me to send you now towards the end of my letter. The queen has the gout a little; I hoped the lord treasurer would have had it too; but Radcliffe told me yesterday it

---

[17] The first *Spectator* was published 1 Mar. 1711, and the paper continued to appear without a break to No. 555, 6 Dec. 1712. In 1714 Addison revived the paper with No. 556, 18 June. The last of this series, No. 635, appeared 20 Dec. 1714. Vols. i and ii of the collected *Spectator*, in 8vo, were published on 8 Jan. 1712. They were published in 12mo on 18 Jan. 1712.

was the rheumatism in his knee and foot; however he mends, and I hope will be abroad in a short time. I am told they design giving away several employments before the parliament sits, which will be the thirteenth instant. I either do not like, or not understand this policy; and if lord treasurer does not mend soon, they must give them just before the sessions. But he is the greatest procrastinator in the world.

3. A fine day this, and I walked a pretty deal; I stufft the secretary's pockets with papers, which he must read and settle at Hampton-Court, where he went to-day, and stays some time. They have no lodgings for me there, so I can't go; for the town is small, chargeable and inconvenient. Lord treasurer had a very ill night last night, with much pain in his knee and foot, but is easier to-day. —And so I went to visit Prior about some business, and so he was not within, and so Sir Andrew Fountain made me dine to-day again with Mrs. Van, and I came home soon, remembering this must go to-night, and that I had a letter of MD's to answer. O Lord, where is it? let me see; so, so, here it is. You grudge writing so soon. Pox on that bill; the woman would have me manage that money for her. I do not know what to do with it now I have it. I am like the unprofitable steward in the gospel: *I laid it up in a napkin; there thou hast what is thine own,*[18] &c. Well, well, I know of your new mayor. (I'll tell you a pun; a fishmonger owed a man two crowns; so he sent him a piece of bad ling and a tench, and then said he was paid: how is that now? find it out; for I won't tell it you: which of you finds it out?) Well, but as I was saying, what care I for your mayor?[19] I fancy Ford[20] may tell Forbes[21] right about my returning to Ireland before Christ-

18 Matthew xxv. 25; Luke xix. 20.
19 See p. 277 n.26
20 Ford was in Ireland, whither he had gone at the end of June (p. 297).
21 The Rev. Thomas Forbes to whom Swift refers in letters, 1713–14, as a manager of his affairs. He was rector of Dunboyne, a parish between

mas, or soon after. I'm sorry you did not go on with your story about *Pray God you be John*; I never heard it in my life, and wonder what it can be.—Ah, Stella, faith you learned upon your Bible to think what to say when you writ that. Yes, that story of the secretary's making me an example is true; 'never heard it before;' why how could you hear it? is it possible to tell you the hundredth part of what passes in our companies here? The secretary is as easy with me as Mr. Addison was. I have often thought what a splutter Sir William Temple makes[22] about being secretary of state; I think Mr. St. John the greatest young man I ever knew; wit, capacity, beauty, quickness of apprehension, good learning, and an excellent taste; the best orator in the house of commons, admirable conversation, good nature, and good manners; generous, and a despiser of money. His only fault is talking to his friends in way of complaint of too great a load of business, which looks a little like affectation; and he endeavours too much to mix the fine gentleman, and man of pleasure, with the man of business. What truth and sincerity he may have I know not: he is now but thirty-two, and has been secretary above a year. Is not all this extraordinary? How he stands with the queen and lord treasurer I have told you before. This is his character; and I believe you will be diverted by knowing it. I writ to the archbishop of Dublin, bishop of Cloyne,[23] and of Clogher together, five weeks ago from Windsor: I hope they had my letters; pray know if Clogher had his.—Fig for your Physician and his advice, madam Dingley; if I grow worse, I will; otherwise I will trust to temperance and exercise: your fall

Dublin and Trim, and there occasionally entertained Swift. In 1713 Swift had him appointed one of the chaplains to the Duke of Shrewsbury, when Lord Lieutenant of Ireland (*Corresp.* ii, *passim*; vi. 234).

[22] Cf. p. 92.

[23] Charles Crow, Bishop of Cloyne since 1702. He died in 1726. The letters to the Bishops of Cloyne and Clogher have not been preserved. For the letter to Archbishop King, *Corresp.* i. 288.

of the leaf; what care I when the leaves fall? I am sorry
to see them fall with all my heart; but why should I take
physick because leaves fall off from trees? that won't
hinder them from falling. If a man falls from a horse,
must I take physic for that?—This arguing makes you
mad; but it is true right reason, not to be disproved.—I
am glad at heart to hear poor Stella is better; use exercise
and walk, spend pattens and spare potions, wear out clogs
and waste claret. Have you found out my pun of the fishmonger? Don't read a word more till you have got it. And
Stella is handsome again, you say? and is she fat? I have
sent to Leigh the set of *Examiners*; the first thirteen were
written by several hands, some good, some bad; the next
three and thirty were all by one hand, that makes forty
six:[24] then that author, whoever he was, laid it down on
purpose to confound guessers; and the last six were written
by a woman. Then there is an account of Guiscard by the
same woman, but the facts sent by Presto. Then *An
Answer to the Letter to the lords about Greg*, by Presto;
Prior's journey, by Presto; *Vindication of the duke of Marlborough*, entirely by the same woman. *Comment on Hare's
Sermon*, by the same woman, only hints sent to the printer
from Presto to give her.[25] Then there's the *Miscellany*, an
apron for Stella, a pound of chocolate without sugar for
Stella, a fine snuff-rasp of ivory, given me by Mrs. St.
John for Dingley, and a large roll of tobacco, which she
must hide or cut shorter out of modesty, and four pair of
spectacles for the Lord knows who. There's the cargo, I
hope it will come safe. Oh, Mrs. Masham and I are very
well; we write to one another, but it is upon business; I
believe I told you so before: pray pardon my forgetfulness
in these cases; poor Presto can't help it. MD shall have
the money as soon as Tooke gets it. And so I think I have
answered all, and the paper is out, and now I have fetcht

[24] For *The Examiner* see p. 76 n.[41]
[25] For notes on Mrs. Manley, and notes on the pamphlets mentioned
by Swift, see pp. 123, 244, 340, 357, 381.

up my week, and will send you another this day fortnight.
—Why, you rogues, two crowns make *tench-ill-ling*: you
are so dull you could never have found it out. Farewel,
&c. &c.

LETTER XXXIV

[SATURDAY]   London, November 3, 1711.

MY thirty-third lies now before me just finished, and I
am going to seal and send it, so let me know whether you
would have me add any thing: I gave you my journal of
this day; and it is now nine at night, and I am going to be
busy for an hour or two.

4. I left a friend's house to-day where I was invited,
just when dinner was setting on, and pretended I was
engaged, because I saw some fellows I did not know, and
went to Sir Matthew Dudley's, where I had the same
inconvenience, but he would not let me go; otherwise I
would have gone home, and sent for a slice of mutton and
a pot of ale, rather than dine with persons unknown, as
bad for aught I know as your deans, parsons, and curates.
Bad slabby weather to-day.—Now methinks I write at
ease, when I have no letter of MD's to answer. But I
mistook, and have got the large paper. The queen is laid
up with the gout at Hampton-Court; she is now seldom
without it any long time together; I fear it will wear her
out in a very few years. I plainly find I have less twitch-
ings about my toes since these ministers are sick and out
of town, and that I don't dine with them. I would compound for a light easy gout to be perfectly well in my
head.—Pray walk when the frost comes, young ladies, go
a frost-biting. It comes into my head, that from the very
time you first went to Ireland I have been always plying
you to walk and read. The young fellows here have begun
a kind of fashion to walk, and many of them have got
swinging strong shoes on purpose; it has got as far as
several young lords; if it hold, it would be a very good

thing. Lady Lucy and I are fallen out: she rails at me, and I have left visiting her.

5. MD was very troublesome to me last night in my sleep; I was adreamed, methought, that Stella was here: I asked her after Dingley, and she said, she had left her in Ireland, because she designed her stay to be short, and such stuff.—Monsieur Pontchartrain,[1] the secretary of state in France, and Monsieur Fontenelle,[2] the secretary of the Royal Academy there (who writ the *Dialogues des morts*, &c.) have sent letters to lord Pembroke, that the Academy have, with the king's consent, chosen him one of their members,[3] in the room of one who is lately dead. But the cautious gentleman has given me the letters to show my lord Dartmouth and Mr. St. John, our two secretaries, and let them see there is no treason in them; which I will do on Wednesday, when they come from Hampton-Court. The letters are very handsome, and it is a great[4] mark of honour and distinction to lord Pembroke. I hear the two French ministers[5] are come over again about the Peace; but I have seen nobody of consequence to know the truth. I dined to-day with a lady of my acquaintance[6] who was sick, in her bed-chamber, upon three herrings and a chicken; the dinner was my bespeaking. We begin now to have chesnuts and Seville oranges; have you the latter yet? 'Twas a terrible windy day, and we had processions in carts of the Pope and the Devil, and

[1] Louis-Phélypeaux, 1643–1727, Comte de Pontchartrain, Chancellor of France since 1699, a friend of men of science and letters.

[2] Bernard le Bovier de Fontenelle, 1657–1757. His *Dialogues des Morts* began to come out in 1683. Swift possessed the work in more than one edition (Williams, *Dean Swift's Library*, pp. 65–6). In 1697 he became secretary to the Académie des Sciences, and after the death of Boileau, 13 Mar. 1711, was in almost undisputed control.

[3] Lord Pembroke (p. 75 n.[39]) had amassed at Wilton, without much judgement or discrimination, a collection of marbles and other antiquities.

[4] Deane Swift reads 'great'; Sheridan, Nichols, Scott, Ryland, Aitken, 'very great'.   [5] See p. 349 n.[12]

[6] Presumably Mrs. Vanhomrigh.

the butchers rang their cleavers; you know this is the fifth of November, popery and gun-powder.

6. Since I am used to this way of writing, I fancy I could hardly make out a long letter to MD without it. I think I ought to allow for every line taken up by telling you where I dined; but that will not be above seven lines in all, half a line to a dinner. Your Ingoldsby is going over, and they say here, he is to be made a lord.—Here was I staying in my room till two this afternoon for that puppy Sir Andrew Fountain, who was to go with me into the city, and never came;[7] and if I had not shot a dinner flying, with one Mr. Murray,[8] I might have fasted, or gone to an alehouse.—You never said one word of goody Stoyte in your letter; but I suppose these winter nights we shall hear more of her.—Does the Provost[9] laugh as much as he used to do? we reckon him here a good-for-nothing fellow.—I design to write to your dean one of these days, but I can never find time, nor what to say. I will think of something: but if DD[10] were not in Ireland, I believe seriously I should not think of the place twice a year. Nothing there ever makes the subject of talk in any company where I am.

7. I went to-day to the city on business; but stopt at a printer's and staid there; it was a most delicious day. I hear the parliament is to be prorogued for a fortnight longer; I suppose, either because the queen has the gout, or that lord treasurer is not well, or that they would do something more towards a Peace. I called at lord treasurer's at noon, and sat a while with lord Harley, but his father was asleep. A bookseller has reprinted or new-titled *A Sermon* of Tom Swift's[11] printed last year, and

---

[7] For Swift's letter chiding Fountaine for failure to keep the appointment see Freeman, *Vanessa and Swift*, p. 196.

[8] Unidentified.   [9] Benjamin Pratt (p. 9 n.[16]).

[10] 'These two initial letters include both *Stella* and *Dingley*.'—Deane Swift.

[11] Thomas Swift (p. 280 n.[4]) published, in 1710, *Noah's Dove. An*

publishes an advertisement calling it Dr. Swift's *Sermon*. Some friend of lord Galway[12] has, by his directions, published a four-shilling book about his conduct in Spain; to defend him; I have but just seen it. But what care you for books, except Presto's *Miscellanies?* Leigh promised to call and see me, but has not yet; I hope he will take care of his cargo, and get your Chester box. A murrain take that box; every thing is spoiled that is in it. How does the strong box do? You say nothing of Raymond: is his wife brought to bed again; or how? has he finished his house; paid his debts; and put out the rest of the money to use? I am glad to hear poor Joe is like to get his two hundred pounds. I suppose Trim is now reduced to slavery again.[13] I am glad of it; the people were as great rascals as the gentlemen. But I must go to bed, sirrahs; the secretary is still at Hampton-Court with my papers, or is come only to-night. They plague me with attending them.

8. I was with the secretary this morning, and we dined with Prior, and did business this afternoon till about eight, and I must alter and undo, and a clutter: I am glad the parliament is prorogued. I staid with Prior till eleven; the secretary left us at eight. Prior, I believe, will be one of those employed to make the Peace, when a Congress is opened.[14] Lord Ashburnham told to-day at the Coffee-house, that lord Harley was yesterday morning married to the duke of Newcastle's daughter, the great heiress,

Earnest Exhortation to Peace: Set forth in a Sermon, Preach'd on the 7th of November, 1710, A Thanksgiving-Day. By Tho. Swift, M.A. formerly Chaplain to Sir William Temple, now Rector of Puttenham in Surrey. The pamphlet, which runs to 24 pages, is undated. The sermon is prefaced by an absurd two-page address to Harley.

[12] For Lord Galway see p. 53 n.[12] The book referred to is *An Impartial Enquiry into the Management of the War in Spain,* which may have been written by Abel Boyer.   [13] See p. 108.

[14] At the end of September St. John had informed Mesnager that Prior was to be the third plenipotentiary (Wickham Legg, *Prior,* p. 168 and n.[1]). Cf. pp. 417, 427.

and it got about all the town.[15] But I saw lord Harley yesterday at noon in his night-gown, and he dined in the city with Prior and others; so it is not true: but I hope it will be so; for I know, it has been privately managing this long time: the lady will not have half her father's estate; for the duke left lord Pelham's son his heir;[16] the widow duchess[17] will not stand to the will, and she is now at law with Pelham. However, at worst, the girl will have about ten thousand pounds a year, to support the honour: for lord treasurer will never save a groat for himself. Lord Harley is a very valuable young gentleman; and they say the girl is handsome, and has good sense, but red hair.

9. I designed a jaunt into the city to-day to be merry, but was disappointed; so one always is in this life; and I could not see lord Dartmouth to-day, with whom I had some business. Business and pleasure both disappointed. You can go to your dean, and for want of him, goody Stoyte, or Walls, or Manley, and meet every where with cards and claret. I dined privately with a friend on a herring and chicken, and half a flask of bad Florence. I begin to have fires now, when the mornings are cold; I have got some loose bricks at the back of my grate for good husbandry. Fine weather. Patrick tells me, my caps are wearing out; I know not how to get others. I want a necessary woman strangely; I am as helpless as an elephant. —I had three pacquets from the archbishop of Dublin,

15 Two years later, 31 Oct. 1713, Edward, Lord Harley, Lord Oxford's only son, married Lady Henrietta Cavendish Holles, only daughter of John, Duke of Newcastle. Swift was supposed to have assisted in negotiations for the apportionment of her inheritance. See *Corresp.* ii. 183; *Portland MSS.* v. 324. Bolingbroke cynically described the marriage as the great end of Oxford's administration (*Corresp.* iii. 113). On the occasion of the marriage Swift addressed verses to Lord Harley (*Poems*, p. 176).

16 The heir was Thomas Pelham Holles, 1693–1768, son of the first Baron Pelham, who married in 1686, as his second wife, Lady Grace Holles, sister of the Duke of Newcastle. Thomas Pelham Holles, succeeding to the barony in 1712, was created Duke of Newcastle in 1715.

17 The widow was Margaret, 1661–1716, third daughter of Henry, second 'Cavendish' Duke of Newcastle.

cost me four shillings, all about Higgins,[18] printed stuff, and two long letters. His people forget to enclose them to Lewis; and they were only directed to Doctor Swift, without naming London or any thing else: I wonder how they reached me, unless the post-master directed them. I have read all the trash, and am weary.

10. Why; if you must have it out, something is to be published of great moment, and three or four great people are to see there are no mistakes in point of fact:[19] and 'tis so troublesome to send it among them, and get their corrections, that I am weary as a dog. I dined to-day with the printer, and was there all the afternoon; and it plagues me, and there's an end, and what would you have? Lady Dupplin, lord treasurer's daughter, is brought to bed of a son.[20] Lord treasurer has had an ugly return of his gravel. 'Tis good for us to live in gravel pits,[21] but not

---

[18] Three letters were written by Archbishop King to Swift in close sequence, 27, probably should be 29, Oct., 31 Oct., and 1 Nov. (*Corresp.* i. 293–9). In the first and second King refers to papers relating to Higgins's affair which he is forwarding. The Rev. Francis Higgins, 1669–1728, a violent High Churchman, was prosecuted for seditious preaching in London in 1707. In 1709 he was superseded as a J.P. for the county of Dublin for offending Lord Sunderland, then Secretary of State. Again he made himself notorious by supporting Dominick Langton, a converted friar, who brought charges against Whig gentlemen of Westmeath. At a sessions at Kilmainham, 5 Oct. 1711, a grand jury presented Higgins as 'a common disturber of her Majesty's peace'. See *Political State of Great Britain*, ii. 346–66; *A Full and Impartial Account of the Tryal of the Reverend Francis Higgins*, 1712; *Corresp.* i. 164 n.[2], 224 n.[1], 294 n.[2]; *Poems*, pp. 1090 ff.

[19] *The Conduct of the Allies.* St. John chiefly supplied Swift with facts and suggestions.

[20] p. 45 n.[39] This son, the second, christened Robert, took the additional surname of Drummond in 1739. He was Bishop of St. Asaph, 1748–61, of Salisbury, 1761, and Archbishop of York, 1761 till his death in 1776.

[21] Kensington Gravel Pits were esteemed a health resort. Cf. Garth's *Dispensary*, Canto iii:

'The Sick to th' Hundreds sooner shall repair,
And change the *Gravel-Pits* for *Essex* Air.'

for gravel pits to live in us: a man in this case should leave
no stone unturned. Lord treasurer's sickness, the queen's
gout, the forwarding the Peace, occasion putting off the
parliament a fortnight longer. My head has had no ill
returns. I had good walking to-day in the city, and take
all opportunities of it on purpose for my health; but I can't
walk in the Park, because that is only for walking sake,
and loses time, so I mix it with business: I wish MD
walked half as much as Presto. If I was with you, I'd
make you walk; I would walk behind or before you, and
you should have masks on, and be tucked up like any
thing, and Stella is naturally a stout walker, and carries
herself firm, methinks I see her strut, and step clever over
a kennel; and Dingley would do well enough, if her petticoats were pinned up; but she is so embroiled, and so
fearful, and then Stella scolds, and Dingley stumbles, and
is so daggled.[22] Have you got the whale-bone petticoats
amongst you yet?[23] I hate them; a woman here may
hide a moderate gallant under them. Pshaw, what's all
this I'm saying? methinks I am talking to MD face
to face.

11. Did I tell you that old Frowde,[24] the old fool, is
selling his estate at Pepperhara, and is skulking about
the town no body knows where? and who do you think

[22] Draggled. Cf. 'Description of a City Shower', l. 33 (*Poems*, p. 138):
'To Shops in Crouds the daggled Females fly'.

[23] The hooped petticoat began to come into fashion about 1708. See
Addison's paper on the trial of the petticoat, *The Tatler*, No. 116, 5 Jan.
1709–10, and *The Petticoat*; *An Heroi-Comical Poem*, 1716, by Joseph
Gay (John Durant Breval).

[24] He was Philip Frowde, father of the Philip Frowde (p. 81 n.[16]),
Addison's friend. Swift's 'old Frowde', the son of Sir Philip Frowde,
knighted in 1665 (Le Neve's *Knights*, Harleian Society, p. 190), was
Deputy Postmaster-General, 1678–88. The manor of Peperharrow, near
Godalming, purchased by Philip Frowde in 1700, was sold by him in 1713
to Alan Brodrick, afterwards Viscount Midleton in the peerage of Ireland
(Manning and Bray, *Hist. of Surrey*, ii. 32; Brayley, v. 231; *Victoria
County History, Surrey*, iii. 51).

manages all this for him, but that rogue Child,[25] the double squire of Farnham? I have put Mrs. Masham, the queen's favourite, upon buying it; but that is yet a great secret; and I have employed lady Oglethorp to enquire about it. I was with lady Oglethorp to-day, who is come to town for a week or two, and to-morrow I will see to hunt out the old fool; he is utterly ruined, and at this present in some blind alley with some dirty wench. He has two sons that must starve, and he never gives them a farthing. If Mrs. Masham buys the land, I will desire her to get the queen to give some pension to the old fool, to keep him from absolutely starving. What do you meddle with other people's affairs for? says Stella. O, but Mr. Masham and his wife are very urgent with me, since I first put them in the head of it. I dined with Sir Matthew Dudley, who, I doubt, will soon lose his employment.

12. Morning. I am going to hunt out old Frowde, and to do some business in the city. I have not yet called to Patrick to know whether it be fair. It has been past dropping these two days. Rainy weather hurts my pate and my purse. He tells me 'tis very windy, and begins to look dark; woe be to my shillings: an old saying and a true; Few fillings, many shillings. If the day be dark, my purse will be light. To my enemies be this curse; A dark day and a light purse. And so I'll rise, and go to my fire, for Patrick tells me I have a fire; yet it is not shaving day, nor is the weather cold; this is too extravagant. What is become of Dilly? I suppose you have him with you. Stella is just now shewing a white leg, and putting it into the slipper.—Present my service to her, and tell her I am engaged to the dean; and desire she will come too: or, Dingley, can't you write a note? This is Stella's morning

[25] He was an attorney in Guildford. In 1725 he bought Waverley Abbey, Farnham, and was succeeded in the property by Charles Child, either a son or nephew, who sold it in 1747 (Manning and Bray, *Surrey*, iii. 152; Brayley, v. 284).

dialogue, no, morning speech I mean.—Morrow, sirrahs, and let me rise as well as you; but I promise you Walls can't dine with the dean to-day, for she is to be at Mrs. Proby's just after dinner, and to go with Gracy Spencer[26] to the shops to buy a yard of muslin, and a silver lace for an under petticoat. Morrow again, sirrahs.—At night. I dined with Stratford in the city, but could not finish my affairs with him; but now I have resolved to buy five hundred pounds South-Sea stock, which will cost me three hundred and eighty ready money; and I will make use of the bill of a hundred pounds you sent me, and transfer Mrs. Walls over to Hawkshaw; or, if she dislikes it, I will borrow a hundred pounds of the secretary, and repay her.[27] Three shillings coach-hire to-day. I have spoken to Frowde's brother,[28] to get me the lowest price of the estate, to tell Mrs. Masham.

13. I dined privately with a friend to-day in the neighbourhood. Last Saturday night I came home, and the drab had just washed my room and my bed-chamber was all wet, and I was forced to go to bed in my own defence, and no fire: I was sick on Sunday, and now have got a swinging cold. I scolded like a dog at Patrick, although he was out with me: I detest washing of rooms: can't they wash them in a morning, and make a fire, and leave open the windows? I slept not a wink last night for hawking and spitting:[29] and now every body has colds. Here's a clutter: I'll go to bed and sleep if I can.

14. Lady Mountjoy sent to me two days ago, so I dined with her to-day, and in the evening went to see lord treasurer. I found Patrick had been just there with a how

26 Probably Mrs. Proby's sister. See pp. 223, 253; and notes.
27 See p. 386 n.[19]
28 Possibly Colonel William Frowde (p. 81 n.[16]), third son of Sir Philip Frowde (pp. 81, 409; and notes).
29 Cf. *As You Like It*, v. 3: 'Shall we clap into't roundly, without hawking or spitting or saying we are hoarse, which are the only prologues to a bad voice?'

d'ye,[30] and my lord had returned answer, that he desired to see me. Mrs. Masham was with him when I came; and they are never disturbed: 'tis well she is not very handsome:[31] they sit alone together, settling the nation. I sat with lady Oxford, and stopt Mrs. Masham as she came out, and told her what progress I had made, &c. and then went to lord treasurer: he is very well, only uneasy at rising or sitting, with some rheumatick pain in his thigh, and a foot weak. He shewed me a small paper, sent by an unknown hand to one Mr. Cook, who sent it to my lord: it was written in plain large letters, thus;

> *Though G————d's knife did not succeed;*
> *A F————n's yet may do the Deed.*

And a little below; *Burn this you Dog*. My lord has frequently such letters as these: once he shewed me one, which was a vision describing a certain man, his dress, his sword, and his countenance, who was to murder my lord. And he told me, he saw a fellow in the chapel at Windsor with a dress very like it. They often send him letters signed Your humble servant, The Devil, and such stuff. I sat with him till after ten, and have business to do.

15. The secretary came yesterday to town from Hampton-Court, so I went to him early this morning; but he went back last night again: and coming home to-night I found a letter from him to tell me, that he was just come home from Hampton-Court, and just returning, and will

---

[30] A formal inquiry after the health of a person. Cf. *Verses on the Death of Dr. Swift*:

> 'When daily Howd'y's come of Course,
> And Servants answer; *Worse and Worse*';

and *The Life and Character of Dean Swift*:

> 'When you are *Sick*, your *Friends*, you say,
> Will send their Howd'ye's ev'ry day'.

(*Poems*, pp. 557, 546; and see Ashton's *Social Life in the Reign of Queen Anne*, i. 78).

[31] She had a red nose.

not be here till Saturday night.[32] A pox take him; he stops
all my business. I'll beg leave to come back when I have
got over this; and hope to see MD in Ireland soon after
Christmas.—I'm weary of courts, and want my journies
to Laracor; they did me more good than all the ministries
these twenty years. I dined to-day in the city, but did no
business as I designed. Lady Mountjoy tells me, that
Dilly is got to Ireland, and that the archbishop of Dublin
was the cause of his returning so soon. The parliament
was prorogued two days ago for a fortnight, which, with
the queen's absence, makes the town very dull, and empty.
They tell me the duke of Ormond brings all the world
away with him from Ireland. London has nothing so bad
in it in Winter, as your knots of Irish folks; but I go to no
Coffee-house, and so I seldom see them. This letter shall
go on Saturday; and then I am even with the world again.
I have lent money, and cannot get it, and am forced to
borrow for myself.

16. My man made a blunder this morning, and let up
a visiter, when I had ordered to see no body, so I was
forced to hurry a hang-dog instrument of mine into my
bed-chamber, and keep him cooling his heels there above
an hour.——I am going on fairly in the common forms
of a great cold; I believe it will last me about ten days in
all.——I should have told you that in those two verses
sent to lord treasurer, the G——d stands for *Guiscard*;
that is easy; but we differed about F——n; I thought it
was for *Frenchman*, because he hates them, and they him:
and so it would be, That although Guiscard's knife missed
its design, the knife of a Frenchman might yet do it. My
lord thinks it stands for *Felton*, the name of him that
stabbed the first duke of Buckingham.—Sir Andrew Fountain and I dined with the Vans to-day, and my cold made
me loiter all the evening. Stay, young women, don't you

[32] This letter has not been preserved. On 16 and 17 Nov. St. John sent
Swift brief notes with a sheet (or sheets) of *The Conduct of the Allies,*
which had been sent for his correction (*Corresp.* i. 304).

begin to owe me a letter? just a month to-day since I had your N. 22. I'll stay a week longer, and then I'll expect like agog; till then you may play at ombre, and so forth, as you please. The Whigs are still crying down our Peace, but we will have it, I hope, in spite of them: the emperor comes now with his two eggs a penny, and promises wonders to continue the war; but it is too late; only I hope the fear of it will serve to spur on the French to be easy and sincere. Night, sirrahs; I'll go early to bed.

17. Morning. This goes to-night; I will put it myself in the post-office. I had just now a long letter from the archbishop of Dublin,[33] giving me an account of the ending your sessions, how it ended in a storm; which storm, by the time it arrives here, will be only *half nature*. I can't help it, I won't hide. I often advised the dissolution of that parliament, although I did not think the scoundrels had so much courage; but they have it only in the wrong, like a bully that will fight for a whore, and run away in an army. I believe, by several things the archbishop says, he is not very well either with the government or clergy.— See how luckily my paper ends with a fortnight.—God Almighty bless and preserve dearest little MD.—I suppose your lord-lieutenant is now setting out for England.[34] I wonder the bishop of Clogher does not write to me; or let me know of his statues,[35] and how he likes them: I will write to him again, as soon as I have leisure. Farewel, dearest MD, and love Presto, who loves MD infinitely above all earthly things, and who will.—My service to Mrs. Stoyte, and Catherine. I'm sitting in my bed; but will rise to seal this. Morrow, dear rogues. Farewel again, dearest MD, &c.

[33] Written 10 Nov. (*Corresp.* i. 300), describing events in the Irish Parliament and Convocation. The Parliamentary session had been stormy. 'We parted in very ill humour', wrote King.

[34] Archbishop King's letter of the 10th informed Swift that the session of the Irish Parliament had ended on the previous day. Ormonde's return to England for a time was therefore probable.

[35] Cf. pp. 250, 395.

LETTER XXXV

[SATURDAY]   London, Nov. 17, 1711.

I PUT my last this evening in the post-office. I dined with Dr. Cockburn. This being queen Elizabeth's birth-day, we have the D— and all to do among us. I just heard of the stir as my letter was sealed this morning; and was so cross I would not open it to tell you. I have been visiting lady Oglethorp and lady Worsley; the latter is lately come to town for the Winter, and with child, and what care you? This is queen Elizabeth's birth-day, usually kept in this town by 'prentices, &c. but the Whigs designed a mighty procession by midnight, and had laid out a thousand pounds to dress up the Pope, Devil, Cardinals, Sacheverell, &c. and carry them with torches about, and burn them. They did it by contribution. Garth gave five guineas, Dr. Garth I mean, if ever you heard of him. But they were seized last night, by order from the secretary: you will have an account of it, for they bawl it about the streets already. They had some very foolish and mischievous designs; and it was thought they would have put the rabble upon assaulting my lord treasurer's house, and the secretary's; and other violences.[1] The Militia[2] was

[1] The Tories alleged that the procession of apprentices and others, which usually took place on Queen Elizabeth's birthday, was, on this occasion, organized by the Whigs as a political conspiracy. It was rumoured that Marlborough was to have been met with the huzzas of the mob, and that the Duke of Montagu, Steele, and other Whigs were to have taken part. In justification of the government's action in seizing the images Swift supplied Mrs. Manley with hints for a pamphlet entitled *A True Relation of the several Facts and Circumstances of the intended Riot and Tumult on Queen Elizabeth's Birth-day* (p. 421), which was published on 29 Nov. (*The Post Boy*, 27–9 Nov.). This ran to a second edition, and was also reprinted in Edinburgh. The writer asserted that one of the effigies was designed to represent Lord Oxford, another Lady Masham; and that 'The *Spectator* [*i.e.* Steele] . . . was to have been an Assistant'. This last accusation is glanced at in *The Spectator*, No. 269. For the order of the procession see 'Biographical Anecdotes' prefixed to Nichols's *Supplement*, 1779.   [2] The London trained bands.

raised to prevent it, and now, I suppose, all will be quiet. The figures are now at the secretary's office at White-hall. I design to see them if I can.

18. I was this morning with Mr. secretary, who just came from Hampton-Court. He was telling me more particulars about this business of burning the Pope. It cost a great deal of money, and had it gone on, would have cost three times as much: but the town is full of it, and half a dozen Grub-street papers already. The secretary and I dined at brigadier Britton's, but I left them at six, upon an appointment with some sober company of men and ladies, to drink punch at Sir Andrew Fountain's. We were not very merry; and I don't love rack punch, I love it better with brandy: are you of my opinion? Why then; twelve-penny weather; sirrahs, why don't you play at shuttle-cock? I have thought of it a hundred times; faith Presto will come over after Christmas, and will play with Stella before the cold weather is gone. Do you read the *Spectators*? I never do; they never come in my way; I go to no Coffee-houses. They say abundance of them are very pretty; they are going to be printed in small volumes;[3] I'll bring them over with me. I shall be out of my hurry in a week, and if Leigh be not gone over, I will send you by him what I am now finishing. I don't know where Leigh is; I have not seen him this good while, though he promised to call: I shall send to him. The queen comes to town on Thursday for good and all.

19. I was this morning at lord Dartmouth's office, and sent out for him from the committee of council, about some business. I was asking him more concerning this bustle about the figures in wax-work of the Pope, and Devil, &c. He was not at leisure, or he would have seen them. I hear the owners are so impudent, that they design to replevin[4] them by law. I am assured that the figure of

---

[3] See p. 399 n.

[4] Recovery of goods upon security given that the ownership shall be tried in a court of justice.

the Devil is made as like lord treasurer as they could. Why; I dined with a friend in St. James's-street. Lord treasurer, I am told, was abroad to-day; I will know to-morrow how he does after it. The duke of Marlborough is come,[5] and was yesterday at Hampton-Court with the queen; no, it was t'other day; no it was yesterday; for to-day I remember Mr. secretary was going to see him, when I was there, not at the duke of Marlborough's, but at the secretary's; the duke is not so fond of me. What care I? I won seven shillings to-night at picquet: I play twice a year or so.

20. I have been so teazed with Whiggish discourse by Mrs. Barton and lady Betty Germain, never saw the like. They turn all this affair of the pope-burning into ridicule; and indeed they have made too great a clutter about it, if they had no real reason to apprehend some tumults. I dined with lady Betty. I hear Prior's com-mission is passed to be ambassador extraordinary and plenipotentiary for the Peace; my lord privy-seal, who you know is bishop of Bristol, is the other; and lord Straf-ford, already ambassador at the Hague, the third: I am forced to tell you ignorant sluts who is who. I was pun-ning scurvily with Sir Andrew Fountain and lord Pem-broke this evening; do you ever pun now? Sometimes the dean, or Tom Leigh.[6] Prior puns very well. Od so, I must go see his excellency, 'tis a noble advancement: but they could do no less, after sending him to France. Lord Strafford is as proud as hell, and how he will bear one of Prior's mean birth on an equal character with him, I know not.[7] And so I go to my business,[8] and bid you good night.

21. I was this morning busy with my printer; I gave him the fifth sheet, and then I went and dined with him

---

[5] Marlborough landed at Greenwich on the 18th, and waited on the Queen the next day (Winston Churchill, *Marlborough*, iv. 495).

[6] p. 9 n.[17]   [7] Swift's doubts were justified (p. 427 n.[38]).

[8] *The Conduct of the Allies.*

in the city, to correct something, and alter, &c. and I walked home in the dusk, and the rain overtook me: and I found a letter here from Mr. Lewis;[9] well, and so I opened it; and he says, The peace is past danger, &c. Well; and so there was another letter inclosed in his; well; and so I looked on the outside of this t'other letter. Well; and so who do you think this t'other letter was from? Well; and so I'll tell you, it was from little MD, N. 23, 23, 23, 23.[10] I tell you it is no more, I have told you so before:[11] but I just looked again to satisfy you. Hie, Stella, you write like an emperor, a great deal together; a very good hand, and but four false spellings in all. Shall I send them to you? I am glad you did not take my correction ill. Well; but I won't answer your letter now, sirrah saucy boxes, no, no; not yet; just a month and three days from the last, which is just five weeks: you see it comes just when I begin to grumble.

22. Morning. Tooke has just brought me Dingley's money. I will give you a note for it at the end of this letter.[12] There was half a crown for entering the letter of attorney: but I swore to stop that. I'll spend your money bravely here. Morrow, dear sirrahs.—At night. I dined to-day with Sir Thomas Hanmer; his wife, the duchess of Grafton,[13] dined with us: she wears a great high head-

---

[9] The letter has not been preserved.

[10] The receipt of No. 23 from Stella is noted by Swift in his account book, Nov. 1711–Nov. 1712 (Forster Collection, 508).

[11] 'Nothing was ever more in *Swift's* style and manner of conversation, than these repetitions and the words following.'—Deane Swift.

[12] Cf. p. 386 n.[10]

[13] Sir Thomas Hanmer (p. 96 n.[21]) married in 1698, as his first wife, Isabella, widow of the first Duke of Grafton (Evelyn's *Diary*, 6 Nov. 1679), who was mortally wounded at the siege of Cork, 1690. She was the only daughter of Henry Bennet, first Earl of Arlington, and became Countess of Arlington, *suo jure*, in 1685. Addison in *The Spectator*, No. 98, 22 June 1711, writing of the *commode*, says: 'There is not so variable a thing in nature as a lady's head-dress. ... About ten years ago it shot up to a very great height, insomuch that the female part of our species were much taller than the men.'

dress, such as was in fashion fifteen years ago, and looks like a mad-woman in it; yet she has great remains of beauty. I was this evening to see lord Harley, and thought to have sat with lord treasurer; but he was taken up with the Dutch envoy[14] and such folks; and I would not stay. One particular in life here different from what I have in Dublin, is, that whenever I come home I expect to find some letter for me, and seldom miss; and never any worth a farthing, but often to vex me. The queen does not come to town till Saturday. Prior is not yet declared; but these ministers being at Hampton-Court I know nothing; and if I write news from common hands, it is always lies. You will think it affectation; but nothing has vexed me more for some months past, than people I never saw, pretending to be acquainted with me, and yet speak ill of me too; at least some of them. An old crooked Scotch countess, whom I never heard of in my life, told the duchess of Hamilton[15] t'other day, that I often visited her. People of worth never do that: so that a man only gets the scandal of having scurvy acquaintance. Three ladies were railing against me some time ago, and said they were very well acquainted with me; two of which I had never heard of; and the third had only seen twice where I happened to visit. A man who has once seen me in a Coffee-house will ask me how I do, when he sees me talking at Court with a minister of state; who is sure to ask me, how I came acquainted with that scoundrel. But come, sirrahs, this is all stuff to you, so I'll say no more on this side the paper, but turn over.

23. My printer invited Mr. Lewis and me to dine at a

---

[14] Monsieur de Buys, Pensionary of Amsterdam, who came to England as Dutch Envoy in consequence of the peace with France negotiated by Prior. He arrived in London on 18 Oct. (Bolingbroke's *Letters*, i. 260). He was the principal representative of Holland at Utrecht. In *The Four Last Years of the Queen* (*Prose Works*, x. 41–2) Swift disparages his ability.

[15] The Duke of Hamilton (p. 323 n.[15]) married, as his second wife, in 1698, Elizabeth, only child of Digby, Lord Gerrard. She died in 1744.

tavern to-day, which I have not done five times since I came to England; I never will call it *Britain*, pray don't call it *Britain*.[16] My week is not out, and one side of this paper is out, and I have a letter to answer of MD's into the bargain: must I write on the third side; faith that will give you an ill habit. I saw Leigh last night: he gives a terrible account of Sterne; he reckons he is seduced by some wencher; he is over head and ears in debt, and has pawned several things. Leigh says he goes on Monday next for Ireland, but believes Sterne will not go with him; Sterne has kept him these three months. Leigh has got the apron and things, and promises to call for the box at Chester; but I despair of it. Good night, sirrahs; I have been late abroad.

24. I have finished my pamphlet[17] to-day, which has cost me so much time and trouble; it will be published in three or four days, when the parliament begins sitting. I suppose the queen is come to town, but know nothing, having been in the city finishing and correcting with the printer. When I came home I found letters on my table as usual, and one from your mother, to tell me, that you desire your writings and a picture should be sent to me, to be sent over to you. I have just answered her letter, and promised to take care of them if they be sent to me. She is at Farnham: it is too late to send them by Leigh; besides, I will wait your orders, madam Stella. I am going to finish a letter to lord treasurer about reforming our language;[18] but first I must put an end to a ballad;[19] and go you to your cards, sirrahs, this is card season.

25. I was early with the secretary to-day, but he was

---

[16] Cf. p. 111; and a letter from Swift to John Barber, 8 Aug. 1738: 'Pox on the modern phrase Great Britain, which is only to distinguish it from Little Britain, where old clothes and books are to be bought and sold' (*Corresp.* vi. 93).

[17] *The Conduct of the Allies.*

[18] See p. 296 n.[8]

[19] Perhaps never printed. For ballads published towards the close of 1711 and beginning of 1712 see *Poems*, pp. 141 ff.

gone to his devotions, and to receive the sacrament; several rakes did the same; it was not for piety, but employments; according to act of parliament. I dined with lady Mary Dudley;[20] and past my time since insipidly, only I was at Court at noon, and saw fifty acquaintance I had not met this long time: that is the advantage of a Court, and I fancy I am better known than any man that goes there. Sir John Walters'[21] quarrel with me has entertained the town ever since; and yet we never had a word, only he railed at me behind my back. The parliament is again to be prorogued for eight or nine days; for the Whigs are too strong in the house of lords: other reasons are pretended, but that is the truth. The prorogation is not yet known, but will be to-morrow.

26. Mr. Lewis and I dined with a friend of his, and unexpectedly there dined with us an Irish knight, one Sir John St. Leger,[22] who follows the law here, but at a great distance: he was so pert, I was forced to take him down more than once. I saw to-day the Pope and Devil, and the other figures of Cardinals, &c. fifteen in all, which have made such a noise. I have put an under-strapper upon writing a two-penny pamphlet to give an account of the whole design.[23] My large pamphlet will be published to-morrow, copies are sent to the great men this night. Domville is come home from his travels; I am vexed at it; I have not seen him yet; I design to present him to all the great men.

₂₀ Sir Matthew Dudley (p. 11 n.²) married Lady Mary O'Bryen, third and youngest daughter of Henry, seventh Earl of Thomond.

₂₁ Deane Swift, Sheridan, Moorhead, read 'Walters"; Nichols, Scott, Ryland, Aitken, 'Walter's'. See p. 374 n.¹⁶

₂₂ John St. Leger, 1674–1743, educated at Westminster School and Christ Church, Oxford, entered the Inner Temple in 1691. He was knighted by William III in 1701. After the accession of George I he went to Ireland as second Baron of the Exchequer (Ball, *Judges in Ireland*, ii. 192–3, *et passim*). His elder brother, Arthur, was created Viscount Doneraile in 1703.

₂₃ p. 415 n.¹

27. Domville came to me this morning, and we dined at Pontack's, and were all day together, till six this evening; he is perfectly as fine a gentleman as I know; he set me down at lord treasurer's, with whom I staid about an hour, till Monsieur Buys, the Dutch envoy, came to him about business. My lord treasurer is pretty well; but stiff in the hips with the remains of the rheumatism. I am to bring Domville to my lord Harley in a day or two. It was the dirtiest rainy day that ever I saw. The pamphlet[24] is published; lord treasurer had it by him on the table, and was asking me about the mottos in the title page; he gave me one of them himself. I must send you the pamphlet if I can.

28. Mrs. Van sent to me to dine with her to-day, because some ladies of my acquaintance were to be there; and there I dined. I was this morning to return Domville his visit, and went to visit Mrs. Masham, who was not within. I am turned out of my lodging by my landlady; it seems her husband and son are coming home; but I have taken another lodging hard by, in Leicester-Fields. I presented Mr. Domville to Mr. Lewis and Mr. Prior this morning. Prior and I are called the two Sosias[25] in a

---

[24] *The Conduct of the Allies,* ... London, *Printed for John Morphew,* ... *1712,* pp. 96, was one of the most effective political pamphlets ever published. It discredited the war, and hastened a decline in Marlborough's popularity. Four more editions appeared before the end of 1711, dated that year; a sixth edition in Jan. 1712; a seventh in April; and an eighth in 1713. There were also Dublin and Edinburgh editions. The three mottoes will be found respectively in Lucan, v. 264–7; Ovid, *Ars Amat.* ii. 147; and Juvenal, i. 50.

[25] See Plautus' *Amphitruo,* Molière's *Amphitryon,* and Dryden's *Amphitryon: Or, The Two Sosia's. The Protestant Post-Boy,* 24–7 Nov. 1711: 'After a Man has once taken leave of a Dirty Road, he is not easily perswaded to turn back into it again, unless an unexperienc'd Traveller, in danger of being mir'd, should demand his Assistance; and then, I think, it is but passable Humanity to return to his Relief: The Application is very obvious, We had, in a Manner, quitted that filthy *Rump* of the Party, ABEL, and the two *Sosia's, Sw—t* and *Pr—r,* and almost determin'd never to Flux our Pen with such stinking Characters.'

Whig news-paper. *Sosias*, can you read it? The pamphlet begins to make a noise: I was asked by several whether I had seen it, and they advised me to read it, for it was something very extraordinary. I shall be suspected: and it will have several paultry answers. It must take its fate, as Savage[26] said of his sermon that he preached at Farnham on Sir William Temple's death. Domville saw Savage in Italy, and says he is a coxcomb, and half mad: he goes in red, and with yellow waistcoats,[27] and was at ceremony kneeling to the Pope on a Palm Sunday, which is much more than kissing his toe; and I believe it will ruin him here when 'tis told. I'll answer your letter in my new lodgings: I have hardly room; I must borrow from the other side.

29. New lodgings.[28] My printer came this morning to tell me he must immediately print a second edition,[29] and lord treasurer made one or two small additions: they must work day and night to have it out on Saturday; they sold a thousand in two days. Our society met to-day, nine of us were present, we dined at our brother Bathurst's,[30] we made several regulations, and have chosen three new members, lord Orrery, Jack Hill, who is Mrs. Masham's

[26] The sermon has not been traced, though Swift's words seem to imply publication. See Julia Longe, *Martha Lady Giffard*, pp. 232, 242. The preacher was probably Dr. John Savage of Emmanuel College, Cambridge, where Temple had been educated. Savage, famed as the Aristippus of the age, is known to have travelled abroad and spent some time in Rome. He was the author of a number of works, including sermons. From 1708 to his death in 1747, at the age of seventy-five, he was rector of Clothall in Hertfordshire. There was also a William Savage, elected master of Emmanuel College in 1719, who died in 1736. See Clutterbuck, *Hist. of Hertfordshire*, iii. 505 n., 507; Nichols, *Lit. Anec.* ii. 141–2.

[27] Spelling probably altered by Deane Swift. See p. 388 n.[24]

[28] The new lodgings were in Little Panton Street (p. 142 n.[16]).

[29] Of *The Conduct of the Allies.*

[30] Allen Bathurst, 1685–1775, Tory M.P. for Cirencester from 1705 till he was raised to the peerage as Baron Bathurst, 1 Jan. 1712 (p. 450 n.[31]). In 1772 he was created an Earl. He remained a lifelong friend of Swift and Pope.

brother, he that lately miscarried in the expedition to Quebeck, and one colonel Disney. We have taken a room in a house near St. James's to meet in. I left them early about correcting the pamphlet, &c. and am now got home, &c.

30. This morning I carried Domville to see my lord Harley, and I did some business with lord treasurer, and have been all this afternoon with the printer, adding something to the second edition. I dined with the printer; the pamphlet makes a world of noise, and will do a great deal of good: it tells abundance of most important facts which were not at all known. I'll answer your letter to-morrow morning; or suppose I answer it just now, though it is pretty late. Come then—You say you are busy with parliaments, &c. that's more than ever I will be when I come back; but you will have none these two years. Lord Santry, &c. yes, I have had enough on't.[31] I am glad Dilly is mended; does not he thank me for shewing him the Court and the great people's faces? He had his glass out at the queen and the rest. 'Tis right what Dilly says; I depend upon nothing from my friends; but to go back as I came. Never fear Laracor, 'twill mend with a Peace; or surely they'll give me the Dublin parish.[32] Stella is in the right; the bishop of Ossory is the silliest, best-natured wretch breathing, of as little consequence as an egg-shell.—Well, the spelling I have mentioned before; only the next time say *at least*, and not *at lest*. Pox on your Newbury:[33] what can I do for him? I'll give his case (I am glad it is not a woman's) to what members I know; that's all I can do. Lord treasurer's lameness goes off daily. Pray God preserve poor good Mrs. Stoyte, she would be a great loss to

[31] Swift refers to the Higgins affair (p. 408 n.[18]). Henry, 1680–1735, third Lord Santry, an ardent Whig, was one of Higgins's chief prosecutors. See *Corresp.* i. 294 n.[2]; *Poems*, pp. 1029, 1091, 1093 and notes. Lord Santry was a small man, and Deane Swift has a footnote illustrating his diminutive size.   [32] See pp. 71, 668.
[33] Probably the same as Colonel Newburgh, p. 504.

us all; pray give her my service, and tell her she has my heartiest prayers. I pity poor Mrs. Manley;[34] but I think the child is happy to die, considering how little provision it would have had. Poh, every pamphlet abuses me, and for things that I never writ. Joe should have written me thanks for his two hundred pounds: I reckon he got it by my means; and I must thank the duke of Ormond, who I dare swear will say he did it on my account? Are they golden pippins, those seven apples? We have had much rain every day as well as you: 7l. 17s. 8d. old blunderer, not 18sh. I have reckoned it 18 times. Hawkshaw's eight pounds is not reckoned; and if it be secure, it may lie where it is, unless they desire to pay it: so Parvisol may let it drop till further orders; for I have put Mrs. Wesley's money into the bank, and will pay her with Hawkshaw's.
———I mean that Hawkshaw's money goes for an addition to MD, you know; but be good houswives. Bernage never comes now to see me; he has no more to ask: but I hear he has been ill.—A pox on Mrs. South's affair; I can do nothing in it, but by way of assisting any body else that solicits it, by dropping a favourable word, if it comes in my way. Tell Walls I do no more for any body with my lord treasurer, especially a thing of this kind. Tell him I have spent all my discretion, and have no more to use.———And so I have answered your letter fully and plainly—And so I have got to the third side of my paper, which is more than belongs to you, young women. It goes to-morrow, To nobody's sorrow. You are silly, not I; I'm a poet, if I had but, &c.———Who's silly now? rogues and lasses, tinder-boxes and buzzards. O Lord, I am in a high vein of silliness; methought I was speaking to dearest little MD face to face. There; so lads, enough for to-night; to cards with the blackguards. Good night, my delight, &c.

Dec. 1. Pish, sirrahs, put a date always at the bottom of the letter as well as the top, that I may know when you

34 Mrs. Isaac Manley.

send it; your last is of Nov. 3d, yet I had others at the same time written a fortnight after. Whenever you would have any money, send me word three weeks before and in that time you will certainly have an answer, with a bill on Parvisol: pray do this; for my head is full and it will ease my memory. Why, I think I quoted to you some of ——'s letter,[35] so you may imagine how witty the rest was; for it was all of a bunch, as goodman Peesley[36] says. Pray let us have no more *Bussiness*, but *Busyness*: the Deuse take me if I know how to spell it, your wrong spelling, madam Stella, has put me out: it does not look right; let me see, *Bussiness, Busyness, Business, Bisyness, Bisness, Bysness*; faith, I know not which is right, I think the second; I believe I never writ the word in my life before; yes, sure I must though; *Business, Busyness, Bisyness.*——I have perplexed myself, and can't do it. Prithee ask Walls. *Business*, I fancy that's right. Yes it is; I looked in my own pamphlet, and found it twice in ten lines, to convince you that I never writ it before. Oh, now I see it as plain as can be; so yours is only an *s* too much. The parliament will certainly meet on Friday next; the Whigs will have a great majority in the house of lords; no care is taken to prevent it; there is too much neglect; they are warned of it, and that signifies nothing: it was feared there would be some peevish address from the lords against a Peace. 'Tis said about the town, that several of the allies begin now to be content that a Peace should be treated. This is all the news I have. The queen is pretty well; and so now I bid poor dearest MD farewel till to-night, then I will talk with them again.

The fifteen images that I saw were not worth forty pounds,[37] so I stretched a little when I said a thousand. The Grub-street account of that tumult is published. The Devil is not like lord treasurer; they were all in your odd

---

[35] See p. 369 n.[1]
[36] See p. 184 n.[19]
[37] See p. 415 and note.

antick masks, bought in common shops. I fear Prior will not be one of the plenipotentiaries.[38]

I was looking over some of this letter, and find I make many mistakes of leaving out words; so 'tis impossible to find my meaning, unless you be conjurers. I will take more care for the future, and read over every day just what I have written that day; which will take up no time to speak of.

LETTER XXXVI

[SATURDAY]   London, December 1, 1711.

MY last was put in this evening. I intended to dine with Mr. Masham to-day, and called at White's Chocolate-house to see if he was there. Lord Wharton saw me at the door, and I saw him, but took no notice, and was going away; but he came through the crowd, called after me, and asked me how I did, &c. This was pretty; and I believe he wished every word he spoke was a halter to hang me. Masham did not dine at home, so I ate with a friend in the neighbourhood. The printer has not sent me the second edition;[1] I know not the reason, for it certainly came out to-day; perhaps they are glutted with it already. I found a letter from lord Harley on my table, to tell me that his father desires I would make two small alterations. I am going to be busy, &c.

2. Morning. See the blunder; I was making it the 37th day of the month from the number above. Well, but I am staying here for old Frowde, who appointed to call this morning: I am ready dressed to go to church; I suppose he dare not stir out but on Sundays.[2] The printer called early this morning, told me the second edition went off yesterday in five hours, and he must have a third ready

---

[38] Lord Strafford bluntly refused to have Prior as a colleague, and the Ministry was compelled to give way (Wickham Legg, *Prior*, p. 169).

[1] Of *The Conduct of the Allies.*

[2] p. 409 n.[24] Debtors could not be arrested on a Sunday.

to-morrow, for they might have sold half another: his men are all at work with it, though it be Sunday. This old fool will not come, and I shall miss church.—Morrow sirrahs.—At night. I was at Court to-day; the queen is well and walked through part of the rooms. I dined with the secretary, and dispatched some business. He tells me, the Dutch envoy designs to complain of that pamphlet. The noise it makes is extraordinary. It is fit it should answer the pains I have been at about it. I suppose it will be printed in Ireland.[3] Some lay it to Prior, others to Mr. secretary St. John, but I am always the first they lay every thing to. I'll go sleep, &c.

3. I have ordered Patrick not to let any odd fellow come up to me; and to-day a fellow would needs speak with me from Sir George Prettyman.[4] I had never heard of him, and would not see the messenger; but at last it proved that this Sir George has sold his estate, and is a beggar. Smithers, the Farnham carrier, brought me this morning a letter from your mother, with three papers inclosed of lady Giffard's writing; one owning some exchequer business of 100*l.* to be Stella's;[5] another for 100*l.* that she has of yours, which I made over to you for Mariston,[6] and a third for 300*l.*; the last is on stampt paper. I think they had better lie in England in some good hand till lady Giffard dies; and I will think of some such hand before I come over. I was asking Smithers about all the people of Farnham. Mrs. White[7] has left off dressing, is troubled with lameness and swelled legs, and seldom stirs out; but her old hang-dog husband as hearty as ever. I was this morning with lord treasurer about

---

[3] *The Conduct of the Allies* was reprinted by two Dublin booksellers, John Hyde and Edward Waters. The latter issued two editions.

[4] Sir George Pretyman, 1638–1715, second baronet. According to Le Neve's *Knights* he was 'living in London and goes a begging, 1712'.

[5] See p. 74 n.33

[6] Unidentified.

[7] See Manning and Bray, *Surrey*, iii. 177, for a pedigree of the family of White of Farnham.

something he would have altered in the pamphlet; but it can't be till the fourth edition, which I believe will be soon; for I dined with the printer, and he tells me they have sold off half the third. Mrs. Percival[8] and her daughter have been in town these three weeks, which I never heard till to-day; and Mrs. Wesley is come to town too, to consult Dr. Radcliffe. The Whigs are resolved to bring that pamphlet into the house of lords to have it condemned, *so I hear*. But the printer will stand to it, and not own the author; he must say, he had it from the penny-post. Some people talk as if the house of lords would do some peevish thing; for the Whigs are now a great majority in it; our ministers are too negligent of such things: I have never slipt giving them warning; some of them are sensible of it; but lord treasurer stands too much upon his own legs. I fancy his good fortune will bear him out in every thing; but in reason I should think this ministry to stand very unsteady: if they can carry a Peace, they may hold; I believe not else.

4. Mr. secretary sent to me to-day to dine with him alone; but we had two more with us, which hindered me doing some business. I was this morning with young Harcourt, secretary to our society, to take a room for our weekly meetings; and the fellow asked us five guineas a week only to have leave to dine once a week; was not that pretty? so we broke off with him, and are to dine next Thursday at Harcourt's (he is lord keeper's son). They have sold off above half the third edition, and answers are coming out: the Dutch envoy refused dining with Dr. D'avenant, because he was suspected to write it: I have

---

8 Wife of John Perceval of Knightsbrook in Swift's parish of Laracor. One of Swift's note-books records games of picquet with Perceval as early as 1702 (Forster, *Life*, p. 269 n.). He was M.P. for the borough of Granard, and later for that of Trim. In 1716 he sold Swift twenty acres for the glebe of Laracor (*Corresp.* ii, *passim*). The editor has one of the original documents signed by Swift and Perceval. He died in 1718. Perceval was related to Sir John Percival (p. 222 n.[20]) who became first Earl of Egmont in 1733.

made some alterations in every edition, and it has cost me more trouble, for the time, since the printing than before. 'Tis sent over to Ireland, and I suppose you will have it reprinted.

5. They are now printing the fourth edition, which is reckoned very extraordinary, considering 'tis a dear twelve-penny book, and not bought up in numbers by the party to give away, as the Whigs do, but purely upon it's own strength. I have got an under spur-leather to write an *Examiner* again, and the secretary and I will now and then send hints; but we would have it a little upon the Grub-street, to be a match for their writers. I dined with lord treasurer to-day at five; he dined by himself after his family, and drinks no claret yet, for fear of his rheumatism, of which he is almost well. He was very pleasant, as he is always; yet I fancied he was a little touched with the present posture of affairs. The elector of Hanover's minister[9] here has given in a violent memorial against the Peace, and caused it to be printed. The Whig lords are doing their utmost for a majority against Friday, and design, if they can, to address the queen against the Peace. Lord Nottingham,[10] a famous Tory and speech-maker, is gone over to the Whig side: they toast him daily, and lord Wharton says, It is *Dismal* (so they call him from his looks) will save England at last. Lord treasurer was hinting as if he wished a ballad was made on him, and I will get up one against to-morrow. He gave me a scurrilous printed paper of bad verses on himself, under the name of the *English*

---

[9] Johann Caspar von Bothmar, 1656–1732, the Elector of Hanover's envoy to the Court of St. James, suspecting his master's right of succession might be endangered, presented a strong memorial against the preliminary articles for peace.

[10] Daniel Finch, 1647–1730, second Earl of Nottingham, was a staunch Tory, but before Parliament reassembled it was known that he had agreed with the Whigs to support their opposition to peace if they would assist him in passing his Occasional Conformity Bill. For Swift's ballad, *An Excellent New Song, Being the Intended Speech of a famous Orator against Peace*, see *Poems*, pp. 141–5.

Catiline,[11] and made me read them to the company. It was his birth-day, which he would not tell us, but lord Harley whispered it to me.

6. I was this morning making the ballad, two degrees above Grubstreet; at noon I paid a visit to Mrs. Masham, and then went to dine with our society. Poor lord keeper dined below stairs, I suppose on a bit of mutton. We chose two members; we were eleven met, the greatest meeting we ever had: I am next week to introduce lord Orrery. The printer came before we parted, and brought the ballad, which made them laugh very heartily a dozen times. He is going to print the pamphlet in small, a fifth edition,[12] to be taken off by friends and sent into the country. A sixpenny answer is come out,[13] good for nothing, but guessing me among others for the author. To-morrow is the fatal day for the parliament meeting, and we are full of hopes and fears. We reckon we have a majority of ten on our side in the house of lords; yet I observed Mrs. Masham a little uneasy; she assures me the queen is stout.[14] The duke of Marlborough has not seen the queen for some days past; Mrs. Masham is glad of it, because she says, he tells a hundred lies to his friends of what she says to him: he is one day humble, and the next on the high ropes. The duke of Ormond, they say, will be in town to-night by twelve.

[11] *A Panegyrick upon the English Cataline. . . . Printed in the Year MDCCXI.* A folio broadside. Copy in the British Museum, 1850. c. 10 (8).

[12] *The Conduct of the Allies.* The fifth and succeeding editions published by Morphew are in smaller letter than the earlier editions and run to only 48 pages, instead of 96.

[13] Either *Remarks On A False, Scandalous, and Seditious Libel, Intituled, The Conduct of the Allies. . . . London, . . . A Baldwin.* 1711 (Advertised in *The Daily Courant*, 7 Dec., and in *The Post-Man*, 6–8 Dec.); or *The Allies And the Late Ministry Defended . . . In Answer to a Pamphlet, Intituled, The Conduct of the Allies. . . . London, . . . A. Baldwin.* 1711 (Advertised in *The Daily Courant*, 6 and 7 Dec.). The second pamphlet was by Dr. Francis Hare, chaplain to the Duke of Marlborough.

[14] Determined.

7. This being the day the parliament was to meet, and the great question to be determined, I went with Dr. Freind[15] to dine in the city, on purpose to be out of the way, and we sent our printer to see what was our fate; but he gave us a most melancholy account of things. The earl of Nottingham began, and spoke against a Peace, and desired that in their address they might put in a clause to advise the queen not to make a peace without Spain; which was debated, and carried by the Whigs by about six voices:[16] and this has happened entirely by my lord treasurer's neglect, who did not take timely care to make up all his strength, although every one of us gave him caution enough. Nottingham has certainly been bribed. The question is yet only carried in the committee of the whole house, and we hope when it is reported to the house to-morrow, we shall have a majority by some Scotch lords coming to town. However, it is a mighty blow and loss of reputation to lord treasurer, and may end in his ruin. I hear the thing only as the printer brought it, who was at the debate; but how the ministry take it, or what their hopes and fears are, I cannot tell until I see them. I shall be early with the secretary to-morrow, and then I will tell you more, and shall write a full account to the bishop of Clogher to-morrow, and to the archbishop of Dublin, if I have time. I am horribly down at present. I long to know how lord treasurer bears this, and what remedy he has. The duke of Ormond came this day to town, and was there.

8. I was early this morning with the secretary, and talkt over this matter. He hoped, that when it was reported

---

[15] John.

[16] Nottingham moved a clause to the Queen's Address representing that 'no Peace could be safe or honourable . . . if Spain and the West Indies were allotted to any branch of the House of Bourbon'. After a long debate this was carried by 62 votes to 54. A like amendment, moved by Robert Walpole the same evening in the Commons, was rejected by 232 votes to 106. *Journals of the House of Lords*, xix. 339; *Commons*, xvii. 1–2.

ESTHER JOHNSON (STELLA)

*From an oil picture in the possession of Cecil H. Villiers Briscoe, Esq., Bellinter House,
Co. Meath, Ireland*

this day in the house of lords, they would disagree with their committee, and so the matter would go off, only with a little loss of reputation to lord treasurer. I dined with Dr. Cockburn, and after a Scotch member came in, and told us that the clause was carried against the Court in the house of lords almost two to one; I went immediately to Mrs. Masham, and meeting Dr. Arbuthnott (the queen's favourite physician) we went together. She was just come from waiting at the queen's dinner, and going to her own. She had heard nothing of the thing being gone against us. It seems lord treasurer had been so negligent, that he was with the queen while the question was put in the house: I immediately told Mrs. Masham, that either she and lord treasurer had joined with the queen to betray us, or that they two were betrayed by the queen: she protested solemnly it was not the former, and I believed her; but she gave me some lights to suspect the queen is changed. For, yesterday when the queen was going from the house, where she sat to hear the debate, the duke of Shrewsbury lord chamberlain asked her, whether he or the great chamberlain Lindsay[17] ought to lead her out; she answered short, Neither of you, and gave her hand to the duke of Somerset, who was louder than any in the house for the clause against Peace. She gave me one or two more instances of this sort, which convince me that the queen is false, or at least very much wavering. Mr. Masham begged us to stay, because lord treasurer would call, and we were resolved to fall on him about his negligence in securing a majority. He came, and appeared in good humour as usual, but I thought his countenance was much cast down. I rallied him, and desired him to give me his staff, which he did; I told him, if he would secure it me a week, I

---

[17] Robert Bertie, 1660–1723, styled Lord Willoughby de Eresby, 1666–1701, fourth Earl of Lindsey, was created Marquis of Lindsey in 1706 and Duke of Ancaster and Kesteven in 1715. Macky characterized him as possessed of 'both wit and learning'. Swift's comment was, 'I never observed a grain of either' (*Prose Works*, x. 279).

would set all right: he asked, How? I said, I would immediately turn lord Marlborough, his two daughters,[18] the duke and duchess of Somerset, and lord Cholmondely[19] out of all their employments; and I believe he had not a friend but was of my opinion. Arbuthnott asked, How he came not to secure a majority? He could answer nothing, but that he could not help it, if people would lie and forswear. A poor answer for a great minister. There fell from him a scripture expression, that *the hearts of kings are unsearchable.*[20] I told him, It was what I feared, and was from him the worst news he could tell me. I begged him to know what we had to trust to; he stuck a little; but at last bid me not fear, for all would be well yet. We would fain have had him eat a bit where he was, but he would go home, it was past six: he made me go home with him. There we found his brother and Mr. secretary. He made his son take a list of all in the house of commons who had places, and yet voted against the Court, in such a manner as if they should lose their places: I doubt he is not able to compass it. Lord keeper[21] came in an hour, and they were going upon business. So I left him, and returned to Mrs. Masham; but she had company with her, and I would not stay.—This is a long journal, and of a day that may produce great alterations, and hazard the ruin of England. The Whigs are all in triumph; they foretold how all this would be, but we thought it boasting. Nay,

---

[18] Lady Sunderland (p. 328 n.[33]) and Lady Rialton, ladies of the bedchamber to the Queen. Henrietta, eldest daughter of the Duke of Marlborough, married in 1698 Francis (Godolphin), Viscount Rialton, who, 15 Sept. 1712, succeeded his father as second Earl of Godolphin. In 1722 she became, *suo jure*, Duchess of Marlborough.

[19] Hugh Cholmondeley, *c.* 1662–1725, succeeding to the title as second Viscount Cholmondeley of Kells in 1681, was created Baron Cholmondeley in the peerage of England in 1689, and Earl of Cholmondeley in 1706. He was Treasurer of the Household, 1708–13, and again, 1714–25. 'Good for nothing as far as I ever knew', was Swift's opinion of him (*Prose Works*, x. 280).

[20] Proverbs xxv. 3.　　　　　　　　[21] Harcourt (p. 18 n.[29]).

they said the parliament should be dissolved before Christmas, and perhaps it may: this is all your d——d duchess of Somerset's doings. I warned them of it nine months ago, and a hundred times since: the secretary always dreaded it. I told lord treasurer, I should have the advantage of him; for he would lose his head, and I should only be hanged, and so carry my body entire to the grave.

9. I was this morning with Mr. secretary; we are both of opinion that the queen is false. I told him what I heard, and he confirmed it by other circumstances. I then went to my friend Lewis, who had sent to see me. He talks of nothing but retiring to his estate in Wales.[22] He gave me reasons to believe the whole matter is settled between the queen and the Whigs; he hears that lord Somers is to be treasurer, and believes, that sooner than turn out the duchess of Somerset, she will dissolve the parliament, and get a Whiggish one, which may be done by managing elections. Things are now in the crisis, and a day or two will determine. I have desired him to engage lord treasurer, that as soon as he finds the change is resolved on, he will send me abroad as queen's secretary somewhere or other, where I may remain till the new ministers recal me; and then I will be sick for five or six months till the storm has spent itself. I hope he will grant me this; for I should hardly trust myself to the mercy of my enemies while their anger is fresh. I dined to-day with the secretary, who affects mirth, and seems to hope all will yet be well. I took him aside after dinner, told him how I had served them, and had asked no reward, but thought I might ask security; and then desired the same thing of him, to send me abroad before a change. He embraced me, and swore he would take the same care of me as himself, &c. but bid me have courage, for that in two days my lord treasurer's wisdom would appear greater than ever; that he suffered all that had happened on purpose,

[22] Erasmus Lewis was born at Abercothy, near Carmarthen, and, at his death, held several estates in Wales.

and had taken measures to turn it to advantage. I said, God send it; but I do not believe a syllable; and as far as I can judge, the game is lost. I shall know more soon, and my letters will at least be a good history to shew you the steps of this change.

10. I was this morning with Lewis, who thinks they will let the parliament sit till they have given the money, and then dissolve them in Spring, and break the ministry. He spoke to lord treasurer about what I desired him. My lord desired him with great earnestness to assure me, that all would be well, and that I should fear nothing. I dined in the city with a friend. This day the commons went to the queen with their address, and all the lords who were for the Peace went with them, to shew their zeal. I have now some further conviction that the queen is false, and it begins to be known.

11. I went between two and three to see Mrs. Masham; while I was there she went to her bed-chamber to try a petticoat. Lord treasurer came in to see her, and seeing me in the outer room fell a rallying me; says he, You had better keep company with me, than with such a fellow as Lewis, who has not the soul of a chicken, nor the heart of a mite. Then he went in to Mrs. Masham, and as he came back desired her leave to let me go home with him to dinner. He asked, whether I was not afraid to be seen with him? I said, I never valued my lord treasurer in my life, and therefore should have always the same esteem for Mr. Harley and lord Oxford. He seemed to talk confidently, as if he reckoned that all this would turn to advantage. I could not forbear hinting, that he was not sure of the queen; and that those scoundrel, starving lords would never have dared to vote against the Court, if Somerset had not assured them, that it would please the queen. He said, That was true, and Somerset did so. I staid till six; then de Buys, the Dutch envoy, came to him, and I left him. Prior was with us a while after dinner. I see him and all of them cast down; though they make the best of it.

12. Ford is come to town; I saw him last night; he is in no fear, but sanguine, although I have told him the state of things. This change so resembles the last, that I wonder they do not observe it. The secretary sent for me yesterday to dine with him, but I was abroad; I hope he had something to say to me. This is morning, and I write in bed. I am going to the duke of Ormond, whom I have not yet seen. Morrow, sirrahs.——At night. I was to see the duke of Ormond this morning: he asked me two or three questions after his civil way, and they related to Ireland: at last I told him, that from the time I had seen him, I never once thought of Irish affairs. He whispered me, that he hoped I had done some good things here; I said, If every body else had done half as much, we should not be as we are: then we went aside, and talked over affairs. I told him how all things stood, and advised him what was to be done. I then went and sat an hour with the duchess; then as long with lady Oglethorp, who is so cunning a devil, that I believe she could yet find a remedy, if they would take her advice. I dined with a friend at court.

13. I was this morning with the secretary; he will needs pretend to talk as if things would be well; Will you believe it, said he, if you see these people turned out?[23] I said, Yes, if I saw the duke and duchess of Somerset out: he swore, if they were not, he would give up his place. Our Society dined to-day at Sir William Wyndham's; we were thirteen present. Lord Orrery, and two other members were introduced; I left them at seven. I forgot to tell you, that the printer told me yesterday, that Morphew, the publisher, was sent for by that lord chief justice,[24] who

---

[23] On 12 Dec. 1711 St. John informed Strafford that, 'her Majesty's resolution is at last taken; the particulars I am not able to inform you of, but an entire turn will be made in favour of those who have obeyed and served her' (Bolingbroke, *Letters*, i. 332).

[24] Thomas Parker, 1666?–1732, a Whig, was violent in his attacks during the impeachment of Sacheverell. In 1710 he became Lord Chief

was a manager against Sacheverell: he shewed him two or three papers and pamphlets; among the rest mine of the *Conduct of the Allies*, threatened him, asked who was the author, and has bound him over to appear next term. He would not have the impudence to do this, if he did not foresee what was coming at court.

14. Lord Shelburn was with me this morning, to be informed of the state of affairs, and desired I would answer all his objections against a Peace, which was soon done, for he would not give me room to put in a word. He is a man of good sense enough; but argues so violently, that he will some day or other put himself into a consumption. He desires that he may not be denied when he comes to see me, which I promised, but will not perform. Leigh and Sterne set out for Ireland on Monday sennight: I suppose they will be with you long before this.——I was to-night drinking very good wine in scurvy company, at least some of them; I was drawn in, but will be more cautious for the future: 'tis late, &c.

15. Morning. They say the *Occasional bill*[25] is brought to-day into the house of lords; but I know not. I will now put an end to my letter, and give it into the post-house myself.[26] This will be a memorable letter, and I shall sigh to see it some years hence. Here are the first steps towards

Justice of England, but declined Oxford's offer of the Lord Chancellorship in Sept. 1711. He came into favour under George I, and was appointed Lord Chancellor in 1718; but in 1725, on conviction of selling places, he resigned the seals. He was created Earl of Macclesfield in 1721.

[25] Nottingham's bill against permitting the practice of occasional conformity. By the Test Act of 1673 no one could hold state or municipal office unless he had first taken communion in accordance with the rites of the Church of England. Many Dissenters, to the indignation of the Tories, received occasionally in order to qualify for office. An attempt to pass an Occasional Conformity Bill in the winter of 1702–3 had failed. See W. H. Hutton's *The English Church from the Accession of Charles I. to the Death of Queen Anne*, pp. 258–63. Cf. Arbuthnot, *The History of John Bull*, Pt. IV.

[26] In Swift's account book for Nov. 1711–Nov. 1712 (Forster Collection 508) letter 36 is entered as dispatched on 14 Dec.

the ruin of an excellent ministry; for I look upon them as certainly ruined; and God knows what may be the consequences.——I now bid my dearest MD farewel; for company is coming, and I must be at lord Dartmouth's office by noon. Farewel, dearest MD; I wish you a merry Christmas; I believe you will have this about that time. Love Presto, who loves MD above all things a thousand times. Farewel again, dearest MD, &c.

LETTER XXXVII

[SATURDAY]   London, Dec. 15, 1711.
I PUT in my letter this evening myself. I was to-day enquiring at the secretary's office of Mr. Lewis, how things went: I there met Prior, who told me, he gave all for gone, &c. and was of opinion the whole ministry would give up their places next week; Lewis thinks they will not till Spring, when the session is over; both of them entirely despair. I went to see Mrs. Masham, who invited me to dinner; but I was engaged to Lewis. At four I went to Masham's. He came and whispered me, that he had it from a very good hand, that all would be well, and I found them both very chearful. The company was going to the Opera, but desired I would come and sup with them. I did so at ten, and lord treasurer was there, and sat with us till past twelve, and was more cheerful than I have seen him these ten days. Mrs. Masham told me, he was mightily cast down some days ago, and he could not indeed hide it from me. Arbuthnott is in good hopes, that the queen has not betrayed us; but only has been frightened, and flattered, &c. But I cannot yet be of his opinion, whether my reasons are better, or that my fears are greater. I do resolve, if they give up, or are turned out soon, to retire for some months, and I have pitched upon the place already: but I will take methods for hearing from MD, and writing to them. But I would be out of the way upon

the first of the ferment; for they lay all things on me, even some I have never read.

16. I took courage to-day, and went to Court with a very chearful countenance. It was mightily crowded; both parties coming to observe each other's faces. I have avoided lord Hallifax's bow till he forced it on me; but we did not talk together. I could not make less than fourscore bows, of which about twenty might be to Whigs. The duke of Somerset is gone to Petworth, and, I hear, the duchess too, of which I shall be very glad. Prince Eugene,[1] who was expected here some days ago, we are now told, will not come at all. The Whigs designed to have met him with forty thousand horse. Lord treasurer told me some days ago of his discourse with the emperor's resident, that puppy Hoffman,[2] about prince Eugene's coming; by which I found my lord would hinder it, if he could; and we shall be all glad if he does not come, and think it a good point gained. Sir Andrew Fountain, Ford and I dined to-day with Mrs. Van by invitation.

17. I have mistaken the day of the month, and been forced to mend it thrice. I dined to-day with Mr. Masham and his lady, by invitation. Lord treasurer was to be there, but came not. It was to entertain Buys, the Dutch envoy, who speaks English well enough: he was plaguy politick, telling a thousand lies, of which none passed upon any of us. We are still in the condition of suspense, and, I think, have little hopes. The duchess of Somerset is not gone to Petworth; only the duke; and that is a poor sacrifice. I believe the queen certainly designs to change the ministry; but perhaps may put it off till the session is over: and I

---

[1] Charles VI, the new Emperor of Austria, in the hope of preventing a peace without Spain, proposed to send to England the celebrated Prince Eugene of Savoy, friend of Marlborough. But Eugene did not reach London till 6 Jan. 1712, too late to influence English policy. See Trevelyan, *England under Queen Anne*, iii. 201–2. St. John appears to have spoken frankly to Hoffmann about the intended visit (*Letters*, i. 333).

[2] Johann Philipp von Hoffmann, the Emperor's Resident in England. See *Prose Works*, x. 129, 132; xi. 82.

think they had better give up now, if she will not deal openly; and then they need not answer for the consequences of a Peace, when it is in other hands, and may yet be broken. They say, my lord privy seal[3] sets out for Holland this week: so the Peace goes on.

18.[4] It has rained hard from morning till night, and cost me three shillings in coach-hire. We have had abundance of wet weather. I dined in the city, and was with the printer, who has now a fifth edition of the *Conduct*, &c. it is in small, and sold for six-pence; they have printed as many as three editions, because they are to be sent in numbers into the country by great men, &c. who subscribe for hundreds.[5] It has been sent a fortnight ago to Ireland; I suppose you will print it there.[6] The Tory lords and commons in parliament argue all from it: and all agree, that never any thing of that kind was of so great consequence, or made so many converts. By the time I have sent this letter, I expect to hear from little MD: it will be a month two days hence since I had your last, and I will allow ten days for accidents. I cannot get rid of the leavings of a cold I got a month ago; or else it is a new one. I have been writing letters all this evening till I am weary, and I am sending out another little thing, which I hope to finish this week, and design to send to the printer in an unknown hand.[7] There was printed a Grub-street speech of lord Nottingham;[8] and he was such an owl to complain of it in the house of lords, who have taken up the printer

---

[3] Robinson, Bishop of Bristol (p. 347 n.[8]).

[4] The first of Swift's letters to Vanessa, so far as can be traced, was written on this day, covering a letter of the same date which was to be forwarded to Miss Anne Long (p. 17 n.[24]) who had written to Swift on 18 Nov. (Freeman, *Vanessa and her Correspondence with Jonathan Swift*, pp. 61–9). No other letters written on this day have survived.

[5] pp. 422, 431 and notes.

[6] p. 428 n.[3]

[7] Presumably *The Windsor Prophecy* (p. 444).

[8] *The Intended Speech of a Famous Orator* (p. 430 n.[10]). See *Poems*, p. 141.

for it. I heard at Court, that Walpole[9] (a great Whig member) said, that I and my whimsical club writ it at one of our meetings, and that I should pay for it. He will find he lies; and I shall let him know by a third hand my thoughts of him. He is to be secretary of state, if the ministry changes: but he has lately had a bribe proved against him in parliament, while he was secretary at war. He is one of the Whigs chief speakers.

19. Sad dismal weather. I went to the secretary's office, and Lewis made me dine with him. I intended to have dined with lord treasurer. I have not seen the secretary this week. Things do not mend at all. Lord Dartmouth despairs, and is for giving up; Lewis is of the same mind; but lord treasurer only says, Poh, poh, all will be well. I am come home early to finish something I am doing; but I find I want heart and humour; and would read any idle book that came in my way. I have just sent away a penny paper to make a little mischief. Patrick is gone to the burial of an Irish footman, who was Dr. King's[10] servant; he died of a consumption, a fit death for a poor starving wit's footman. The Irish servants always club to bury a countryman.

20. I was with the secretary this morning, and for aught I can see we shall have a languishing death: I can know nothing, nor themselves neither. I dined, you know, with our Society, and that odious secretary would make me

9 Sir Robert Walpole was at this time M.P. for King's Lynn and leader of the opposition in the House of Commons. He held office as Secretary at War from Feb. 1708 to Sept. 1710, and as Treasurer of the Navy from Jan. 1710 to the end of that year.

10 William King, 1663–1712, educated at Westminster and Christ Church, Oxford, was admitted advocate at Doctors' Commons, and was Judge of the Admiralty Court in Ireland, 1701–7. He wrote a number of satirical or humorous pieces, including *Dialogues of the Dead, Mully of Mountown, Voyage to the Island of Cajamai,* and *The Art of Cookery.* John Nichols edited his *Works* in three volumes, 1776. Poems by him have been attributed to Swift (*Poems,* pp. 1074–5, 1082, 1150). See also Johnson's *Lives of the Poets,* ed. Birkbeck Hill, ii. 26–31.

president next week, so I must entertain them this day
sennight at the Thatched-house Tavern,[11] where we dined
to-day; it will cost me five or six pounds; yet the secretary
says, he will give me wine. I found a letter[12] when I came
home from the bishop of Clogher.

21. This is the first time I ever got a new cold before
the old one was going: it came yesterday, and appeared
in all due forms, eyes and nose running, &c. and is now
very bad, and I cannot tell how I got it. Sir Andrew
Fountain and I were invited to dine with Mrs. Van.—I
was this morning with the duke of Ormond; and neither
he nor I can think of any thing to comfort us in present
affairs. We must certainly fall, if the duchess of Somerset
be not turned out; and no body believes the queen will
ever part with her. The duke and I were settling when
Mr. secretary and I should dine with him, and he fixt upon
Tuesday; and when I came away I remembered it was
Christmas day. I was to see lady[13] ——, who is just up
after lying-in; and the ugliest sight I have seen, pale, dead,
old and yellow, for want of her paint. She has turned my
stomach. But she will soon be painted, and a beauty again.

22. I find myself disordered with a pain all round the
small of my back, which I imputed to Champagne I had
drunk; but find it to have been only my new cold. It was
a fine frosty day, and I resolved to walk into the city. I
called at lord treasurer's at eleven, and staid some time
with him. He shewed me a letter from a great presbyterian parson[14] to him, complaining how their friends had

11. The Thatched House, a fashionable tavern during the eighteenth
century, stood in St. James's Street on the present site of the Conservative
Club. The original building was demolished in 1844. Cf. *Poems*, p. 313;
and see E. B. Chancellor's *St. James's Street*, pp. 157–62.

12. This letter has not been preserved.

13. Possibly Lady Pembroke (p. 384 n.[12]), at this time about forty-three.
She had married first Sir Richard Mauleverer, Bart., of Alleston, and
secondly John, second Baron Arundell of Trerice, who died in 1698. She
married Lord Pembroke in 1708.

14. John Shower, 1657–1715, pastor of a Presbyterian congregation at

betrayed them by passing this *Conformity Bill*; and he shewed me the answer he had written; which his friends would not let him send; but was a very good one. He is very chearful; but gives one no hopes, nor has any to give. I went into the city, and there I dined.

23. Morning. As I was dressing to go to church, a friend that was to see me, advised me not to stir out; so I shall keep at home to-day, and only eat some broth, if I can get it. It is a terrible cold frost, and snow fell yesterday, which still remains, look, there you may see it from the pent-houses. The lords made yesterday two or three votes about Peace, and Hanover, of a very angry kind, to vex the ministry, and they will meet sooner by a fortnight than the commons:[15] and they say, are preparing some knocking addresses. Morrow, sirrahs. I'll sit at home, and when I go to bed, I will tell you how I am.—I have sat at home all day, and eaten only a mess of broth and a roll. I have written a *Prophecy*, which I design to print; I did it to-day, and some other verses.[16]

24. I went into the city to-day in a coach, and dined there. My cold is going. It is now bitter hard frost, and has been so these three or four days. My *Prophecy* is printed, and will be published after Christmas day; I like it mightily; I don't know how it will pass. You will never

Curriers' Hall, London Wall. Sheridan (*Works*, 1784, xi. 210) printed Shower's letter and Oxford's reply; and in a footnote affirmed that the answer 'was written by Dr. Swift, as appears from his handwriting, and particularly from a correction in the original draught'. Swift's praise of this answer, the style, and derisive sarcasm, make it very probable that he was the author. The letters are printed by Ball, *Corresp.* i, Appendix vii.

[15] On 22 Dec. both Houses adjourned for the Christmas holidays. Before separating the Lords approved an Address that the Queen should instruct her plenipotentiaries to consult with and act in unison with the other allies in Holland (*Journals of the House of Lords*, xix. 351). The House of Lords adjourned till the 2nd, the Commons till the 14th of January.

[16] *The Windsor Prophecy* (*Poems*, pp. 145–8), a fierce attack on the Duchess of Somerset, appeared as a broadside printed in black and roman letter. The 'other verses', which may never have been printed, cannot be safely identified.

understand it at your distance, without help. I believe every body will guess it to be mine, because it is somewhat in the same manner with that of *Merlin*[17] in the *Miscellanies.* My lord privy-seal set out this day for Holland: he'll have a cold journey. I gave Patrick half a crown for his Christmas-box, on condition he would be good, and he came home drunk at midnight. I have taken a memorandum of it; because I never design to give him a groat more. 'Tis cruel cold.

25. I wish MD a merry Christmas, and many a one; but mine is melancholy: I durst not go to church to-day, finding myself a little out of order, and it snowing prodigiously, and freezing. At noon I went to Mrs. Van, who had this week engaged me to dine there to-day: and there I received the news, that poor Mrs. Long[18] died at Lynn in Norfolk on Saturday last, at four in the morning; she was sick but four hours. We suppose it was the asthma, which she was subject to as well as the dropsy, as she sent me word in her last letter, written about five weeks ago; but then said she was recovered. I never was more afflicted at any death. The poor creature had retired to Lynn two years ago, to live cheap, and pay her debts. In her last letter she told me she hoped to be easy by Christmas; and

17 *A Famous Prediction of Merlin* (*Poems*, pp. 101–5), published as a half-sheet in 1709, and reprinted in the *Miscellanies* of 1711.

18 p. 17 n.[24]; and cf. p. 441 n.[4] On the following day Swift wrote to the Rev. Thomas Pyle (Nichols, *Lit. Anec.* ix. 433–44) of King's Lynn asking him to place 'a plain marble stone' on the wall of his church to the memory of Miss Long. In his account book for 1711–12 (Forster, 508), on a page otherwise blank, Swift made the following entry:

'Decbr. 22. 1711

'On Saterday. at 4 in the morn. dyed Mrs. Ann Long at Lynn in Norfolk, where | she had retired about 2 years before, and lived under the Name of Smyth. the | News of it came to Town on Monday night following, wch was Xmas Eve and I | heard of it on Xmas day at Noon, wch was Tuesday. She was the most beautifull | Person of the Age, she lived in, of great Honr and Virtue, infinite Sweetness and | Generosity of Temper, and true good Sense.

J. Swift.'

she kept her word, although she meant it otherwise. She had all sorts of amiable qualities, and no ill ones, but the indiscretion of too much neglecting her own affairs. She had two thousand pounds left her by an old grandmother,[19] with which she intended to pay her debts, and live on an annuity she had of one hundred pounds a year, and New-burg-house, which would be about sixty pounds more. That odious grandmother living so long, forced her to retire; for the two thousand pounds was settled on her after the old woman's death, yet her brute of a brother, Sir James Long,[20] would not advance it for her; else she might have paid her debts, and continued here, and lived still: I believe melancholy helped her on to her grave. I have ordered a paragraph to be put in the *Post-boy*,[21] giving an account of her death, and making honourable mention of her; which is all I can do to serve her memory: but one reason was spite; for, her brother would fain have her death a secret, to save the charge of bringing her up here to bury her, or going into mourning. Pardon all this, for the sake of a poor creature I had so much friendship for.

26. I went to Mr. secretary this morning, and he would have me dine with him. I called at noon at Mrs. Masham's, who desired me not to let the *Prophecy* be published, for fear of angering the queen about the duchess of Somerset; so I writ to the printer to stop them. They have been printed and given about, but not sold.[22] I saw lord treasurer there, who had been two hours with the queen;

---

[19] Dorothy, daughter of Sir Edward Leach, one of the Masters in Chancery.

[20] Sir James Long, Bart., of Draycot, Wiltshire, who succeeded to the baronetcy in 1697. He was M.P. for Chippenham, 1705–13, for Wootton Bassett, 1715–22, and for Wiltshire, 1727 till his death in 1729.

[21] A paragraph appeared in the *Post Boy* for 27 Dec., announcing the death of 'Mrs. Anne Long . . . celebrated . . . for her beauty, virtue, and good sense'.

[22] Cf. also 4 Jan. 1711–12, 'it is not published here, only printed copies given to friends'. Copies, however, got abroad, and it was twice reprinted in broadside form (*Poems*, pp. 145–6).

and Mrs. Masham is in hopes things will do well again. I went at night again, and supped at Mr. Masham's, and lord treasurer sat with us till one o'clock. So 'tis late, &c.

27. I entertained our Society at the Thatched-house Tavern to-day at dinner; but brother Bathurst sent for wine, the house affording none. The printer had not received my letter, and so he brought us dozens a piece of the *Prophecy*; but I ordered him to part with no more. 'Tis an admirable good one, and people are mad for it. The frost still continues violently cold. Mrs. Masham invited me to come to-night and play at cards; but our Society did not part till nine. But I supped with Mrs. Hill, her sister, and there was Mrs. Masham and lord treasurer, and we stayed till twelve. He is endeavouring to get a majority against next Wednesday, when the house of lords is to meet, and the Whigs intend to make some violent addresses against a Peace, if not prevented. God knows what will become of us.—It is still prodigiously cold; but so I told you already. We have eggs on the spit, I wish they may not be addle. When I came home to-night I found, forsooth, a letter from MD, N. 24, 24, 24, 24;[23] there, do you know the number now? and at the same time one from Joe, full of thanks: let him know I have received it, and am glad of his success, but won't put him to the charge of a letter. I had a letter some time ago from Mr. Warburton, and I beg one of you will copy out what I shall tell you, and send it by some opportunity to Warburton. 'Tis as follows; The Dr. has received Mr. Warburton's letter, and desired he will let the Dr. know, where[24] that accident he mentions is like soon to happen, and he will do what he can in it.——And pray, madam, let them know, that I do this to save myself the trouble,

[23] The receipt of this letter is noted by Swift in his account book for Nov. 1711–Nov. 1712 (Forster Collection, 508).

[24] Possibly a misreading; but 'where' in the sense of 'whether' is recorded in *O.E.D.* as late as 1660, and may have survived to Swift's time in familiar speech.

447

and them the expence, of a letter.—And I think this is enough for one that comes home at twelve from a lord treasurer and Mrs. Masham. Oh, I could tell you ten thousand things of our mad politicks, upon what small circumstances great affairs have turned. But I will go rest my busy head.

28. I was this morning with brother Bathurst to see the duke of Ormond. We have given his grace some hopes to be one of our Society. The secretary and I and Bathurst are to dine with him on Sunday next. The duke is not in much hopes, but has been very busy in endeavouring to bring over some lords against next Wednesday. The duchess catched me as I was going out; she is sadly in fear about things, and blames me for not mending them by my credit with lord treasurer; and I blame her. She met me in the street at noon, and engaged me to dine with her, which I did; and we talked an hour after dinner in her closet. If we miscarry on Wednesday, I believe it will be by some strange sort of neglect. They talk of making eight new lords, by calling up some peers eldest sons; but they delay strangely. I saw judge Coote[25] to-day at the duke of Ormond's: he desires to come and see me, to justify his principles.

29. Morning. This goes to-day. I will not answer yours, your 24th, till my next, which shall begin to-night, as usual. Lord Shelburn has sent to invite me to dinner, but I am engaged with Lewis at Ned Southwell's. Lord Northampton[26] and lord Aylesbury's[27] sons are both made

[25] The soundness of Coote's (p. 391 n.[36]) politics was suspect, and he was under some apprehension of removal from the bench (Ball, *Judges in Ireland*, ii. 61).

[26] James Compton, 1687–1754, eldest son of the fourth Earl of Northampton, was at this time styled Lord Compton and was M.P. for Warwickshire. He was summoned to the House of Lords as Baron Compton, 28 Dec. 1711. In 1727 he succeeded his father as fifth Earl of Northampton.

[27] Charles Bruce, 1682–1747, M.P. for Marlborough, eldest surviving son of the second Earl of Ailesbury, was, 29 Dec. 1711, summoned in his

peers; but we shall want more. I write this post to your dean.[28] I owe the archbishop a letter this long time.[29] All people that come from Ireland complain of him, and scold me for protecting him. Pray, madam Dingley, let me know what Presto has received for this year, or whether any thing is due to him for last: I cannot look over your former letters now. As for Dingley's own account of her exchequer money,[30] I will give it on t'other side. Farewel, my own dearest MD, and love Presto; and God ever bless dearest MD, &c. &c. I wish you many happy Christmasses and New-Years.

I have owned to the dean a letter I just had from you; but that I had not one this great while before.

Dingley's account.

Received of Mr. Tooke,	—	—	—	—	6	17	6
Deducted for entering the letter of attorney,					0	2	6
For the three half crowns it used to cost you, I don't know why nor wherefore,			—	—	0	7	6
For exchange to Ireland,	—	—	—	—	0	10	0
For coach-hire,	—	—	—	—	—	0	2	6
In all, just					8	0	0

So there's your money, and we are both even: for I'll pay you no more than that eight pounds Irish, and pray be satisfied.

Churchwarden's accounts, boys.

Saturday night. I have broke open my letter, and tore it into the bargain; to let you know, that we are all safe;

father's barony of Bruce of Whorlton. In 1741 he succeeded his father as third Earl of Ailesbury.

[28] Dean Stearne, *Corresp.* i. 309. A letter recounting the political situation. Swift broke the seal and added a postscript to inform Stearne of the creation of twelve new peers.

[29] Swift's last letter to Archbishop King was written from Windsor on 1 Oct. (*Corresp.* i. 288).

[30] For Mrs. Dingley's exchequer business see pp. 386 n.[19], 387.

the queen has made no less than twelve lords to have a majority; nine new ones, the other three peers sons;[31] and has turned out the duke of Somerset. She is awaked at last, and so is lord treasurer: I want nothing now but to see the duchess out. But we shall do without her. We are all extremely happy. Give me joy, sirrahs. This is written in a Coffee-house. Three[32] of the new lords are of our Society.

LETTER XXXVIII

[SATURDAY]   London, Dec. 29, 1711.

I PUT my letter in this evening, after coming from dinner at Ned Southwell's, where I drank very good Irish wine, and we were in great joy at this happy turn of affairs. The queen has been at last persuaded to her own interest and security, and I freely think she must have made both herself and kingdom very unhappy, if she had done otherwise. It is still a mighty secret that Masham is to be one of the new lords; they say he does not yet know it himself;

---

[31] To form a group of twelve new peers necessary to ensure a majority in the Upper House the Queen, advised by her ministers, took the following steps. The eldest sons of two Earls, Northampton and Ailesbury (p. 448, and notes), were called up by writ. A barony was conferred on Henry Paget, eldest son of Lord Paget (p. 642 n.[56]), and another barony on Viscount Dupplin (p. 45 n.[39]), Lord Oxford's son-in-law. Viscount Windsor (p. 451 n.[3]), an Irish peer, was created Baron Mountjoy in the English peerage. Two baronets, Sir Thomas Mansell (p. 201 n.[1]), and Sir Thomas Willoughby, became respectively Baron Mansell and Baron Middleton. Sir Thomas Trevor, Chief Justice of the Common Pleas, became Baron Trevor. George Granville (p. 168 n.[4]) was created Baron Lansdown, Thomas Foley (p. 253 n.[23]), Baron Foley, Allen Bathurst (p. 423 n.[30]), Baron Bathurst, and Samuel Masham (p. 169 n.[6]), husband of the Queen's favourite, Baron Masham.

[32] Swift should have written 'Four', unless he did not count Viscount Dupplin, now created Baron Hay of Pedwardine in the peerage of the United Kingdom, as a 'new lord'. The other three were Lords Lansdown, Bathurst, and Masham. Four days later (p. 453) he speaks of 'four'.

but the queen is to surprise him with it.[1] Mr. secretary will be a lord at the end of the session; but they want him still in parliament. After all, it is a strange unhappy necessity of making so many peers together; but the queen has drawn it upon herself, by her confounded trimming and moderation. Three, as I told you, are of our Society.

30. I writ the dean and you a lie yesterday; for the duke of Somerset is not yet turned out. I was to-day at Court, and resolved to be very civil to the Whigs; but saw few there. When I was in the bed-chamber talking to lord Rochester, he went up to lady Burlington,[2] who asked him, who I was; and lady Sunderland and she whispered about me: I desired lord Rochester to tell lady Sunderland, I doubted she was not as much in love with me as I was with her; but he would not deliver my message. The duchess of Shrewsbury came running up to me, and clapt her fan up to hide us from the company, and we gave one another joy of this change; but sighed, when we reflected on the Somerset family not being out. The secretary and I, and brother Bathurst, and lord Windsor,[3] dined with the duke of Ormond. Bathurst and Windsor are to be two of the new lords. I desired lord Radnor's brother,[4] at Court to-day, to let my lord know I would call on him at six, which I did, and was arguing with him three hours to bring him over to us, and I spoke so closely,

[1] Masham came in as an afterthought. The place was designed for Sir Miles Wharton, a country gentleman of ancient family; but he declined it on the ground that it looked 'like serving a turn'. The Queen, furthermore, did not approve making Mrs. Masham, who was a 'useful servant', into a 'great lady'. At last, however, she was persuaded to consent. See Dartmouth's note in Burnet's *Own Time*, vi. 33.

[2] Juliana, 1672–1750, daughter of the Hon. Henry Noel of North Luffenham, Rutland, and widow (1704) of Charles Boyle, second Earl of Burlington. She was Mistress of the Robes.

[3] The Hon. Thomas Windsor, *c.* 1670–1738, created Viscount Windsor of Blackcastle in the peerage of Ireland in 1699, now became Baron Mountjoy of the Isle of Wight.

[4] The Hon. Russell Robartes, brother of Lord Radnor (p. 13 n.[10]), was a Teller of the Exchequer, and M.P. for Bodmin.

that I believe he will be tractable; but he is a scoundrel, and though I said I only talked for my love to him, I told a lie; for I did not care if he were hanged: but every one gained over is of consequence. The duke of Marlborough was at Court to-day, and no body hardly took notice of him. Masham's being a lord begins to take wind: nothing at Court can be kept a secret. Wednesday will be a great day: you shall know more.

31. Our frost is broken since yesterday, and it is very slabbery;[5] yet I walked to the city and dined, and ordered some things with the printer. I have settled Dr. King in the *Gazette*; it will be worth two hundred pounds a year to him.[6] Our new lords patents are passed: I don't like the expedient, if we could have found any other. I see I have said this before. I hear the duke of Marlborough is turned out of all his employments:[7] I shall know to-morrow, when I am to carry Dr. King to dine with the secretary.—These are strong remedies; pray God the patient is able to bear them. The last ministry people are utterly desperate.

Jan. 1. Now I wish my dearest little MD many happy New-years; yes, both Dingley and Stella, aye and Presto too, many happy new-years. I dined with the secretary, and it is true that the duke of Marlborough is turned out of all. The duke of Ormond has got his regiment of Foot-guards, I know not who has the rest. If the ministry be not sure of a Peace, I shall wonder at this step, and do not approve it at best. The queen and lord treasurer mortally hate the duke of Marlborough, and to that he owes his

---

[5] Slabbery, or slabby: Wet, slushy.

[6] In a letter to Archbishop King, 8 Jan. 1711–12 (*Corresp.* i. 316), Swift puts it at two hundred and fifty pounds. For an amusing account of the occasion see King's *Works*, 1776, vol. i, pp. xxiii–xxiv. The post was uncongenial to Dr. William King, and he retained it only a few months. See p. 543.

[7] *The London Gazette* of 31 Dec. announced the dismissal of Marlborough from all his employments and the creation of twelve new peers. The Whigs, though furious, were helpless in the face of Tory enthusiasm and the national longing for peace.

fall, more than to his other faults; unless he has been tampering too far with his party, of which I have not heard any particulars; however it be, the world abroad will blame us. I confess my belief, that he has not one good quality in the world besides that of a general, and even that I have heard denied by several great soldiers. But we have had constant success in arms while he commanded. Opinion is a mighty matter in war, and I doubt but the French think it impossible to conquer an army that he leads, and our soldiers think the same; and how far even this step may encourage the French to play tricks with us, no man knows. I do not love to see personal resentment mix with public affairs.

2. This being the day the lords meet, and the new peers to be introduced. I went to Westminster to see the sight; but the crowd was too great in the house. So I only went into the robing-room, to give my four brothers joy, and Sir Thomas Mansel, and lord Windsor; the other six I am not acquainted with. It was apprehended the Whigs would have raised some difficulties, but nothing happened. I went to see lady Masham at noon, and wish her joy of her new honour, and a happy New-year. I found her very well pleased; for peerage will be some sort of protection to her upon any turn of affairs. She engaged me to come at night, and sup with her and lord treasurer; I went at nine, and she was not at home, so I would not stay.—No, no, I won't answer your letter yet, young women. I dined with a friend in the neighbourhood. I see nothing here like Christmas, except brawn or mincepies in places where I dine, and giving away my half-crowns like farthings to great men's porters and butlers. Yesterday I paid seven good guineas to the fellow at the tavern, where I treated the Society. I have a great mind to send you the bill. I think I told you some articles. I have not heard whether any thing was done in the house of lords after introducing the new ones. Ford has been sitting with me till peeast tweeleve a clock.

3. This was our Society day, lord Dupplin[8] was president; we chuse every week; the last president treats and chuses his successor. I believe our dinner cost fifteen pounds besides wine. The secretary grew brisk, and would not let me go, nor lord Lansdown, who would fain have gone home to his lady, being newly married to lady Mary Thynne.[9] It was near one when we parted; so you must think I can't write much to-night. The adjourning of the house of lords yesterday, as the queen desired, was just carried by the twelve new lords, and one more. Lord Radnor was not there; I hope I have cured him. Did I tell you, that I have brought Dr. King in to be Gazeteer? it will be worth above two hundred pounds a year to him: I believe I told you so before, but I am forgetful. Go, get you gone to ombre, and claret, and toasted oranges. I'll go sleep.

4. I cannot get rid of the leavings of my cold. I was in the city to-day, and dined with my printer, and gave him a ballad made by several hands, I know not whom. I believe lord treasurer had a finger in it; I added three stanzas; I suppose Dr. Arbuthnott had the greatest share.[10] I have been over-seeing some other little prints, and a pamphlet made by one of my understrappers.[11] Somerset is not out yet. I doubt not but you will have the *Prophecy* in Ireland, although it is not published here, only printed copies given to friends. Tell me, do you understand it? No, faith, not without help. Tell me what you stick at, and I'll explain. We turned out a member of our Society

---

[8] One of the new peers under the title Baron Hay of Pedwardine.

[9] George Granville (p. 168 n.[4]), now Lord Lansdown, married, in Dec. 1711, Mary, widow of Thomas Thynne, daughter of Edward Villiers, first Earl of Jersey. She died on 17 Jan. 1734–5, thirteen days before her husband.

[10] This was, almost certainly, a broadsheet ballad, entitled *A Fable of the Widow and her Cat*, attacking Marlborough (*Poems*, pp. 151–4). It was quickly reprinted at least three times. Cf. p. 477 n.[13]

[11] Mr. Paul Vern Thompson (*Notes and Queries*, clxxv. 79) suggests that this was *The Representation of the Loyal Subjects of Albinia*, which was published, as advertisements in *The Post Boy* show, on 4 Jan. 1711–12.

yesterday for gross neglect and non-attendance. I writ to him by order to give him notice of it. It is Tom Harley, secretary to the treasurer, and cousin-german to lord treasurer. He is going to Hanover from the queen. I am to give the duke of Ormond notice of his election as soon as I can see him.

5. I went this morning with a parishioner of mine, one Nuttal,[12] who came over here for a legacy of one hundred pounds, and a roguish lawyer had refused to pay him, and would not believe he was the man. I writ to the lawyer a sharp letter, that I had taken Nuttal into my protection, and was resolved to stand by him; and the next news was, that the lawyer desired I would meet him, and attest he was the man, which I did, and his money was paid upon the spot. I then visited lord treasurer, who is now right again, and all well, only that the Somerset family is not out yet. I hate that; I don't like it, as the man said by, &c. Then I went and visited poor Will. Congreve, who had a French fellow tampering with one of his eyes; he is almost blind of both. I dined with some merchants in the city, but could not see Stratford, with whom I had business. Presto, leave off your impertinence, and answer our letter, sayth MD. Yes, yes, one of these days, when I have nothing else to do. Oh, faith, this letter is a week written, and not one side done yet.—These ugly spots are not tobacco, but this is the last gilt sheet I have of large paper, therefore hold your tongue. Nuttal was surprised, when they gave him bits of paper instead of money; but I made Ben Tooke put him in his geers:[13] he could not reckon ten pounds, but was puzzled with the Irish way. Ben. Tooke and my printer have desired me to make them stationers to the ordnance, of which lord Rivers is master[14] instead of the

---

12 Probably Christopher Nuttall, who lived in or near Kells, co. Meath. In 1710 his name appears as an officer in Philips's Foot. Through the marriage of his daughter Agnes he was grandfather of Laurence Sterne.

13 Harness. Generally used in the plural. Cf. pp. 111, 598.

14 He succeeded Marlborough as Master of the Ordnance.

duke of Marlborough. It will be a hundred pounds a year a-piece to them, if I can get it. I will try to-morrow.

6. I went this morning to earl Rivers, gave him joy of his new employment, and desired him to prefer my printer and bookseller to be stationers to his office. He immediately granted it me; but, like an old courtier, told me it was wholly on my account, but that he heard I had intended to engage Mr. secretary to speak to him, and desired I would engage him to do so; but that however he did it only for my sake. This is a court trick, to oblige as many as you can at once. I read prayers to poor Mrs. Wesley (who is very much out of order) instead of going to church; and then I went to Court, which I found very full, in expectation of seeing prince Eugene, who landed last night, and lies at Leicester-House;[15] but he was not to see the queen till six this evening. I hope and believe he comes too late to do the Whigs any good.[16] I refused dining with the secretary, and was like to lose my dinner, which was at a private acquaintance's. I went at six to see the prince at Court; but he was gone in to the queen; and when he came out, Mr. secretary, who introduced him, walked so near him, that he quite screened him from me with his great periwig. I'll tell you a good passage: As prince Eugene was going with Mr. secretary to Court, he told the secretary, that Hoffman, the emperor's resident, said to his highness, that it was not proper to go to Court without a long wig, and his was a tyed-up one; Now, says the prince, I knew not what to do; for I never had a long periwig in my life; and I have sent to all my valets and footmen to see whether any of them have one, that I might borrow it; but none of them has any.[17]—Was not this spoken very greatly with some sort of contempt? But the secretary said, It was a thing of no consequence, and

[15] Leicester House, *c.* 1630–1790, stood on the north side of the present Leicester Square.   [16] See p. 440 n.[1]

[17] Swift tells this story again in 'A Treatise of Good Manners and Good Breeding' (Delany, *Observations*, 1754, p. 303; *Prose Works*, xi. 82).

only observed by gentlemen-ushers. I supped with lord Masham, where lord treasurer and Mr. secretary supped with us; the first left us at twelve, but the rest did not part till two; yet I have written all this, because it is fresh: and now I'll go sleep, if I can; that is, I believe I shall, because I have drank a little.

7. I was this morning to give the duke of Ormond notice of the honour done him to make him one of our Society, and to invite him on Thursday next to the Thatched-house: he has accepted it with the gratitude and humility such a preferment deserves; but cannot come till the next meeting, because prince Eugene is to dine with him that day; which I allowed for a good excuse, and will report accordingly. I dined with lord Masham, and sat there till eight this evening; and came home, because I was not very well, but a little griped: but now I am well again, I will not go, at least but very seldom, to lord Masham's suppers. Lord treasurer is generally there, and that tempts me; but late sitting up does not agree with me; there's the short and the long, and I won't do it; so take your answer, dear little young women; and I have no more to say to you to-night, because of the archbishop; for I am going to write a long letter to him;[18] but not so politickly as formerly: I won't trust him.

8. Well; then come, let us see this letter; if I must answer it, I must. What's here now? Yes faith, I lamented my birth-day[19] two days after, and that's all; and you rhyme, madam Stella; were those verses made upon my birth-day?[20] Faith, when I read them, I had them running

[18] *Corresp.* i. 312. The letter is dated the 8th, and gives the Archbishop an account of political events, but reveals nothing he might not have learned elsewhere.

[19] Swift's birthday fell on the 30th of November. 'Dr. *Swift*, upon his birth-day, used always to read the third chapter of *Job*.'—Deane Swift. Cf. *Corresp.* vi. 103, 27 Nov. 1738; Swift, writing to Mrs. Whiteway of his birthday: 'I read the third chapter of Job that morning'.

[20] For poems attributed to Stella see *Poems*, pp. 736–9. Among these is one addressed to Swift on his birthday in 1721.

in my head all the day, and said them over a thousand times; they drank your health in all their glasses, and wished, &c. I could not get them out of my head. What; no, I believe it was not: what do I say upon the eighth of December? Compare, and see whether I say so. I am glad of Mrs. Stoyte's recovery, heartily glad: your Dolly Manley's[21] and bishop of Cloyne's child I have no concern about: I am sorry in a civil way, that's all. Yes, yes, Sir George St. George[22] dead. Go, cry, madam Dingley; I have written to the dean.[23] Raymond will be rich, for he has the building itch. I wish all he has got may put him out of debt. Poh, I have fires like light'ning; they cost me twelvepence a week, besides small-coal. I have got four new caps, madam, very fine and convenient, with striped cambrick, instead of muslin; so Patrick need not mend them, but take the old ones. Stella snatched Dingley's word out of her pen; Presto a cold? why all the world here is dead with them: I never had any thing like it in my life; 'tis not gone in five weeks. I hope Leigh is with you before this, and has brought your box: how do you like the ivory rasp? Stella is angry; but I'll have a finer thing for her. Is not the apron as good? I'm sure I shall never be paid it: so all's well again. What the quarrel with Sir John Walters?[24] Why, we had not one word of quarrel; only he railed at me when I was gone. And lord keeper and treasurer teazed me for a week: it was nuts to them: a serious thing with a vengeance. The Whigs may sell their estates then, or hang themselves, as they are disposed; for a Peace there will be. Lord treasurer told me, that Conolly was going to Hanover. Your provost[25] is a coxcomb. Stella is a good girl for not being angry when

---

[21] Mrs. Isaac Manley.

[22] Sir George St. George of Dunmore, co. Galway, M.P. for co. Leitrim, 1661–92, and afterwards for co. Galway. One of his daughters married Dillon Ashe, another Bishop Ashe.

[23] See p. 449 n.[28]

[24] See pp. 374, 421.

[25] Dr. Benjamin Pratt.

I tell her of spelling; I see none wrong in this. God Almighty be praised that your disorders lessen, it encreases my hopes mightily that they will go off. And have you been plagued with the fear of the plague? Never mind those reports; I have heard them five hundred times. *Replevi*; Replevin,[26] simpleton, 'tis Dingley I mean; but it is a hard word, and so I'll excuse it. I stated Dingley's accounts in my last. I forgot Catherine's sevenpenny dinner. I hope it was the beef-steaks; I'll call and eat them in Spring: but goody Stoyte must give me coffee, or green tea, for I drink no bohea. Well, aye, the pamphlet; but there are some additions to the fourth edition: the fifth edition was of four thousand, in a smaller print, sold for sixpence.[27] Yes, I had the twenty pound bill from Parvisol; and what then? Pray now eat the Laracor apples; I beg you not to keep them, but tell me what they are. You have had Tooke's bill in my last. And so there now, your whole letter is answered. I tell you what I do; I lay your letter before me, and take it in order, and answer what is necessary; and so, and so. Well; when I expected we were all undone, I designed to retire for six months, and then steal over to Laracor; and I had in my mouth a thousand times two lines of Shakspear, where cardinal Wolsey says;

'A weak old man, battered with storms of state,
Is come to lay his weary bones among you.'[28]

I beg your pardon, I have cheated you all this margin; I did not perceive it; and I went on wider and wider like Stella; aukward sluts, *she writes so so, there*:[29] that's as like

---

[26] p. 416 n.[4]   [27] pp. 422, 431, and notes.
[28] *King Henry VIII*, Act iv, sc. 2 :
          'An old man, broken with the storms of state,
          Is come to lay his weary bones among ye'.
On Swift's knowledge of Shakespeare see H. Williams, *Dean Swift's Library*, pp. 74–5, and notes; D. Nichol Smith, *Letters of Swift to Ford*, p. 7 n.[4]
[29] 'These words in the manuscript imitate *Stella*'s writing, and are sloped the wrong way.'—Deane Swift. On Stella's writing see p. 183, n.[16]

as two eggs a penny.—*A weak old man*, now I am saying it, and shall till to-morrow.—The duke of Marlborough says, There is nothing he now desires so much as to contrive some way how to soften Dr. Swift. He is mistaken; for those things that have been hardest against him were not written by me. Mr. secretary told me this from a friend of the duke's; and I'm sure now he is down, I shall not trample on him; although I love him not, I dislike his being out.[30]—Bernage was to see me this morning, and gave some very indifferent excuses for not calling here so long. I care not two-pence. Prince Eugene did not dine with the duke of Marlborough on Sunday, but was last night at lady Betty Germain's assemblée, and a vast number of ladies to see him. Mr. Lewis and I dined with a private friend.[31] I was this morning to see the duke of Ormond, who appointed me to meet him at the Cockpit at one, but never came. I sat too some time with the duchess. We don't like things very well yet. I am come home early, and going to be busy. I'll go write.

9. I could not go sleep last night till past two, and was waked before three by a noise of people endeavouring to break open my window; for a while I would not stir, thinking it might be my imagination; but hearing the noise continued, I rise[32] and went to the window, and then it ceased: I went to bed again, and heard it repeated more violently; then I rise,[32] and called up the house, and got a candle: the rogues had lifted up the sash a yard; there are great sheds before my windows, although my lodgings be a story high; and if they get upon the sheds, they are almost even with my window. We observed their track, and panes of glass fresh broken. The watchmen told us to-day, they saw them, but could not catch them: they attacked others in the neighbourhood, about the same

[30] On Swift's attitude towards Marlborough see *Poems*, p. 155.
[31] Possibly Arbuthnot, a close friend both of Lewis and of Swift.
[32] Deane Swift's reading is 'rise . . . rise'; Sheridan, Nichols, Scott, Ryland, Aitken, read 'rose . . . rose'.

time, and actually robbed a house in Suffolk-Street, which
is the next street but one to us. It is said, they are seamen
discharged from service. I went up to call my man, and
found his bed empty; it seems he often lies abroad. I
challenged him this morning as one of the robbers. He
is a sad dog; and the minute I come to Ireland I will dis-
card him. I have this day got double iron bars to every
window in my dining-room and bed-chamber; and I hide
my purse in my thread stocking between the bed's head
and the wainscot. Lewis and I dined with an old Scotch
friend,[33] who brought the duke of Douglas,[34] and three
or four more Scots upon us.

10. This was our Society day you know; but the duke
of Ormond could not be with us, because he dined with
prince Eugene. It cost me a guinea contribution to a poet,
who had made a copy of verses upon monkies,[35] applying
the story to the duke of Marlborough; the rest gave two
guineas, except the two physicians,[36] who followed my
example. I don't like this custom; the next time I will
give nothing. I sat this evening at lord Masham's with
lord treasurer: I don't like his countenance; nor I don't
like the posture of things well. We cannot be stout, Till
Somerset's out; as the old saying is.

11. Mr. Lewis and I dined with the chancellor of the
exchequer,[37] who eats the most elegantly of any man I
know in town: I walkt lustily in the Park by moon-shine
till eight, to shake off my dinner and wine; and then went
to sup at Mr. Domville's with Ford, and staid till twelve.
It is told me to-day as a great secret, that the duke of
Somerset will be out soon; that the thing is fixt; but what
shall we do with the duchess? They say, the duke will
make her leave the queen out of spight if he be out. It has

33 Perhaps Arbuthnot.
34 Archibald Douglas, 1694–1761, styled Earl of Angus till 1700, when
he succeeded his father as third Marquis of Douglas. In 1703 he was
created first Duke of Douglas.   35 Not identified.
36 Arbuthnot and Freind.   37 Robert Benson.

stuck upon that Fear a good while already. Well, but Lewis gave me a letter from MD, N. 25.[38] O Lord, I did not expect one this fortnight, faith. You are mighty good, that's certain; but I won't answer it, because this goes to-morrow, only what you say of the printer being taken up; I value it not; all's safe there;[39] nor do I fear any thing, unless the ministry be changed; I hope that danger is over. However, I shall be in Ireland before such a change; which could not be, I think, till the end of the session, if the Whigs designs had gone on. Have not you an apron by Leigh, madam Stella? have you all I mentioned in a former letter?

12. Morning. This goes to-day as usual. I think of going into the city; but of that at night. 'Tis fine moderate weather these two or three days last. Farewel, &c. &c.

LETTER XXXIX

[SATURDAY]   London, Jan. 12, 1711–12.

WHEN I sealed up my letter this morning, I lookt upon myself to be not worth a groat in the world. Last night, after Mr. Ford and I left Domville, Ford desired me to go with him for a minute upon earnest business, and then told me that both he and I were ruined:[1] for he had trusted Stratford with five hundred pounds for tickets for the lottery, and he had been with Stratford, who confessed he had lost fifteen thousand pounds by Sir Stephan Evans,[2] who broke last week; that he concluded Stratford must

[38] The receipt of this letter was noted by Swift in his account book for Nov. 1711–Nov. 1712 (Forster Collection, 508).

[39] Presumably Stella had expressed fears for the printer of *The Conduct of the Allies.* Cf. p. 472.

[1] Years later, 14 Aug. 1725, Swift recalled the occasion to Ford: 'I remember when you expected to be undone in all your ready money by Stratford' (*Letters of Swift to Ford,* ed. D. Nichol Smith, p. 121).

[2] Sir Stephen Evance, a goldsmith, knighted in 1690 (Shaw, *Knights of England,* ii. 266). In *The Tatler,* No. 43, 'Sir *Francis* [Child], Sir *Stephen* [Evance], and the Bank', are named together.

break too; that he could not get his tickets, but Stratford made him several excuses, which seemed very blind ones, &c. And Stratford had near four hundred pounds of mine, to buy me five hundred pounds in the South-Sea company. I came home reflecting a little; nothing concerned me but MD. I called all my philosophy and religion up; and, I thank God, it did not keep me awake beyond my usual time above a quarter of an hour. This morning I sent for Tooke, whom I had employed to buy the stock of Stratford, and settle things with him. He told me, I was secure; for Stratford had transferred it to me in form in the South-Sea house, and he had accepted it for me, and all was done on stampt parchment. However, he would be further informed; and, at night, sent me a note to confirm me. However, I am not yet secure; and, besides, am in pain for Ford, whom I first brought acquainted with Stratford. I dined in the city.

13. Domville and I dined with Ford to-day by appointment: the lord Mansel told me at court to-day, that I was engaged to him: but Stratford had promised Ford to meet him and me to-night at Ford's lodgings. He did so; said he had hopes to save himself in his affair with Evans. Ford asked him for his tickets: he said he would send them to-morrow; but looking in his pocket-book, said he believed he had some of them about him, and gave him as many as came to two hundred pounds, which rejoiced us much; besides, he talked so frankly, that we think[3] there is no danger. I asked him, Was there any more to be settled between us in my affair; he said, no; and answered my questions just as Tooke had got them from others; so I hope I am safe. This has been a scurvy affair. I believe Stella would have half laughed at me, to see a suspicious fellow, like me, over-reached. I saw prince Eugene to-day at Court: I don't think him an ugly faced fellow, but well enough, and a good shape.

3 Deane Swift and Sheridan read 'we think'; Nichols, Scott, Ryland, Aitken, 'we might think'.

14. The parliament was to sit to-day; and met; but were adjourned by the queen's directions till Thursday. She designs to make some important speech then. She pretended illness: but I believe they were not ready, and they expect some opposition; and the Scotch lords are angry,[4] and must be pacified. I was this morning to invite the duke of Ormond to our Society on Thursday, where he is then to be introduced. He has appointed me at twelve to-morrow about some business: I would fain have his help to impeach a certain lord;[5] but I doubt we shall make nothing of it. I intended to have dined with lord treasurer, but I was told he would be busy; so I dined with Mrs. Van; and at night I sat with lord Masham till one. Lord treasurer was there, and chid me for not dining with him: he was in very good humour: I brought home two flasks of Burgundy in my chair: I wish MD had them. You see it is very late; so I'll go to bed, and bid MD good night.

15. This morning I presented my printer and bookseller to lord Rivers, to be stationers to the Ordnance;[6] *Stationers*, that's the word; I did not write it plain at first. I believe it will be worth three hundred pounds a year between them. This is the third employment I have got for them. Rivers told them, the Doctor commanded him, and he durst not refuse it. I would have dined with lord treasurer to-day again, but lord Mansel would not let me, and forced me home with him. I was very deep with the duke of Ormond to-day at the Cockpit, where we met to be private; but I doubt I cannot do the mischief I intended. My friend Penn came there, Will Pen the quaker, at the head of his brethren, to thank the duke for his kindness

---

[4] The House of Lords refused a writ of summons to the Duke of Hamilton (p. 323 n.[15]), a Scottish peer, who had been created Duke of Brandon in the English peerage, 10 Sept. 1711, though he continued to sit as a representative peer of Scotland. See G. E. C., *Complete Peerage*, iv. 447 n.; vi. 267 n.   [5] Doubtless Somerset is meant.
[6] Barber and Tooke. Lord Rivers was Master of the Ordnance.

to their people in Ireland. To see a dozen scoundrels with their hats on, and the duke complimenting with his off, was a good sight enough. I sat this evening with Sir William Robinson,[7] who has mighty often invited me to a bottle of wine: and it is past twelve.

16. This being Fast-day, Dr. Freind and I went into the city to dine late, like good fasters. My printer and bookseller want me to hook in another employment for them in the Tower, because it was enjoyed before by a stationer, although it be to serve the Ordnance with oil, tallow, &c. and is worth four hundred pounds *per annum* more: I will try what I can do. They are resolved to ask several other employments of the same nature to other offices; and I will then grease fat sows, and see whether it be possible to satisfy them. Why am not I a stationer? The parliament sits to-morrow, and Walpool, late secretary at war, is to be swinged for bribery, and the queen is to communicate something of great importance to the two houses, at least they say so. But I must think of answering your letter in a day or two.

17. I went this morning to the duke of Ormond about some business; and he told me he could not dine with us to-day, being to dine with prince Eugene. Those of our Society of the house of commons could not be with us, the house sitting late on Walpool. I left them at nine, and they were not come. We kept some dinner for them. I hope Walpool will be sent to the Tower, and expelled the house: but, this afternoon the members I spoke with in the court of requests talked dubiously of it. It will be a leading card to maul the duke of Marlborough for the

---

[7] Aitken is mistaken in identifying him with Sir William Robinson, Bart., of Newby, Yorkshire. Swift's acquaintance was the William Robinson who served jointly with Bartholomew Vanhomrigh, Vanessa's father, as Commissary-General of Ireland, and was knighted by William III. He also sat in the Irish Parliament; held other public offices in Ireland; and designed Marsh's Library in Dublin. He died 22 Oct. 1712. See *Corresp.* i. 56 n.³; iii. 455–7; Le Neve, *Monumenta*, 1700–15, p. 253.

same crime, or at least to censure him. The queen's message was only to give them notice of the Peace she is treating,[8] and to desire they will make some law to prevent libels against the government; so farewel to Grub-street.

18. I heard to-day that the commoners of our Society did not leave the parliament till eleven at night, then went to those I left, and stay'd till three in the morning. Walpool is expelled, and sent to the Tower.[9] I was this morning again with lord Rivers, and have made him give the other employment to my printer and bookseller; 'tis worth a great deal. I dined with my friend Lewis privately, to talk over affairs. We want to have this duke of Somerset out, and he apprehends it will not be; but I hope better. They are going now at last to change the commissioners of the customs: my friend Sir Matthew Dudley will be out, and three more, and Prior will be in. I have made Ford copy out a small pamphlet, and send it to the press, that I might not be known for author; 'tis *A Letter to the October Club*,[10] if ever you heard of such a thing.——Methinks this letter goes on but slowly for almost a week; I want some little conversation with MD, and to know what they are doing just now. I am sick of politicks. I have not dined with lord treasurer these three weeks; he chides me, but I don't care; I don't.

[8] The Queen was, at this time, suffering from gout, and prevented from making her speech to Parliament on the 14th. On the 17th, her illness continuing, she sent a message to both Houses announcing that the Congress was about to open, and that her Plenipotentiaries had arrived at Utrecht (*Journals of the House of Commons*, xvii. 28).

[9] The Commissioners of Public Accounts had charged Walpole with illicit gains from forage contracts. Despite an able defence he was, by a majority of 57, voted guilty of corruption. His expulsion from the House was, however, carried by 22 votes only, and his committal to the Tower by 12 (*Journals of the House of Commons*, xvii. 29–30, 128). He was released from the Tower in July.

[10] See pp. 159, 194, and notes. *Some Advice Humbly Offer'd to the Members of the October Club, In a Letter from a Person of Honour*. This cleverly phrased pamphlet of 16 pages, published by Morphew, was designed to appease extreme Tory dissatisfaction with the Ministry.

19. I dined to-day with lord treasurer; this is his day of choice company; where they sometimes admit me, but pretend to grumble. And to-day they met on some extraordinary business; the keeper, steward, both secretaries, lord Rivers, and lord Anglesey; I left them at seven, and came away, and have been writing to the bishop of Clogher.[11] I forgot to know where to direct to him since Sir George St. George's death; but I have directed to the same house: you must tell me better; for the letter is sent by the bell-man. Don't write to me again till this is gone, I charge you; for I won't answer two letters together. The duke of Somerset is out, and was with his yellow liveries at parliament to-day. You know he had the same with the queen, when he was master of the horse: we hope the duchess will follow, or that he will take her away in spite. Lord treasurer, I hope, has now saved his head. Has the dean received my letter?[12] ask him at cards to-night.

20. There was a world of people to-day at Court to see prince Eugene, but all bit, for he did not come. I saw the duchess of Somerset talking with the duke of Buckingham; she looked a little down, but was extreamly courteous. The queen has the gout, but is not in much pain. Must I fill this line[13] too? well then, so let it be. The duke of Beaufort[14] has a mighty mind to come into our Society; shall we let him? I spoke to the duke of Ormond about it, and he doubts a little whether to let him in or no. They say the duke of Somerset is advised by his friends to let his wife stay with the queen; I am sorry for it. I dined with the secretary to-day, with mixt company; I don't love it. Our Society does not meet till Friday, because Thursday

---

[11] Letter not preserved.   [12] p. 449 n.[28]

[13] 'It is the last of the page, and written close to the edge of the paper.'— Deane Swift.

[14] Henry Somerset, 1684–1714, second Duke of Beaufort, nephew of the Duchess of Ormonde. He was a strong Tory. *Wentworth Papers, passim.* He died in his thirty-first year of drinking a quantity of small beer after over-heating himself.

will be a busy day in the house of commons; for then the duke of Marlborough's bribery is to be examined into about the pension pay'd him by those that furnished bread to the army.

21. I have been five times with the duke of Ormond about a perfect trifle, and he forgets it: I used him like a dog this morning for it. I was asked to-day by several in the court of requests, Whether it was true that the author of the *Examiner*[15] was taken up in an action of twenty thousand pounds by the duke of Marlborough? I dined in the city, where my printer showed me a pamphlet called *Advice to the October Club*, which he said was sent him by an unknown hand; I commended it mightily; he never suspected me; 'tis a twopenny pamphlet. I came home and got timely to bed; but about eleven one of the secretary's servants came to me, to let me know that lord treasurer would immediately speak with me at lord Masham's upon earnest business; and that if I was abed, I should rise and come. I did so; lord treasurer was above with the queen; and when he came down he laughed, and said it was not he that sent for me: the business was of no great importance, only to give me a paper, which might have been done to-morrow. I stay'd with them till past one, and then got to bed again. Pize[16] take their frolicks. I thought to have answered your letter.

22. Doctor Gastrel was to see me this morning; he is an eminent divine, one of the canons of Christ-church, and one I love very well: he said, he was glad to find I was not with James Broad.[17] I asked what he meant; Why, says he, have you not seen the Grub-street paper, that says

[15] 'Upon the 10th and 17th of this month the *Examiner* was very severe upon the duke of *Marlborough*, and in consequence of this report pursued him with greater virulence in the following course of his papers. But *Swift* was not the writer of the *Examiner* at that period.'—Deane Swift. And see the *Examiner* for 7 Feb. 1711-12.

[16] A word used in various forms of mild imprecation. See Wright's *Dialect Dictionary*; and O.E.D.

[17] James Broad, a bailiff, is mentioned in *The Tatler*, No. 39.

Dr. Swift was taken up as author of the *Examiner* on an action of twenty thousand pounds, and was now at James Broad's (who, I suppose, is some bailiff). I knew nothing of this; but at the court of requests twenty people told me they heard I had been taken up. Lord Lansdown observed to the secretary and me, that the Whigs spread three lies yesterday; that about me; and another, that Macartney, who was turned out last Summer, is again restored to his places in the army; and the third, that Jack Hill's commission for lieutenant of the Tower is stopt, and that Cadogan is to continue. Lansdown thinks they have some design by these reports; I cannot guess it. Did I tell you that Sacheverell has desired mightily to come and see me; but I have put it off: he has heard that I have spoken to the secretary in behalf of a brother whom he maintains, and who desires an employment. T'other day at the court of requests Dr. Yalden[18] saluted me by name; Sacheverell, who was just by, came up to me,[19] and made me many acknowledgements and compliments. Last night I desired lord treasurer to do something for that brother of Sacheverell's: he said he never knew he had a brother; but thanked me for telling him, and immediately put his name in his table-book. I will let Sacheverell know this, that he may take his measures accordingly; but he shall be none of my acquaintance. I dined to-day privately with the secretary, left him at six, paid a visit or two, and came home.

23. I dined again to-day with the secretary; but could

---

18 Thomas Yalden, 1670–1736, educated at Magdalen College, Oxford, obtained a fellowship there in 1699. He took orders and held several ecclesiastical preferments. A minor poet, his *Hymn to Darkness* was praised by Johnson. See Johnson's *Lives of the English Poets*, ed. Birkbeck Hill, ii. 297–303. At Oxford he formed friendships with Addison and Sacheverell.

19 The first time the two met. On 31 Jan. Sacheverell wrote to thank Swift for recommending his brother (*Corresp.* i. 316; *post*, p. 477). The recommendation was successful (*post*, pp. 515–6). Sacheverell had two brothers, of whom one only, Thomas, is known by name.

not dispatch some business I had with him, he has so much besides upon his hands at this juncture; and preparing against the great business to-morrow, which we are all top full of. The ministers' design is, that the duke of Marlborough shall be censured as gently as possible, provided his friends will not make head to defend him; but if they do, it may end in some severer votes. A gentleman who was just now with him, tells me he is much cast down, and fallen away; but he is positive, if he has but ten friends in the house, that they shall defend him to the utmost, and endeavour to prevent the least censure upon him; which I think cannot be, since the bribery is manifest: Sir Solomon Medina[20] paid him six thousand pounds a year to have the employment of providing bread for the army, and the duke owns it in his letter to the commissioners of accounts. I was to-night at lord Masham's; lord Dupplin took out my new little pamphlet,[21] and the secretary read a great deal of it to lord treasurer; they all commended it to the skies, and so did I, and they began a health to the author. But I doubt lord treasurer suspected: for he said, This is Dr. Davenant's style; which is his cant when he suspects me. But I carried the matter very well. Lord treasurer put the pamphlet in his pocket to read at home. I'll answer your letter to-morrow.

24. The secretary made me promise to dine with him to-day after the parliament was up; I said I would come; but I dined at my usual time; knowing the house would sit late on this great affair. I dined at a tavern with Mr. Domville and another gentleman; I have not done so before these many months. At ten this evening I went to

[20] Bread contractor for the allied armies. Knighted in 1700. The Commissioners of Public Accounts reported (21 Dec. 1711) to the House of Commons that between 1702 and 1711 Marlborough had received over £63,000 from Sir Solomon Medina and his predecessor (*Journals of the House of Commons,* xvii. 15–18). The Duke, admitting the fact, declared that he had only followed precedent, and that the money had been devoted to the public service.

[21] *Some Advice to the October Club.*

the secretary, but he was not come home; I sat with his lady till twelve, then came away; and he just came as I was gone, and he sent to my lodgings, but I would not go back; and so I know not how things have passed; but hope all is well; and I will tell you to-morrow day. It is late, &c.

25. The secretary sent to me this morning to know whether we should dine together; I went to him, and there I learnt, that the question went against the duke of Marlborough by a majority of a hundred;[22] so the ministry is mighty well satisfied, and the duke will now be able to do no hurt. The secretary and I and lord Masham, &c. dined with lieutenant-general Withers,[23] who is just going to look after the army in Flanders: the secretary and I left them a little after seven, and I am come home, and will now answer your letter, because this goes to-morrow: let me see.——The box at Chester; oh, burn that box, and hang that Sterne; I have desired one to enquire for it who went towards Ireland last Monday, but am[24] in utter despair of it.—No, I was not splenetick; you see what plunges the Court has been at to set all right again. And that duchess is not out yet, and may one day cause more mischief. Somerset shews all about a letter from the queen, desiring him to let his wife continue with her. Is not that rare! I find Dingley smelt a rat; because the Whigs are *upish*; but if ever I hear that word again, I'll *uppish* you. I am glad you got your rasp safe and sound; does Stella

[22] After a long debate in the House of Commons it was declared by 265 votes to 155 that the payments made to Marlborough by the bread contractors were 'unwarrantable and illegal' (*Journals of the House of Commons*, xvii. 37–8; Winston Churchill, *Marlborough*, iv. 529–30).

[23] Henry Withers had a long and distinguished career in the army. He was appointed a Brigadier in 1702 and Lieutenant-General in 1707 (Dalton's *Army Lists*, i–iii, v, vi, *passim*). He died in 1729, and was buried in Westminster Abbey. He was a friend of 'Duke' Disney (p. 196 n.[25]). In *The Tatler*, No. 46, there is a generous tribute to his character.

[24] Deane Swift and Sheridan read 'am'; Nichols, Scott, Ryland, Aitken, 'I am'.

like her apron? Your criticks about guarantees of succession are puppies; that's an answer to the objection. The answerers here made the same objection, but it[25] is wholly wrong. I am of your opinion, that lord Marlborough is used too hardly: I have often scratched out passages from papers and pamphlets sent me before they were printed; because I thought them too severe. But, he is certainly a vile man, and has no sort of merit beside the military. The *Examiners* are good for little: I would fain have hindered the severity of the two or three last, but could not. I will either bring your papers over, or leave them with Tooke, for whose honesty I will engage.[26] And I think it is best not to venture them with me at sea. Stella is a prophet, by foretelling so positively that all would be well. Duke of Ormond speak against Peace? No, simpleton: he is one of the stanchest we have for the ministry. Neither trouble yourself about the printer: he appeared the first day of term, and is to appear when summoned again; but nothing else will come of it.[27] Lord Chief Justice is cooled since this new settlement. No; I will not split my journals in half; I will write but once a fortnight: but you may do as you will; which is, read only half at once, and t'other half next week. So now your letter is answered. (Pox on these blots!) What must I say more? I will set out in March, if there be a fit of fine weather; unless the ministry desire me to stay till the end of the session, which may be a month longer; but I believe they will not: for I suppose the Peace will be made, and they will have no further service for me. I must make my canal fine this Summer, as fine as I can. I am afraid I shall see great neglects among my quick-sets. I hope the cherry-trees on the river-walk are fine things now. But no more of this.

26. I forgot to finish this letter this morning, and am come home so late I must give it to the bell-man; but I would have it go to-night, lest you should think there is

[25] 'it', omitted by Deane Swift, is supplied by Sheridan and later editors.
[26] p. 449 n.[30]   [27] Cf. p. 462 n.[39]

any thing in the story of my being arrested in an action of twenty thousand pounds by lord Marlborough, which I hear is in Dyer's letter,[28] and consequently, I suppose, gone to Ireland. Farewel, dearest MD, &c. &c.

LETTER XL

[SATURDAY]   London, Jan. 26, 1711–12.

I HAVE no gilt paper left of this size, so you must be content with plain. Our Society dined together to-day, for it was put off, as I told you, upon lord Marlborough's business on Thursday. The duke of Ormond dined with us to-day, the first time; we were thirteen at table; and lord Lansdown came in after dinner, so that we wanted but three. The secretary proposed the duke of Beaufort, who desires to be one of our Society; but I stopt it, because the duke of Ormond doubts a little about it; and he was gone before it was proposed. I left them at seven, and sat this evening with poor Mrs. Wesley, who has been mighty ill to-day with a fainting fit: she has often convulsions too; she takes a mixture with *assa fœtida*, which I have now in my nose; and every thing smells of it. I never smelt it before, 'tis abominable. We have eight pacquets, they say, due from Ireland.

27. I could not see prince Eugene at Court to-day, the crowd was so great. The Whigs contrive to have a crowd always about him, and employ the rabble to give the word, when he sets out from any place. When the duchess of Hamilton came from the queen after church, she whispered me that she was going to pay me a visit: I went to lady Oglethorp's, the place appointed; for ladies always visit me in third places, and she kept me till near four: she

28 Dyer's *News Letter*, edited by the Jacobite John Dyer, a purveyor of sensational news. *The Tatler*, No. 18, 21 May 1709, ridicules him as 'particularly famous for dealing in Whales; insomuch that in Five Months Time . . . he brought Three into the Mouth of the River *Thames*, besides Two Porpusses and a Sturgeon'.

talks too much, is a plaguy detractor, and I believe I shall not much like her. I was engaged to dine with lord Masham; they staid as long as they could, yet had almost dined, and were going in anger to pull down the brass peg for my hat, but lady Masham saved it. At eight I went again to lord Masham's; lord treasurer is generally there at night: we sat up till almost two. Lord treasurer has engaged me to contrive some way to keep the archbishop of York[1] from being seduced by lord Nottingham. I will do what I can in it to-morrow. 'Tis very late, so I must go sleep.

28. Poor Mrs. Manley the author is very ill of a dropsy and sore leg; the printer[2] tells me he is afraid she cannot live long. I am heartily sorry for her; she has very generous principles for one of her sort; and a great deal of good sense and invention: she is about forty, very homely and very fat. Mrs. Van made me dine with her to-day. I was this morning with the duke of Ormond, and the pro-locutor,[3] about what lord treasurer spoke to me yesterday; I know not what will be the issue. There is but a slender majority in the house of lords; and we want more. We are sadly mortified at the news of the French taking the town in Brasil from the Portuguese.[4] The sixth edition of three thousand of the *Conduct of the Allies* is sold, and the printer talks of a seventh; eleven thousand of them have been sold; which is a most prodigious run. The little two-penny *Letter of Advice to the October Club* does not sell; I know not the reason; for it is finely written, I assure you;

---

[1] John Sharp, 1645–1714, was chaplain in ordinary to James II, but was suspended for preaching against Roman Catholicism. In 1689 he was installed Dean of Canterbury, and promoted to the Archbishopric of York in 1691. Swift attributed the Queen's unwillingness to bestow English preferment upon him to Sharp's having represented that he was unfit for the episcopal bench. Nottingham, who had 'gone over to the Whig side', was, apparently, attempting to placate the Archbishop.

[2] John Barber.   [3] Atterbury. Cf. p. 156, and note.

[4] Rio de Janeiro was entered by the French, under Duguay-Trouin, on 21 Sept. 1711.

and, like a true author, I grow fond of it, because it does not sell: you know that is usual to writers, to condemn the judgment of the world: if I had hinted it to be mine, every body would have bought it, but it is a great secret.

29. I borrowed one or two idle books of *Contes de Fées*,[5] and have been reading them these two days, although I have much business upon my hands. I loitered till one at home; then went to Mr. Lewis at his office; and the vice chamberlain told me, that lady Ryalton had yesterday resigned her employment of lady of the bed-chamber, and that lady Jane Hyde, lord Rochester's daughter, a mighty pretty girl, is to succeed; he said too, that lady Sunderland would resign in a day or two. I dined with Lewis, and then went to see Mrs. Wesley, who is better to-day. But you must know, that Mr. Lewis gave me two letters, one from the bishop of Cloyne, with an inclosed from lord Inchequin[6] to lord treasurer; which he desires I would deliver and recommend. I am told, that lord was much in with lord Wharton, and I remember he was to have been one of the lords justices by his recommendation; yet the bishop recommends him as a great friend to the church, &c. I'll do what I think proper. T'other letter was from little saucy MD, N. 26.[7] O Lord, never saw the like, under a cover too, and by way of journal; we shall never have done. Sirrahs; how durst you write so soon, sirrahs? I won't answer it yet.

30. I was this morning with the secretary, who was sick and out of humour; he would needs drink Champagne some days ago, on purpose to spite me, because I advised him against it, and now he pays for it; Stella used to do

5 *Contes des Fées* by Marie-Catherine Le Jumel de Berneville, Comtesse d'Aulnoy (or Aunoy), *c.* 1650–1705.

6 William O'Brien, *c.* 1666–1719, third Earl of Inchiquin, who succeeded to the title in 1692. According to Swift Lord Wharton bargained with him to accept a Lord Justiceship of Ireland at less than the official salary (*Prose Works*, v. 26–7).

7 The receipt of this letter is noted by Swift in his account book for Nov. 1711–Nov. 1712 (Forster Collection, 508).

such tricks formerly; he put me in mind of her. Lady Sunderland has resigned her place too. It is lady Catherine Hyde that succeeds lady Ryalton; and not lady Jane. Lady Catherine is the late earl of Rochester's daughter.[8] I dined with the secretary, then visited his lady; and sat this evening with lady Masham; the secretary came to us; but lord treasurer did not; he dined with the master of the rolls,[9] and staid late with him. Our Society does not meet till to-morrow sennight, because we think the parliament will be very busy to-morrow upon the state of the war; and the secretary, who is to treat as president, must be in the house. I fancy my talking of persons and things here, must be very tedious to you, because you know nothing of them; and I talk as if you did. You know Kevin's-street, and Werburgh-street, and (what do you call the street where Mrs. Walls lives?) and Ingoldsby, and Higgins, and lord Santry; but what care you for lady Catherine Hyde? Why do you say nothing of your health, sirrah? I hope it is well.

31. Trimnel, bishop of Norwich,[10] who was with this lord Sunderland at Moor-park in their travels, preached yesterday before the house of lords; and to-day the question was put to thank him, and print his sermon; but passed against him; for it was a terrible Whig sermon. The Bill

[8] She was an unmarried daughter of Laurence Hyde, first Earl of Rochester (p. 84 n.25). Not to be confused with her niece, Lady Catherine Hyde (p. 317 n.34), afterwards Duchess of Queensberry, who was, at this time, under twelve years old.

[9] Sir John Trevor, 1637–1717, called to the Bar in 1661, was knighted in 1671, and first entered Parliament in 1673. In 1685 he was chosen Speaker by unanimous vote, and in the same year was appointed to the Mastership of the Rolls. On the accession of William III he was displaced; but in 1690 he was again chosen Speaker, and reinstated as Master of the Rolls in 1693. In 1695 he was expelled the house for corruption, but held the Mastership of the Rolls till his death.

[10] Charles Trimnell, 1663–1723, Bishop of Norwich since 1708. In 1721 he became Bishop of Winchester. He had been chaplain to the Earl of Sunderland; and Swift suggests that the Earl learned 'his politics from his tutor' (*Prose Works*, x. 27).

to repeal the *Act for naturalizing protestant foreigners*,[11] passed the house of lords to-day by a majority of twenty, though the Scotch lords went out, and would vote neither way, in discontent about duke Hamilton's patent,[12] if you know any thing of it. A poem is come out to-day, inscribed to me, by way of a flirt; for it is a Whiggish poem, and good for nothing.[13] They plagued me with it in the court of requests. I dined with lord treasurer at five alone, only with one Dutch man. Prior is now a commissioner of the customs.[14] I told you so before, I suppose. When I came home to-night, I found a letter from Dr. Sacheverell, thanking me for recommending his brother to lord treasurer and Mr. secretary for a place. Lord treasurer sent to him about it: so good a solicitor was I, although I once hardly thought I should be a solicitor for Sacheverell.

Feb. 1. Has not your dean of St. Patrick's received my letter? you say nothing of it, although I writ above a month ago.[15] My printer has got the gout, and I was forced to go to him to-day, and there I dined. It was a most delicious day; why don't you observe whether the same days be fine with you? To-night at six Dr. Atterbury and Prior, and I, and Dr. Freind, met at Dr. Robert Freind's house at Westminster, who is master of the school: there we sat till one, and were good enough company. I here take leave to tell politick Dingley, that the passage in the *Conduct of*

---

11 An Act for Naturalizing Foreign Protestants received the royal assent on 23 Mar. 1708–9. An attempt to repeal, which passed the Commons on 31 Jan. 1710–11, was thrown out by the Lords on 5 Feb. Again, on 17 Jan. 1711–12 (*Journals*, xvii. 28), the Commons passed a Bill of repeal, to which the Lords consented, with some amendments, on 31 Jan. (*Journals*, xix. 368).   12 p. 464 n.[4]

13 *When the Cat's away, The Mice may play. A Fable, Humbly inscrib'd to Dr. Sw—t*, four pages folio, advertised in *The Spectator* for 31 Jan., No. 289. This poem, in defence of Marlborough, was a reply to *A Fable of the Widow and her Cat* (p. 454 n.[10]).

14 The promised transfer of Prior to the customs was slow of fulfilment. It is first mentioned by Swift on 26 June 1711; again 15 Oct.; again 18 Jan. 1711–12.

15 p. 449 n.[28]

the Allies is so far from being blameable,[16] that the secretary designs to insist upon it in the house of commons, when the Treaty of Barrier[17] is debated there, as it now shortly will, for they have ordered it to be laid before them. The pamphlet of *Advice to the October Club* begins now to sell; but I believe it's fame will hardly reach Ireland: 'tis finely written, I assure you. I long to answer your letter; but won't yet; you know 'tis late, &c.

2. This day[18] ends Christmas;[19] and what care I? I have neither seen, nor felt, nor heard any Christmas this year. I passed a lazy dull day: I was this morning with lord treasurer, to get some papers from him, which he will remember as much as a cat, although it be his own business. It threatened rain, but did not much; and Prior and I walked an hour in the Park, which quite put me out of my measures. I dined with a friend hard by; and in the evening sat with lord Masham till twelve. Lord treasurer did not come; this is an idle dining day usually with him. We want to hear from Holland how our Peace goes on; for we are afraid of those scoundrels the Dutch, lest they

[16] The passage in *The Conduct of the Allies*, which Rebecca Dingley found 'blameable', was a paragraph (*Prose Works*, v. 83–4) in which Swift, commenting on the Dutch undertaking, in the second article of the Barrier Treaty, to 'assist and maintain' the Hanoverian succession in England, concluded by observing that the guarantee might 'put it out of the power of our own legislature' to change the succession, 'how much soever the necessities of the kingdom may require it'. Lord Chief Justice Parker (p. 437 n.24) pronounced the passage capable of treasonable interpretation. In the fourth edition of *The Conduct of the Allies* Swift altered the passage and added an explanatory postscript (*Prose Works*, v. 123). Cf. p. 488.

[17] By the terms of the Barrier Treaty between the Netherlands and England, signed 29 Oct. 1709, the Dutch were to be allowed to garrison a defensive line of cities and fortresses on the French border and in the Spanish Netherlands. In return the Dutch promised armed support of the Hanoverian succession. The full text of the treaty is printed in *The Dutch Barrier*, Geike and Montgomery, pp. 377–86.

[18] The word 'day' is omitted by Nichols, Scott, Ryland, and Aitken.

[19] 2 Feb. is the Feast of the Purification of the Virgin, also known as Candlemas.

should play us tricks. Lord Marr, a Scotch earl, was with us at lord Masham's; I was arguing with him about the stubbornness and folly of his countrymen; they are so angry about the affair of duke Hamilton, whom the queen has made a duke of England, and the house of lords will not admit him: he swears he would vote for us, but dare not; because all Scotland would detest him if he did; he should never be chosen again, nor be able to live there.

3. I was at Court to-day to look for a dinner; but did not like any that were offered me; and I dined with lord Mountjoy. The queen has the gout in her knee, and was not at chapel. I hear we have a Dutch mail, but I know not what news, although I was with the secretary this morning. He shewed me a letter from the Hanover envoy, Mr. Bothmar, complaining that the Barrier Treaty is laid before the house of commons; and desiring that no infringement may be made in the Guarantee of the Succession; but the secretary has written him a peppering answer. I fancy you understand all this, and are able state-girls, since you have read the *Conduct of the Allies*. We are all preparing against the birth-day,[20] I think it is Wednesday next. If the queen's gout encreases, it will spoil sport. Prince Eugene has two fine suits made against it; and the queen is to give him a sword worth four thousand pounds, the diamonds set transparent.

4. I was this morning soliciting at the house of commons' door for Mr. Vesey, a son of the archbishop of Tuam,[21] who has petitioned for a Bill to relieve him in some difficulty about his estate; I secured him about[22]

---

[20] The Queen was born on 6 Feb. 1665.

[21] The Archbishop of Tuam (p. 132 n.[63]) had 'a numerous issue'. This son was probably Agmondisham Vesey (*Poems*, p. 1033 n.), who later went over to the Whigs and was rewarded by his appointment as Accountant-General of Ireland (Lodge, *Peerage of Ireland*, vi. 33–4). For the bill in Vesey's favour see *Journals of the House of Commons*, xvii. 69, 74, 105, 117, 147, 152, 158, 185, 235). It received the royal assent on 22 May 1712.

[22] Nichols, Scott, Ryland, Aitken, and Moorhead read 'above'.

fifty members. I dined with lady Masham. We have no pacquet from Holland, as I was told yesterday; and this wind will hinder many people from appearing at the birth-day, who expected cloaths from Holland. I appointed to meet a gentleman at the secretary's to-night, and they both failed. The house of commons have this day made many severe votes about our being abused by our allies.[23] Those who spoke, drew all their arguments from my book, and their votes confirm all I writ; the Court had a majority of a hundred and fifty: all agree, that it was my book that spirited them to these resolutions; I long to see them in print. My head has not been as well as I could wish it for some days past, but I have not had any giddy fit, and I hope it will go over.

5. The secretary turned me out of his room this morn-ing, and shewed me fifty guineas rolled up, which he was going to give to some French spy.[24] I dined with four Irishmen at a tavern to-day; I thought I had resolved against it before, but I broke it. I played at cards this evening at lady Masham's, but I only played for her while she was writing; and I won her a pool; and supt there. Lord treasurer was with us, but went away before twelve. The ladies and lords have all their cloaths ready against to-morrow: I saw several mighty fine, and I hope there will be a great appearance, in spite of that spiteful French fashion of the Whiggish ladies not to come, which they have all resolved to a woman; and I hope it will more spirit the queen against them for ever.

6. I went to dine at lord Masham's at three, and met all the company just coming out of Court; a mighty crowd; they staid long for their coaches: I had an opportunity of seeing several lords and ladies of my acquaintance in their fineries. Lady Ashburnham looked the best in my eyes. They say, the Court was never fuller nor finer.

[23] *Journals of the House of Commons*, xvii. 68.
[24] Apparently a man named Mézière (Bolingbroke's *Letters*, i. 395, 406).

Lord treasurer, his lady, and two daughters,[25] and Mrs. Hill dined with lord and lady Masham; the five ladies were monstrous fine. The queen gave prince Eugene the diamond sword to-day; but no-body was by when she gave it, except my lord chamberlain. There was an entertainment of Opera songs at night, and the queen was at all the entertainment, and is very well after it. I saw lady Wharton, as ugly as the Devil, coming out in the crowd all in an undress; she had been with the Marlborough daughters and lady Bridgwater[26] in St. James's, looking out of the window all undressed, to see the sight. I do not hear that one Whig lady was there, except those of the bed-chamber. Nothing has made so great a noise as one Kelson's[27] chariot, that cost nine hundred and thirty pounds, the finest was ever seen. The rabble huzzaed him as much as they did prince Eugene. This is birthday chat.

7. Our Society met to-day, the duke of Ormond was not with us; we have lessened our dinners, which were grown so extravagant, that lord treasurer and every body else cried shame. I left them at seven, visited for an hour, and then came home, like a good boy. The queen is much better after yesterday's exercise: her friends wish she would use a little more. I opposed lord Jersey's election into our Society, and he is refused: I likewise opposed the duke of Beaufort; but I believe he will be chosen in spite of me: I don't much care; I shall not be with them above two months; for I resolve to set out for Ireland the beginning

---

[25] Lord Oxford's two daughters were Elizabeth (p. 135 n.[72]), who married the Marquis of Caermarthen, and Abigail, married in 1709 to Viscount Dupplin (p. 45 n.[39]). See Collins, *Peerage of England*, ed. Brydges, iv. 80.

[26] In 1703 Scroop Egerton, fifth Earl and (1720) first Duke of Bridgewater, married Lady Elizabeth Churchill, third daughter of the Duke of Marlborough. She died in 1714.

[27] He may have been a member of the Kelson family residing at Shipley, near Exeter, in the eighteenth century; but it has not been possible to identify him.

of April next (before I treat them again) and see my willows.

8. I dined to-day in the city; this morning a scoundrel dog, one of the queen's musick, a German, whom I had never seen, got access to me in my chamber by Patrick's folly, and gravely desired me to get an employment in the customs for a friend of his, who would be very grateful; and likewise to forward a project of his own, for raising ten thousand pounds a year upon Operas: I used him civiller than he deserved; but it vexed me to the pluck.[28] He was told, I had a mighty interest with lord treasurer, and one word of mine, &c.——Well; I got home early on purpose to answer MD's letter, N. 26; for this goes to-morrow.——Well; I never saw such a letter in all my life; so saucy, so journalish, so sanguine, so pretending, so every thing.——I satisfied all your fears in my last; All is gone well, as you say; yet you are an impudent slut to be so positive; you will swagger so upon your sagacity that we shall never have done. Pray don't mislay your reply; I would certainly print it, if I had it here: how long is it? I suppose, half a sheet: was the Answer written in Ireland? Yes, yes, you shall have a letter when you come from Baligall.[29] I need not tell you again who's out and who's in: we can never get out the duchess of Somerset.——So, they say Presto writ the *Conduct*, &c. do they like it? I don't care whether they do or no; but the Resolutions printed t'other day in the Votes,[30] are almost quotations from it; and would never have passed, if that book had not been written. I will not meddle with the Spectator, let him fair-sex[31] it to the world's end. My disorder is over, but blood was not from the p–les.——Well, madam

[28] The heart.

[29] An entry by Rebecca Dingley in Swift's account book for 1709–10 (Forster, 507) shows that she and Stella were at Ballygall (p. 28 n.[12]) from 23 Jan. to 1 Feb. 1711–12.   [30] p. 480 n.[23]

[31] In allusion to the feminine interest of *The Spectator* and constant mention of the 'fair sex'.

Dingley, the frost; why we had a great frost, but I forget how long ago; it lasted above a week or ten days: I believe about six weeks ago; but it did not break so soon with us I think as December 29; yet I think it was about that time, on second thoughts. MD can have no letter from Presto, says you, and yet four days before you own you had my thirty-seventh, unreasonable sluts! The bishop of Gloucester[32] is not dead, and I am as likely to succeed the duke of Marlborough as him if he were; there's enough for that now. It is not unlikely that the duke of Shrewsbury will be your governour;[33] at least I believe the duke of Ormond will not return.—Well, Stella again: why really three editions of the *Conduct*, &c. is very much for Ireland; it is a sign you have some honest among you.—Well; I will do Mr. Manley[34] all the service I can: but he will ruin himself. What business had he to engage at all about the city? can't he wish his cause well, and be quiet, when he finds that stirring will do it no good, and himself a great deal of hurt? I cannot imagine who should open my letter; it must be done at your side.—If I hear of any thoughts of turning out Mr. Manley, I will endeavour to prevent it. I have already had all the gentlemen of Ireland here upon my back often, for defending him. So now I have answered your saucy letter. My humble service to goody Stoyte and Catherine; I will come soon for my dinner.

9. Morning. My cold goes off at last; but I think I have got a small new one. I have no news since last. They say we hear by the way of Calais, that Peace is very near concluding. I hope it may be true. I'll go and seal up my

---

[32] Edward Fowler, a Whig in politics and a latitudinarian in doctrine, had been Bishop of Gloucester since 1691. He died in 1714.

[33] Subsequent allusions to Shrewsbury in the *Journal* and mention of him in Swift's correspondence (*Corresp.* i. 315, 319–21, 323, 325–6) show that his appointment as Lord Lieutenant of Ireland was generally expected. He was offered the viceroyalty when Ormonde was appointed Captain-General of the Forces in Flanders, but declined it (*MSS. of the Marquis of Bath*, i. 218). He was, however, induced to accept it in Sept. 1713.

[34] Isaac Manley.

letter, and give it myself to-night into the post-office; and so I bid my dearest MD farewel till to-night. I heartily wish myself with them, as hope saved. My willows, and quicksets, and trees will be finely improved, I hope, this year. It has been fine hard frosty weather yesterday and to-day. Farewel, &c. &c. &c.[35]

LETTER XLI

41 [SATURDAY]   London. Febr. 9. 1711-12

When my Letter is gone, and I have none of yours to answer, My Conscience is so clear, and my shoulders so light, and I go on with such courage to prate upon nothing to deerichar Md, oo would wonder. I dined with Sir Mat Dudley, who is newly turnd out of Commissn of the Customs; he affects a good Heart, and talks in the extremity of Whiggery, which was always his Principle,[1] thō he was gentle a little while he kept in Employnt; We can yet get no Pacquets from Holld. I have not been with any of the Ministry these 2 or 3 days. I keep[2] out of their way on purpose, for a certain Reason, for some time: thō I must dine with the Secrty to morrow, the chusing of the Company being left to me; I have engagd Ld Anglesea and Ld Carteret, and have promisd to get 3 more but I have a mind tht none else should be admitted: however, if I like any body at Court to morrow I may perhaps invite them. I have got another cod; but not very bad. ⌐Nite my Md⌐

---

[35] Here ends that part of the *Journal* edited in 1768 by Deane Swift, on whom, save for Letter I, we are dependent for the text. The latter part of the *Journal*, consisting of twenty-five letters, was edited by Hawkesworth in 1766. These letters, save for LIV, survive, and the text is here printed from the originals. See, however, Introduction, p. lix.

[1] Sir Matthew Dudley (p. 11 n.[2]) was definitely a Whig in politics.

[2] A word, apparently 'have', is struck out before 'keep'. Presumably Swift first intended to write 'have kept'.

10. I saw Pr Eugene at Court to day very plain; he is plaguy yellow, and tolerably ugly besides.³ The Court was very full, and People had their Birthday Cloaths. I dined with the Secty to day, I was to invite 5, but I only invited 2, Ld Anglesea & Ld Carteret. pshaw, I told you this but yesterday. We have no Pacquets from Hold yet. Here are a parcel of drunken whiggish Lds like your Ld Santry who come into Chocolate House & rail aloud at the Toryes, and have Challenges sent them, and the next morning come and beg Pardon. Genll Ross⁴ was like to. swinge the Marquis of Winchester⁵ for this Trick tother day, and we have nothing else now to talk of, till the Parlmt has had another Bout with the State of the War, as they intend in a few days. They have orderd the Barrier Treaty to be layd before them, and it was talkt some time ago, as if there were a design to impeach Ld Townshend⁶ who made it. I have no more Politicks now. Nite dee Md.

11. I dind with Ld Anglesea to day, who had 7 Irishmen to be my Companions, of which 2 only were Coxcombs, one I did not know, and tother was young Blith,⁷

---

³ In *The Spectator*, No. 340, 31 Mar. 1712, Steele gives a very different description of his appearance.

⁴ Charles Ross, son of the eleventh Baron Ross, Colonel of the Royal Irish Dragoons from 1695 to 1705. In Apr. 1712 he was appointed Lieutenant-General of the Horse under the Duke of Ormonde in Flanders. He died in 1732 (Dalton, *Army Lists*, ii. 212; iii. 34).

⁵ Charles Paulet, or Powlett, 1685–1754, eldest son of the second Duke of Bolton (p. 369 n.²), called Marquis of Winchester, succeeded his father in 1722. He married in 1751, as his second wife, Lavinia Fenton, who, in 1728, had taken the part of Polly Peachum in Gay's *Beggar's Opera*.

⁶ Charles Townshend, 1674–1738, second Viscount Townshend, was sent in 1709, by the Whig Ministry, as plenipotentiary to The Hague. In October of that year, when Marlborough refused to countenance it, he alone signed the Barrier Treaty for Great Britain.

⁷ John Bligh, or Blith, 1683–1728, son of the Rt. Hon. Thomas Bligh (p. 34 n.³⁸), of Rathmore, co. Meath, married in 1713 (cf. *Wentworth Papers*, p. 353) Lady Theodosia Hyde, daughter of the third Earl of Clarendon,

who is a Puppy of figure here, with a fine Chariot. He askt me one day at Court, when I had been just talking with some Lds, who stood near me, Dr, when shll we see you in the County of Meath, I whisprd him to take care wht he sd, for the People would think he was some Barbarian. He nevr would speak to me since, till we mett to day. I went to Ldy Mashams to night, & sate with Ld Treasr & the Secrty there till past 2 a clock, and when I came home, found some Letters from Ireld, which I read, but can say nothing of them till to morrow, tis so very late, but ⌐. .¬ must always be ⌐s . . . d¬ late or Early. ⌐Nite delest Sollahs¬.[8]

12. One Lettr from the Bp of Cl.[9] last night, and tother from Walls, about Mrs Souths Sallary,[10] and his own Pension of 18ll for his Tyths of the Park. I will do nothing in either, the first I cannot serve in, & the other is a Trifle; only you may tell him I had his Lettr, and will speak to Ned Southwell about what he desires me. You say nothing of your Deans receiving my Letter. I find, Clements whom I recommended to Ld Anglesy[11] last year at Walls desire, or rather the Bp of Cl-'s[12] is mightily in Ld Anglsea's favor; You may tell the Bp & Walls so; I sd to Ld Anglesea, that I was[13] I had the good Luck to recommend him &c I dined in the City with my Printer; to consult with him about some Paprs[14] Ld Tr— gave me

---

and *suo jure* Baroness Clifton. In 1721 he was created Baron Clifton; and in 1725 Earl of Darnley.

[8] Of the concluding eleven words for the day the first, the fifth, and the last three have been struck through. The first does not seem to be 'I', or 'it' as might naturally be conjectured. The fifth begins with 's' and ends with 'd', and cannot be 'oors dee MD' (Forster), or 'found' (Ryland, Aitken). The last three can be deciphered confidently.

[9] Bishop of Clogher.

[10] p. 369 n.[1]   [11] See pp. 242-3.

[12] Bishop of Clogher.

[13] The word 'glad' omitted?

[14] Materials for *Some Remarks on the Barrier Treaty* (pp. 489, 492), which Swift was engaged in writing.

last night, as he always does, too late; However, I will do something with them. My third Cold is a little bettr; I never had any thing like it before, three Colds successively. I hope I shall have the 4th; ⌜. .⌝[15] Those Messengrs came from Holld to day, and they brought over the 6 Pacquets that were due; I know not the particulars yet, for when I was with the Secrty at noon, they were just opening; but one thing I find, that the Dutch are playing us Tricks, and tampering with the French, they are dogs. I shll know more ⌜to mollow . . Md⌝

13. I dined to day privately with my Friend Lewis at His Lodgings, to consult about some Observations on the Barrier Treaty Our News from Holland is not good: The French raise difficultyes, and make such Offers to the Allyes as cannot be acceptd. And the Dutch are uneasy that we are like to get any thing for ourselves; and the Whigs are glad at all this. I came home early, and have been very busy 3 or 4 hours. I had a Letter from Dr Prat to day by a private hand, recommending the Bearer to me, for something that I shall not trouble my self about: Wesly[16] writ to recommend the same Fellow to me; His[17] Expression is that hearing I am acquainted with My Ld Treasr, he desires I would do so, and so: A matter of nothing. What Puppyes are Mankind.. I hope I shall be wiser when I have once done with Courts. I think you han't troubled me much with your Recommendations. I would do you all the Saairs[18] I could. Pray have you got your Apron Maran[19] ppt; I pd for it but yesterday, that puts me in mind of it. I writ an Inventory of what things

---

[15] Forster reads 'eugc, euge, euge'. But, comparing 30 Mar. 1712, it seems probable that 'urge, urge, urge' is the correct reading. Pons (*Du nouveau sur le 'Journal à Stella'*, pp. 11–12) confidently suggests 'rouge, rouge, rouge'. The word rendered 'uth' by Deane Swift, 22 Jan. 1710–11, was probably the same.

[16] Garret Wesley (p. 3 n.[15]).

[17] Before 'His' a word is scrawled out.

[18] Services.

[19] 'Maran', or 'Maram', is little language for 'Madam'.

I sent by Lee, in one of my Letters; did you compare it with what you got? I hear nothing of your Cards now; do you never play; yes at Baligawl.[20] go to bed ⌐Nite deelest Md¬.

14. Our Society dined to day at Mr Secrtys house; I went there at 4, but hearing the House of Comms would sit late upon the Barrier Treaty, I went for an hour to Kensington to see Ld Masham's Children. My young Nephew[21] his son of 6 months old has got a swelling in his Neck, I fear it is the Evil. We did not go to dinner till 8 at night, & I left them at 10; the Commons have been very severe on the Barrier Treaty; as you will find by their Votes. A Whig Membr took out the Conduct of the Allyes, and read that Passage about the Succession,[22] with great Resentmt, but none seconded him. The Church Party carryed every Vote by a great Majority. The A.B. Dublin[23] is so raild at by all who come from Ired, that I can defend him no longer. Ld Anglesea assured me that the Story of applying Piso out of Tacitus to Ld Treasrs being wounded, is true.[24] I believe, the D. of Beaufort will be admitted to our Society next meeting; To day I published the Fable of Midas, a Poem printed in a loose half sheet of Paper:[25] I know not how it will sell. But it passed wonderfully at our Society to night; & Mr Secty read it before me tother night to Ld Tr. at Ld Mashams, where they equally approvd of it. tell me how it passes with you. I think this Paper is larger than ordinary, for here is 6 days Journall and no nearer the Bottom. I fear these Journals are very dull. Nite my deelest lives.

15. Mr Lewis & I dined by Invitation with a Scotch

---

[20] Ballygall, Thomas Ashe's place (p. 28 n.[12]).

[21] As the son of a brother of the Society Swift calls the child a 'Nephew'.

[22] p. 478 n.[16]

[23] Archbishop of Dublin.

[24] p. 236.

[25] *Poems*, p. 155. As in *The Examiner*, No. 28, Swift attacks Marlborough for his love of money.

acquaintance,[26] after I had been very busy in my Chamb till 2 afternoon. My third Cold is now very troublesome upon my Breast, especially in the Morning; This is a great Revolution in my Health, Colds never used to return so soon with me, or last so long. Tis very surprising this News to day of the Dauphin and Dauphiness both dying within 6 days.[27] They say the old King is almost heartbroke. He has had prodigious mortifications in his Family. The Dauphin has left 2 little Sons of 4 and 2 years old, the eldest is sick. There is a foolish Story got about the Town, tht Ld Strafford one of our Plenipotentryes is in the Interests of France; and it has been a good while sd that Ld Privy Seal[28] and he do not agree very well. They are both long practised in Business, but neither of them of much Parts; Strafford has some Life and Spirit, but is infinitely proud, & wholly illiterate. Nite Md.

16. I dined to day in the City with my Printer to finish something I am doing about the Barrier Treaty but it is not quite done.[29] I went this Evening to Ld Masham's, where Ld Treasr sate with us till past 12; the Lds have voted an[30] Adress to the Qu,[31] to tell her they are not satisfyed with the K. of France's Offers. The Whigs brought it in of a sudden, and the Court could not prevent it, and therefore did not oppose it. The H. of Lds is too strong in

---

[26] Probably Arbuthnot.

[27] The Dauphin had died 13 Apr., N.S., 1711 (p. 238 n.[6]). His son, then heir to the throne, Louis, Duke of Burgundy, died 18 Feb. 1712, a few days after the death (12 Feb.) of his wife, Marie-Adelaide, daughter of Victor Amadeus, Duke of Savoy. They left two sons, the Dukes of Brittany and Anjou, five and two years old respectively. The elder died 8 Mar. 1712, leaving a sickly infant, afterwards Louis XV, as heir to the throne of France. A difficult political situation thus arose, for the next heir in strict succession to the Duke of Anjou was Philip V, King of Spain. The difference between the New Style and the Old accounts for Swift's knowledge of the deaths on 15 Feb.

[28] Robinson, Bishop of Bristol.

[29] *Some Remarks on the Barrier Treaty* (p. 478 n.[17]).

[30] Swift first wrote 'and', struck this through, and wrote the correct 'an'.

[31] *Journals of the House of Lords*, 15 Feb. 1711–12, xix. 379.

Whigs notwithstanding the new Creations. For they are very diligent, and the Toryes as la[zy,]³² the side that is down has always most Industry: the Whigs intended to have made a Vote tht would reflect on Ld Treasr; but their Project was not ripe: I hitt my face such a Rap by calling the Coach to stop to night that it is plaguy sore, the bone beneath the Eye. Nite deel.³³

17. The Court was mighty full to day and has been these many Sundays, but the Qu was not at Chappel; she has got a little fitt of the Gout in her foot. The good of going to Court is tht one sees all ones Acquaintance, whom otherwise I should hardly meet twice a year. Prince Eugene dines with the Secretary to day, with about 7 or 8 Genrll officers or forein Ministers. They will be all drunk I am sure. I never was in company with this Prince; I have proposed to some Lds that we should have a sober Meal with him, but I cant compass it. It is come over in the Dutch News Prints, that I was arrested on an action of 20000ll by D Marlbrow. I did not like my Court Invitation to day; so Sr A Fountn and I went and dined with Mrs Van; I came home at 6, and have been very busy till this minute, and it is past 12. So I got into bed to write to ⌈Md; for . . . .⌉.³⁴ We reckon, the Dauphin's Death, will put forward the Peace a good deal. Pray is Dr. Griffith³⁵ reconcild to me yet? have I done enough to soften him? ⌈. . . . . Nite deelest logues⌉.³⁶

----

³² Hawkesworth's reading, followed by later editors. The word is at the outer corner of the sheet and rubbed, but the 'la' is clearly legible.

³³ All that is written.

³⁴ Eight or nine words have been obliterated, and are illegible, save for 'Md; for'. The last appears to be 'Md', although Pons (*Du nouveau sur le 'Journal à Stella'*, p. 15) reads it 'bed'. Forster has no hesitation in discovering, 'MD MD, for we must always write to MD MD MD, awake or aseep'.

³⁵ p. 128 n.⁴⁶

³⁶ A number of words scored through. There is little semblance to Forster's reading: 'Go to bed. Help pdfr. Rove pdfr. MD MD. Nite

18. Lewis had Guiscard's Picture, he bought it, and offerd it Ld Treasr who promised to send for it, but never did; so I made Lewis give it me, and I have it in my Room. & nw Ld Treasr says he will take it from me, is that fair? He designs to have it at Length in the cloathes he wore when he did the Action & a Pen knife in his hand; & Kneller is to copy it from this that I have. I intended to dine with Ld Treasr to day; but he has put me off till tomorrow; so I dined with Ld Dupplin; you know Ld Dupplin very well, he is a Brother of the Society. Well, but I have receivd a Lettr from the Bp of Cloyn[37] to sollicite an Affair for him with Ld Treasr, and with the Parlnt, which I will do as soon as fly. I am not near so keen[38] about other Peoples affairs, as ⌐. . . . ppt⌐[39] used to reproach me about; it was a Judgnt on me. Hearkee, . . .[40] both. Meetinks I begin to want a Rettle flom Md,[41] fais, and so I do. I doubt you have been in pain about the Report of my being arrested. The Pamphleteers have let me alone this month, which is a great wonder, only the 3d part of the Answer to the Conduct,[42] wch is lately come

darling rogues'. Pons (op. cit., p. 16) succeeds in finding, 'sans hésitation, et avec une certitude totale', the words 'deelest rife MD'. But the only words which admit of little doubt are the last three.

37 Hawkesworth printed '*Clogher*', and Moorhead reads 'Clogh'. But the word is quite clearly 'Cloyn'. On 29 Jan. (p. 475) Swift mentions a request from the Bishop of Cloyne, with an enclosure directed to Oxford, with which he had little sympathy, and his attitude on this occasion is the same. For Charles Crow, Bishop of Cloyne, see p. 401 n.[23]

38 A word before 'keen' is struck out.

39 Forster reads this obliteration as 'saucy Ppt'. The last three letters are clearly 'ppt'. The others are very doubtful.

40 This word is not blotted out; but it is difficult to make anything of it. Forster finds 'Idledearies'. There is, however, no 'd' in the earlier part, and it looks more like 'Jutledearies'.

41 Letter from Md.

42 *The Allies and the Late Ministry Defended* (p. 431 n.[13]). The third part of this reply to *The Conduct of the Allies* was advertised as published on 11 Feb. (*The Daily Courant*); and a fourth part was advertised on 10 Mar.

out (Did I tell you of it already?) The H. of Commons goes on in mauling the late Ministry & their Proceedings. ⌜Nite deelest Md⌝.[43]

19. I dind with Ld Treasr to day, & sate with him till 10 inspight of my Teeth; thô my Printer waited for me to correct a Sheet. I told him of 4 Lines I writt extempore with my Pencil, on a bitt of Paper[44] in his House while he lay wounded; Some of the Servant[s] I suppose. made wastpaper of them; and he never had heard of them. Shall I tell them you; They were inscribed, To Mr Harleys Physicians. Thus. On Europe Britain's Safety lyes;[45] Britain is lost if Harley dyes; Harley depends upon your Skill: Think what You save, or what You kill.—Are not they well enough to be done off hand; for that is the meaning of the Word extempore, wch you did not know; did you? I proposed tht some Company should dine with him on the 8th of March, which was the day he was wounded, but he says he designs tht the Lds of the Cabinet who then sate with him, should dine that day with them;[46] however, he has invited me too.—I can not get rid of my cold, it plagues me in the morning chiefly. Nite Md.

20. Aftr waiting to catch the Secrty coming out from Sr Ts Hanmer for 2 hours, in vain, about some Business I went into the City to my Printer, to correct some sheets of the Barrier Treaty and Remarks, wch must be finished to morrow; I have been horrible busy for some days past with this and some other Things; & I wanted some very necessary Papers wch the Secty was to give me, and the Pamphlet must now be publishd without them. But they are all busy too; Sr Tho. Hanmer is Chairman of the Committee for drawing up a Representation of the State

---

[43] Blotted out, but easily legible.

[44] The 'bitt of Paper' is preserved among the manuscripts of the Marquis of Bath at Longleat (*Poems*, p. 140).

[45] Swift meant to write 'On Britain Europe's safety lies'. Hawkesworth corrected the mistake.

[46] Presumably a slip for 'him'.

of the Nation[47] to the Qu— where all the wrong Steps of the Allyes & late Ministry about the War will be mentiond. the Secty I suppose was helping him about it to day. I believe it will be a Pepperer. Nite dee Md.

21. I have been 6 hours to day morning writing 19 Pages of a Lettr to day to Ld Treasr, about forming a Society or Academy to correct and fix the English Language.[48] (Is English a Speech or a Language?) it will not be above five or 6 more, I will send it him to morrow, and will print it if he desires me. I dined, you know, with our Society to day, Thursday is our day, we had a new Membr admitted; it was the D. of Beaufort. We were 13 met,, Brother Ormd was not there; but sent his Excuse that Prince Eugene dined with him. I left them at 7, being engaged to go to Sr Tho. Hanmer, who desired I would see him at that Hour; His business was, that I would hoenlbp ihainm italoi dsroanws ubpl tohne sroeqporaensiepnotlastoiqobn;[49] which I consented to do, but know not whether I shall succeed; because it is a little out of my way. However I have taken my Share. Nite Md.

22. I finished the rest of my Lettr to Ld Treasr to day;[50] and sent it to him about one a Clock, and then dind privately with my friend Mr Lewis, to talk over some Affairs of moment.. I have gotten the 13th volume of Rymers Collection of the Records of the Tower[51] for the

---

[47] Swift printed the Representation, which was presented to the Queen on 4 Mar., in *The Four Last Years of the Queen* (*Prose Works*, x. 101–14). He there describes it as 'written with much energy and spirit', and 'supposed to be the work of Sir Thomas Hanmer's pen'. There can, however, as appears below, be little doubt that Swift shared in its composition. See also *Journals of the House of Commons*, xvii. 119–23.

[48] p. 296 n.[8]

[49] 'Help him to draw up the representation'. Omit every other letter, not counting the 'l' in 'italoi', which is blotted.

[50] The date 'Feb. 22. 1711, 12' appears on the last page of the printed pamphlet.

[51] See p. 271 n.[11] Vols. xiii and xiv of Rymer's *Foedera* were published in 1712.

University of Dublin; I have 2 Volumes now; I will write to the Provost, to know how I shall send them to him; No, I won't for I'll bring them my self among my own Books. I was with Hanmer this morning, & there was the Secrty & Chancllr of the Excheqr very busy with him laying their Heads togethr about the Representation. I went to Ld Mashams to night, & Lady Masham made me read to her a pretty 2 penny Pamphlet calld the St Albans Ghost..[52] I thought I had writt it my self; so did they, but I did not. Ld Treasr came down to us from the Queen: and we staid till 2 a Clock; That is the best night place I have, the usually[53] Company are Ld & Lady Masham, Ld Treasr, Dr Arbuthnot, & I; sometimes the Secrty; & sometimes Mrs Hill of the Bedchambr, Ldy Masham's Sister.. I assure oo it im vely rate now. But zis goes to morrow; and I must have time to converse with own richar Md. ⌐Nite deelest sollahs.⌐[54]

23. I have no news to tell you this last day. nor do I know where I shll dine; I hear the Secrty is a little out of order; perhaps I may dine there. phaps not. I sent Hanmer what he wanted from me, I know not how he will approve of it. I was to do more of the same sort; I am going out; & must carry zis in my Pottick to give it at some generall Posthouse. I will talk furthr with oo at night. I suppose in my next I shll answer a Lettr from Md that will be sent me: on Tuesday it will be 4 weeks since I hd your last. N. 26. this day sennight I expect one, for that will be something more than a full Month.

[52] The Story of the St. Alb—ns Ghost, Or the Apparition of Mother Haggy, an octavo pamphlet of sixteen pages, published 19 Feb. (The Post Boy, 16–19 Feb.). The pamphlet reached a fifth edition by the middle of July (The Post Boy, 17–19 July); another London edition appeared in 1712, and a Dublin reprint. The Story was an attack on the Duke and Duchess of Marlborough (Aitken, Arbuthnot, pp. 43–4). It has been assigned to Swift and to Arbuthnot; but there is no evidence to support these attributions.

[53] Sic, for 'usual'.

[54] Struck through, but easily legible.

Farewell ⌐mine deelest rife . . . . . Md Md Md
Md . . . . . .
. . . . Lazy all . . . lele.⌐55

Address: To ⌐Mrs Johnson, at her⌐56
    Lodgings over against St Mary's
    Church near Capell Street
      Ireland   Dublin

Postmark: $\dfrac{FE}{23}$

Endorsement by   41
Rebecca Dingley: Recd. Mar. 1st.

LETTER XLII

42. [SATURDAY]   London. Feb. 23. 1711–12

After having disposed my last Lettr in the Post office,
I am now to begin this with telling Md, that I dind with
the Secty to day, who is much out of Order with a cold,
and fevorish, yet he went to the Cabinet Council to night
at 6, agst my will. The Secrty is much the greatest Com-
moner in Engld, and turns the whole Parlmt, who can do
nothing without him, and if he lives & has his health, will
I believe be one day at the Head of Affairs. I have told
him sometimes, that if I were a dozen years younger,
I would cultivate his Favor, and trust my Fortune with
his. But, what care oo for all this; I am sorry when I came

55 A lengthy obliteration, which Forster reads as, 'mine deelest rife
deelest char Ppt, MD MD MD Ppt, FW, Lele MD, ME, ME, ME, ME
aden, FW MD, Lazy Ones, Lele, Lele, all a Lele'. Pons (op. cit., pp.
16–17) accepts 'mine deelest rife', and, linking it with 'deelest rife MD',
which he succeeds in reading in the entry for 17 Feb. (p. 490 n.³⁶), he
believes the word intended for Stella, and Stella only, to interpret as 'wife'.
See Introduction, p. liv.

56 The words 'Mrs Johnson, at her' are scrawled out. Beneath the
address two editorial notes, reading the other way up, have been written.
One has been blotted out save for the two first words, 'Letters from'. The
other reads: 'No 41 | from 9. Feb: to 23d: | inclusive | Dr Swift to Mrs
Johnson | & Mrs Dingley.'

first acquainted with this Ministry, that I did not send you their Names & Characters, and then you would have relisht would[1] I would have writ; especially if I had let you into the particulars of Affairs. but enough of this. Nite deelest Logues.

24. I went early this morning to the Secrty, who is not yet well; Sr T. Hanmer, and the Chancelr of the Excheqr came while I was there; and he would not let me stir; so I did not go to Church; but was busy with them till noon, about the Affairs I told you in my last. The other two went away; & I dined with the Secrty, and found my head very much out of Order, but no absolute fitt, and I have not been well all this day. It has shook me a little, I sometimes sit up very late at Ld Mashams and have writt much for severall days [past];[2] but I will amend both; for I have now very little Business: and hope, I shall have no more, and I am resolved to be a great Rider this Summer in Ired. I was to see Mrs Wesly this evening, who has been somewhat better for this month past, and talks of returning to the Bath in a few Weeks. Our Peace goes on but slowly: The Dutch are playing Tricks, and we do not push it as strongly as we ought. The fault of our Court is delay, of wch the Qu— has a great deal, & Ld Tr— is not without his Share.—But pay ri char Md ret us know a little of your Life and tonvelsesens.[3] do you play at Ombre, or visit the Dean, & goody Walls & Stoit and Manlys as usuall. I must have a Lettr from oo to fill the other side of this Sheet. Let me know what you do. Is my Aunt alive yet. Oh, pray now I think of it, be so kind to step to my Aunt,[4] and take notice of my great

---

[1] Apparently a slip for 'what'.

[2] The word is obliterated by damp. Hawkesworth, followed by later editors, reads 'past', which is almost certainly right.

[3] Conversation.

[4] Godwin Swift, who died in 1695, married, as his fourth wife, Elinor, daughter of Colonel William Meade. She survived her husband, and married secondly, in 1702, the Rev. Theophilus Harrison, Dean of Clonmacnoise.

Grandfathers⁵ Picture, You know he has a Ring on his
finger with a Seal of an Anchor & Dolphin⁶ about it; but
I think there is besides at the Bottom of the Picture the
same Coat of Arms quartered with another, wch I suppose
was my great Grandmothers.⁷ If this be so, it is a stronger
Argument than the Seal. & pray see whether you think
that Coat of Arms was drawn at the same time with the
Picture, or whether it be of a Later hand; and ask my
Aunt what she knows about it. But, perhaps there is no
such Coat of Arms on the Picture, and I onely dreamt it.
My reason is, because I would ask some Herald here,
whethr I should chuse that Coat, or one in Guillim's large
Folio of Heraldry,⁸ where my Uncle Godwin⁹ is named
with another Coat of Arms, of 3 Stags.¹⁰ This is sad stuff
to rite; so Nite Md.

    25. I was this morning again with the Secrty, & we

---

  ⁵ The Rev. William Swift, 1566–1624, rector of St. Andrew's, Canterbury. He was buried in Canterbury Cathedral. See also Forster, *Life*, p.
5 and note. According to Deane Swift (*Essay*, 1755, Appendix, p. 7):
'His picture was drawn in the year 1623, ætatis suæ 57: His wife's picture
was drawn the same year, ætatis suæ 54.'

  ⁶ According to Swift's Fragment of Autobiography (Deane Swift,
op. cit., Appendix, p. 7; Forster, op. cit., p. 6) William Swift altered the
family coat of arms to the device of 'a dolphin (in those days called a
Swift) twisted about an anchor, with this motto, *Festina Lente*'.

  ⁷ William Swift married Mary, daughter of a Mr. Philpott of Kent.
She died on 5 Mar. 1625, aged 58, and was buried with her husband. For
some account of her, not altogether correct, see the Fragment of Autobiography (Deane Swift, op. cit., Appendix, p. 5; Forster, op. cit., p. 5).

  ⁸ John Guillim, 1565–1621, published *A Display of Heraldrie* in 1610,
of which a number of editions subsequently appeared. The last before the
date at which Swift is writing was issued in 1679.

  ⁹ Eldest brother of Swift's father. Godwin Swift was baptized at
Goodrich, 23 Jan. 1627, emigrated to Ireland *c.* 1660, and died 7 Dec.
1695. To his charitable help Swift owed his education.

  ¹⁰ The coat of arms appears in Guillim's work (ed. 1724, p. 158), and
is thus described: 'He beareth *Or*, a Chevron, *Nebule*, *Argent* and *Azure*,
between three Bucks in full Course, *Vert*, by the Name of *Swift*, and is born
by *Godwin Swift* of *Goodridge*, in the County of *Hereford*, Esq.; one of the
Society of *Gray's Inn*, descended from the *Swifts* of *Yorkshire*.'

were 2 hours busy; and then went togethr to the Park, Hide park I mean, & he walkt to cure his Cold, and we were looking at 2 Arabian Horses sent some time ago to Ld Treasr. The D. of Marlbr's Coach overtook us, with His Grace, & Ld Godolphin in it; but they did not see us, to our great Satisfaction, for neither of us desired that either of those 2 Lds should see us together. There were half a dozen Ladyes riding like Cavaliers to take the Air. My Head is bettr to day. I dind with the Secrty, but we did no Business after dinner: and at 6 I walkt into the Fields, these [?] days are grown pure & long: then I went to visit Percivll & his Family, whom I had seen but twice since they came to Town; they too are going to the Bath next Month. Countess Doll of Meath[11] is such an Owl, that wherever I visit people are asking me whethr I know such an Irish Ldy; and her Figure & her Foppery; I came home early; & have been amusing my Self with looking into one of Rimer's Volumes of the Records of the Towr; & am mighty easy to think I have no urgent Business upon my Hands. My 3d Cold is not yet off; I sometimes cough, and am not right with it in the morning: did I tell you that I believe it is Ldy Masham's hot room that gives it me; I never knew such a Stove; and in my Conscience, I believe, both my Ld & she; my Ld Treasr, Mr Secrty & my self, have all suffered by it. We have all had cold together, but I walk home on foot. Nite deelogues.

26. I was again busy with the Secrty; ⌈. . . . .⌉[12] we read over some Papers, and did a good deal

---

[11] Edward Brabazon, fourth Earl of Meath, married in 1704, as his second wife, Dorothea, daughter of James Stopford of Tara Hill. He died in 1708, and she married in 1716, as his second wife, Lieut.-Gen. Richard Gorges of Kilbrew (p. 653 n.[51]). They both died in Apr. 1728, within four days of each other, and were buried at Kilbrew, co. Meath. For Swift's 'Elegy on Dicky and Dolly' see *Poems*, p. 429; and cf. p. 1074.

[12] Several words blotted out. Forster deciphers 'giving help promised, iss oo Ppt'. The second and third words are possible; and there may be an allusion here to Swift's promised help in the composition of the Representation to the Queen (p. 493 n.[47]).

of Business; and I dind with him, & we were to do more business after dinner. But after dinner is after dinner— An old saying and a true, Much drinking little thinking; We had company with us, and nothing could be done, & I am to go there agn to morrow. I have now nothing to do; and the Palnt[13] by the Qu—'s Recommendation is to take some Method for preventing Libells &c,[14] which will include Pamphlets I suppose: I don't know what Method they will take, but it comes on in a day or two. To day in the morning I visited upwards: First I saw the D. of Ormd below Stairs, and gave him Joy of his beig declard Genll in Flandrs, then I went up one pair of Stairs, & sate with the Dutchess; then I went up another pr of Stairs, and pd a visit to Ldy Betty, and desired her woman to go up to the Garret, that I might pass half an hour with her, but she was young and handsom, & would not. The Duke is our President[15] this week, & I have bespoke a smal dinner on purpose for good Example. Nite mi deelest Logues.

27. I was again with the Secrty this morning; but we onely read over some Papers with Sr. T. Hanmer; then I cald at Ld Treasr's it was his Levee day but I went up to his Bedchamber; & sd what I had to say; I came down & peept in at the Chambr where a hundred Fools were waiting, and 2 Streets were full of Coaches: I dined in the City with my Printer, and came back at 6 to Ld Treasr, who had invited me to dinner, but I refused him, I sate there an hour or 2, and then went to Ld Mashams they were all abroad; so truly I tame[16] home, & read whatever stuff was next me. I can sitt and be idle now. which I have not been above a year past.. However, I will stay out the Session, to see if they have any further Commands for me,

---

13 Parliament.

14 The Queen, in a message to the Commons, 17 Jan. 1711–12, recommended them to find a remedy for the mischief of 'scandalous Libels' (*Journals of the House of Commons*, xvii. 28).

15 Of the Society.　　　　16 Came.

and tht I suppose will end in April, but I may go somewhat before, for I hope all will be ended by then, & we
shall have eithr a certain Peace, or certain War. The
Ministry is contriving new Funds for Money by Lotteryes,
and we go on as if the war were to continue, but I believe
it will not. Tis pretty late now ung oomens, so I bid oo[17]
Nite own deedallars.

28. I have been packing up some Books in a great Box
I have bought; & must by another for Cloaths & Luggage:
This is a beginning towards a Removall. I have sent to
Holld for a dozen Shirts,[18] & design to buy another new
Gown & hat, I'll come over like a Zinkerman,[19] and lay
out nothing in Cloaths in Ireld this good while. I have
writ this Night to the Provost.[20] Our Society mett to day
as usuall, and we were 14, besides the E. of Arran,[21] whom
his Brother the D. of Ormd brought among us agst all
order. We were mightily shockt; but after some whispers
it ended in chusing Ld Arran one of our Society; wch I
opposed to his Face, but it was carryed by all the rest
against me.

29. This is leap year, and this is leap day. Prince
George[22] was born on this day. People are mistaken and
some here think it is St Davids day; but they do not understand the Virtue of Leap-year. I have nothing to do now
boys; & have been reading all this day like Gum-dragon;[23]

17 Or 'ee'.
18 The fine linen manufactured in the Netherlands was in repute, and
called 'Holland'.
19 Not Dutch, but little language for 'Gentleman'.
20 Dr. Benjamin Pratt.
21 Charles Butler, 1671–1758, second son of Thomas, Earl of Ossory,
eldest son of the first Duke of Ormonde, was created Earl of Arran, in the
peerage of Ireland, in 1693, and, in 1694, Baron Butler in the English
peerage. In Macky's *Characters* he was described as possessed 'of very good
sense, though [he] seldom shows it'. Swift observed: 'This is right; but
he is most negligent of his own affairs' (*Prose Works*, x. 281). For an
interesting letter addressed to him by Swift see *Corresp*. vi. 193.
22 The late consort of the Queen.
23 Gum-dragon is a colloquial form of gum-tragacanth. Tragacanth is

and yet I was dictating some Trifles[24] this morning to a Printer. I dined with a Friend hard by; & the Weathr was so discouraging, I could not walk. I came home early, and have read 200 Pages of Arrian,[25] Alexdr the great is just dead; I do not think he was poisoned. Betwixt you and me all those are but idle Storyes, tis certain that neither Ptolomy nor Aristobulus thought so, and they were both with him when they[26] died. Tis a Pity we have not their Historyes. The Bill for limiting Membrs of Parlmt to have but so many Places past the H. of Commons, & will pass the H. of Lds[27] inspight of the Ministry wch you know is a great Lessening of the Qu—'s Power. 4 of the new Lds voted against the Court in this Point. It is certainly a good Bill in the Reign of an ill Prince; but I think things are not settled enough for it at present: & the Court may want a Majority upon a Pinch. Nite deelest Logues rove Pdfr.

Mar. 1. I went into the City to enquire after poor Stratford, who has put himself a Prisonr into the Queens Bench,[28] for wch his Friends blame him much: because

the name given to certain shrubs and the gum derived from them. Swift uses the word for the sake of its sound.

[24] Presumably this refers to the Representation to the Queen (pp. 493, 498).

[25] In the manuscript list of his books (H. Williams, *Dean Swift's Library*, p. 7) drawn up by Swift in 1715 there are two editions of Arrian's *De Expeditione Alexandri* in Greek and Latin. The earlier, published at Amsterdam in 1687 and edited by Nic. Blankaerts, disappeared later; but the sale catalogue has the other edition (No. 362), a small folio edited by Gronovius and published at Leyden in 1704.

[26] A slip for 'he'.

[27] In Nov. 1710 the Lords had thrown out a Place Bill limiting posts under the Crown which could be held by any member of the House of Commons. But on the day on which Swift wrote the Lords agreed to the second reading of a bill for 'limiting the number of Officers in the House of Commons' (*Journals of the House of Lords*, xix. 389).

[28] One of the eight prisons of London enumerated by Strype. The King's Bench stood in the Borough High Street, Southwark, adjoining the Marshalsea. Debtors were often allowed to live in lodgings 'within the rules of King's Bench'. It was pulled down in 1869.

his Creditors designed to be very easy with him. He graspt at too many things togethr, and that was his Ruin. There is one circumstance relating to Lt Genrll Meredith that is very melancholy. Meredith was turned out of all his Employmts last Year, and had about ten thousd Pds left to live on; Stratford upon Friendship desired he might have the managemt of it for Meredith, to putt it into Funds & stocks for the best Advantage; and now he has lost it all. You have heard me often talk of Stratford; we were Classfellows at School & University. I dined with some Merchants his friends to day; & they sd they expected his breaking this good while. I gave him notice of a Treaty of Peace, while it was a Secret; of wch he might have made good use, but that helpt to ruin him. for he gave money, reckoning there would be actually a Peace by this Time, & consequently Stocks rose high; Ford narrowly scapt losing 500ll by him; and so did I too. Nite my two deelest Rives Md.

2. Morn. I was wakend at 3 this morning, my man & the People of the House tellig me of a great Fire in the Hay-market. I slept again, and 2 hours after my man came in again and told me it was my poor Brothr Sr Wm Windham's house was burnt; and that 2 maids leaping out of an upper room to avoyd the Fire, both fell on their Heads; one of them upon the Iron Spikes before the door; and both lay dead in the Streets; it is supposed to have been some Carelessness of one or both those Maids. The D. of Ormd was there, helping to put out the Fire. Brothr Windham gave 6000 Pound, only but[29] a few Months ago, for that House, as he told me, & it was very richly furnisht.[30] I shall know more particulars at night. He marryed Ldy Kathrine Seymor, the D. of Sommersts

---

[29] 'only' written at the end of a line. A word at the beginning of the next line, followed by 'but', is blotted out.

[30] According to letters printed in *The Wentworth Papers*, pp. 274–6, the total loss was above £20,000, despite the fact that a box of jewels, most of the plate, and all Sir William Wyndham's writings were saved.

Daughter; you know her I believe. At Night. Windhams young Child escapt very narrowly. Ldy Kathrne escaped barefoot; they all went to Northumbld House.[31] Mr Briges[32] house at next door is damaged much, & was like to be burnt. Windham has lost above 10000ll by this accident: His Ldy above a thousd Pds worth of Cloaths. He was not at Court to day. It was a terrible Accidt;[33] I dined with Ld Masham. the Qu was not at Church. Nite Md.

3. Pray tell Walls; that I spoke to the D. of Ormd, & Mr Southwell about his Friends Affair; who I find needed not me for a Sollicitor; for thy both told me the thing would be done. I likewise mentiond his own Affair to Mr Southwell; & I hope that will be done too; for Southwell seems to think it reasonable: and I will mind him of it again. Tell him this nakedly; you need not know the Particulars, they are Secrets; one of them is about Mrs South having a Pension: the othr about his Sallary from the Govemnt for the Tythe of the Parts that ly in his Parish, to be put upon the Establishmt; but oo must not know zees sings, zey are Secrets, & we must keep them flom nauty dallars. I dind in the City with my Printer, with whom I had some small Affair, but I have no large work on my Hands now. I was with Ld Treasr this morning and hat care oo for zat, oo dined with the Dean to day. Monday is Parsons Holyday, and oo lost oo money at Cards & dice ze Givars[34] device. So I'll go to bed. Nite my twodeelest Logues.

[31] The original house was built, *c.* 1605, by Henry Howard, Earl of Northampton. It passed to the Percy family and was inherited by the Lady Elizabeth Percy, who became Duchess of Somerset, from her father, the eleventh and last Earl of Northumberland. The house was pulled down in 1874 for the formation of Northumberland Avenue (Wheatley and Cunningham, *London Past and Present*, ii. 603).

[32] James Brydges (p. 21 n.[40]).

[33] This sentence was omitted by Hawkesworth and Sheridan. Nichols, Scott, Ryland, and Aitken, reversing the sequence of the manuscript, print it before 'He was not at Court to day'.

[34] 'Devil's', or rather, 'Divel's'. Cf. *Polite Conversation*, Dialogue III

4. I sate to day with poor Mrs Wesly, who made me dine with her; she is much better than she was. I heartily pray for her health out of the entire Love I bear to her worthy Husband. This day has passt very insignificantly; but it is a great Comfort to me now that I can come home & read, and have nothing upon my hands to write. I was at Ld Mashams to night and staid there till one; Ld Treasr was there; but I thought thought[35] he lookt melancholy; just as he did at the Beginning of the Sessions; and he was not so merry as usuall. In short, the Majority in the H. of Lds is a very weak one, & he has much ado to keep it up, and he is not able to make those Removes he would, & oblige his Friends; & I doubt to[36] he does not take care enough about it. or rather cannot do all himself: and will not employ others; wch is his great Fault,[37] as I have often told You. Tis late. Nite Md.

5. I wish you a merry Lent; I hate Lent, I hate different diets, and Furmity & Butter, & herb Porrige, and sour devout Faces of People who onely put on Religion for 7 Weeks.. I was at the Secrtys Office this morning, and there a Gentleman brought me 2 Letters dated last Octobr, one from the Bp of Cloghr; tother from Walls;[38] The Gentleman is calld Coll Newburgh;[39] I think you mentiond him to me sometime ago; he has business in the H. of Lds; I will do him what Service I can, The Representation of the H. of Comms is printed;[40] I have not seen it yet. It is plaguy severe they say; I dined with Dr

(*Prose Works*, xi. 295): 'Damn your cards, said he, they are the devil's books'.

[35] Swift wrote 'I thought' twice, struck out the second 'I', but left the second 'thought' standing.

[36] Too.

[37] With this thought in mind, and probably at this time, Swift addressed to Oxford the verses entitled 'Atlas' (*Poems*, pp. 159–60).

[38] Neither letter has survived.

[39] Presumably the same as the Newbury mentioned 30 Nov. 1711 (p. 424).

[40] Printed by S. Keble by order of the Speaker.

Arbuthnott; and had a true Lenten dinner; Not in point
of Vittals, but Spleen, for his Wife and a Child or two
were Sick in the House, and that was full as mortifying
as Fish. We have had mighty fine cold frosty weather for
some days past; I hope you take the Advantage of it, and
walk now and then. You never answer that Part of my
Letters where I desire you to walk. I must keep my
Breath to cool my Lenten Porridge. Tell Jemmy Leigh
that his Boy that robd him now appears about the Town;
Patrick has seen him once or twice. I knew nothing of his
being robbd till Patrick told me had seen the Boy. I wish
it had been Stearn[41] that had been robbd to be revengd
for the Box that he lost & be p—xd to him. Nite Md.

6. I hear Mr Prior has sufferd by Stratford's breaking;
I was yesterday to see Prior, who is not well; and I thought
he lookt melancholy, he can ill afford to lose money. I
walkt before dinner in the Mall a good while with Ld
Arran, & Ld Dupplin two of my Brothrs, & then we
went to dinner; where the D. of Beaufort was our President. We were but eleven to day; we are now in all 9 Lds,
& ten Commonrs. the D. of Beaufort had the Confidence
to propose his Brother in law the E. of Danby[42] to be a
Membr, but I opposed it so warmly that it was waved:
Danby is not above 20, and we will have no more Boys;
and we want but 2 to make up our Numbr.[43] I stayd till

41 Enoch Stearne.
42 Peregrine Hyde Osborne, 1691–1731, younger son of the second
Duke of Leeds. He became Earl of Danby on the death of his elder
brother (p. 337 n.²²) in Aug. 1711. From 1712 to 1729 he was styled
Marquis of Caermarthen. In the latter year he succeeded his father as
third Duke of Leeds. The Duke of Beaufort had married, 14 Sept. 1711,
as his third wife, Mary, youngest daughter of the second Duke of Leeds
and sister of Lord Danby.
43 The 'Society,' beginning with twelve (p. 294 n.²), finally numbered
twenty-two members: Sir William Wyndham, Lord Harley, 'young'
Harcourt (son of the Lord Keeper), Sir William Raymond, the Duke of
Shrewsbury, George Granville (Lord Lansdown), Samuel Masham (Lord
Masham), Lord Dupplin, the Earl of Jersey, St. John (Lord Bolingbroke),
Lord Orrery, 'Duke' Disney, Major-General John Hill, Lord Bathurst,

8, and then we all went away soberly. The D. of Ormds treat last week cost 20 Pound; tho it was only four dishes and 4, without a Dessert; and I bespoke it in order to be cheap. Yet I could not prevail to change the House. Ld Treasr is in a Rage with us for being so extravagant, and the Wine was not recknd neither; for that is always bought by him that is President. Ld Orrery is to be Presidt next week; and I'll see whethr it cannot be cheapr, or else we will leave the House. ⌐........⌐[44] Ld Masham made me go home with him to night to eat boild Oysters. Take Oysters; wash them clean, that is wash their Shells clean; then put your Oysters into an Earthen Pot, with their Hollow sides down. then Put this Pot into a great Kettle with Water, and so let them boyl. Your Oysters are boyld in their own Liquor, and not mixt Water. Ld Treasr was not with us, he was very ill to day with a Swimming in the Head, and is gone home to be Cuppt & sent to desire Ldy Masham to excuse him to the Qu— Nite dee Md.

7. I was to day at the H. of Lds about a Friends bill;[45] then I crosst the Water at Westminstr Stairs, to South-wick,[46] went thro St George's fields to the Mint; wch is the Dominions of the K.[47] Bench Prison, where Stratford lodges in a blind Alley, & writt to me to come to him, but

the Duke of Ormonde, the Duke of Beaufort, the Earl of Arran, Robert Benson (Chancellor of the Exchequer), Swift, Prior, Arbuthnot, Dr. John Freind. Thomas Harley, Lord Oxford's cousin, who was for a time a member, was turned out, 3 Jan. 1711–12, 'for gross neglect and non-attendance'. Lord Oxford was excluded from membership, presumably from motives of policy, and accepted the exclusion in good humour (pp. 294, 306).

[44] Words blotted out and undecipherable. Forster reads, 'Pidy pdfr, deelest sollahs'; but there is scarcely space for this, and there may be no reference to the ladies.

[45] A petition to vest the estate of Mrs. Vanhomrigh's late husband in trustees to be sold, and the purchase money to be divided into five equal parts. It received the royal assent on 22 May 1712 (*Journals of the House of Lords*, xix. 363, 394, 396, 405–6, 411, 456; *Commons*, xvii, Mar., Apr., May, 1712, *passim*).

[46] Southwark.   [47] Should be 'Q.' for 'Queen's'.

he was gone to the Change. I thought he had something to say to me about his own Affairs—I found him at his usuall Coffee house and went to his old Lodgings, & dined with him & his Wife & othr Company. His Business was onely to desire I would intercede with the Ministry about his Brother in Law Ben Burton of Dublin, your[48] Banker, who is like to come in trouble as we hear about spreading false whiggish News. I hate Burton, & told Stratford so, and I will advise the D. of O. to make use of it to keep the Rogue in awe. Mrs. Stratford tells me Her husbands Creditors have consented to give him Liberty to get up his debts abroad, & she hopes he will pay them all. He was cheerfullr than I have seen him this great while. I have walkt much to day Nite deelest Logues.

8. This day Twelvemonth Mr Harley was stabbd. but he is ill & takes Physick to day. I hear (tis now morning) and can't have the Cabinet Councillors with him as he intended; nor me to say Grace. I am going to see him. Pray read the Representation; tis the finest that ever was writt. Some of it is pdfr's[49] Style, but not much.[50] This is the day of the Qu—'s Accession to the Crown. So it is a great day. I am going to Court; & will dine with Ld Masham. but I must go this moment to see the Secrty about some Business: so I will seal up this, and put it in the Post my own self. Farewell deelest hearts & Souls Md. Farewell Md Md Md FW FW FW Me Me Lele Lele Lele Lele Sollahs lele.

Address: [The outer half of the sheet containing the address is missing].
Endorsement by Rebecca Dingley at the top left-hand corner of the first page: Recd. Mar. 19.

48 All editors before Moorhead print 'the'. Swift wrote 'yr' because Burton was a Dublin banker.
49 Deane Swift printed 'Presto' where Swift wrote 'pdfr'. The pronunciation was, apparently, 'Podefar' (p. 552 n.¹). Hawkesworth here prints 'my'. 50 A word obliterated before 'much'.

LETTER XLIII

43. [SATURDAY]　　　　　　London. Mar. 8. 1711-12

I carryed my 42d[1] Lettr in my Pocket till evening, &
then put it in the generll Post.[2] I went in the morning
to see Ld Treasr; who had taken Physick, and was drinking his Broth; I had been with the Secty before, to recommend a Friend one Dr Friend[3] to be Physician Genll, &
the Secrty promisd to mention it to the Qu— I can serve
every body but my self[4] then I went to Court, and carryed
Ld Keepr & the Secrty to dine with Ld Masham, where
we drank the Qu— & Ld Treasr with every health,
because this was the day of his Stabbing. Then I went
and playd Pools at Picquet with Ldy Masham & Mrs
Hill, won 10 sh, gave a Crown to the Box, & came home.
I mett at my Lodgings a Lettr from Jo, with a Bit annexd
from ppt, what Jo asks is entirely out of my way; and I
take it for a foolish whim in him; Beside I know not who
is to give a Patent; if the D. of Ormd; I would speak to
him; & if it comes in my Head I will mention it to Ned
Southwell. They have no Patent that I know of for such
Things here; but good Security is all, & to think tht I
would speak to Ld Treasr for any such Matter at Random,
is a Jest. Did I tell you of a race of Rakes calld the
Mohacks[5] that play the devil about this Town every Night,

---

[1] '42d' is added above the line.

[2] Entered as dispatched on 8 Mar. in Swift's account-book (Forster
Collection, 508).　　　　　　　[3] Dr. John Freind.

[4] At this time Swift hoped for the Deanery of Wells, vacant by the
death of William Graham on 4 Feb. 1711-12. On 5 Feb. Swift wrote to
Oxford informing him of the vacancy, adding: 'I entirely submit my poor
fortunes to your Lordship' (*Bath MSS.* i. 228; *Corresp.* ii. 4; in both
instances incorrectly dated 5 Jan. 1712-13). It was generally reported,
both in England and Ireland (*post*, p. 518; *Corresp.* i. 322, 335), that
Swift was to have Wells; but the Deanery was finally bestowed on Dr.
Brailsford, chaplain to the Duke of Newcastle. On the whole affair see
Sir Charles Firth's paper, 'Dean Swift and Ecclesiastical Preferment', in
The Review of English Studies, ii. 6–9.

[5] Young bloods who roamed the midnight streets are described in

slitt peoples noses, & beat them &c. Nite sollahs, and
rove pdfr. Nite Md.

9. I was at Court to day, and nobody invited me to
dinner, except one or 2 whom I did not care to dine with
so I dined with Mrs Van. Young D'avenant[6] was telling
us at Court how he was sett upon by the Mohacks; and
how they ran his Chair thro with a Sword, It is not safe
being in the Streets at night for them.. the Bp of Salsbry's
son[7] is sd to be of the Gang. They are all Whigs; and a
great Ldy sent to me, to speak to her Fathr and to Ld
Treasr to have a Care of them, and to be carefull likewise
of my self; for she had heard they had malicious Intentions
agst the Ministers & their Friends; I know not whether
there be any thing in this, thô others are of the Same
Opinion.[8] The weath still continues very fine & frosty.
I walkt in the Park this evening; & came home early
to avoid the Mohaks. Ld Treasr is better. Nite my own
two deelest Md.

10. I went this morning agn to see Ld Treasr, who is

Shadwell's play *The Scowrers* (1691); but, if accounts be true, the Mohocks
were a much more dangerous gang. The papers were filled with stories of
their atrocities; broadsides and pamphlets were printed; and on 17 Mar.
1711–12 a proclamation offering £100 reward for the discovery of any of
the offenders was issued. To what extent the public excitement was
justified remains in doubt. Lord Chesterfield questioned the very existence
of the Mohocks. See *The Spectator*, Nos. 324, 332, 347; *Wentworth
Papers*, pp. 277–8; Gay's play, *The Mohocks* (1712), *Trivia*, iii. 321–34;
and R. J. Allen's *Clubs of Augustan London*, pp. 105–18.

6 Henry Molins Davenant, son of Charles Davenant (p. 82 n.[17]), was at
this time Resident at Frankfort (Bolingbroke, *Letters*, i. 263). Macky
described him as 'A very giddy-headed young fellow, with some wit', to
which Swift added, 'He is not worth mentioning' (*Prose Works*, x. 284).

7 Thomas Burnet, 1694–1753, youngest son of Gilbert Burnet, Bishop
of Salisbury. Hearne (*Collections*, iii. 327) also had heard that 'Bp. Burnett's
Son' was 'one of the principal of the Mohocks'. The rumour was unjustified. See *Letters of Thomas Burnet to George Duckett*, 1914, ed. D. Nichol
Smith, pp. 209–10.

8 In the *Four Last Years of the Queen* Swift asserts that these disturbances
were encouraged by Prince Eugene to conceal a 'main design' for the
assassination of Lord Oxford (*Prose Works*, x. 45–6).

quite recovered, and I stayd till he went out. I dined with a Friend in the City, about a little Business of printing; but not my own. You must buy the small 2 penny Pamphlet calld, *Law is a bottomless Pitt*,[9] tis very prettily written, & there will be a second Part. The Commons are very slow in bringing in their Bill to limit the Press,[10] and the Pamphleteers make good use of their Time for there come out 3 or 4 every day,—Well, but is not it time methinks to have a Lettr from MD. tis now 6[11] weeks since I had your numbr 26. I can assure oo I expect one before this goes, and I'll make shorter days Journalls than usuall, cause I hope to fill up a good deal of tothr side with my answer. Our fine weathr lasts yet, but grows a little windy: we shall have rain soon I dispose. Go to cards Sollah, & I to seep, Nite Md.

11. Ld Treasr has lent the long Lettr[12] I writt him, to Prior, and I can't get Prior to return it; and I want to have it printd, and to make up this Academy for the Improvemt of our Language. Fais[13] we nevr shall improve it as much as FW has done. Sall we? No fais, ourrichar Gangridge.[14] I dined privatly with my Friend Lewis, and then went to see Ned Southwell, and talk with him about Walls Business, & Mrs South's, the Latter will be done; but his own not. Southwell tells me, tht it must be layd before Ld

---

[9] Written by Arbuthnot in support of the negotiations for peace, and published 6 Mar. 1711-12 (*The Examiner*). The full title of the pamphlet reads: *Law is a Bottomless-Pit. Exemplify'd in the Case of the Lord Strutt, John Bull, Nicholas Frog, and Lewis Baboon. Who spent all they had in a Law-Suit.* It was priced on the title-page at 3*d.* This was the first of five pamphlets by Arbuthnot, afterwards printed together as 'The History of John Bull' in vol. ii. of the Pope and Swift *Miscellanies*, 1727. It is not unlikely that the friend with whom Swift dined was Arbuthnot himself. [10] p. 499 n.[14]

[11] Swift began to write 'seven', and then scored it out.

[12] The *Proposal for Correcting . . . the English Tongue*, which was sent to Oxford on 22 Feb.

[13] 'Fais . . . Gangridge.' Omitted by Hawkesworth and Sheridan.

[14] 'Our little language.' Swift suggests playfully the superiority of their little language to any academic improvements.

Treasr, and the nature of it explaind; and a great deal of Clutter, which is not worth the while, and may be Ld Treasr won't do it last.[15] & it is as Walls says himself not above fourty shill a year difference. You must tell Walls this, unless he would have the Business a Secret from you; in that Case, onely say, I did all I could with Ned Southwell, & it cant be done; [fo]r[16] it must be layd before Ld Treasr &c, who will not do it, and besides it is not worth troubling his Ldship. So Nite my two deelest nuntyes nine[17] Md.

[1]2.[18] Here is the D— and all to do with these Mohocks,,[19] Grubstreet Papers about them fly like Lightning; and a List Printed of near 80 put into [se]vrll[20] Prisons, and all a Lye; and I begin almost to think there is no Truth or very little in the whole Story. He that abusd D'avenant was a drunken gentleman, none of that Gang. My Man tells me, tht one of the Lodgers heard in a Coffee-house publickly, tht one design of the Mohocks was upon me, if [the]y[21] could catch me. And tho I believe nothing of it, yet I forbear walking late, and they have put me to the Charge of some Shillings already. I dined [t]o[22] day with Ld Treasr, and two Gentlemen of the Highlands of Scotland, yet very polite men; I sate there till 9, and then went to Ld Mashams, where Ld Treasr followd me, & we sate till 12, and I came home in a Chair for fear of

---

15 'at' omitted before 'last'.

16 Part of word caught in by the binder.

17 Forster reads: 'So nite my two deelest nauty nown MD'. But· the sentence has not been blotted, and Forster's reading is wrong. 'Nuntyes nine' is probably little language for 'monkies mine'. Cf. 2 Nov. 1710, p. 79.   18 Partly caught in by the binder.

19 The night of 11 Mar. was signalised by a great outbreak of Mohock rioting. Many arrests were made, including Lord Hinchinbroke, Sir Mark Cole, and other well-known people. Among the 'Grubstreet Papers' published the next morning, were two broadsides, one entitled *The Town Rakes: Or, The Frolicks of the Mohocks or Hawkubites,* the other giving a list of those who had been taken up (R. J. Allen, *Clubs of Augustan London,* pp. 108–11).

20. 21. 22 Parts of words caught in by the binder.

the Mohocks; and I have given him warning of [it t]o.[23] little Harrison whom I sent to Holld is now actually made Qu—s Secrty at the Hague, it will be in the Gazett to morrow, tis worth [1]2[24] hundred Pounds a Year. Here is a young Fellow has writt some Sea Eclogues, Poems of Mermen, resembling Pastoralls of Shepherds, & they are very pretty, and the Thought is new. Mermen are he Mermaids; Tritons; Natives of the Sea; do you understand me. I think to recommend him to our Society to morrow. His Name is Diaper..[25] P— on him, I must do something for him. & get him out of the Way. I hate [t]o[26] have any new Witts rise; but when they do rise I would encourage them. but they tred on our Heels, & thrust us off the Stage. Nite deelest Md.

[1]3.[27] You would laugh to see our Printer constantly attending our Society after dinner, and bringing us whatever new thing he has printed, wch he seldom fails to do. Yet he had nothing to day. Ld Lansdown one of our Society was offended at a Passage in this days Examiner,[28] wch he thinks reflects on him, as I believe it does thô in

[23, 24] Partly caught in by the binder.

[25] William Diaper, the son of Joseph Diaper of Bridgewater, was sent to Balliol College, Oxford, in 1699. He took orders in 1715, became curate of Brent, Somerset, and died in 1717. The *Nereides: Or, Sea-Eclogues* are re-printed in Nichols's *Select Collection*, v. 209–55. He also wrote *The Dryades: Or, The Nymph's Prophecy* (p. 586). In 1714 he addressed to Swift an imitation of 'Horace, Book I. Ep. xvii', published as a quarto pamphlet, and reprinted in Nichols's *Supplement to Swift's Works*, 1779. For a letter to him from Swift see *Corresp.* ii. 24. See *Alumni Oxonienses*, i. 400; *Notes and Queries*, clxiii. 33; Curll's *Miscellanea*, 1727, i. 120. Pope introduced Diaper into the 1728 edition of *The Dunciad* (ii. 217–18), but afterwards removed him. See *The Dunciad*, ed. Sutherland, 1943, p. 137 n.

[26, 27] Partly caught in by the binder.

[28] A letter addressed to *The Examiner*, printed in the issue of 6–13 Mar., which could be read to refer to Lord Lansdown and the Department of War, while complimenting the principal as 'a man of undoubted honour and virtue . . . and every way qualified for the execution of any office', complained that there was 'no where more *bribery* and *oppression*' practised than among his subordinate officials.

a mighty civil way, tis onely that is[29] Underlings cheat, but that he is a very fine Gentleman every way &c. Ld Orrery was President to day; but both our Dukes were absent. Brothr Windham recommended Diaper to the Society; I believe We shall make a Contribution among our selves; wch I dont like. Ld Treasr has yet done nothing for us; but we shall try him soon. The Company parted early; but Friend & Prior & I sate a while longer, & reformed the State, and found fault with the Ministry. Prior hates his Commission of the Customs because it spoils his Witt. He says he dreams of nothing but Cockets, & Dockets and Drawbacks,[30] and other Jargon words of the Custom house. Our good weathr went away yesterday, & the nights are now dark, & I came home before ten. Night nown deelest Sollahs.

14. I have been plagud this Morning with Sollicitors, and with no body more than my Brothr, Dr Friend; who must needs have to gett old Dr Lawrence[31] the Physician Genrll turnd out, & himself in.. He has argued with me so long upon the reasonableness of it; that I am fully convinced it is very unreasonable: & so I would tell the Secty, if I had not already made him speak to the Qu. Besides; I know not but my friend Dr Arbuthnott would be content to have it himself, and I love him ten times better than Friend. What's all this to you; but I must talk of things as they happen in the day, whether you know any thing of them or no. I dined in the City, & coming

29 i.e. his.
30 Cockets and dockets were official certificates of the payment of duty. Drawbacks were remissions of import duty when the merchandise on which it had been paid was exported.
31 Sir Thomas Lawrence, who was probably born about 1645, was appointed physician to the garrison at Tangiers by Charles II. He attended William III in his last illness. In June 1702 he was appointed physician to Queen Anne, and became first physician on the death of Sir Thomas Millington in Jan. 1703-4. He was among the physicians attending the Queen on her death-bed. His daughter, Elizabeth, was the second wife of Charles, fifth Baron Mohun (p. 570).

back. one Parson Richardson of Ired overtook me, he was here last Summer upon a Project of converting the Irish, & printing Bibles &c in that Language, & is now returnd to pursue it on. He tells me, Dr Coghill came last night[32] Town; I will send to see how he does to morrow. He gave me a Lettr from Walls about his old Business. Nite deelest Md.

15. I had intended to be early with the Secrty this morning, when my man admitted up Stairs one Mr Newcomb,[33] an Officer, who brought me a Letter from the Bp of Clogher, with 4 Lines added by Mrs Ash, all about that Newcomb. I think indeed his Case is hard; but Gd knows whether I shall be able to do him any Service. People will not understand; I am a very good Second; but I care not to begin a Recommendation unless it be for an intimate Friend. However, I will do what I can. I misst the Secrty; and then walkt to Chelsea to dine with the Dean of Christchurch;[34] who was engagd to Ld Orrery, with some other Christ Church men.[35] He made me go with him whethr I would or no, for they have this long time admitted me a Christchurch man. Ld Orrery generally every Winter gives his old Acquaintance of that Colledge a Dinner. There were nine Clergy-men at Table and 4 Lay men. The Dean and I soon left them,[36] and after a Visit or two, I went to Ld Mashams; & Ld Treasr, Arbuthnott & I sate till twelve, and now I am come home

---

[32] 'to' omitted.

[33] No officer of the name of Newcomb appears in Dalton's *Army Lists*; but, as Aitken suggests, the allusion to General Ross, below (16 Mar.), makes it probable that Swift's acquaintance was Beverly Newcomen (Dalton, iii. 52; iv. 60), who served as a Lieutenant at Killiecrankie, and had been in Major-General Ross's regiment since 1695. He was a son of Sir Thomas Newcomen, Bart., who was killed at the siege of Enniskillen.

[34] Atterbury.

[35] It was as a young man at Christ Church that Orrery (p. 99 n.[33]), then the Hon. Charles Boyle, entered into the famous controversy with Bentley in which he received assistance from the Christ Church wits, including Aldrich and Atterbury.   [36] There is a pen-mark through 'left them'.

& got to bed— I came afoot, but had my man with me. Ld Treasr advised me not to go in a Chair, because the Mohocks insult Chairs more than they do those on Foot. They think there is some mischievous design in those Villains; Severall of them Ld Treasr told me, are actually taken up. I heard at dinner that one of them was killed last night—we shall know more in a Little time. I dont like them as the man sd. Nite Md.[37]

16. This morning at the Secrtys I met Genll Ross and recommended Newcombs Case to him, who promises to joyn with me in working up the D. of Ormd to do something for him. Ld Winchelsea told me to day at Court, that two[38] of the Mohocks caught a maid of old Ldy Winchelseas just at the door of their House in the Park where she was with a Candle,[39] and had just lighted out somebody. They cutt all her Face, & beat her without any Provocation. I hear my Friend Lewis has got a Mohock, in one of the Messengers hands; the Qu— was at Church to day, but was carryed in an open Chair. She has got an ugly Cough, Arbuthnott her Physician says. I dined with Crow, late Governr of Barbadoes; an acquaintance of Stearns: after dinner, I askt him whethr he had heard of Stearn.[40] Here he is sd he, at the Door in a Coach, and in came Stearn, he has been here this Week; he is byying a Captainship in his Cousin Stearns[41] Regimt. He told me, he left Jemmy Leigh playing Cards with you. He is to give 800 Guinneas for his Commission. I suppose you know all this better than I. How shall I have room to answer oo Rettle hen I get it. I am gone so far already. Nite deelest Logues Md.

17. Dr Sachevrell came this morning to give me thanks

---

[37] Forster reads, quite incorrectly: 'I don't like them. But the more I lite MD'.   [38] Written above 'one', which is struck through.
[39] Three letters, which look like 'Can' struck out before 'Candle'.
[40] Enoch Stearne.
[41] A Lieut.-Col. Robert Stearne was in Col. Frederick Hamilton's regiment in 1695.

for getting his Brothr an Employmt; it was but 6 or 7 weeks since I spoke to Ld Treasr for him. Sachevrll brought Trap along with him, we dined togeth at my Printers, and I sate with them till 7. I little Thought, & I believe so did he, that ever I should be his Sollicitor to the present Ministry, when I left Ireld. this is the 7th I have now provided for since I came, & can do nothing for my self. I dont care: I shall have Ministryes & other People obliged to me, Trap is a Coxcomb, and the tother is not very deep, and their Judgmt in things of Witt or Sense is miraculous. The 2d Part of *Law is a bottomless Pitt*[42] is just now printed, and better I think than the first. Nite my two deel sawcy dallars.

18. There is a Proclamation out against the Mohocks. one of those that are[43] taken is a Baronet.[44] I dined with poor Mrs Wesley who is returning to the Bath. Mrs Percivlls young[45] Daughter has got the Small Pox but will do well. I walkt this evenig in the Park, & mett Prior, who made me go home with him, where I staid till past 12, and could not get a Coach, and was alone, and was afraid enough of the Mohocks; I will do so no more, thō I got home safe. Prior & I were talking discontentedly of some Managemts; that no more People are turnd out, wch get Ld Tr— many Enemyes; but whethr the Fault be in him or the Qu— I know not. I doubt, in both. Ung oomens it is now 7 weeks since I receivd oor last: but I expect one next Irish Pacquet, to fill the rest of this Paper; but if it dont come, I'll do without it. So I wish oo good Luck at Ombre with the Dean. Nite nuntyes nine.[46]

19. Newcomb came to me this morning, & I went to

[42] See p. 510 n.[9] *John Bull In his Senses: Being the Second Part of Law is a Bottomless-Pit.* Apparently published on this or the following day. See *The History of John Bull*, H. Teerink, p. 6.

[43] A word scrawled out before 'are'.

[44] Sir Mark Cole, 1687–1720, who succeeded his brother as fourth Baronet in 1711. He died childless and the baronetcy became extinct.

[45] Nichols and Scott incorrectly read 'youngest'. Hawkesworth and Sheridan omit the whole sentence.   [46] Cf. 11 Mar. *ad fin.*

the D. of Ormd to speak for him, but the D. was just going
out to take the Oaths for Genrll, The D. of Shrewsbury is
to be Ld Lt of Ireld. I walkt with Domvil & Ford to
Kensington, Where we dind and it cost me above a
Crown. I dont like it, as the man sd. I saw there Ld
Masham's Children. the youngest my Nephew, I fear has
got the Kings evil,[47] the othr 2 are Daughters of 3 and 4
years old. Twas very windy walking, the Gardens there
are mighty fine. I passt the eveing at Ld Mashams with
Ld Treasr & Arbuthnot, as usuall, and we stayd till past
one; but I had my Man to come with me. & at home I
found 3 Letters, one from one Fetherston[48] a Parson, with
a Postscript of Tisdalls to recommend him; & Fetherston
whom I never saw has been so kind to give me a Lettr of
Attorney to recover a debt for him. Another from Ld
Abercorn, to get him the Dukedom of Chattelheraut from
the K. of France; in wch I will do what I can. For his
Pretensions are very just.[49] the third I warrant from our
Md. Tis a great Stir this of getting a Dukedom from the
K. of France; but it is onely to speak to the Secty; & get
the D. of Ormd to engage in it; & mention the Case to
Ld Treasr &c & this I shall do. Nite deelest richar Md.

[47] Scrofula. See p. 264 n.[20]
[48] The receipt of this letter is noted by Swift in one of his account books
(Forster Collection, 508). The Rev. Thomas Fetherston became a prebendary of St. Patrick's Cathedral. There are a number of references to
him in Swift's letters, 1713–14 (*Corresp.* ii, *passim*).
[49] In 1549, during the minority of Mary, Queen of Scots, James
(Hamilton), second Earl of Arran, then regent of the kingdom, received
a grant of the Duchy of Châtelherault from Henry II of France. His eldest
son died without issue; the male line of his second son became extinct when
William, second Duke of Hamilton, fell mortally wounded at the battle of
Worcester, 1651; and the succession then passed to the female line in the
person of Lady Anne Hamilton (who married the Earl of Selkirk), with
the estate and title of Duchess of Hamilton. Her son, James, fourth Duke
of Hamilton, is often mentioned in the *Journal*. But the Earl of Abercorn
was the lineal descendant of Lord Claud Hamilton, third son of James,
first Duke of Châtelherault, and, as heir-male, he based his claim on the
French law of inheritance. See also, *Complete Peerage,* i. Appendix B.

20. I was with the D. of Ormd this morning about Ld Abercorn, Dr Friend & Newcomb; some will do, & some will not do: that's wise Maram: the D. of Shrewsbury is certainly to be your Governr.[50] Ill go in a day or two, & give the Dutchess Joy & recommend the A.B of Dublin to her. I writ to the A.Bp some Months ago that it would be so; & told him I would speak a good word for him to the Dutchess; & he says he has a great respect for her &c.[51] I made our Society change their House; & we met to day at the Star & Garter[52] in the Pallmall. Ld Arran was President. The other Dog was so extravagant in his Bills, that for four dishes and four 1st & second Course, without wine or Dessert; he chargd 2 1ll 6s 8d to the D. of Ormd: We design when all have been Presidents this turn, to turn it into a Reckoning of so much a Head; but we shall break up when the Session ends. Nite deelest Md.

21. Morning. Now I will answr Md s Rettle. N. 27. You that are adding to your Numbers, & grumbling: had made it 26; & then cobled[53] it to 27. Y[54] believe it is above a Month since your last; yes, it is above 7 weeks since I had your last, but I ought to consider that this was 12 days right[55] so that makes it pretty even. O the Sirry Zade[56] with her Excuses of a fortnight at Balligawl, seeing their Friends, & landlord running away. O Rold hot a Cruttle[57] & a Bustle—No—if you will have it, I am not Dean of Wells,[58] nor know any thing of being so; nor is there any thing in the Story; & that's enough. It was not

---

[50] *Corresp.* i. 315. [51] *Corresp.* i. 319.

[52] The Star and Garter stood on the north side of Pall Mall, opposite Schomberg House.

[53] The word looks like 'called', but the 'to' would then be redundant. Forster's reading, 'cobbled' is almost certainly right, save that there should be only one 'b'. Nichols, Scott, Ryland, Aitken read 'altered', which is manifestly wrong. Hawkesworth and Sheridan omit the first part of the day's entry, beginning at 'I am not Dean of Wells'.

[54] Nichols, Scott, Ryland, Aitken read 'I'. But 'Y' stands for 'You'.

[55] Apparently a mistake for 'writing'. The letter was begun on 8 Mar.

[56] Silly Jade. [57] O Lord, what a clutter. [58] See p. 508 n.⁴

Roper[59] sent that News, Roper is my humble Slave. Yes, I heard of your Resolves, & that Burton was embroyld. Stratford spoke to me in his behalf; but I sd I hated the Rascal. Poor Catherine gone to Wales. but she'll come back again I hope; I would see her in my Journey if she wear near the Road; & bring her over. Jo is a Fool; that sort of Business is not at all in my way: Pray put him off it. People laugh when I mention it. Bed oo paadon Maram, I'm drad oo rike oo Aplon,[60] no harm I hope.— And so [te ung][61] Dd wonders she has not a Letter at the day; oo'll have it soon [marn].[62]—the D— he is! marryed to that Vengeance![63] Men are not to be believed. I don't think her a Fool. Who would have her? Dilly will be governd like an Ass, & she will govern like a Lyon. En't that true ppt.—Why; Stearn told me he left you at Ombre with Lee,[64] & yet you never saw him. I know nothing of his Wife being here. It may cost her a Clap[65] (I dont care to write that Word plain) He is a little in doubt about buying his Commission. Iss I'll bring oo over all the little Papers I can[66] think on; I thought I sent you by Lee all that were good at that time. The Authr of the Sea Eclogues, sent Books to the Society yesterday; & we give him Guinneas a piece, & may[67] will do furthr from him. for him I mean. So the Bp of Cl.[68] & Ldy were your Guests for a Night or two.—Why, Ppt, you are grown a great Gamester, & Company-keeper. I did say to my self

[59] Abel Roper, 1665–1726, a Tory journalist, started *The Post Boy* (p. 237 n.[4]) in 1695. Apparently Swift occasionally contributed a paragraph to *The Post Boy*. See under 17 Nov. 1712.

[60] Beg your pardon, Madam. I'm glad you like your apron.

[61], [62] Scarcely decipherable.

[63] Dillon Ashe married a cousin, a daughter of Sir George St. George of Dunmore (p. 458 n.[22]). His brother, the Bishop of Clogher, had previously married one of her sisters (*Corresp.* i. 375 n.[3], 376 n.[4]).

[64] Leigh.　　[65] Smudged by Swift from motives of delicacy.

[66] A word before 'can' is blotted out.

[67] Presumably Swift meant to write 'maybe'.

[68] Ashe, Bishop of Clogher.

when I read those Names, just what you guess, & you clear up the matter wonderfully. You may converse with those 2 Nymphs if you please but the —— take me if I ever do. Iss fais it is delightfull to hear tht Ppt is every way Ppt now, in Health & looks, and all. Pray Gd keep her so many many many Years. . I doubt the Session will not be over till towards the End of April. However I shall not wait for it, if the Ministry will let me go sooner. I wish I were just now in my Garden at Laracor; I would set out for Dublin early on Monday, & bring you an Account of my young Trees, which you are better acquainted with than the Ministry, and so am I. Oh, now you have got numbr 41, have you so? Why perhaps I forgot & kept it to the next Post in my Pocket;[69] I have done such Tricks. My Cold is better, but not gone. I want Air and Riding. Hold ee Tongue oo ppt about Colds at Moorpark; the Case is quite different. I will do what you desire me for Tisdal when I next see Ld Anglesea. Pray give him my Service. The Weath is warm these 3 or 4 days and rainy. I am to dine to day with Lewis and Dartenuff at Sommers's the Clerk of the Kitchin at Court. Dartenuff loves good Bits and good Sups.—Good mollows richar Sollahs.—At Night.—I dined as I sd, & it cost me a Shilling for a Chair. It has raind all day, and is very warm. Ldy Mashams young Son my Nephew is very ill, & she is ⌜out of order⌝[70] with grief. I pity her mightily. I am got home early, and going to write to the Bp of Cl— but have no Politicks to send him. Nite my own two deelest sawcy doxes.[71]

22. I am going into the City this morning with a Friend about some Business, so I will immediatly seal up

---

[69] At the beginning of Letter 42 Swift mentions posting 41 on 23 Feb., and he records the same date of posting in his account book (Forster Collection, No. 508). ·

[70] Obliterated, but the word is almost certainly 'order' (Pons, op. cit., p. 8), not 'mind', as conjectured by previous editors.

[71] Previous editors read 'd ones', for 'dear ones', but the word is certainly 'doxes'. Cf. 17 June 1712, where Swift addresses Stella as 'sawci doxi'.

this, and keep it in my Pottick till evening, & zen put it in the Post. The Weathr continues warm and gloomy; I have heard no news since I went to bed, so can say no more. Pray send ⌐. . . . . . .⌐⁷² that I may have time to write to ⌐. . . .⌐⁷³ about it. I have here underneath given orders⁷⁴ for fourty Shill for Mrs Brent, wch you will send to Parvisol. Farewell deelest deel Md, and rove pdfr dearly dearly. Farewell Md Md FW FW FW Me Me Me Lele lele lele lele lele—& lele and lele aden.

Address: To Mrs Johnson, at her Lodgings
      over against St. Mary's Church, near
      Capel-street
        Ireland   Dublin

Postmark: $\frac{MR}{22}$

                43.
Endorsement by   Mar-30.⁷⁵
Rebecca Dingley:

LETTER XLIV

44 [SATURDAY]   London. Mar. 22d. 1711–12

Ugly nasty Weather. I was in the City to day with Mrs Wesly & Mr¹ Percivll to get money from a Banker for Mrs Wesly, who goes to the Bath on Thursday. . I left them there, & dined with a friend, & went to see ·Ld Treasr: but he had People with him I did not know, so I went to Ldy Mashams, and lost a Crown with her at Picquet, and then sate with Ld Masham, & Ld Treasr &c there till past one. But I had my Man with me to come hom; I gave in my 43d² and one for the Bp. of Cl. to

---

⁷², ⁷³ Obliterated and undecipherable. Forster professes to read 'Pdfr the ME account', and 'Parvisol'.   ⁷⁴ Cut off.

⁷⁵ In another hand below Rebecca Dingley's endorsement: 'From Mar 8th to 22d'

¹ Former editors, except Moorhead, read 'Mrs'. But there is no 's'.

² Entered as dispatched on the 22nd in Swift's account book (Forster Collection, 508).

the Post office as I came from the City, and so oo know tis late now, and I have nothing to say for this day, Our Mohocks are all vanisht; however I shall take care of my Person. Nite my own two deelest nuntyes Md.

23. I was this morning before Church with the Secrty about Ld Abercorn's Business, & some others. My Solliciting Season is come, and will last as long as the Sessions. . I went late to Court, and the Company was almost gone. The Court serves me for a Coffee-house, once a week I meet acquaintance there that I should not otherwise see in a quarter. There is a flying Report that the French have offerd a Cessation of Arms, and to give us Dunkerk, & the Dutch Namur for security till the Peace is made. The D. of Ormd thy say goes in a week. Abundance of his Equipage is already gone. Is[3] Friends are afraid the Expence of this Employmt will ruin him, since he must lose the Governmt of Ireld. I dined privately with a Friend, and refused all Dinners offerd me at Court, wch however were but two, and I did not like eithr Did I tell you of a Scoundrel about the Court, that sells Employnts to ignorant People, and cheats them of their Money. he lately made a Bargain for the Vicechamberlns Place for 7000ll, and had receivd some Guinneas Earnest, but the whole Thing was discoverd tothr day, and Examination taken of it by Ld. Dartmouth, & I hope he will be swingd.[4] The Vicechambrln[5] told me sevrll Particulars of it last night at Ld Mashams. Can dd play at Ombre yet? ⌐enough hod te Cards while ppt steps into next Room—Nite deelest sollahs⌐.[6]

24. This morning I recommended Newcomb agn to

---

[3] A slip for 'His'.

[4] A pamphlet, *A New Way of Selling Places at Court*, giving an account of this 'Great Stock-Jobber', was published by Morphew in May 1712 (*Post Boy*, 10–13 May). Reprinted by Nichols, *Supplement*, 1779.

[5] Thomas Coke (p. 327 n.[28]).

[6] Lightly obliterated from the question mark after 'yet' to the end of the entry. 'hod' stands for 'to hold'.

the D. of Ormd, and left Dick Stewart to [do][7] it furthr; then I went to visit the Dutchess of Hamilton who was not awake: so I went to the Dutchess of Shrewsbury and sate an hour at her Toilet. I [spoke][8] to her about the Dukes being Ld Lt; she sayd she knew nothig of it, but I rallyd her out of that, and she resolves not to stay behind the Duke. I intend to recommd the Bp of Cl— to her for an Acquaintance. He will like her very well. She is indeed a most agreeable woman, & a great Favorite of mine. I know not whethr the Ladyes in Ireld will like her. I was at the Court of Requests to get some Lds to be at a Commttee to morrow about a Friends Bill;[9] & there[10] the Duke of Beaufort gave me a Poem finely bound in Folio, printed at Stamford, & writt by a Country Squire. Ld Exetr[11] desired the Duke to give it the Qu— because the Authr is his Friend: but the Duke desird I would let him know whethr it was good for any thing; I brought it home & will return it to morrow, as the dullest thing I ever read; & advise the Duke not to present it. I dind with Domvile at his Lodgings by Invitation, for he goes in a few days for Ireld. Nite dee Md.

25. There is a mighty Feast at a Tory Sheriffs to day in the City, 12 hundred dishes of meat, about[12] 5 Lds, and sevll hundrd Gentlemen will be there, and give 4 or 5 Guinneas a Piece, according to Custom. Dr Coghill & I dined by Invitation at Mrs Van's. It has raind or mizzled all day as my Pockets feel. There are two new Answers come out to the Conduct of the Allyes[13] The last years

7, 8 Probable readings. There is a hole in the paper.

9 p. 506 n.[45]   10 The word should possibly be read as 'then'.

11 John Cecil, 1674–1721, sixth Earl of Exeter. His interest in the poem is explained by the family connexion with Stamford, near which stands Burleigh House.

12 Hawkesworth gave the correct reading, 'about', subsequent editors, except Moorhead, 'above'.

13 Swift perhaps refers to *A Full Answer to the Conduct of the Allies*, 1712, pp. 95; and *A Further Search into The Conduct of the Allies, And the Late Ministry, As to Peace and War*, 1712, pp. 77.

Examiners printd togethr in a small Volume,[14] go off but slowly. The Printer overprintd himself by[15] at least a thousand, so soon out of Fashion are Party papers however so well writt. The Medlys[16] are coming out in the same Volume, & perhaps may sell better. Our news about a Cessation of Arms begins to flag; and I have not these two[17] days since[18] any body in Business, to ask them about it. We had a terrible Fire last night in Drury lane, or thereabouts, and 3 or 4 People destroyd. One of the Maids of Honr has the Small-pox, but the best is, she can lose no Beauty, & we have one new handsom Md of Honr. Nite Md.

26. I forgot to tell you that on Sunday last about 7 at night, it lightend above 50 times as I walkt the Mall, wch I think is extdy at this time of the Year. & the Weathr was very hot. Had you any thing of this in Dublin? I intended to dine with Ld Treasr to day: but Ld Mansel & Mr Lewis made me dine with them at Kit Musgrave's. Now you don't know who Kit Musgrave is. I sate the Evening with Mrs Wesley who goes to morrow morning to the Bath. She is much better than she was. The News of the French desiring a Cessation of Arms &c was but Town talk.. We shall know in a few days as I am told, whethr there will be a Peace or no. The D. of Ormd will go in a Week for Flanders, they say: Our Mohawks go on still, & cut Peoples faces evry night; fais they shan't

---

[14] *The Examiners For the Year 1711. To which is prefix'd, A Letter to the Examiner.... Printed for John Morphew, ... and A. Dodd, ... 1712.* Published in the form of a small pocket volume about the middle of March (*The Post-Man,* 13–15 Mar.).   [15] 'by' written above the line.

[16] *The Medley* appeared in two portions, 5 Oct. 1710–6 Aug. 1711 and 3 Mar.–7 Aug. 1712, running in all to 90 numbers. The earlier run was reprinted in 1712 as *The Medleys for the Year 1711.* This volume contained the five *Whig Examiners* of 1710.

[17] All editors before Moorhead incorrectly read 'three'.

[18] The word 'since' has been read by editors (except Moorhead) as 'seen'. It is certainly 'since'. Swift omitted to write 'seen', which he intended should follow 'since'.

cut mine, I like it better as it is, the Dogs will cost me at least a Crown a Week in Chairs. I believe the souls of your Houghers of Cattle[19] have gott into them, and now they don't distinguish between a Cow and a Christian. I forgot to wish you yesterday a happy new Year, you know the 25 of March is the first day of the Year, And now you must leave of Cards, and put out your fire: I'll put out mine the 1st of April, cold or not cold. I believe I shall lose Credit with you by not coming over at the Beginning of April: but I hoped the Session would be ended, and I must stay till then, & yet I would fain be at the Beginning of my Willows growing. Percivll tells me that the Quicksetts upon the flatt in the Garden, do not grow so well as those famous ones on the Ditch. They want digging about them; The Cherry trees by the River side my Heart is sett upon; Nite Md.

27. Society day. You know that I suppose. Dr. Arthburnett was Presidt. His dinner was dresst in the Qu—s Kitchin, and was mighty fine; & we eat it at Ozinda's Chocolate house[20] just by St James's. We were never merryer nor bettr company, and did not part till after 11 I did not summon Ld Lansdown: He and I are fallen out. There was something in an Examinr a fortnight ago that he thought reflected on the Abuses in his Office, (he is Secrtry at War) & he writt to the Secty that he heard I had inserted that Paragraph.[21] This I resented highly, that he should complain of me before he spoke to me; and I sent him a peppering Letter, and would not summon him by a Note as I do the rest; nor ever will have any thing to say to him till he begs my Pardon. I mett Ld

[19] The practice of houghing or slaughtering cattle broke out in co. Galway early in 1711, and spread rapidly to other counties. It ceased suddenly in 1713. See Lecky, *Hist. of England in the Eighteenth Century* (edn. 1879), ii. 351–6. In writing to Archbishop King, 29 Mar. 1712, Swift again compared the Mohocks with the houghers (*Corresp.* i. 323).

[20] Situated at the bottom of St. James's Street by the Palace, but whether on the east or west side of the street is not known. It was a favourite Tory resort. [21] p. 512 n.[28]

Treasr to day at Ldy Masham's he would have fain carryed me home to dinner, but I beggd his Pardon; what? upon a Society day? No no. Tis rate Sollahs; I ant dlunk. Nite Md.

28. I was with my Friend Lewis to day getting Materials for a little Mischief;[22] and I dined with Ld Treasr, and 3 or 4 fellows I never saw before: I left them at 7, and came home, and have been writing to the A.Bp Dubln,[23] and Cozn Dean[24] in answer to one of his of 4 months old, that I spied by chance routing among my Papers. I have a Pain these 2 days exactly upon the Top of my left Shouldr, I fear it is something Rheumatick, it winches[25] now and then. Shall I putt Flannell to it? Domvile is going to Ireld; he came here this morning to take leave of me; but I shall dine with him to morrow. Does the Bp of Cl talk of coming for Engd this Summer? I think Ld Molesworth[26] told me so about 2 Months ago.

[22] The only piece of 'mischief' published within the next few months for which 'Materials' from Lewis might have been useful to Swift was *A Letter from the Pretender, To a Whig-Lord* (*Prose Works*, v. 257), which appeared on 19 July, and is mentioned on that day (p. 551). The verse pieces published in June and July (*Poems*, 161-9) would not call for Lewis's help nor would *A Hue and cry after Dismal*. The pamphlet, *Letter to a Whig-Lord* (3 June), is not 'Mischief'; and the occasion for writing *A Letter of Thanks from my Lord W[harto]n to the Lord Bp of S. Asaph* came later.

[23] Swift's letter, dated 29 Mar., was an answer to King's letter of 16 Feb. (*Corresp.* i. 318, 322).

[24] The letter has not been preserved. The reference is to Deane Swift, the first son of Godwin Swift by his third wife, Hannah, daughter of Major Richard Deane of Castle Rickard. Deane Swift, born in 1674, was a merchant in Lisbon, whence he returned to Ireland about 1705. He died on 17 Apr. 1714. His son, Deane Swift, born in 1706, was Swift's future biographer and editor of the earlier part of the *Journal to Stella*.

[25] Twinges.

[26] This is difficult to understand. Robert Molesworth, 1656-1725, of Brackanstown, co. Dublin, the first of the title, was raised to the peerage by George I in 1716, as Baron of Philipstown and Viscount Molesworth of Swords, in reward for his support of the Hanoverian succession (Lodge, *Peerage of Ireland*, v. 135).

The weathr is bad again, rainy and very cold this Evening. Do you know what the Longitude is? a Projector[27] has been applying himself to me to recommend him to the Ministry, because he pretends to have found out the Longitude. I believe He has no more found it out, than he has found out mineᵣ. . . .ˡ[28] However I will gravely hear what he says, and discover him a Knave or Fool. Nite Md.

29. I am plagued with these Pains in my Shouldr; I believe it is Rheumatick: I will do something for it to Night. Mr Lewis & I dined with Mr Domvile to take our Leave of him: I drunk 3 or 4 Glasses of Champigne[29] by perfect teazing; thô it is bad for my Pain; but if it continues I will not drink any wine without Water till I am well. The Weathr is abominably cold and wet.—I am got into bed and have put some old Flannel for want of new to my Shouldr, and rubbd it with Hungary water.[30]— Tis plaguy hard; I never would drink any Wine if it were not for my Head, and drinking has given me this Pain. I will try Abstemiousness for a while. How does Md do now? how does Dd & ppt? You must know I hate Pain, as the old woman sd—But I'll try to go seep; My Flesh sucks up Hungary water rarely. My Man's an awkward Rascal, and makes me peevish. Do you know that tother day he was forced to beg my Pardon that he could not shave my Head, his Hand shook so. He is drunk every day & I design to turn him off soon as ever I get to

[27] In his letter to King (*supra*) Swift mentioned this 'Projector'. The reference may be to William Whiston, 1667–1752, a divine who, in 1710, had been deprived for heresy of his professorship at Cambridge. He also pursued mathematical and scientific studies; and, in the hope of winning a reward offered by Parliament, made various attempts to discover a means of finding the longitude. In 1714 he published, in collaboration with Humphry Ditton, *A New Method for Discovering the Longitude.*

[28] Swift has blotted out a word which is not in doubt.

[29] The word 'and', following 'Champigne', is scrawled through.

[30] A distilled water, named after a Queen of Hungary, made by infusing rosemary flowers in rectified spirit of wine.

Ireld. I ll write no more now, but go to Sleep, and see whether Sleep & Flannell will cure my Shouldr. Nite deelest Md.

30. I was not able to go to Church or Court to day, for my Shouldr; the Pain has left my Shouldr and crept to my neck and Collar bone. It makes me think of pooppt's bladebone. Urge urge urge,[31] dogs gnawing.. I went in a Chair at 2 and dined with Mrs Van, where I could be easy; & came back at 7. My Hungary water is gone, & to night I use Spirits of wine, wch my Landlady tells me is very good. It has raind terribly all day long; & is extreamly cold: I am very uneasy, and such cruell Twinges every moment. Nite deelest Md.

31. Ap. 1, 2, 3, 4, 5, 6, 7,—8. All these days I have been extreamly ill, tho I twice crawld out a week ago; but am now recovering, thô very weak. The violence of my Pain abated the night before last; I will just tell you how I was & then send away this Lettr wch ought to have gone Saterday last. The Pain encreasd with mighty Violence in my left Shouldr & Collar bone & that side my Neck. On Thursday morning appeared great Red Spots in all those Places where my Pain was, & the violence of the Pain was confined to my Neck behind a little on the left side; which was so violent that I[32] not a minutes ease nor hardly a minutes sleep in 3 days & nights. the Spots encreasd every day & had little Pimples which are now grown white & full of corruption [tho'][33] small. the Red still continues too, and most prodigious hott & inflamed. The Disease is the Shingles. I eat nothing but Water gruell; I am very weak but out of all violent Pain. The Doctrs say it would have ended in some violent Disease if it had not come out thus. I shall now recover fast. I have been in no danger of Life, but miserable Torture.

[31] Cf. p. 487.

[32] 'Had' omitted.

[33] The reading of Hawkesworth and later editors. There is a hole in the paper.

I must[34] not write too much—so adieu deelest Md Md Md FW FW Me Me Me Lele I can say lele yet oo see— Fais I dont conceal a bitt.[35] as hope savd.

[Note written on fold of cover][36]
I must purge & clystr after this; and my next Lettr will not be in the old order of Journall till I have done with Physick. An't oo surprised to see the Lettr want half a side.[37,38]

Address: To Mrs Dingley, at her Lodgings
over against St Mary's Church
near Capel-street
                                        Dublin
             Ireland

Postmark: $\dfrac{AP}{8}$

Endorsement by   44.
Rebecca Dingley: Apr. 14.

34 Word, or part of word, obliterated before 'must'.

35 No attempt has here been made to score out the endearments of the little language, and Pons (op. cit., p. 18) takes the words 'Fais I dont conceal a bitt' for a declaration from Swift that he is, for once in a way, hiding nothing. But these words are separated from the little language by a dash, and may more naturally be read to mean that nothing has been kept back, that the full gravity of the illness has been confessed.

36 The verso of the sheet on which this letter is written is little more than a third covered with writing. This last paragraph was written on a corner of the covering sheet, or the fourth page as the letter was folded.

37 Patrick's constant drunkenness, his condition on 29 Mar., and Swift's illness, evidently brought matters to a head. The account book for 1711–12 (Forster, 508) has this entry:
'Apr. 8. 1712. Patrick left me
— 11 William came'.
There are references to William Geddes in Swift's letters between 1713 and 1716 (*Corresp.* ii. 48, 263–4, 347, 349–51, 355).

38 In his account book for Nov. 1711–Nov. 1712 (Forster Collection, 508) Swift notes letter 44 as posted on 10 Apr.

LETTER XLV

45.[1] [THURSDAY]   London. Apr. 24. 1712

I had your 28th[2] 2 or 3 days ago. I can hardly answer
it now—Since my last I have been extremely ill. Tis this
day just a Month since I felt a small pain on the tip of my
left Shoulder, which grew worse & spread for 6 days;
then broke all out by my collar, & left side of my neck in
monstrous red Spotts, inflamed, & these grew to small
Pimples. for 4 days I had[3] no rest nor nights for a Pain
in my neck; then I grew a little bettr; afterwards where
my Pains were a cruell Itching seised me beyond what
ever I could imagine, & kept me awake severall Nights;
I rubbd it vehemently but did not scratch it. Then it
grew into three or for great Sores like Blisters and run;
at last I advised the Dr to use it like a Blister; so I did,
with Melilot[4] Plaisters, which still run, and I am now in
pain enough; but am daily mendeng: I kept my Chambr
a fortnight: then went out a day or 2; but then confined[5]
my self again. 2 days ago, I a went to a Neighbr to dine,
but yesterday again kept at home. to day I will venture
abroad a little; and hope to be well in a week or ten days.
I never suffered so much in my life; I have taken my
Breeches in above 2 Inches, so I am leaner, wch answers
one Question in your Letter. The Weather is mighty fine,[6]
I write in the morning, because I am better then. I will
go and try to walk a little; I will give Dd's Certificate to

---

[1] This short letter is written in a larger hand, and the lines are more
widely spaced.

[2] Noted by Swift in his account book for Nov. 1711–Nov. 1712
(Forster Collection, 508) as received on 21 Apr.

[3] A word, or part of word, scratched out before 'had'.

[4] A kind of clover, the dried flowers of which were formerly used for
making soothing plasters and poultices.

[5] Swift first wrote 'kept', then noticing that it came just below 'kept' in
the line above he scratched it through and wrote 'confined'.

[6] A blot obscured Swift's first attempt at 'fine', and he has written it
again at the beginning of the next line.

Took to morrow farewell Md Md Md Me Me FW FW
Me Me—[7]

Address (part   [To] Mrs Johnson, att her
missing, and   [Lodgin]gs over against St Mary's
not in Swift's   [Church,] near Capel street
hand):   Dublin
                    [Ire]land

Postmark: $\frac{AP}{2[\ ]}$

Endorsed by   45
Rebecca Dingley: May. 1st.

LETTER XLVI

46 [SATURDAY]   London. May. 10. 1712.

I have not yet ease or Humor enough to go on in my
Journall Method, thô I have left my Chambr these 10
days. My Pain continues Still in my Shouldr and Collar
I keep Flannel on it, and rub it with Brandy; and take a
nasty dyet Drink I still Itch terribly, & have some few
Pimples; I am weak & sweat, & then the Flannell makes
me mad with Itching; but I think my Pain lessens. A
Journall while I was sick would have been a noble thing,
made up of Pain; and Physick, & Visits & Messages.
The 2 last were almost as troublesom as the 2 first. One
good Circumstance is that I am grown much leaner, I
believe I told you, that I have taken in my Breeches 2
Inches. I had your N. 29[1] last night. In answer to your
good opinion of my Disease, the Drs sd they never saw
any thing so odd of the Kind; they were not properly
Shingles, but Herpes miliaris, and 20 other hard names..
I can never be sick like othr People, but always something

---

[7] This letter was posted on 25 Apr. Swift's account book (Forster
Collection, 508) marks it 'short'.

[1] Swift's account book for Nov. 1711–Nov. 1712 (Forster Collection,
508) enters Stella's No. 29 as received on 9 May.

out of the common way; and as for your notion of it coming without Pain, it neither came, nor stayd, nor went without Pain, & the most pain I ever bore in my Life— Madameris[2] is retired in the Country with the Beast her Husband long ago—I thank the Bp of Cl for his Proxy; I will write to him soon. Here is Dilly's Wife in Town, but I have not seen her yet—No, Sinkerton[3] tis not a Sign of Health, but a Sign that if it had not come out some terrible Fitt of Sickness would have followd. I was at our Society last Thursday, to receive a new Membr, the Chancellor of the Exchequr;[4] but I drink nothing above wine & water—We shall have a Peace I hope soon, or at least entirely broke, but I believe the first. My Lettr to Ld Treasr about the Engl. Tongue is now printing, and I suffer my name to be put at the End of it,[5] wch I nevr did before in my Life. The Appendix to the 3d Part of John Bull[6] was published[7] yesterday; tis equall to the rest. I hope you read John Bull. It was a Scotch Gentleman a friend of mine that writ it; but they put it upon me. The Parlmt will hardly be up till June. We were like to be undone some days ago with a Tack,[8] but we carryed it bravely, and the Whigs came in to help us. Poor Ldy Masham I am afraid will lose her onely son, about a twelve Month old, with the King's Evil. I never would let Mrs Fenton see me in my Illness, tho she often came,

---

[2] This seems to stand for 'Madam Ayris', or a similar name; but the allusion cannot definitely be traced. Presumably to be identified with 'M—', who had retired to the country with her husband, a 'surly brute' (pp. 30, 186, and notes).

[3] Simpleton. ᴧ ᴧ

[4] Robert Benson.

[5] Swift's name is printed at the end of the letter and on the half-title.

[6] *An Appendix to John Bull still in his Senses: Or, Law is a Bottomless-Pit.* p. 510 n.[9] This was the fourth of the *John Bull* pamphlets.

[7] 'to the v' scratched out after 'published'.

[8] In parliamentary language a clause appended (tacked) to a money bill in order to secure its passage because the money bill must pass. The procedure has long been invalid.

but she has been once here since I recovered.. Bernage
has been twice to see me of late. His Regimt will be
broke, and he onely upon half pay; so perhaps he thinks
he will want me again. I am told here that the Bp of
Cloghr & Family are coming over, but he says nothing
of it himself.—I have been returning the Visits of those
that sent Howdees[9] in my Sickness, particularly the
Dutchess of Hamilton, who came & satt with me 2 hours;
I make Bargains with all People that I dine with, to let me
scrub my Back agst a Chair, & the Dutchess of Ormd
was forced to bear it tother day: Many of my Friends are
gone to Kensington where the Qu— has been removed
for some time—This is a long Lettr for a kick[10] body; I
will begin the next in the Journall way, thô my Journals
will be sorry ones.—My left Hand is very weak &
trembles; but my right side has not been toucht This is
a pitifull Letter for want of a better, but plagud with a
Tetter, my Fancy does fetter—Ah my poor willows &
Quicksets.[11]—Well, but you must read John Bull. Do
you understand it all? Did I tell you that young Parson
Geree[12] is going to be marryed, and asked my Advice
when it was too late to break off. He tells me Elwick[13]
has purchasd 40ll a year in Land adjoyning to his Living.
—Ppt does not say one word of her own little Health.
I'm angry almost; but I won't tause see im a dood dallar
in odle sings,[14] iss and so im DD too. Gd bless Md &

[9] p. 412 n.[30]
[10] Sick.
[11] The beginning of a word before 'Quicksets' is scrawled out.
[12] The Rev. John Geree, who is said to have lived 'in Sir William
Temple's family' (*Portland MSS.* vii. 186), became a fellow of Corpus
Christi College, Oxford, and was presented by his college to the living of
Letcombe Bassett, Berkshire. Thither Swift, despairing of the political
situation, retired in the summer of 1714 (*Poems*, pp. 191–2). In 1734
Geree was appointed a Canon of Hereford. He died in 1761. *Alumni
Oxonienses*, Early Series, ii. 558.
[13] He married Geree's sister, Elizabeth (p. 586).
[14] Because she is a good girl in other things.

FW & Me, ay & pdfr too. farewell Md Md Md FW
FW FW Me

Lele I can say lele it ung oomens
iss I tan, well as oo.[15]

Address: To Mrs Dingley, att her
Lodgings over against St Mary's
Church, near Capel street
Dublin
Ireland

Postmark: $\dfrac{\text{MA}}{\text{10}}$

Endorsed by   46.
Rebecca Dingley: May. 15.

LETTER XLVII

47 [SATURDAY]   London May. 31. 1712

I cannot yet arrive to my Journall Letters. My Pains
continuing still thô with less Violence, but I dont love to
write Journals while I am in pain, and above all, not
Journalls to Md; But however I am so much mended that
I intend my next shall be in the old way; and yet I shall
perhaps break my Resolution when I feel Pain. I believe
I have lost Credit with you in relation to my coming over;
but I protest, it is impossible to one who has any thing to
do with this Ministry, to be certain, when he fixes any
time. There is a Business which till it takes some Turn
or other, I cannot leave this Place in Prudence or Honr.
And I never wished so much as now that I had staid in
Ireld, but the Dye is cast, and is now a spinning, and till
it settles I can not tell whethr it be an Ace or a Sise.[1] I
am confident by what you know your selves, that You will
justify me in all this. The moment I am used ill, I will

---

[15] This letter was posted on 10 May. It is entered as 'short' in Swift's
account book (Forster Collection, 508).

[1] Sice, the number six at dice.

leave them; but know not how to do it while Things are in suspense. The Session will soon be over (I believe in a fortnight) and the Peace we hope will be made in a short time; and then there will be no further Occasion for me, nor I have any thing to trust to but Court Gratitude; so that I expect to see my Willows[2] a Month after the Parlmt is up; but I will take Md in the way, and not go to Laracor like an unmannerly Spreenekick Ferrow.[3] Have you seen my Ld[4] to Ld Treasr; there are 2 Answers[5] come out to it already, thô tis no Politicks, but a harmless Proposall about the Improvemt of the Engl. Tongue. I believe if I writt an Essay upon a Straw some Fool would answer it. About ten days hence I expect a Lettr from Md N.30. You are now writing it near the End as I guess. I have not received Dd's money; but I will give you a Note for it on Parvisol, & bed oo Paadon[6] I have not done it before— I am just now thinking to go lodge at Kensington for the Air.[7] Ldy Masham has teazd me to do it, but Business had hindred me; but now Ld Treasr has removed thither. Fifteen[8] of our Society dined together under a Canopy in an Arbour[9] at Parsons Green[10] last Thursday: I never saw any Thing so fine and Romantick. We got a great Victory last Wednesday in the H. of Lds by a Majority I think of 28,[11] And the Whigs had desired their Friends to

---

[2] By the banks of a small stream at Laracor, which he cut out to form a canal, Swift planted rows of willows. See Forster, *Life*, pp. 121-2.

[3] Splenetic fellow.

[4] 'Ld' intended for 'Letter'.

[5] One of these, by John Oldmixon, was *Reflections on Dr. Swift's Letter to the Earl of Oxford, About the English Tongue.*

[6] Beg your pardon.

[7] For Kensington as a health resort see p. 408 n.[21]

[8] Swift began to write 'Fourteen', and scratched it out.

[9] A word, or part of a word, struck out before 'Arbour'.

[10] Lord Peterborough was at the time abroad; but during his absence he gave St. John the use of his house and gardens at Parson's Green (p. 349). In a letter to Peterborough of 27 May 1712 St. John says, 'I visit Parson's Green very often' (Bolingbroke, *Letters*, i. 518).

[11] Ormonde, now commanding in Flanders, had received secret orders

bespeak Places to see Ld Treasr carryed to the Tower. I mett your Higgins here yesterday: He roars at the Insolence of the Whigs in Ireld; talks much of his own Sufferings and expences in asserting the Cause of the Church; and I find he would fain plead merit enough to desire that his Fortune should be mended. I believe he designs to make as much noise as he can in order to Prefermt. Pray let the Provost,[12] when he sees you, give you ten English Shillings, and I will give as much here to the Man that delivred me Rimers Books he knows the meaning: Tell him I will not trust him, but that you can order it to be pd me here; And I will trust you till I see you; Have I told you that the Rogue Patrick has left me these two Months, to my great Satisfaction. I have got anothr, who seems to be much better, if he continues it. I am printing a threepenny Pamphlet,[13] and shall print anothr in a fortnight; and then I have done, unless some new Occasion starts. Is my Curate Warburton marryed to Mrs Melthrop[14] in my Parish: So I heeear; Or is[15] a

to 'avoid engaging in any siege, or hazarding a battle' (Bolingbroke, *Letters*, 10 May 1712; i. 500). When, however, he was compelled reluctantly to refuse assistance to Eugene in attacking Villars the nature of his orders became apparent. Expostulations reached England; indignation was aroused; and on 28 May the matter was debated in both Houses. Halifax led in the Lords, and received the support of Wharton, Cowper, Nottingham, and Marlborough. Oxford succeeded, however, in turning the tide, and the Ministry carried the day by 68 votes to 40 (*Journals of the House of Lords*, xix. 460–61). In the Commons William Pulteney moved that Ormonde be instructed to prosecute the war with vigour, but he was defeated by 203 votes to 73 (*Journals of the House of Commons*, xvii. 246).

12 Dr. Benjamin Pratt.

13 *Some Reasons to Prove, That no Person is obliged by his Principles, as a Whig, To Oppose Her Majesty Or Her Present Ministry. In a Letter to a Whig-Lord* (*Prose Works*, v. 237–55). It is probable that Swift, in the first instance, addressed the letter to Lord Ashburnham (p. 65 n.³) who, having been a Whig, became a doubtful Tory. The other pamphlet was a satirical *Letter of Thanks from my Lord W[harto]n To the Lord Bp of S. Asaph* (*Prose Works*, v. 259–68).

14 p. 31 n.²⁴ Warburton did not marry till 1717.

15 The word 'it' omitted.

Lye. Has Raymd got to his new House:[16] Do you see Jo
now and then. What luck have you at Ombre; How
stands it with the Dean? ⌐........⌐[17] My Service to
Mrs Stoit, and Catharine if she be come from Wales. I
have not yet seen Dilly Ash's wife I calld once but she
was not at home; I think she is under the Doctor's Hand;
⌐......⌐[18] I believe this News of the D. of Ormd[19] producing Letters in the Council of War, with orders not to
fight, will surprise you in Ireld. Ld Treasr sd in the House
of Lds that in a few days the Treaty of Peace should be
layd before them; And our Court thought it wrong to
hazard a Battle, and sacrifice many Lives in such a Juncture. If the Peace holds all will do well, otherwise I
know not how we shall weather it. And it was reckoned
as a wrong Step in Politicks for Ld Treasr to open himself
so much.[20] The Secrty would not go so far to satisfy the
Whigs in the H. of Commons: but there all went swim-
mingly.—I'll say no more to oo to nite sollohs; becase
I must send away the Lettr, not by the Bell,[21] but early:
and besides I have not much more to say, at zis plesant
liting. Does Md never read at all now, pee? but oo walk
plodigiousry I suppose, oo make nothing of walking to
too to to ay, to Donibrook: I walk too as much as I can:
because sweating is good; but I'll walk more if I go to
Kensington.[22] I suppose I shall have no Apples this year
neithr; for I dined tothr day with Ld Rivers[23] who is sick,.
at his Country house; and he shewd me all his Cherryes
blasted; Nite deelest Sollahs; farwell deelest Rives;

---

[16] Raymond had 'the building itch' (p. 458).

[17, 18] Several words heavily obliterated.

[19] 'te D.' scratched out before 'Ormd'.

[20] Oxford declared that no separate peace was contemplated, and that
for 'so villainous a thing ... every servant of the Queen must answer for it
with his head'. It is also alleged that he added, 'The Allies know of our
proceedings and are satisfied with them' (Stanhope's *Queen Anne*, chap. xv).

[21] p. 11 n.[23]

[22] Swift moved to Kensington on 5 June (p. 142 n.[16]).

[23] 'Rivers' written twice. The first struck out.

rove poopoopdfr farwell deelest richar Md, Md Md FW FW FW FW FW Me Me Lele, Me, lele lele richar Md.

Address: [T]o Mrs Dingley, at her
      [Lodg]ings over against St Mary's
      [Chur]ch near Capel street
                    Dublin
    [I]reland

Postmark: $\dfrac{MA}{31}$

Endorsed by   47.
Rebecca Dingley: June. 5.[24]

LETTER XLVIII

48. [TUESDAY]   Kensington. Jun. 17. 1712.

I have been so tosticated[1] about since my last, that I could not go on in my Journall manner, thô my Shoulder is a great deal better; However I feel constant pain in it, but I think it diminishes, and I have cutt off some slices from my Flannel. I have lodged here near a fortnight, partly for the Air and Exercise; partly to be near the Court, where dinners are to be found. I generally get a lift in a Coach to Town, and in the evening I walk back. On Saterday I dined with the Dutchess of Ormd at her Lodge near Sheen; and thought to get a Boat back as usuall; I walkt by the Bank to Cue[2]; but no Boat; then to Mortlack, but no boat; & it was 9 a clock: at last a little sculler calld, full of nasty People; I[3] made him sett me down at Hammersmith; so walkt 2 miles to this Place, & got here by 11.

---

[24] Rebecca Dingley endorsed this letter 'June. 5', which might be taken to confirm the date of posting, 29 May, entered by Swift in his account book (Forster Collection, 508). On the other hand, the postmark clearly reads '31', the date with which Swift heads the letter.

[1] 'Intoxicated.' Swift means worried and troubled with his complaint.
[2] Kew.
[3] An obliteration before 'I'.

Last night I had anothr such difficulty; I was in the City till past 10 at night; it raind hard; but no Coach to be had; It gave over a little and I walkt all the way here and gott home by 12. I love these shabby difficultyes when they are over; but I hate them because they rise from not having a thousd[4] pd a year—I had your N. 30 about 3 days ago.[5] wch I will now Answer. And first, I did not relapse; but found[6] I came out before I ought, and so and so, as I have told you in some of my last. The first coming abroad made People think I was quite recovered; & I had no more messages afterwards.—Well but John Bull is not writt by the Person you imagine,[7] as hope[8]—It is too good for anothr to own, had it been Grubstreet, I would have let People think as they please; and I think that's right, is not it now? so flap ee hand, & make wry mouth ee self sawci doxi. Now comes Dd: why sollah I did write in a fortnight, my 47th, and if it did not come in due time, can I help Wind and Weathr; am I a Laplander, am I witch,[9] can I work Miracles, can I make Easterly winds. Now I am agst Dr Smith;[10] I drink little water with my Wine: yet I believe he is right: Yet Dr Cockburn told me a little

[4] The word 'thousd' has been written twice, once at the end of a line, once at the beginning of the next line. The first 'thousd' is struck through.

[5] On 13 June. See Swift's account book (Forster Collection, 508).

[6] Ryland reads 'second', but this is certainly wrong.

[7] In *The History of John Bull*, 1925, H. Teerink argues the case for Swift's authorship of the *John Bull* pamphlets. There can, however, be no doubt that Arbuthnot was the author. See *John Arbuthnot*, Lester M. Beattie, pp. 36–58; Émile Pons, *Revue Anglo-Américaine* iv. 354; and T. F. Mayo, *PMLA*. xlv. 274.

[8] 'saved' is to be understood.

[9] Swift refers again to '*Lapland* Witches' in 'The Bubble' (*Poems*, p. 254). The publication of the *Historia de Gentibus Septentrionalibus* of Olaus Magnus in 1555 gave vogue to the connexion of Lapland with witches.

[10] William Smith, or Smyth, a Dublin physician (see p. 541) whose opinion Stella had evidently quoted. He was at Trinity College, Dublin; M.B. 1688, M.D. 1692. He was five times President of the College of Physicians. He died in 1732.

wine would not hurt me: But it is so hot and dry, and water is so dangerous. The worst thing here is my Evenings at Ld Mashams, where Ld Treasr comes, and we sitt till after 12, but it is convenient I should be among them for a while as much as possible; I need not tell ee why. But I hope that will be at an End in a Month or two one way or othr; and I am resolved it shall. But I can't go to Tunbridge nor any where else out of the way in this Juncture. So Ppt designs for Templeoag[11] (what a name is that) where abouts is that place; I hope not very far from——[12] [Higgins is here roaring that all is wrong in Irld; & would have me gett him an Audience of Ld Treasr to tell him so. But I will have nothing to do in it; no not I fais.] Dublin. We have had no Thundr till last night; and till then we were dead for want of rain; but there fell a great deal. No field lookt green. I reckon the Qu— will go to Windsor in 3 or 4 weeks; and if the Secty takes a House there, I shall be sometimes with him. but how affecteedly ppt talks of my being here all Summer; wch I do not intend; nor to stay one Minute longr in Engld than becomes the Circumstances I am in. I wish you would go soon into the Country, & take a good deal of it; & where bettr than Trim. Jo will be your humble Servt; Parvisol your Slave, & Raymd at your Command, for he picques himself on good manners. I have seen Dilly's wife,—And I have seen once or twice old Bradly[13] here. He is very well, very old, and very wise: I believe I must go see his Wife when I have Leisure. I should be glad to see Goody Stoit, and her Husband; pray give them my humble Service; and to Katharine; and to Mrs Walls:

[11] Templeogue, about five miles to the south-west of Dublin, boasted a chalybeate spring, and was just becoming a fashionable resort. After 1730 the popularity of the place declined (Ball, *History of County Dublin*, Pt. iii. 26–7).

[12] Swift had evidently turned over the sheet. 'Dublin' is the first word on the next page. The sentence in square brackets was added later, in two lines, at the foot of the first page.

[13] See p. 362 n.[16]

I am not the least bit in love with Mrs Walls. I suppose the Cares of the Husband encrease with the fruitfullness of the Wife. I am grad at halt[14] to hear of Ppts good Health: pray let her finish it by drinking Waters. I hope Dd had her Bill, & has her money. Remembr to write a due time before Me money is wantd; & be good galls, dood dallars I mean, & no crying dallars.. I heard somebody coming up stairs, and forgot I was in the Country; & I was afraid of a Visiter; that's one Advantage of being here; that I am not teazd with Sollicitors.—My Service to Dr Smith; Molt the Chymist is my Acquaintance.[15] I sent the Questions to him about Sr W. Raleighs Cordial, and the Answer he returned is in these words *It is directly after Mr Boyle's Receit.*[16] That Commission is performd; If he wants any of it, Molt shall use him fairly. I suppose Smith is one of your Physicians. So now oor Lettr is fully and impartially answerd, not as rascals answr me: I believe if I writt an Essay upon a Straw, I should have a Shoal of Answerers; but no mattr for that; You see I can answr you without making any Reflections, as becomes men of Learning. Well; but now for the Peace: why, we expect it daily; but the French have the Staff in their own Hands, & we trust to their Honesty: I wish it were otherwise. Things are now in the way of being soon in the Extreams of well or ill. I hope and believe the first. Ld Wharton is gone out of Town in a Rage, and curses himself & friends for ruining themselves in defending Ld Marl— and Godolphin, & taking Nottinghm into their favor. He swears he will meddle no more during this

---

14 Glad at heart.

15 Hawkesworth (followed by Sheridan) edited the passage, making 'my Service to Dr. *Smith*' the first part of Molt's answer, following directly on 'these words'. Nichols, Scott, Ryland, Aitken, place 'My service to Dr. Smith' after 'Molt, the chemist, is my acquaintance', inverting Swift's sequence.

16 The reference is to Robert Boyle, the natural philosopher and chemist, not to Henry Boyle (p. 24 n.[49]), who had been principal Secretary of State till 1710, when he was succeeded by St. John.

Reign, a pretty Speech at 66, & the Qu— is 20 years youngr: & now in very good Health. For you must know her Health is fixt by a certain Reason, that she has done with Braces (I must use the Expression) and nothing ill has happend to her since; so she has a new Lease of her Life. Read the Lettr to a Whig Lord.[17] Do you ever read; why dont you say so; I mean does Dd read to ppt. Do you walk. I think ppt should walk to[18] Dd, as Dd reads to ppt. for ppt oo must know is a good walker; but not so good as pdfr. I intend to dine. to day with Mr Lewis but it threatens rain, & I shall be too late to get a Lift; & I must write to the Bp of Cl.[19] tis now 10 in the morning, & this is all writt at a heat. Farewell deelest lole deelest Md Md Md Md Md FW FW FW Me Me Lele Me lele Me lele Me lele lele lele Me.[20]

Address: For Mrs Rebecca Dingley att
      her Lodgings over against St Mary's
      Church near Capel street
                    Dublin
    Ireland

Postmark: $\dfrac{IV}{17(?)}$

Endorsed by   48.
Rebecca Dingley: June 23d.

[17] *Some Reasons to Prove, That no Person is obliged by his Principles, As a Whig, To Oppose Her Majesty . . . In a Letter to a Whig-Lord.* See p. 536 n.[13]

[18] i.e. 'for'.

[19] Swift's account book (Forster Collection, 508) contains an entry for this day, 'Bp. of Clogher'.

[20] This letter was posted on the day of writing. See Swift's account book (Forster Collection, 508).

LETTER XLIX

49 [TUESDAY]   Kensington. Jul. 1. 1712

I never was in a worse Station for writing Letters, than
this, especially for writing to Md, since I left off my
Journals; For I go to Town early, and when I come home
at night, I generally go to Ld Masham, where Ld Tr.
comes and we stay till past twelve. But I am now resolved
to write Journals again, thô my Shouldr is not yet well,
for I have still one or two itching Pimples, and a little Pain
now and then. It is now high Cherry time with us; take
notice is it so soon with you; & we have early Apricocks, &
Goseburyes are ripe. On Sunday Archdeacon Parnel
came here to see me. It seems he has been ill for grief of
his Wives death, & has been 2 Months at the Bath. He
has a mind to go to Dunkirk with Jack Hill, and I persuade
him to it, & have spoke to Hill to receive him; but I doubt
he wont have spirit to go. I have made Ford Gazeteer,
and got 200ll a year settled on the Employmt by the Secrtys
of States beside the Perquisites. It is the prettyest Employmt in Engd of its bigness: yet the Puppy does not
seem satisfyed with it. I think People keep some Follyes
to themselves till they have Occasion to produce them.
He thinks it not genteel enough, & makes 20 difficultyes.
Tis impossible to make any man easy: His salary is pd
him every week if he pleases, without Taxes or Abatemts;
he has little to do for it; He has a pretty Office, with Coals,
Candles, Paper &c; can frank what Lettrs he will, and
his Perquisites if he takes Care may be worth 100ll more.
I hear the Bp of Cl is landing, or landed in Engld; & I
hope to see him in a few days. I was to see Mrs Bradley[1]
on Sunday night. Her youngest son is marry to somebody
worth nothing; & her Daughtr was forced to leave Ldy
Giffrd; because she was striking up an Intrigue with a Footman,, who playd well upon the Flute. This is the Mothers

1 See p. 362 n.16

Account of it. Yesterday the old Bp of Worcester,[2] who pretends to be a Prophet, went to the Queen by Appointmt, to prove to Her Majesty out of Daniel and the Revelations, that 4 years hence there would be a War of Religion: that the K. of France would be a Protestant, and fight on their side, that the Popedom[3] would be destroyd, &c, and declared he would be content to give up His Bishoprick if it were not true; Ld Tr. who told it me was by, and some others; and I am told, Ld Treasr confounded him sadly in his own Learning, wch made the old Fool very quarrelsom; he is near ninety years old. Old Bradley is fat and lusty, and has lost his Palsy: Have you seen Toland's Invitation to Dismal;?[4] How do you like it? but it is an Imitation of Horace, and perhaps you don't understand Horace. Here has been a great Sweep of Employmts; and we expect still more Removalls. the Court seems resolved to make thorow work. Mr Hill[5] intended to sett out to morrow for Dunkirk of wch he is appointed Governr, but He tells me to day, that he can not go till Thursday or Fryday. I wish it were over. Mr Secrty tells me he is[6] no fear at all that France will play tricks with us; If we have Dunkirk once, all is safe. We rayl now all against the Dutch, who indeed have acted like Knaves Fools and

---

[2] William Lloyd, 1627–1717, one of the famous seven bishops of 1688, had been Bishop of Worcester since 1700. He was a good scholar; but constant study of the Apocalypse disturbed his mind. Cf. Dartmouth's note in Burnet's *Own Time*, i. 327; and Evelyn's *Diary*, 26 Apr. 1689; 18 June, 15 Aug. 1690.

[3] 'dom' is added above the line.

[4] *T—l—nd's Invitation to Dismal, to Dine with the Calves-Head Club. Imitated from Horace, Epist.* 5. *Lib.* 1., a broadside published a few days before (*Poems*, p. 161). In this lampoon Swift represented Lord Nottingham, the Tory and champion of the clergy, invited by John Toland, the deistical writer, to dine with Whigs and republicans in celebration of the execution of Charles I. The Calf's (or Calves') Head Club dined annually on 30 Jan., the date of the execution.

[5] The Duke of Ormonde had been informed of the appointment in a letter from St. John dated 27 June 1712 (Bolingbroke's *Letters*, i. 557).

[6] A mistake for 'has'.

Madmen. Mr Secrty is soon to be made a Vicount; He desired I would draw the Preamble of his Patent; but I excused my self from a Work that might lose me a great deal of Reputation, and get me very little. we would fain have the Court make him an Earl, but it will not be,[7] and[8] therefore he will not take the Title of Bullenbrook,[9] which is lately extinct in the elder Branch of his Family. I have[10] advised him to be called Ld Pomfret; but he thinks that Title is already in some other Family,[11] and besides he objects that it is in Yorkshire where he has no Estate, but there is nothing in that; And I love Pomfret; Don't you love Pomfret? why, tis in all our Historyes, they are full of Pomfret Castle.[12] But what's all this to you; you dont care for this. Is goody Stoit come to London; I have not heard of her yet. Your Dean of St Patr— never had the manners to answer my Letter. I was tothr day to see Stearn[13] and his Wife; she is not half so handsom, as when I saw her with you in Dublin. They Design to pass the Summer at a House Near Ld Sommers's, about a dozen

---

  [7] St. John was jealous and incensed at receiving a Viscounty only, whereas Harley had been created an Earl. In *A Letter to Sir William Windham*, 1753, p. 31, he commented, 'I was dragged into the house of lords in such a manner, as to make my promotion a punishment, not a reward.'

  [8] An obliteration before 'and'.

  [9] Oliver St. John, third Baron St. John of Bletso, was created Earl of Bolingbroke in 1624. He was succeeded by his grandson, Oliver, who was, in turn, succeeded in the title by his brother, Paulet St. John. The third Earl died unmarried, 5 Oct. 1711, when the earldom of Bolingbroke became extinct. For a tabular pedigree, showing the relationship of Henry St. John to the St. Johns of Bletso, see G. E. C. *Complete Peerage*, ed. Vicary Gibbs, ii. 206.

  [10] An obliteration before 'have'.

  [11] George Fitzroy, 1665–1716, Duke of Northumberland, a natural son of Charles II by Barbara, Duchess of Cleveland, also held the titles of Baron Pontefract and Viscount Falmouth. Against Macky's mention of him in his *Memoirs* Swift noted : 'He was a most worthy Person, very good-natured and had very good Sense' (*Prose Works*, x. 274.)

  [12] Pontefract Castle. See p. 550 n.[11]

  [13] Enoch Stearne.

miles off.[14] You never told me how my Lettr to Ld Treasr passes in Ireld. I suppose you are drinking at this time Temple-somethings[15] Waters. Steel was arrested[16] tother[17] day for making a Lottery, directly agst an Act of Parlmt. He is now under Prosecution, but they think it will be droppt out of Pity. I believe he will very soon lose his Employmt, for he has been mighty impertinent of late in his Spectators, and I will never offer a Word in his behalf. Raymd writes me Word, that the Bp of Meath,[18] was going to summon me in order to Suspension, for absence; if the Provost[19] had not prevented him. I am prettily rewarded for getting them their first fruits with a P——. We have had very little hot weathr during the whole Month of June; And for a Week past we have had a great deal of rain; tho not every day.[20] I am just now told that the Governr of Dunkirk has not orders yet to deliver up the Town to Jack Hill and his Forces, but expects them daily, this must putt off Hills Journy a while, and I do not

---

[14] In 1701, or 1702, Lord Somers purchased the manor of Brookmans, North Mimms, in Hertfordshire. A new house had been erected on the manor in 1682. He was buried in the chancel of North Mimms Church. See Clutterbuck, *History of the County of Hertford*, i. 454–5; *Victoria County History*, ii. 256.   [15] Templeogue.

[16] There is no evidence that Steele was arrested, although he had placed himself in a dangerous position. On 24 June 1712 he inserted in *The Spectator*, No. 413, which was written by Addison, a signed letter inviting subscriptions of half-a-guinea towards a scheme called the Multiplication Table, which was to be worked in conjunction with the State Lottery, assuring subscribers of the possibility from 'that small sum' of raising themselves 'an easy fortune'. But on the same day an Act against illicit lotteries came into force, and an advertisement appeared in *The Spectator* of 28 June withdrawing the proposal (Aitken, *Life of Steele*, i. 347–8; Rae Blanchard, *Correspondence of Richard Steele*, p. 276 n.).

[17] Swift began to write 'to day' before 'tother', and scratched it out.

[18] William Moreton, 1641–1715, Swift's diocesan, by whom also he had been ordained. Moreton came to Ireland in 1677 as chaplain to the first Duke of Ormonde, Lord Lieutenant. He became Bishop of Kildare in 1682; and was translated to Meath in 1705.

[19] Dr. Benjamin Pratt.

[20] 'but to day' scratched out after 'every day'.

like these Stoppings in such an Affair— Go get ee gone
& drink ee waters if this Rain²¹ has not spoild them,
sawci doxi I have no more to say to oo at plesent but rove
Pdfr; & Md, & Me, & Podefr will rove pdfr & Md &
Me—I wish you had taken any Account when I sent
mony to Mrs Brent; I believe I hant done it a great while
and pray send me notice when²² ⌐............⌐ Farewell
dearest MD FW FW FW Me Me Me.²³

Address: To Mrs Dingley, att her
           Lodgings over against St Mary's
           Church near Capel street
                              Dublin
             Ireland
No Postmark.
Endorsed by   49.
Rebecca Dingley: July. 8.

LETTER L

50 [THURSDAY]   Kensington. July. 17. 1712.
I am weary of living in this Place, and glad I am to leave
it so soon. The Qu— goes on Tuesday to Windsor, and
I shall follow in 3 or 4 days after. I can do nothing here,
going early to London, and coming late from it and supping
at Ldy Mashams. I din'd to day with the D. of Argyle at
Cue, and would not go to the Court to night because of
writing to Md. the Bp of Clogher has been here this fortnight; I see him as often as I can. poor Master Ash¹ has
a sad Redness in his Face, it is St Anthony's fire, his face

---

²¹ 'and' scratched out after 'Rain'.
²² The words 'and pray send me notice when' are missed by Moorhead.
They are followed by the obliteration of half a line, which Forster professes
to read as 'ME wants me to send. She ought to have it when it is due'; but
this is purely conjectural and almost certainly wrong.
²³ This letter was not posted (or finished?) till 3 July. See Swift's
account book (Forster Collection, 508).
¹ Son of the Bishop of Clogher.

all swelld; and will break in his Cheek, but no danger.—
Since Dunkirk has been in our Hands, Grubstreet has
been very fruitfull: pdfr has writt 5 or 6 Grubstreet papers
this last week.. Have you seen Toland's Invitation to
Dismal, or a Hue & cry after Dismal, or a Ballad on
Dunkirk, or an Argument that Dunkirk is not in our
Hands[2] Poh, you have seen nothing.—I am dead here with
the Hot weathr, yet I walk every night home, & believe it
does me good. but my Shouldr is not yet right, itchings, &
scratchings, and small akings. Did I tell you that I have
made Ford Gazeteer, with 200ll a year Salary, besides
Perquisites. I had a Lettr lately from Parvisol, who says
my Canal looks very finely; I long to see it; but no Apples;
all blasted again. He tells me there will be a Triennial
Visitation in August. I must send Raymd another Proxy.
So now I will answr ee Rettle N. 33.[3] dated Jun. 17. Ppt
writes as well as ever for all her waters I wish I had never
come here, as often and as heartily as Ppt, what had I to
do here? I have heard of the Bp's making me uneasy, but
I did not think it was because I never writt to him. A little
would make me write to him; but I don't know what to
say. I find I am obliged to the Provost for keeping the
Bp from being impertinent.—Yes Maram Dd, but oo

---

[2] For *Toland's Invitation to Dismal* see p. 544 n.[4] *A Hue and cry after
Dismal,* a prose satire on Nottingham, advertised in successive numbers of
The Examiner, 17, 24, 31 July, appeared as a broadside. Another edition
was published under the title, *Dunkirk to be Let, ... With A Hue-and-Cry
after Dismal* (*Poems,* p. 1097; *Review of English Studies,* vi. 195–6). The
'Ballad on Dunkirk' was a verse broadside with the title, *Peace and Dunkirk;
Being an Excellent New Song upon the Surrender of Dunkirk to General Hill*
(*Poems,* p. 167). It was advertised in *The Examiner,* 10, 17, 24, 31 July.
No copy of 'an Argument that Dunkirk is not in our Hands' has been discovered. It was presumably the piece advertised in *The Examiner,* 17 July,
as: 'Dunkirk still in the Hands of the French, being a plain and true Discovery of a most notorious Falshood, invented by Jacobites and Tories,
that the Town of Dunkirk was lately delivered to the English.'

[3] 'N. 33' is a mistake. 'N. 31' was the last received by Swift before the
date of writing. It reached him on 4 July. No. 33 did not reach him till
23 Sept. See Swift's account book (Forster Collection, 508).

would not be content with Letters flom pdfr of 6 lines, or
12 either fais. I hope Ppt will have done with the waters
soon, and find benefit by them; I believe if they were as
far off as Wexford they would do as much good; For I
take the Journy to contribute as much as any thing. I can
assure you the Bp of Cloghers being here does not in the
least affect my staying or going. I never talkt to Higgins
but once in the Street; and I believe he and I shall hardly
meet but by chance. What care I whethr my Lettr to Ld
Treasr be commended there or no? why does not somebody among you answer it, as 3 or 4 have done here (I am
now sitting with nothing but my Nightgown for heat).
Ppt shall have a great Bible. I have put it down in my
memlandums,⁴ just now. and Dd shall be repaid her tother
Book; but patience, all in good time; you are so hasty a
dog would &c. So Ppt has neither won nor lost. Why
mun, I play sometimes too, at Picket that is, Picquett I
mean; but very seldom.—Out late, why 'tis onely at Ldy
Mashams, and that's in our Town: but I never come late
here from London, except once in rain⁵ when I could not
get a Coach.—We have had very little Thunder here;
none these 2 Months; why pray, Madam Philosopher,
how did the Rain hinder the Thunder from doing harm,
I suppose it ssquencht it.—So here comes ppt aden⁶ with
her little watry postscript; o Rold, dlunken Srut⁷ drink
pdfrs health ten times in a molning; you are a whetter, fais
I sup Mds 15 times evly molning in milk porridge. lele's
fol oo now, and lele's fol ee Rettle, & evly kind of sing;⁸
and now I must say something else.—You hear Secty
St John is made Vicount Bullinbrook;⁹ I could hardly
persuade him to take that Title, because the eldest Branch
of his Family had it in an Earldom, & it was last Year
extinct; If he did not take it I advised him to be Ld

---

⁴ Memoranda.   ⁵ 'in rain' written above the line.
⁶ Again.   ⁷ O Lord, drunken slut.
⁸ There's for you now, and there's for your letter, and every kind
of thing.   ⁹ Bolingbroke.

Pomfret, wch I think is a noble Title; you hear of it often
in the *Chronicles*[10] Pomfret Castle:[11] but we believed it was
among the Titles of some other Ld. Jack Hill sent his
Sister a Pattern of a head-dress from Dunkirk; it was like
our Fashion 20[12] years ago, onely not quite so high, and
lookt very ugly. I have made Trap Chapln to Ld Bullin-
broke, and he is mighty happy & thankfull for it.—Mr
Addison returnd me my visit this morning; He lives in
our Town.. I shall be mighty retired and mighty busy for
a while at Windsor. Pray why dont Md go to Trim, and
see Laracor; and give me an Account of the Garden & the
River, & the Holly, & the Cherry trees on the River
walk.———[13]

19. I could not send this Lettr last Post, being called
away before I could fold or finish it. I dined yestrday with
Ld Treasr, satt with him till 10 at night, yet could not
find a Minute for some Business I had with him. He
brought me to Kensington, and Ld Bulingbrook would
not let me go away till 2, and I am now in bed very lazy
and sleepy at nine. I must shave head & Face, & meet
Ld Bullinbrook[14] at 11; and dine again with Ld Tr.[15] To

10 Underlined.

11 At Pontefract, or Pomfret, in the West Riding of Yorkshire, a
Norman castle was built by Ilbert de Lacy about 1076. Here Thomas,
Earl of Lancaster, was executed, 1322; Richard II came to a violent end,
1400; and Anthony Woodville, Earl Rivers, was executed, 1483. The
castle was taken in the Pilgrimage of Grace, 1536; during the Great
Rebellion it stood four sieges, and was finally dismantled after its capture
by Lambert, 1649.

12 '20' is written above the line in place of a number which has been
obliterated.

13 After a long dash Swift began '19' on the same line.

14 Swift first wrote 'Bulinbrk', with one 'l', but scratched it out in
favour of this form.

15 Swift's account book for 1711–12 (Forster, 508) has this note: 'Jul.
19. left Kensington. went to Windsr.' If the date be correct perhaps Lord
Oxford took him down to Windsor after dinner. But there may be a
mistake; for the Queen did not move to Windsor till 22 July (*Wentworth
Papers*, p. 292).

day there will be anothr Grub; a Letter from the Pretendr to a Whig Ld.[16] Grubstreet has but ten days to live, then an Act of Parlmt takes place, that ruins it, by taxing every half sheet at a halfpenny:[17] We have news just come, but not the Particulars, that the Earl of Albermarle[18] at the head of 8 thousd Dutch is beaten lost the greatest part of his men, & himself a Prisoner. This perhaps may cool their Courage, & make them think of a Peace. the D. of Ormd has got abundance of Credit by his good Conduct of Affairs in Flanders. We had a good deal of Rain last night, very refreshing—Tis late & I must rise. Don't play at Ombre in your waters Sollah—Farewel deelest Md Md Md Md FW FW Me Me Me lele lele lele—[19]

Address: To Mrs Dingley, att
her Lodgings over against St
Marys Church near Capel street
Dublin.

Ireland

Postmark: $\dfrac{IY}{19}$

Endorsed by   5.0.
Rebecca Dingley: July. 23.

[16] *A Letter from the Pretender, To a Whig-Lord.* A broadside, dated at the top: '*S. Germain, July 8.* 1712', and signed at the foot, 'James R.' (*Prose Works,* v. 257).

[17] See p. 553 n.[9]

[18] Arnold Joost van Keppel, 1670–1718, came to England with William of Orange in 1688, was created Earl of Albemarle in 1696, and returned to Holland after the King's death. On 24 July, N.S., 1712, Villars made a surprise attack on Albemarle, who had been stationed at Denain in command of 8,000 men, routed his force, and took 3,000 prisoners, including Albemarle himself and the Princes of Anhalt and Nassau-Siegen.

[19] This letter was posted 19 July. See Swift's account book (Forster Collection, 508).

LETTER LI

51. [THURSDAY]   London. Aug. 7.[1] 1712

I had your N. 32[2] at Windsor; I just read it, and immediatly seald it up again, and shall read it no more this twelvemonth at least. the Reason of my Resentmt at it is, because you talk as glibly of a Thing as if it were done, which for ought I know, is further from being done than ever,[3] since I hear not a word of it; thô the Town is full of it, and the Court always giving me Joy and Vexation. You might be sure I would have let you know as soon as it was done; but I believe you fancyed I would affect not to tell it you, but let you learn it from News Papers, and Reports. I remember onely there was something in your Letter about Me's money, and that shall be taken care of on the other side. I left Windsor on Monday last,[4] upon Ld Bolingbrokes being gone to France,[5] and somebodyes being here that I ought often to consult with in an Affair I am upon;[6] but that Person talks of returning to Windsor

[1] The date originally written, either 17 or 11, is obliterated, and above it Rebecca Dingley has written in watery ink, '7'. Above that again, in the same ink, she has written, 'Podefar was misken', meaning that Swift was mistaken. The letter was posted on 7 Aug., as Swift's account book (Forster Collection, 508) shows.

[2] Stella's No. 32 was received on 29 July. See Swift's account book (Forster Collection, 508).

[3] The reference is to the vacant Deanery of Wells (p. 508 n.[4]).

[4] The 4th of August. Swift wrote to Vanessa from Windsor, 'I will come as early on Monday as I can find opportunity.' He hoped, furthermore, while in London, to dine with the Vanhomrighs 'thrice a week' (Freeman, *Corresp. of Swift and Vanessa*, p. 70; *Corresp.* i. 335).

[5] Bolingbroke's mission to Paris was designed to clear up with Torcy outstanding points in the negotiations for peace. He returned at the end of August, leaving Prior as Chargé d'Affaires.

[6] The reference is to the composition of his *History of the Four Last Years of the Queen* with which Swift constantly occupied himself until May 1713, when, for the time being, the manuscript was laid aside. On the history of this piece see further 'Jonathan Swift and the *Four Last Years of the Queen*', by Harold Williams, in *The Library*, 1935, xvi. 61–90.

again, and I believe I shall follow him. I am now in a
hedge Lodging, very busy, as I am every day till noon;
so that this Lettr is like to be short, and you are not to
blame me these 2 Months, for I protest If I study ever so
hard, I believe I can not in that time compass what I am
upon. We have a Feaver both here and at Windsor, which
hardly any body misses, but it lasts not above 3 or 4 days,
and kills nobody. The Qu— had 40 Servants down of it
at once. I dined yesterday with Lord Tr— but could do
no Business, thô he sent for me, I thought on purpose;
but he desires I will dine with him again to day. Windsor
is a most delightfull Place,[7] and at this time abounds in
Dinners, My Lodgings there look upon Eaton and the
Thames, I wish I were Owner[8] of them, they belong to a
Prebend. Gd knows what is in your Letter, and if it be
not answered, whose fault is it, sawcidallars..—Do you
know, that Grubstreet is dead and gone last Week;[9] No
more Ghosts or Murders now for Love or Money. I
plyed it pretty close the last Fortnight, and publisht at
least 7 penny Papers of my own, besides some of other
Peoples.[10] But now, every single half Sheet pays a half-

---

[7] In his letter to Vanessa from Windsor, referred to above, Swift
describes himself as 'weary of this place'.

[8] 'Owner' was first written with a small 'o'. The capital 'O' was then
written above the word.

[9] An Act was passed, 10 June 1712, to come into force on 1 Aug.,
whereby all newspapers printed on a half-sheet, or less, were to be taxed
a halfpenny, if on a whole sheet, and not more, one penny. The intention
of the Act was the suppression of libels.

[10] By 'the last Fortnight' Swift means, apparently, the last two weeks
before the Act came into force, not two weeks before the date on which
he was writing. Four papers are mentioned by name on 17 July: (1)
Toland's Invitation to Dismal; (2) *A Hue and cry after Dismal* (p. 548 n. [2]);
(3) 'Ballad on Dunkirk', the verse broadside *Peace and Dunkirk*; and
(4) 'an Argument that Dunkirk is not in our Hands' (p. 548 n. [2]). On
19 July 'another Grub' is named—(5) *A Letter from the Pretender, to a
Whig-Lord* (p. 551 n. [16]). This leaves two other papers to be found, unless
the two editions of *A Hue and cry after Dismal* are to be counted separately.
Although this was priced at twopence one of the two may have been *A*

penny to the Qu——. The Observator is fallen, the Medleys are jumbled together with the Flying-post, the Examiner is deadly sick, the Spectator keeps up, and doubles it price. I know not how long it will hold. Have you seen the red Stamp the Papers are marqued with. Methinks it is worth a halfpenny the stamping it. Ld Bolinbroke & Prior set out for France last Saterday, My Lds business is to hasten the Peace before the Dutch are too much mauld: and to hinder France from carrying[11] the Jest of beating them, too far. Have you seen the 4th part of John Bull:[12] it is equall to the rest, and extremely good. The Bp of Cloghrs son has been ill of St Antony's Fire, but is now quite well; I was afraid his Face would be spoild, but it is not. Dilly is just as he used to be, and puns as plentifully and as bad; the two Brothers see one anothr, but I think not the two

Letter of Thanks . . . To the Lord Bp of S. Asaph. In *The Examiner* for 10–17, 17–24, 24–31 July four penny papers are advertised, *Dunkirk still in the Hands of the French, A Hue and cry after Dismal,* (4) and (2) above, *It's Out at Last: Or, French Correspondence Clear as the Sun,* and *A Dialogue upon Dunkirk, between a Whig and a Tory.* No copy of the last has been traced, and it may be either (6) or (7). In *The Athenaeum,* 8 Nov. 1902, pp. 619–20, Mr. Lavers-Smith, who had procured a copy of *It's Out at Last,* reprinted it *in extenso* and pronounced it to be from Swift's pen. This prose broadside carries no printer's name; and, although ably written, the style and choice of words do not suggest Swift. Further, no ordinary reader of the day could take it for anything but an attack on the Ministry. The surrender of Dunkirk is attributed to clandestine understanding with France; Parliament is exhorted to call the Ministry to account; Lady Masham is singled out for her 'great Service' to France; and the writer wishes that 'the Nation had open'd their Eyes before it was too late'.

[11] There is a small obliteration before 'carrying'.

[12] *Lewis Baboon Turned Honest, And John Bull Politician. Being the Fourth Part of Law is a Bottomless-Pit*; published 31 July (*The Daily Courant,* 30 July; *The Post Boy,* 29–31 July). This pamphlet was really the fifth of the series. Lester M. Beattie, *John Arbuthnot,* p. 166, accepts the possibility that the satirical 'Preface' may, as argued by Teerink, *The History of John Bull,* pp. 70–81, have been written by Swift, and should be regarded as one of the papers with which he plied the press 'pretty close the last fortnight'. See also Pons, *Revue Anglo-Américaine,* iv. 356, Apr. 1927.

Sisters.[13] Raymd writ[14] to me, that he intended to invite you to Trim. are you, have you, will you be there? won't oo see pool laratol;[15] Parvisol says I shall have no fruit. Blasts have taken away[16] all. Pray observe the Cherry Trees on the River walk; but oo are too lazy to take such a Journy. If you have not your Letters in due time for 2 Months hence, impute it to my being tosticated between this and Windsor. And pray send me again the State of Md's money; for I will not look in to your Lettr for it; Poor Ld Winchelsea is dead,[17] to my great Grief, he was a worthy honest Gentleman, & particular Friend of mine; and what is yet worse, my old Acquaintance Mrs Finch is now Countess of Winchelsea, the Title being fallen to her Husband, but without much Estate.—I have[18] been poring my Eyes all this morning, and it is now past 2 afternoon, so I shall take a little walk in the Park. Do you play at Ombre still, or is that off by Mrs Stoits absence, and Mrs Manly's Grief Somebody was telling me of a strang[19] Sister that Mrs Manly has got in Ireld, who disappointed you all, about her being handsom; My Service to Mrs Walls—Farewell deelest Md Md Md FW FW FW Me Me Me Me Me lele logues both, rove poo pdfr—

Address: [To M]rs Dingley att her
      [Lodgings] over against St Mary's
      [Church n]ear Capel street
                 Dublin
        [Irelan]d
Postmark: AV
Endorsed by   51.
Rebecca Dingley: Augst. 14.

13 Dillon Ashe and his brother, the Bishop of Clogher, had married sisters (p. 519 n. 63), daughters of Sir George St. George.
14 'told' struck out before 'writ'.   15 poor Laracor.
16 There is a small obliteration before 'away'.
17 Charles, third Earl of Winchilsea (p. 138 n. 4), died on 5 Aug. The title passed to his uncle, Heneage Finch (p. 282 n. 9).
18 First written 'having'.   19 Strange.

LETTER LII

52. [MONDAY]   Windsor. Sepbr. 15th.[1] 1712

I never was so long without writing to Md as now, since I left them, nor ever will again while I am able to write. I have expected from one week to anothr, that something would be done in my own Affairs, but nothing at all is nor I dont know when any thing will, or whethr ever at all, so slow are people at doing Favors.—I have been much out of order of late with the old giddyness in my Head. I took a vomit for it 2 days ago, and will take another about a day or two hence. I have eat mighty little Fruit, yet I impute my disorder to that little, and shall henceforth wholly forbear it. I am engaged in a long work,[2] and have done all I can of it, and wait for some Papers from the Ministry for materialls for the rest, & they delay me as if it were a Favor I asked of them; so that I have been idle here this good while, and it happened in a right time, when I was too much out of order to study. One is kept constantly out of humor by a thousand unaccountable things in publick Proceedings and when I reason with some Friends, we cannot conceive how Affairs can last as they are; God only knows; but it is a very melancholy Subject for those who have any near concern in it. I am again endeavouring as I was last year to keep People from breaking to pieces, upon a hundred misunderstandings. One cannot withold them from drawing different ways while the Enemy is watching to destroy both. See how my Stile is altered by living & thinking & talking among these People., instead of my Canal & river walk, and Willows. I lose all my money here among the Ladyes, so that I never play when I can help it, being sure to lose; I have lost 5ll the five weeks I have been here, I hope Ppt is luckyer at Picquet with the Dean & Mrs Walls. The Dean never answerd my Letter thô. I have clearly

[1] The date was first written '14', and then Swift wrote '5' over the '4'.
[2] See p. 552 n.6

forgot whethr I sent a Bill for Me in any of my last Letters; I think I did; pray let me know, & always give me timely Notice. I wait here but to see what they will do for me; and whenever Prefermts are given from me, as hope saved I will come over.———[3]

18th. I have taken a Vomit to day; and hope I shall be bettr: I have been very giddy since I writ what[4] is before, yet not as I used to be, more frequent, but not so violent. Yesterday we were allarmed with the Queens being ill. She had and Aguish & feaverish Fitt and you never saw such Countenances as we all had; such dismal Melancholy. Her Physicians from Town were sent for; but towards night she grew better, to day she misst her Feet,[5] and was up; We are not now in any Fear It will be at worst but an Ague; and we hope even that will not return. Ld Treasr would not come hear from London because it would make a Noise, if he came before his usuall time, which is Saterday, & he goes away on Mondays. The whigs have lost a great support in the E. of Godolphin.[6] Tis a good Jest to hear the Ministers talk of him now with Humanity and Pity, because he is dead, and can do them no more hurt. Ldy Orkney the late King's Mistress,[7] who lives at a fine place 5 miles from hence calld Cliffden,[8] and I are grown

---

[3] Swift wrote '18th' on the same line after a dash.

[4] There is an obliteration before 'what'.

[5] Fit.

[6] Died 15 Sept. 1712.

[7] Elizabeth Villiers, 1657?–1733, daughter of Sir Edward Villiers, Knight Marischal of England, accompanied Princess Mary to Holland, and became mistress of the Prince of Orange. As William III he granted her a large estate in Ireland; but cast her off in 1694. In the following year she married Lord George Hamilton (fifth son of William, third Duke of Hamilton), who, in 1696, was created Earl of Orkney in the peerage of Scotland. Lady Orkney and Swift were attracted to each other. She gave him various presents; and seems to have assisted him in writing the *Four Last Years of the Queen* (*Corresp.* i. 352). In a character of her from Swift's hand (*Bath MSS.* i. 226) it is said that, 'Her advice hath many years been asked and followed in the most important affairs of state.'

[8] Cliefden, or Cliveden, near Taplow. The original house was built

mighty Acquaintance. She is the wisest woman I ever saw, & Ld Treasr made great use of her Advise in the late change of Affairs. I hear, Ld Marlbrow is growing ill of his Diabetis, which if it be true, may soon carry him off; and then the Ministry will be something more at ease. Md has been a long time without writing to pdfr thō they have not the same Cause; tis seven weeks since your last came to my hands, wch was N. 32,[9] that you may not be mistaken, I hope ppt has not wanted her health; You were then drinking waters. The Doctor tells me I must go into a Course of Steel, tho I have not the Spleen; for that they can never give me thō I have as much Provocation to it as any man alive. Bernage's Regimt is broke, but he is upon half pay: I have not seen him this long time; but I suppose he is overrun with Melancholy. My Ld Shrewsbury is certainly designed to be Governor of Ireld; and I believe the Dutchess will please the people there mightily. The Irish whig Leaders promise great Things to themselves from His Governmt; but care shall be taken, if possible, to prevent them. Mrs Fenton has writ to me that she has been forced to leave Ldy G—[10] and come to Town for a Rheumatism; that Ldy does not love to be troubld with Sick People. Mrs Fenton writes to me as one dying, & desires I would think of her son; I have not answered her Lettr: She is retired[11] to Mrs Povey's.—Is my Aunt[12] alive yet; and do you ever see her. I suppose she has forgot the Loss of her son.[13] Is Raymds new house quite finished; and does he squander as he used to do? Has he yet spent

by George Villiers, Duke of Buckingham. See Lipscomb's *Buckingham*, iii. 296–7.

[9] He received Stella's 32 on 29 July. No. 33 reached him on 23 Sept. See Swift's account book (Forster Collection, 508).

[10] Lady Giffard.

[11] Forster (*Life of Swift*, p. 432) reads 'returned', which is certainly wrong. [12] Mrs. Theophilus Harrison (p. 496 n. 4).

[13] This may be a reference to Thomas, one of Mrs. Harrison's sons by her first husband, Godwin Swift. Thomas was killed in 1707 at the battle of Almanza.

all his Wive's Fortune? I hear there are 5 or 6 People
putting strongly in for my Livings; God help them. But
if ever the Court should give me any thing, I woud
recommend Raymd to the D. of Ormd, not for any particular Friendship to him, but because it would be proper
for the Ministr of Trim to have Laracor. You may keep the
gold studded Snuffbox now, for my Brothr Hill, Governr
of Dunkirk has sent me the finest that ever you saw; tis
allowed at Court, that none in Engld comes near it, thō
it did not cost above 2oll.[14] And the Dutchess of Hamilton
has made me Pockets for[15] like a womans, with a Belt and
Buckle, for you know I wear no wastcoat in Summer; &
there are severall divisions, and one on purpose for my
box, oh ho,— We have had most delightfull Weathr this
whole week, but illness and vomiting have hindred me
from sharing in a great Part of it. Ldy Masham made the
Queen send to[16] Kensington for some of her preserved
Ginger for me, wch I take in the morning, and hope it
will do me good. Mrs Brent sent me a Letter by a young
Fellow a Printer, desiring I would recommend him here,
which you may tell her, I have done; but I cannot promise
what will come of it, for it is necessary they should be made
free here[17] before they can be employd; I remembr I putt
the Boy prentice to Brent. I hope Parvisol has sett my
Tyths well this year: He has writt nothing to me about it;
pray talk to him of it when you see him: & lett him give
me an Account how Things are. I suppose the Corn is

---

[14] General Hill had taken possession of Dunkirk on 19 July. For
Swift's letter of thanks to Hill, 12 Aug. 1712, containing some description
of the box, see *Corresp.* i. 336. Deane Swift (*Essay*, 1755, pp. 163–4),
who also mentions the goose and snail device on the bottom of the box,
further tells us that a 'prospect of the rialto of *Venice*' with many figures in
carnival dress, was painted inside the lid. Two snuff-boxes are mentioned
in Swift's will, neither, apparently, this gift from Hill.

[15] 'it' omitted?   [16] Swift wrote 'to' twice, and obliterated the first.

[17] That is, obtain the freedom of the city of London. The old guild
system jealously guarded the practice of a trade against any who were not
free of the town or locality.

now off the Ground. I hope he has sold that great ugly Horse. Why don't you sell to him? He keeps me at Charges for Horses that I can never ride; yours is lame, and will never be good for any thing. The Qu will stay here about a Month longer I suppose, but Ldy Masham will go in ten days to lye in at Kensington, poor Creature she fell down in the Court here t'other day, she woud needs walk a cross it, upon some displeasure with her Chair men; and was like to be spoild, so near her time, but we hope all is over, for a black Eye and a sore side; tho I shall not be at ease till she is brought to bed.—I find I can fill up a Lettr some way or other without a Journall. If I had not a Spirit naturally chearfull, I should be very much dis-contented at a thousand Things. Pray God preserve Md's Health, & Pdfrs; and that I may live far from the Envy and discontent that attends those who are thought to have more Favor at Courts than they really possess. Love pdfr, who loves Md above all things. farewell deelest ten thousand times deelest Md Md Md FW FW Me Me Me Me lele lele lele lele—[18]

Address: To Mrs Dingley, att her
    Lodgings over against St Mary's
    Church, near Capel Street
                                Dublin
    Ireland
                                SE[19]
Postmarks: WINDSOR   ――
                                20
Endorsed by   52.
Rebecca Dingley: Octr. 1st.
        At Portraune[20]

[18] Perhaps the whole of the entry under the 18th was not written on that day, for Swift's account book (Forster Collection, 508) shows that the letter was not posted (or finished?) till the 20th, and this date is corroborated by the postmark.

[19] In England only London was permitted date-stamps. Swift posted on 20 Sept. in Windsor, where the place-stamp was impressed. The date was stamped in the London office. Swift's account book (Forster, 508) records 20 Sept. as the date of dispatch.

[20] This and the next letter were received at Portraine. In Swift's

LETTER LIII

53. [THURSDAY]   London. Octbr. 9. 1712.

I have left Windsor these ten days,¹ and am deep in
Pills with Assa fetida, and a Steel bitter drink; and I find
my Head much better than it was; I was very much dis-
couraged, for I used to be ill for 3 or 4 days together,
ready to totter as I walked. I take 8 pills a day, and have
taken I believe 150 already. The Qu, Ld Treasr, Ldy
Masham and I were all ill together; but are now all better;
onely Ldy Masham expects every day to ly in att Kensington. There was never such a Lump of Lyes spread about
the Town togethr as now; I doubt not, but you will have
them in Dublin before this comes to you; and all without
the least grounds of Truth.— I have been mightily put
backward in something I am writing,² by my Illness, but
hope to fetch it up so as to be ready when the Parlmt
meets. Ld Treasr has hd an ugly fit of the Rheumatism,
but is now near quite well, I was playing at one and thirty³
with him and his Family tother night. he gave us all 12
pence apiece to begin with: it put me in mind of Sr W T.⁴
I askt both him & Lady Masham seriously whethr the
Qu— were at all inclined to a Dropsy, and they positively
assured me she was not, so did Her Physician Arbuthnot
who always attends her. yet these Devils have spread, that
she has holes in her Legs, and runs at her Navel; and I

account book for 1709-10 (Forster, 507) entries by Rebecca Dingley for
1712 show that the two ladies, with their maid, Margaret, visited Portraine
twice in that year. The first visit extended from 20 Aug. to 9 Sept., the
second visit from 18 Sept. to 26 Nov. Cf. the endorsement to letter LV.

¹ From Swift's account book for 1711-12 (Forster, 508) we learn that
in September (the day is not given) he 'left Windsor' and 'came to Mrs
Hubbots in Rider Street'. See p. 142 n.¹⁶

² His *History of the Four Last Years of the Queen*.

³ A card game popular in Ireland, whither it seems to have been carried
from Spain (W. A. Chatto, *Origin and History of Playing Cards*, pp.
114–15). It resembled Vingt-un.

⁴ Sir William Temple.

know not what. Arbuthnot has sent me from Windsor a pretty Discourse upon Lying,[5] and I have ordered the Printer to come for it. It is A Proposall for publishing a curious Piece calld the Art of Politicall Lying, in two Volumes &c. And then there is an Abstract of the first[6] Volume, just like those Pamphlets thy call the works of the Learnd.[7] Pray get it when it comes out. The Qu has a little of the Gout in one of her Hands; I believe she will say[8] a Month still at Windsor. Ld Tr shewd me the kindest Lettr from her in the World. by which I pickt out one Secret, that there will be soon made some Knights of the Garter: you know anothr is fallen by Ld Godolphin's Death: He will be buryed in a day or two at Westminster Abby. I saw Tom Leigh in Town once; the Bp Cl. has taken his[9] Lodging for the Winter; they are all well.. I hear there are in Town abundance of People from Ireld; half a dozen Bishops at least. The poor old Bp of London[10] at past fourscore fell down backwards, going up Stairs, and I think broke or crackt his Scull; yet is now recovering. The Town is as empty as at Midsummer; & if I had not occasion for Physick I would be at Windsor still. Did I tell you of Ld Rivers's Will; He has left Legacy to about 20 paultry old whores by name, and not a Farthing to any Friend, Dependent or Relation; he has left from his onely Child Ldy Barrimore[11] her Mothers Estate, and given the

---

[5] *Proposals for Printing a very Curious Discourse, in Two Volumes in Quarto, Intitled Ψευδολογία Πολιτική; Or, A Treatise of the Art of Political Lying.* It was reprinted in the Pope and Swift *Miscellanies,* 1727, ii. 297–318.

[6] An obliteration before 'first'.

[7] *The History of the Works of the Learned,* a periodical in small quarto, published from 1699 to 1712. Volumes 1–8 have been ascribed to Samuel Parker; the later volumes to G. Ridpath and others.

[8] stay.

[9] The word is lightly scratched over.

[10] Henry Compton (p. 341 n.[32]).

[11] Elizabeth, who, in 1706, married, without her father's knowledge, James Barry, fourth Earl of Barrymore.

whole to his Heir male a Popish Priest, a Second Cousin, who is now Earl Rivers,[12] and whom he used in his Life like a Footman. after him it goes to his chief Wench and Bastard. Ld Treasr & Ld Chambrln[13] are Executors of this hopefull Will. I loved the Man, and detest his Memory. We hear nothing of Peace yet. I believe verily the Dutch are so wilfull because they are told the Qu— cannot live.—I had poor Md Letters. N. 3[14] at Windsor; ⌐but I could not answr it then poopdfr wam vely kick[15] then, and besides it was a very inconvenient place to send Lettrs from. Oo thought to come home the same day, and stayd a month; that was a sign your Place was agreeable;⌐[16] I should love such a sort of Jaunt. Is that lad Swanton[17] a little more fixed than he used to be? I think you like the Girl very well. She has left off her grave airs I suppose.— I am now[18] told Ld Godolphin was buryed last night—⌐O poo ppt, lay down ee heads aden; fais I flodive[19] ee: I always reckon if y are ill I shall hear it; & therefore hen oo are silent, I reckon all is well.⌐[20]—I believe I scaped the new feaver[21] for the same reason that pooppt did because I am not well, but why should Dd scape it pray. she is

---

[12] John Savage, born in 1665, cousin of the fourth Earl, succeeded to the title. He was a Roman Catholic priest. On his death (*c.* 1735) the title became extinct.

[13] The Duke of Shrewsbury.

[14] No. 33. Received 23 Sept. (Swift's account book, Forster Collection, 508).

[15] very sick.

[16] From 'but I' to 'agreeable' is lightly scored through.

[17] Mrs. Swanton, whose Christian name was Honoria, the elder daughter of Willoughby Swift (Swift's cousin), married Ferdinand Swanton of Lisbon. The Swantons were now living at Portraine. It is probable that Swift is referring to Swanton himself and his wife, and not to their children. See *Corresp.* v. 11 n.²; vi. 213. Deane Swift (*Essay*, pp. 53–5) relates, on Mrs. Swanton's authority, an anecdote of Swift's early life.

[18] 'now' is written above the line.

[19] forgive.

[20] From 'O poo ppt' to 'all is well' is lightly struck through.

[21] See p. 553.

melthigal[22] oo know and ought to have the Feavr; but I hope it is now too late & she won't have it at all. Some Physicians here talk very melancholy, & think it foreruns the Plague; wch is actually at Hamburgh. I hoped ⌜ppt would have done with her illness⌝;[23] but I think we both have tht Faculty never to part with a Disorder for ever: we are very constant. I have had my Giddiness 23 years by fits —Will Mrs Raymd never have done lying in. He intends to leave Beggars enough; for I dare say he squandred away the best part of his Fortune already, & is not out of debt. I had a Lettr from him lately ——————

Oct. 11. Ld Tr sent for me yesterday & the day before to sit with him, because he is not yet quite well enough to go abroad; & I could not finish my Lettr—How the duce come I to be so exact in Me Money; just 17s & 8d more than due. I believe you cheat me. If Hawkshaw does not pay the Interest,[24] I will have the Principle. pray speak to Parvisol, & have his Advice what I should do about it. Service to Mrs Stoit & Catharine & Mrs Walls—Ppt makes a petition with meny Apologyes. John Danvers[25] you know is Ldy G—'s[26] Friend. The rest I never heard of. I tell you what. as things are at present I cannot possibly speak to Ld Tr for any[27] body. I need tell you no more.— Something or nothing will be done in my own Affairs: if the former, I will be a Sollicitr for your Sister.[28] if the Latter, I have done with Courts for ever. Opportunityes will often fall in my way if I am us'd well. and I will then make it my business: It is my delight to do good Offices for people who want & deserve, and a tenfod delight to do it to a relation ⌜of Ppts whose Affairs she has so at

---

[22] a healthy girl.

[23] 'ppt' to 'illness' lightly struck through.

[24] 'Interest' is written above 'Principle', which Swift wrote by mistake and then struck through.

[25] Possibly husband of, or related to, the Mrs. Danvers who was one of the women of the royal bedchamber (*Wentworth Papers*, p. 416).

[26] Lady Giffard's.

[27] An obliteration before 'any'.

[28] Mrs. Filby.

heart⌐.²⁹ I have taken down his name & his Case (not her Case) and whenever a proper time comes. I will do all I can—zats enough to say when I can do no more. and ⌐I beg ee pardon a sousand times that I cannot⌐³⁰ do bettr. I hope the Dean of St P—³¹ is well of his Feaver. He has never writ to me; I am glad of it, pray don't³² desire him to write.—I have dated your Bill late, because it must not commence ung oomens till the 1st of November next. O ⌐fais⌐³³ I must be ⌐ise iss fais must I, else Me will cheat pdfr.⌐³⁴ Are you good Huswifes, & Readers, are you walkers? I know you are Gamesters; Are you drinkers? Are you—⌐O Rold, I must go no further³⁵ fear of aboozing fine Radyes⌐³⁶—Parvisol has never sent me one word how he sett this years Tyths; pray ask whethr Tyths sett well or ill this year. Bp Killaloo tells me Wool bears a good rate in Ired; but how is Corn. I dined yestrday with Ldy Orkney, & we sate alone from 2 till 11 at night. You have heard of her I suppose. I have 20 Lettrs on my hands, & am so lazy & so busy I cant answr them; & they grow upon me for severall months. Have I any Apples at Laracor? Tis strange every year should blast them when I took so much care for Shelter. Ld Bolingbroke has been idle at his Country house this Fortnight wch puts me backwards in a Business I have. I am got into an ordinary room two pair of Stairs, & see no body if I can help it, yet some Puppyes have found me out, and my Man is not such an Artist as Patrick at denying me. Patrick has been solliciting to come to me again: but in vain—The Printer has been here with some of the new whims printd; & has

---

²⁹ 'of' to 'heart' partially obliterated.

³⁰ A slight score of the pen through the line from 'I' to 'cannot'.

³¹ St. Patrick's. Dr. Stearne.

³² Swift wrote 'don't' twice, once at the end of a line and again at the beginning of the next. The former is struck out.

³³ The word is scrawled over.

³⁴ 'ise' to 'pdfr' partially obliterated.

³⁵ 'for' omitted.

³⁶ From 'O' to 'Radyes' partially obliterated.

taken up my time. I am just going out, & can only bid ee farewell ⌐Farewell deelest ickle Md Md Md Md FW FW FW FW Me Me Me Me lele deel Me lele lele lele sollahs bose⌐[37,38]

Address: [To] Mrs Dingley, att her Lodgings
 [over a]gainst St Mary's Church
 [near] Capel street
                    Dublin
         Ireland
Postmark: OC
Endorsed by   53.
Rebecca Dingley: Octr. 18.
         At Portraune.

LETTER LIV

[TUESDAY]   London, Oct. 28, 1712.[1]

I HAVE been in physic this month, and have been better these three weeks. I stop my physic, by the doctor's orders, till he sends me farther directions. D.D. grows politician, and longs to hear the peace is proclaimed.[2] I hope we shall have it soon, for the Dutch are fully humbled; and Prior is just come over from France for a few days; I suppose, upon some important affair. I saw him last night, but had no private talk with him. Stocks rise upon his coming. As for my stay in England, it cannot be long now, and so tell my friends. The parliament will not meet till after Christmas, and by that time the work I am doing will

---

[37] 'Farewell' to 'bose' obliterated. 'bose' means 'both'.

[38] In Swift's account book for 1711–12 (Forster Collection, 508) the date of this letter is given as 9 Oct. He generally gives the date of dispatch, or last diary date.

[1] The text of this letter is that of Hawkesworth, 1766. The original has disappeared.

[2] Presumably a reference to Stella's No. 34, which was received on 22 Oct. See Swift's account book (Forster Collection, 508).

be over, and then nothing shall keep me. I am very much discontented at Parvisol, about neglecting to sell my horses, &c.

Lady Masham is not yet brought to-bed; but we expect it daily. I dined with her to-day. Lord Bolingbroke returned about two months ago, and Prior about a week; and goes back (Prior I mean) in a few days. Who told you of my snuff-box[3] and pockets? did I? I had a letter to-day from Dr. Coghill, desiring me to get Rapho for dean Sterne,[4] and the deanry for myself. I shall indeed, I have such obligations to Sterne. But, however, if I am asked, who will make a good bishop, I shall name him before any body. Then comes another letter, desiring I would recommend a provost, supposing that Pratt (who has been here about a week) will certainly be promoted; but I believe he will not. I presented Pratt to lord treasurer, and truly young Molyneux[5] would have had me present him too; but I directly answered him I would not, unless he had business with him. He is the son of one Mr. Molyneux,[6] of Ireland. His father wrote a book; I suppose you know

3 See p. 559.

4 Twelve days before, 16 Oct., John Pooley, Bishop of Raphoe, had died. Swift responded to Coghill's letter by pressing the claims of Stearne to the vacant bishopric. Lord Harcourt recommended to Oxford Dr. Delaune, President of St. John's College, Oxford (*Portland MSS.* v. 239, 359; vii. 113, 172, 175). The bishopric was, however, filled by the translation of Thomas Lindsay (p. 62 n.[53]) from Killaloe (p. 666).

5 Samuel Molyneux had taken his M.A. degree at Trinity College, Dublin, in 1710. He became secretary to the Prince of Wales, successively M.P. for three English constituencies, and in 1727 M.P. for Dublin University in the Irish Parliament. But he devoted himself chiefly to astronomical research, and was a friend and correspondent of Locke. He died in 1728 at the early age of thirty-nine.

6 William Molyneux, 1656–98, educated at Trinity College, Dublin, applied himself to the study of philosophy and mathematics. He was M.P. for Dublin University in 1692 and 1695. In 1698 he published *The Case of Ireland's Being Bound by Acts of Parliament in England, Stated*, a work which produced a great sensation, for he declared boldly that it was 'against Reason and the Common Rights of all Mankind' that Ireland should be bound by the Acts of an English Parliament.

it. Here is the duke of Marlborough going out of England[7] (Lord knows why), which causes many speculations. Some say he is conscious of guilt, and dare not stand it. Others think he has a mind to fling an odium on the government, as who should say, that one, who has done such great services to his country, cannot live quietly in it, by reason of the malice of his enemies. I have helped to patch up these people together once more.[8] God knows how long it may last. I was to-day at a trial between lord Lansdown and lord Carteret,[9] two friends of mine. It was in the Queen's-Bench, for about six thousand pounds a year (or nine I think). I sat under lord chief justice Parker, and his pen falling down, I reached it up. He made me a low bow; and I was going to whisper him that *I had done good for evil; for he would have taken mine from me.* I told it to lord treasurer and Bolingbroke. Parker would not have known me, if several lords on the bench, and in the court, bowing, had not turned every body's eyes, and set them a-whispering. I owe the dog a spite, and will pay him in two months at farthest, if I can. So much for that. But you must have chat, and I must say every sorry thing that comes into my head. They say the queen will stay a month longer at Windsor. These devils of Grubstreet rogues, that write the *Flying-Post* and *Medley* in one paper, will not be quiet. They are always mauling lord treasurer, lord Bolingbroke, and me. We have the dog under prosecution, but Bolingbroke is not active enough; but I hope to swinge him. He is a Scotch rogue, one Ridpath.[10] They

7 Marlborough left England at the end of November, and was joined by the Duchess in Holland. They returned, landing at Dover, on the evening of the day of Queen Anne's death, and were received with enthusiasm. 8 Oxford and Bolingbroke.

9 Carteret's mother was conducting a lawsuit with Lord Lansdown about her father Lord Bath's estates. A decision, largely in her favour, was not reached till 1714. See Basil Williams, *Carteret & Newcastle*, 1943, pp. 11–12.

10 George Ridpath, a Scotsman, for some years editor of the Whig *Flying-Post*, was committed to Newgate, 8 Sept. 1712, for writing libels

get out upon bail, and write on. We take them again, and get fresh bail; and so it goes round. They say, some learned Dutchman has wrote a book, proving, by civil law, that we do them wrong by this peace; but I shall shew, by plain reason, that we have suffered the wrong, and not they. I toil like a horse, and have hundreds of letters still to read; and squeeze a line perhaps out of each, or at least the seeds of a line. Strafford goes back to Holland in a day or two, and I hope our peace is very near. I have about thirty pages more to write[11] (this is to be extracted) which will be sixty in print. It is the most troublesome part of all, and I cannot keep myself private, tho' I stole into a room up two pair of stairs, when I came from Windsor; but my present man has not yet learned his lesson of denying me discreetly.

30th. The duchess of Ormond found me out to-day, and made me dine with her. Lady Masham is still expecting. She has had a cruel cold. I could not finish my letter last post for the soul of me. Lord Bolingbroke has had my papers these six weeks, and done nothing to them. Is Tisdall yet in the world? I propose writing controversies, to get a name with posterity. The duke of Ormond will not be over these three or four days. I design to make him join with me in settling all right among our people. I have ordered the duchess to let me have an hour with the duke at his first coming, to give him a true state of persons and things. I believe the duke of Shrewsbury will hardly be declared your governor yet; at least I think so now; but resolutions alter very often. Duke Hamilton gave me a pound of snuff to-day, admirable good. I wish D.D. had it; and Ppt. too, if she likes it. It cost me a quarter of an hour of his politics, which I was forced to hear. Lady Orkney is making me a writing table of her own con-

in the *Observator* and *Flying-Post*. On 23 Oct. he appeared before the Court of the Queen's Bench, and was allowed bail. He was brought to trial, 19 Feb. 1713, and found guilty, but fled the country.
11 Of the *History of the Four Last Years of the Queen.*

trivance, and a bed night-gown. She is perfectly kind, like a mother. I think the d— was in it the other day, that I should talk to her of an ugly squinting cousin of her's, and the poor lady herself, you know, squints like a dragon. The other day we had a long discourse with her about love; and she told us a saying of her sister Fitzharding,[12] which I thought excellent, that *in men, desire begets love; and in women, love begets desire.* We have abundance of our old criers still hereabouts.[13] I hear every morning your woman with the old sattin and taffata, &c. the fellow with old coats, suits, or cloaks. Our weather is abominable of late. We have not two tolerable days in twenty. I have lost money again at ombre, with lord Orkney and others; yet, after all, this year I have lost but three and twenty shillings; so that, considering card-money, I am no loser.

Our society hath not yet renewed their meetings. I hope we shall continue to do some good this winter; and lord treasurer promises the academy for reforming our language shall soon go forward. I must now go hunt those dry letters for materials. You will see something very notable, I hope. So much for that. God Almighty bless you.[14]

LETTER LV

55 [SATURDAY] London. Novbr. 15th. 1712

Before this comes to your Hands, you will have heard of the most terrible Accident that hath almost ever happened. This morning at 8, my man brought me word that D. Hamilton had fought with Ld Mohun, & killd

---

[12] Barbara Villiers, eldest daughter of Sir Edward Villiers, married John Berkeley, fourth Viscount Fitzhardinge. She died in 1708; and on his death, 19 Dec. 1712, the title became extinct.

[13] On London cries see Addison's paper in *The Spectator*, No. 251, 18 Dec. 1711.

[14] In Swift's account book for 1711–12 (Forster Collection, 508) the date of this letter is given as 31 Oct., presumably the date of posting.

him, and was brought home wounded.[1] I immediatly sent him to the Dukes house in St James's Square, but the Porter could hardly answer for tears; and a great Rabble was about the House. In short, they fought at 7 this morning the Dog Mohun was killd on the Spot, and wile the Duke was over him Mohun shortening his Sword stabbd him in[2] at the Shoulder to the heart: the Duke was helpt towards the Cake-house[3] by the Ring in Hide park (where they fought,[4] and dyed on the Grass before he could reach the House, & was brought home in his Coach by 8, while the poor Dutchess was asleep. Mackartney & one Hamilton were the Seconds; who fought likewise, and are both fled.[5] I am told, that a footman of Ld Mohun's

[1] The details of this tragic event, distorted at the time by party feeling, are in some doubt. The Duke of Hamilton, a Jacobite in sympathy, had been proposed as Ambassador to Paris; Lord Mohun, a notorious rake, had taken to politics in the Whig interest. Their immediate quarrel, however, sprang out of a protracted family lawsuit. The Duke's second was Colonel John Hamilton of the Scots Foot Guards; Lord Mohun was accompanied by Maccartney (p.120 n.[17]). The principals engaged furiously. The Duke killed Mohun, but himself received a wound which the doctors considered to be the cause of his death. Three days later, however, Colonel Hamilton swore before the Privy Council that, while he held the wounded Duke, Maccartney came up with a sword and stabbed at him. This evidence was not confirmed by servants, who were looking on; but Tories regarded Hamilton as the victim of a Whig plot. In *The Four Last Years of the Queen* Swift accuses Maccartney of stabbing the Duke in the breast 'most barbarously' (*Prose Works*, x. 178). For a Whig account see Boyer's *Political State*, iv. 377–418. See also *A Noble Rake, The Life of Charles, Fourth Lord Mohun*, R. S. Forsythe, 1928; and *Portland MSS.* v. 256.

[2] An obliteration before 'in'.

[3] Later called the Cheesecake House. An engraving representing its appearance in 1801 will be found in *The Gentleman's Magazine*, lxxi. 401. See also lxxii. 105.

[4] The close of the parenthesis is omitted.

[5] Maccartney escaped to Holland, but, on the accession of George I, he returned to England, and, in June 1716, was tried for murder. Although Colonel Hamilton's evidence against him was discredited Maccartney was found guilty as an accessory and 'burnt' in the hand. He was, however, almost immediately given an appointment in the army, and promoted to be Lieutenant-General. He died in 1730.

stabbd D. Hamilton, & some say Macartney did so too. Mohun gave the affront, & yet sent the Challenge. I am infinitly concerned for the poor Duke who was a frank honest good natured man, I loved him very well, & I think he loved me better. He that[6] the greatest mind in the world to have me go with him to France, but durst not tell it me; & those he did sd I could not be spared, wch was true. They have removed the poor Dutchess to a Lodging in the Neighborhood, where I have been with her two hours, and am just come away. I never saw so melancholy a Scene For indeed all Reasons for real grief belong to her, nor is it possible[7] for any one to be a greater loser in all regards. She has moved my very soul. The Lodging was inconvenient, & they would have removed her to anothr; but I would not suffer it; because it had no room backwards; and she must have been tortured with the noise of the Grubstreet Screamers,[8] mention her Husbands murder to her Ears. I believe you have heard the Story of my Escape in opening the Banbox sent to Ld Treasr, the Prints have told a thousand Lyes of it but at last we gave them a true account of it at length, printed in the Evening: onely I would not suffer them to name me, having been so often named before, & teazed to death with Questions.[9] I wonder how I came to have so much

---

[6] A mistake for 'had'; or some words are missing.

[7] Swift first wrote 'easy', scratched it out, and wrote 'possible' above.

[8] The account was possibly a quarto sheet with the title: 'A full and true Account of a Desperate and Bloody Duel: which was Fought this Morning in *High-Park* .... London, Printed by *Edw. Midwinter*, ... price one I penny'.

[9] The story of the bandbox plot was related at length in the Tory *Post Boy*, 11–13 Nov. According to this account Oxford received by post on the morning of Tuesday, 4 Nov., a box within which, as he began to open it, he caught sight of a pistol. A gentleman present [Swift himself] carried the box to the window, and, continuing to open it with extreme care, found it to contain two pistols with 'artificial barrels' of 'two large ink-horns charged with powder and ball'. The barrels pointed in opposite directions and a thread was attached to a trigger. Swift, however, succeeded in opening the box without mishap. The Whig *Flying-Post*, 20–22 Nov.,

presence of mind, which is usually not my talent; but so it pleased God, and I saved my self and him, for there was a Bullet a piece. A Gentleman told me, that if I had been killd, the Whigs would have calld it a Judgmt, because the Barrells were of Inkorns, with which I had done them so much mischief. There was a pure Grubstreet of it full of Lyes and Inconsistencyes.[10] I do not like these things at all; and I wish my self more and more among my Willows: There is a Devilish Spirit among People; & the Ministry must exert themselves or sink. ⌐Nite dee sollahs, I'll go seep—⌐[11]

16. I thought to have finished this yesterday but was too much disturbed. I sent a Letter early this morning to Ldy Masham to beg her to write some comforting words to the poor Dutchess; I dined to[12] with Ldy Masham, at Kensington where she is expecting these 2 months to lye in she has promised me to get the Qu—to write to the Dutchess kindly on this Occasion; and to morrow I will beg Ld Treasr to visit and[13] comfort her. I have been with her 2 hours again; and find her worse. Her violence not so frequent, but her melancholy more formal and settled. She has abundance of witt and Spirit; about 33 year old, handsom, and airy, and seldom spared any body

ridiculed the whole affair; and some suggested that Swift invented the design with a view to winning credit for himself. A contemporary ballad, *Plot upon Plot*, expresses the hope for Swift that,

'—surely now the Bandbox whim
Will help him down to Wells'.

Abel Boyer gives an account of the incident from a Whig point of view in the *Political State of Great Britain*, iv. 370–4. See also Nichols's *Supplement*, 1779, 4to edn., p. 25 n.

10 The reference may be to *An Account of the Duel . . . with Previous Reflections on Sham Plots*, 1712, by Abel Boyer. Thomas Burnet's *A Letter to the People*, . . . *With a Word or Two of the Bandbox Plot*, 1712, appeared later. See *Letters of Thomas Burnet*, ed. D. Nichol Smith, pp. 223–4.

11 Scored through, but not illegible.

12 Either 'too', or a slip for 'to-day'.

13 Swift began to write 'her' before 'and', then obliterated it.

that gave her the least Provocation; by which she had many Envyers[14] and few Friends: Ldy Orkney her Sister in Law[15] is come to Town on this Occasion, and has been to see her; and behaved her self with great humanity; They have been always very ill togethr; and the poor Dutchess could not have Patience when people told her I went often to Ldy Orkneys. But I am resolved to make them Friends; for the Dutchess is now no more an object of Envy, and must learn humility from the severest Master Affliction. I design to make the Ministry put out a Proclamation[16] (if it can be found proper) against that Villain Macartney: What shall we do with these Murderers? I cannot end this letter to night; and there is no occasion, for I cannot send it till Tuesday, and the Crowner's inquest on the Duke's Body is to be to morrow, and I shall know more: but what care oo for all this; ⌈iss poo Md⌉ im sorry for ⌈poopdfrs⌉ friends; and this is a very surprising Event. Tis late, and I'll go to bed. This looks like Journalls. ⌈Nite.⌉

17. I was to day at Noon with the Dutchess of Hamilton again, after I had been with Ldy Orkney, & chargd her to be kind to her Sister in her Affliction; the Dutchess told me Ldy Orkney had been with her, & tht she did not treat her as gently as she ought. They hate one anothr; but I will try to patch it up. I have been drawing up a Paragraph for the Post boy, to be out to morrow, and as malicious as possible, and very proper for Abel Roper te Printer of it.[17] I Dined at Ld Treasrs at 6 in the Evenig;

[14] All editors before Moorhead incorrectly read 'enemies'.

[15] The Earl of Orkney was a younger brother of the Duke of Hamilton.

[16] A Royal Proclamation, dated 24 Nov., offering a reward of £500 for the apprehension of Maccartney, was published. The text of the proclamation is given by R. S. Forsythe in *A Noble Rake*, Appendix E.

[17] The paragraph, which appeared in *The Post Boy*, No. 2734, 15–18 Nov., reads: 'On Saturday Morning last, about 7 of the Clock, the Duke of Hamilton and the Lord Mohun fought a Duel in Hide-Park; his Grace's Second was Col. Hamilton, and his Lordship's Major-Gen. Mackartney. The Ld Mohun died on the Spot; and my Ld Duke soon

wch is his usuall hour returning from Windsor. he promises
to visit the Dutchess to morrow, and say he has a message
to her from the Qu——.[18] I have stayd till past one with
him; ⌐so Nite deelest Md.⌐

18. The Commttee of Council is to sitt this afternoon
upon the Affair of D. Hamiltons murder: and I hope a
Proclamation will be out agst Macartney. I was just now
(tis now Noon) with the Dutchess to let her know. Ld
Tr will see her. She is mightily ⌐out of order.⌐[19] The Jury
have not yet brought in their Verdict upon the Crowners
Inquest; we suspect Macartney stabbd the Duke while he
was fighting. the Qu—— and Ld Treasuer are in great
Concern at this Event. I dine to day agn with Ld Tr; but
must send this to the Post office before; because else I shall
not have time, he usually keeping me so late. Ben Took bid
me write to Dd to send her Certificate, for it is high time
it should be sent, he says. Pray make Parvisol write to
me & send me a generll account of my Affairs and to let
him know tht I shall be over in Spring. & tht by all means
he sells the Horses. Prior has kisst the Qu—— hand & will
return to France in a few days, & Ld Straffd to Holld: &
now the K. of Spain has renounced his Pretensions to
France, the Peace must follow very soon unavoidably.
You must no more call Philip Duke of Anjou, for we now
acknoledge him K. of Spain. Dr Prat tells me you are all

after he was brought home, who receiv'd the following Wounds, one on
the Right side of his Leg, about 7 inches long; another in his Right Arm;
the third in the upper part of his Left Breast, running downwards into his
Body, which was lookt upon to be the immediate Occasion of his Death;
the fourth Wound was on the outside of his Left Leg. My Ld Mohun
receiv'd a very large wound in his Groin; another on the Right Side
through his Body, up to the Hilt of the Sword; and the third in his Arm;
and other Wounds. As to further Particulars. we shall refer them to our
next.' This paragraph was printed in small type. The 'further particulars', in full-sized type, appeared in the number for 18–20 Nov.

18 The words 'Th Court', scrawled through, apparently the beginning
of an unfinished sentence, follow 'te Qu'. Hawkesworth, Sheridan, Nichols,
and Scott read 'Tis late'; Ryland and Aitken 'Thank God'.

19 The words 'out of order' are struck through, but easily legible.

mad in Ireld with your Play-house Frolicks & Prologues; & I know not what. Bp Cl. & Family are well; They have heard from you, or you from them lately, I have forgot which; I dined there tother day; but the Bp came not till after dinner; & our meat & drink was very so so. Mr Vedeau was with me yesterday; & inquired aftr you he was a Lieutenant, and is now broke & upon half pay: He asked me nothing for himself; but wanted an Employmt for a Friend, who would give a handsom pair of Gloves: One Hales sent me up a Letter tothr day; which[20] sd you lodged in his House, & therefore desired I would get him a civil Employmt; I would not be within; and have directed my man to give him an answer, that I never open Letter brought me by the Writers &c. I was complaining to a Lady that I wanted to mend an Employmt from fourty to 60ll a year in the Salt Office; & thought it hard I could not do it. She told me one Mr Griffin[21] should do it, & afterwards I mett Griffin at her Lodgings, & he was as I found, one I had been acquainted with; I named Filby[22] to him, & his abode somewhere near Nantwich: He sd frankly, he had formerly examined the man, & found he understood very little of his Business; but if he heard he mended, he would do what I desired. I will let it rest awhile, & then resume it, and if ppt writes to Filby she may advise him to diligence &c. I told Griffin positively I would have it done, if the man mended. This is an account of ⌈pooppt's⌉ Commission to her most humble

[20] '& sd he' scratched out before 'which'.

[21] Presumably Humphrey Griffith, one of the Commissioners of Salt, although Swift always calls him 'Griffin'. Perhaps a son, or other relation, of Edward Griffith, died 11 Feb. 1710–11, who became a Commissioner of the Salt Office in 1704. See R. S. Forsythe, *A Noble Rake*, p. 135 n.

[22] Stella's sister, Anne (p. 39 n.[19]), married a man called Filby, whom Swift was now recommending for an employment. According to a manuscript genealogy in a copy of Deane Swift's *Essay*, 1755, in the possession of Lord Rothschild, Anne Johnson married, 'Filby a Baker in London; fail'd & became a Salt Officer in ye West of England. They had 18 or 19 Children'. Cf. *Gentleman's Magazine*, xxvii. 488.

ESTHER JOHNSON (STELLA)

From an oil picture attributed to Charles Jervas, in the National Portrait Gallery of Ireland

⌐Servant Pdfr⌐. I have a world of writing to finish:²³ &
little time; these Toads of Ministers are so slow in their
helps. This makes me sometimes steal a week from the
exactness I used to write to ⌐Md. Farewell dee logues
deelest Md Md Md Md Md FW FW FW Me Me Me
lele.⌐

Smoak the folding of my Letters of late.²⁴

Address: To Mrs Dingley, att her
          Lodgings, over against St Mary's
          Church near Capel-street
          Ireland   Dublin

Postmark: $\frac{NO}{18}$

Endorsed by   55.
Rebecca Dingley: Novr. 26.
             just come from
             Portraine.

LETTER LVI

56 [FRIDAY]   London. Decbr. 12. 1712.

Here is now ⌐a stlange ting,¹ 2 Rettles flom Md un-
answered,² never was before⌐; I am slower ⌐& Md is
faster⌐: but the last was owing ⌐to Dd's Certificate⌐;³ why
could it not be sent before pay now; is it so hard for Dd
to prove she is alive: I protest solemnly I am not able to
write to Md for othr Business:⁴ but I will resume my
Journall method next time; I find it is easyer, thô it contains
nothing but where I dine, & the occurrences of the day:

²³ His *History of the Four Last Years of the Queen.*

²⁴ This letter was sent away 18 Nov. according to Swift's account book
(Forster Collection, 509).

¹ Or 'sing'. The words 'a' to 'before' are scored through, but for the
most part lightly.

² Stella's No. 35 was received on 2 Dec., No. 36 on 11 Dec. See
Swift's account book (Forster Collection, 509).

³ 'Dd's Certificate', lightly scored over.

⁴ The composition of his *History* and other affairs of the moment.

I will write now but once in 3 weeks till this Business is off my hands which must be in six I think at furthest. Oh Ppt, I remembr your Reprimanding me for medling in othr Peoples Affairs I have enough of it now with a Wannion.[5] Two Women have been here 6 times a piece, I never saw them yet: the first I have dispatcht with a Lettr; the othr I must see and tell her I can do nothig for her. She is wife of one Mr Connor an old College Acquaintance,[6] and comes on a foolish Errand for some old Pretensions that will succeed when I am Ld Treasr. I am got[7] 2 pair of Stairs in a private Lodging; & have orderd all my Friends not to discovr where I am; yet every mornig 2 or 3 Sotts are plaguing me, & my present Servant has not yet his Lesson perfect of denying me. I have written 130 Pages in folio to be printed, & must write 30 more, which will make a large Book of 4s[8]—I wish I knew an Opportunity of sending you some Snuff I will watch who goes to Ired, & do it if possible. I had a Lettr from Parvisol, & find he has sett my Livings very low. Coll Hamilton[9] who was secnd to D. Hamilton is tryed to day; I suppose he is come off, but have not heard. I dined with Ld Treasr; but left him by nine, & visited some People. Ldy Betty is[10] Daughtr[11] will be marryed on Monday next (as I suppose) to the Marquis of Caermarthen.—I did not know your Country place had been

5 Vengeance. See *O.E.D.*

6 He would be Charles Connor, who came from co. Kerry. He took his B.A. degree in the same year as Swift, 1686, and proceeded M.A. in 1691 (*Alumni Dubl.*, p. 169).

7 Possibly 'up' is omitted. But see 20 Dec. 1712.

8 The *History of the Four Last Years of the Queen.*

9 Colonel John Hamilton surrendered to justice and was examined at the inquests on the Duke of Hamilton and Lord Mohun, 15–22 Nov. He also gave evidence before the Privy Council on 21 Nov. On the 27th he was committed to Newgate, indicted for murder, and tried at the Old Bailey, 12 Dec. 1712. He was convicted of manslaughter, but, pleading his clergy, was released (R. S. Forsythe, *A Noble Rake*, pp. 231–2).

10 For 'his'.

11 p. 135 n.[72]

Portrain till you tod me so in your last. Has Swanton taken it of Wallis.[12] that Wallis was a grave wise Coxcomb. Gd be thankd that Ppt im bettr of her disoddles;[13] pray God keep her so: The Pamphlet of Politicall Lying is writt by Dr Arbuthnot the Authr of John Bull, tis very pretty; but not so obvious to be understood—Higgins first Chapln to D. Hamilton—why D. Hamilton never dreamt of a Chapln; nor I believe ever heard of Higgins. you are glorious newsmongrs in Ireld—Dean Francis[14] Sr R. Leving[15] Stuff Stuff: & Prat more Stuff. We have lost our fine Frost here, & Abel Roper tells us you have had flouds in Dublin, ho brave you. Oh ho Swanton Seised Portrain, now I understand ee. Ay ay, now I see Portraune on the top of your Lettr. I never minded it before. Now to your second. N. 36. So you read one of the Grubstreets about the Bandbox: The Whig Papers have abused me about the Bandbox; God help me; what could I do; I fairly ventured my Life: there is a particular Account of it in the Post boy, & evening Post of that day. Ld Treasr has had the Seal sent him that seald the Box, and directions where to find the tothr Pistol in a Tree in St James's Park, which Ld Bolinbrokes Messengrs found accordingly; but who sent the Present is not yet known. D Hamilton avoided the quarrell as much as possible according to the foppish Rules of Honor in practice. What signifyed your writing angry to Filby: I hope you said nothing of hearing any thing from me. High[16] do oo write by tandle light nauti nauti nauti dallar a hundld times fol doing so. O fais Dd, I'll take care of my Self. the Queen is in Town, &

---

[12] Probably the Rev. Thomas Wallis, who in 1713 became vicar of Athboy. He appears to have entertained Swift, Stella, and Rebecca Dingley; and on several occasions he acted as Swift's proxy at diocesan visitations (*Corresp.* iii. 82, 86, 105, 236, 385; iv. 460).   [13] Disorders.

[14] John Francis, rector of St. Mary's, Dublin, opposite Stella's lodgings. He was Dean of Leighlin from 1696 to 1705, when he resigned his stall. He died in 1724. *Fasti Eccl. Hib.* i. 170; ii. 66.

[15] Sir Richard Levinge (p. 93 n.[13]).

[16] For 'Why', or perhaps 'Heigh!'

Lady Mashams month of lying in is within 2 days of being out. I was at the Christnig a Monday: I could not get the Child[17] namd Robin aftr Ld Treasr: it is Samuel after the Father. My Brothr Ormd sent me some Chocolate to day; I wish you had share of it. but thy say tis good for me, & I design to drink some in a morning Our Society meets next Thursday now the Qu is in town. & Ld Treasr assures me that the Society for reforming the Language shall soon be established I have given away ten shill to day, to Servants; tant be help if one should cry ones Eyes out.[18] Hot a stir is here about your Company & visits; charmig company no doubt. ⌐. .⌐[19] I keep no Company at all. nor have I any desire to keep any: I never go to a Coffee-house nor a Tavern, nor have touched a Card since I left Windsor. I make few Visits, nor go to Levees; My onely debauhig is sitting late when I dine if I like the Company; I have almost dropt the Dutchesses of Shrewsbury & Hamilton & sevrll othrs Ld Treasr, the D. of Ormd & Ldy Orkney are all that I see very often, o yes, & Ldy Masham, & Ld Bolinbroke. & one or 2 private Friends. I make no figure but at Court, where I affect to turn from a Lord to the meanest of my Acquaintance. and I love to go there on Sundays, to see the World. But to say the truth I am growing weary of it. I dislike a million of things in the course of publick Affairs; & if I were to stay here much longr I am sure I shoud ruin my self with endeavoring to mend them. I am every[20] invited into Schemes of doing this, but I cannot find any that will probably succeed. Tis impossible to save People against their own will; and I have been too much engaged in Patch-work already. Do you understand all this Stuff?— No—well zen you are now returnd to Ombre & the Dean, & Christmas, I wish oo a very merry one. & pray don't lose oo money, nor play upon Watt Welch's Game. Nite

---

[17] Swift began to write 'Child' a second time, and struck it out.
[18] Early editors omitted 'tant' to 'out'; and Ryland missed the sentence.
[19] A small illegible obliteration before 'I'.   [20] 'day' omitted?

Sollahs, tis rate, I'll go to seep, I don't seep well, & there-
fore never dare to drink Coffee or Tea after dinner; but
I am very seepy in a molning.[21] This is the Effect of Time
& Years. Nite deelest Md.

13. Morn. I am so very seepy in the mornings, that
my man wakens me above ten times, and now I can tell oo
no News of this day (here is a restless dog crying Cabbages
and Savoys plagues me every morning about this time, he
is now at it, I wish his largest Cabbage was sticking in his
Throat) I lodge over against the House in little Rider
street where Dd lodged, dont oo lememble Maram.[22]—To
Night I must see the Abbè[23] Gautier, to get some particulars for my History: it was he who was first employd by
France in the Overtures of Peace. & I have not had time
this month to see him. He is but a Puppy too.—Ldy
Orkney has just sent to invite me to dinner. She has not
given me the Bed nightgown; besides I am come very
much off from writing in bed tho I am doing it this Minute,
but I stay till my fire is burnt up. My grate is very largely,
2 bushell of Coals a week, but I save it in lodgings. Ld
Abercorn is come to London, & will plague me,[24] & I
can do him no Service—D Shrewsbury goes in a day or
2 for France, perhaps to day; We shall have a Peace very
soon, the Dutch are almost entirely agreed, & if they stop
we shall make it without them; that has been long resolved.
One Squire Jones,[25] a scoundrel in my Parish has writt to
me to desire I would engage Jo Beaumnt to give him his
Interest for Parlmt man for Trim: pray tell Jo this; & if
he designed to vote for him already, then he may tell Jones,
that I received his Letter, & that I writt to Jo to do it; if

[21] Morning.
[22] Remember, Madam.
[23] Thus written by Swift with the wrong accent.
[24] p. 517 n.[49]
[25] Thomas Jones, M.P. for Trim, 1713–14. Probably one of the family
resident at Dollardstown, co. Meath. At this time the head of the family
was Richard Jones, of Dollardstown, M.P. for Donegal, 1703–13; and
High Sheriff of co. Meath, 1708. Richard died in 1729.

Jo be engaged for any othr, then he may do what he will;
& Parvisol may say he spoke to Jo, but Jo's engaged &c.
I receivd 3 pair of fine thread Stockins from Jo lately,
Pray thank him when you see him, & that I say they are
very fine & good (I never lookt at them yet, but that's no
matter) This is a fine day. I am ruined with Coaches &
Chairs this 12 penny weathr. I must see my Brothr Ormd
at 11, & then the Dutchess of Hamilton, with whom I
doubt I am in disgrace, not having seen her these ten days.
—I send this to day, and must finish it now, & phaps some
People may come & hinder me, for it im ten a Clock, (but
not shaving day) & I must be abroad at 11. Abbe Gautier
sends me word I can't see him to night pots cake[26] him.
I don't value any thing but one Letter he has, of Petcum's,[27]
shewing the Roguery of the Dutch. Did not the Conduct
of the Allyes make you great Politicians, fais I believe you
are not quite so ignorant as I thought you. I am glad to
hear oo walked so much in the Country: does Dd ever
read to you ung ooman. O fais I shall find strange doings
hen I tum ole.[28]—Here is somebody coming that I must
see, that wants a little place, the Son of Coz Rooks[29] eldest
Daughtr, tht dyed many years ago.—He's here;—farewell
deelest Md Md Md Me Me Me FW FW FW lele—[30]

Address: To Mrs Dingley at her Lodgings
over against St Mary's Church near
Capel Street
                    Dublin
        Ireland
No Postmark.
Endorsed by   5.6.
Rebecca Dingley: Decr. 18.

[26] Pox take.   [27] A Dutch diplomatic agent.
[28] Come 'ore' for 'over'. The reading is not certain. It may be 'orb'.
[29] In a letter to Thomas Swift, 6 Dec. 1693 (*Corresp.* i. 367), Swift
mentions 'Matt. Rooke'; and, in a postscript, 'cousin Rooke and Matt.'
[30] This letter was posted on 13 Dec. See Swift's account book
(Forster Collection, 509).

LETTER LVII

57. [THURSDAY]　　London. Decbr. 18. 1712.

Our Society was to meet to day, but Ld Harley, who was President this week could not attend, being gone to Wimbleton with his new Brothr in Law the young Marquess of Caermarthen, who marryed Ldy Betty Harley on Monday last, and Ld Treasr is at Wimbleton too. However half a dozen of us mett, & I proposed our meetings should be onely once a fortnight, for betwixt you & me, we do no good. It cost me 19¹ Shillings to day for my Club at Dinner; I don't like it ⌐fais⌐. We have terrible snowey Slobbery weathr. Ld Abercorn is come to Town, & will see me whether I will or no. You know he has a Pretence to a Dukedom in France; wch D. Hamilton was solliciting for; but Abercorn resolves to spoil their Title if they will not allow him a 4th Part; and I have advised the Dutchess to compound with him, & have made the Ministry of my Opinion. ⌐Nite dee sollahs Md Md⌐.

19. ⌐Ay mally zis im sumsing rike a pdfr to write⌐² Journals again, tis as naturall as Mothers milk, now I am got into it. Ld Tr. is returned from Wimbleton (tis not above 8 miles off) and sent for me to dine with him at 5, but I had the Grace to be abroad and dined with some othrs with honest Ben Took by Invitation. the Dutchess of Ormd promised me her Picture, & comig home to night I found hers & the Dukes both in my Chamber, was not that a pretty civil surprise; yess & thy are in fine gilded Frames too. I am writing a Letter to thank her, which I will send to morrow morning. I'll tell her she is such a Prude that she will not let so much as her Picture

---

¹ Moorhead reads '13', but the figure is undoubtedly a '9'.

² 'Ay' to 'write' lightly scored through. The meaning is, 'Ay, marry! this is something like a'. Ryland and Aitken, without justification, read for' for 'a'. Nichols and Scott turn it into 'How agreeable it is in a morning for Pdfr to write'. Hawkesworth and Sheridan omit the whole sentence, 'Ay . . . into it.'

be alone in a room with a MAN, unless the Dukes be with it, and so forth.[3]—We are all full of snow, & dabbling; Ldy Masham has come abroad these 3 days, and seen the Qu. I dined with her tothr day at her Sister Hill's. I hope she will remove in a few days to her new Lodgings at St James's from Kensington. Nite dee logues Md.

20. I lodge[4] 2 pair of Stairs, have but one Room, & deny my self to every body almost, yet I cannot be quiet and all my mornings are lost with People who will not take answers below Stairs, such as Dilly, & the Bp & Provst[5] &c. Ldy Orkney invited me to dinner to day, wch hindred me from dining with Ld Tr this is his day that his chief Friends in the Ministry dine with him. However I went there about 6, and sate with them till past nine when thy all went off; but he kept me back; and told me the Circumstances of Ldy Betty's Match.[6] the young Fellow has 60 thousand Pounds ready money; 3 great Houses furnished, 7 thousand Pounds a year at present, and aboute 5 more after his Father & Mother dye. I think Ldy Betty's Prtion is not above 8 thousd Pd. I remembr eithr Tisdal writt to me in somebody's Lettr, or you did it for him, that I should mention him on occasion to Ld Anglesea, with whom he sd, he had some little Acquaintance; Ld Anglesea was with us to night at Ld Treasr and there I asked him about Tisdal, & described him, he sd he never saw him, but that he had sent him his Book.[7] See what it is to be a Puppy. Pray tell Mr Walls, that Ld Anglesea thanked me for recommending Clements to him, that he says he is 20 thousand Pds the better for knowing Clements. But pray don't let Clements go and

---

[3] This conceit appears in Swift's letter of thanks to the Duchess (*Corresp.* i. 358–9).

[4] See p. 578 n.[7]   [5] The Bishop of Clogher and Benjamin Pratt.

[6] Lady Betty Harley's marriage to the Marquis of Caermarthen.

[7] His *Conduct of the Dissenters of Ireland with Respect to the Church and State*, published in Dublin in 1712.

write a Lettr of thanks, & tell My Ld that he hears so & so &c. Why, tis but like an Irish Understanding to do so. Sad weather, 2 Shill in Coaches to day, and yet I am dirty. I am now going to read over somethig & correct it so Nite.

21. Puppyes have got a new way of plaguing me; I find Lettrs directed for me at Ld Tr's, sometims with inclosed ones to him, & some times with Projects, & sometimes with Libels. I usually keep them 3 or 4 days without opening—I was at Court to day, as I allways am on Sundays instead of a Coffee house, to see my Acquaintance This day sennight after I had been talking at Court with Sr Wm Windham the Spanish Ambasdr[8] came to him, & sd he heard that was Dr S— and desired him to tell me, that His Mastr & the K. of Fr, and the Qu— were more obligd to me than any man in Europe, so we bowd & shook hands &c I took it very well of him I dind with Ld Tr., & must again to morrow, thō I had rather not (as Dd says) but now the Qu. is in Town he does not keep me so late. I have not had time to see Fanny Manly[9] since she came, but intend it one of these days. Her Uncle Jack Manly, I hear can not live a Month,[10] which will be a great loss to Her Father In Ireld; for I believe he is one of his chief Supports. Our Peace now will be soon determind; for Ld Bolinbroke tells me this morning, that 4 Provinces of Holland[11] have complyd with the Q—, & we expect the rest will do so immediatly. Nite Md.

22. Ld Keepr promised me yesterday the first convenient Living to poor Mr Geree, who is marryed, &

[8] The Marquis de Monteleon, who had recently arrived in England as Spanish Ambassador.

[9] Frances, daughter of Isaac Manley. She married the Rev. Samuel Holt, mentioned by Swift in a letter of 15 May 1716 (*Corresp.* ii. 316). Holt matriculated at Trinity College, Dublin, 6 Mar. 1694–5. He was a prebendary of St. Patrick's from 1723 to 1763, the year of his death.

[10] He did not die till 1714.

[11] Utrecht, North and South Holland, and West Friesland.

wants some Addition to what he has; he is a very worthy
Creature.. I had a Letter some weeks ago from Elwick
who marryed Betty Geree. It seems the poor woman dyed
some time last Summer. Elwick grows rich, and purchases
lands. I dined with Ld Treasr to day, who has engaged
me to come again to morrow. I gave Ld Bolinbroke a
Poem of Parnels,[12] I made Parnel insert some Complimts
in it to His Ldship; He is extreamly pleasd with it, &
read some parts of it to day to Ld Treasr who liked it as
much; & indeed he outdoes all our Poets here a Barrs
Length. Ld Bolingbr— has ordered me to bring him to
dinner on Christmas Day, & I made Ld Tr— promise to
see him; and it may one day do Parnel a Kindness. You
know Parnel; I believe I have told you of that Poem.
Nite deel Md.

23. This morning I presented one Diaper a Poet to
Ld Bolinbroke, with a new Poem,[13] which is a very good
one; and I am to give him a Sum of money from my Ld;
and I have contrivd to make a Parson of him; for he is
half a one already, being in Deacons Orders, and serves
a small Cure in the Country, but has a sword at his A—
here in Town. Tis a poor little short Wretch, but will do
best in a Gown, & we will make Ld Keepr give him a
Living. Ld Bolingbroke writ to Ld Treasr to excuse me to
day, so I dined with the former, and Monteleon the Spanish

[12] Ryland and Aitken presume this to be a reference to Parnell's poem
On Queen Ann's Peace. But the treaty of peace, after delays and procrastinations, was not signed till 31 Mar., O.S., 1713, that is more than
three months later. The reference is to *An Essay on the Different Stiles of
Poetry*, which contained elaborate compliments to Bolingbroke. On
Friday, 20 Mar. 1712–13, Swift writes, 'Parnel's Poem will be published
on Monday', and the *Essay* was published, as an octavo pamphlet, on that
or the following day. The latter part of *On Queen Ann's Peace* (*Posthumous
Works of Thomas Parnell*, 1758, pp. 248–65) was clearly composed after
the signing of the treaty; and Bolingbroke receives no more praise than
several notabilities. If anything he is assigned second place to Oxford.

[13] The poem was 'The Dryades: Or, the Nymph's Prophecy.' Cf.
p. 512 n.[25]

Ambassador, who made me many Complimts, I staid till nine; and now it is past ten and my man has lockt me up, and I have just called to mind that I shall be in disgrace with Tom Leigh; That Coxcomb had got into Acquaintance with one Eckershall Clerk of the Kitchin to the Qu— who was civil to him at Windsor on my Account; for I had done some service to Ekershall. Leigh teases me to pass an Evening at His Lodgings with Eckershall; I putt it off sevrall times but was forced at last to promise I would come to night, and it never was in my head till I was lockt up, and I have called and called; but my Man is gone to bed; so I will write an Excuse to morrow. I detest that Tom Leigh, and am as formal to him as I can when I happen to meet him in the Park. The Rogue frets me if he knew it. He asked me why I did not wait on the Bishop of Dromore,[14] I answrd I had not the Honr to be acquaintd with him; & would not presume &c. He takes me seriously, says the Bishop is no proud man &c—He tells me of a Judge in Ireld that has done ill things, I ask why he is not out: Says he, I think the Bishops & you & I, and the rest of the Clergy shoud meet & consult about it: I beg his Pardon, & say I cannot be serviceable that way, he answers, yes, every body may help something. Don't you see how curiously he contrives to vex me, for the dog knows that with half a word I could do more than all of them together. Butt he onely does it from the Pride & envy of his own heart, and not out of a humorous design of teazing, he is one of those, that would rather a Service should not be done, than done by a private man and of his own Country. You take all this, don't you.. Nite dee sollahs, I'll go seep a dazey.

24. I dined to day with the Chancllr of the Excheqr, in order to look over some of my Papers, but nothing was

14 Tobias Pullein, 1648–1713, fellow of Trinity College, Dublin, 1671–7. Bishop of Cloyne in 1694, whence he was translated to Dromore in the following year. Swift names him as one who had a special regard for Stella (*Prose Works*, xi. 134).

done. I have been also mediatig between the Hamilton Family & Ld Abercorn, to have them compound with him, and I believe they will do it. Ld Selkirk[15] the late Duke's Brother is to be in Town in order to go to France to make the demands: & the Ministry are of Opinion thy will get some Satisfaction, and they empowred me to advise the Hamilton side to agree with Abercorn, who asks a 4th Part, & will go to France & spoil all if they won't yield it. Nite sollahs.

25. ⌐A melly Tlismas; melli Tlismas, I sd it first. I wish oo a sousand' zoll, with halt and soul⌐.[16] I carryed Parnel to dine at Ld Bolingb— and he behaved himself very well, & Ld Bol— is mighily pleased with him. I was at St James Chappel by 8 this morning, and Church & Sacramt were done by ten. The Qu— has the Gout in her Hand, & did not come to Church to day; and I stayd so long in my Chambr that I misst going to Court. did I tell you that the Qu— designs to have a drawing-Room and Company every day. Nite deelogues.

26. I was to wish the D. Ormd a happy Christmas, & give half a Crown to his Porter. it will cost me a dozen half Crowns among such Fellows; I dind with Ld Treasr, who chid me for being absent 3 days, mighty kind with a P— less of Civility and more of his Interest. We here Macartney is gone over to Ireld. Was not it Comical, for a

---

[15] Charles Douglas, 1663–1739, second Earl of Selkirk, was the third son of William, the first Earl, who, marrying Anne, *suo jure* Duchess of Hamilton, was created Duke of Hamilton for life in 1660. In 1688 the Duke resigned the Earldom of Selkirk, under a *novodamus*, to Charles and other his younger sons. The second Earl, held in favour for his support of the Revolution, was Lord of the Bedchamber to William III, George I, and George II. The difference between Selkirk and Abercorn arose out of the claim to the Dukedom of Châtelherault (p. 517 n.[49]).

[16] The sentence, heavily scored through, is difficult to decipher. This, which is also Moorhead's reading, seems to be justified. Ryland and Aitken read: 'All melly Titmasses—melly Titmasses—I said it first—I wish it a souzand [times] zoth with halt and soul.' If 'zoll' be right it probably means 'fold'; 'halt' stands for 'heart'.

Gentleman to be sett upon by Highway men, & to tell them he was Macartney; upon wch they brought him to a Justice of Peace in hopes of the reward;[17] and the Rogues were sent to Gail; was it not great Presence of Mind. But may be you heard this already, for there was a Grubstreet of it. Ld Bol— told me I must walk away to day when dinner was done, because Ld Tr and he and anothr were to enter on Business: but I sd it was as fit I should know their Business as any body; for I was to justify;[18] so the rest went, and I stayd and it was so important I was like to sleep over it. I left them at nine & tis now 12. Nite Md.

27. I dined to day with Genrll Hill, Governr of Dunkirk, Ldy Masham & Mrs Hill his 2 Sisters were of the Company; & some others; and there have I been sitting this evening till 11 looking over others at Play; for I have left off loving play my self, and I think ppt is now a great Gamester. I have a great Cold on me, not quite at its height, I have them seldom, and therefore ought to be Patient. I mett Mr Addison and pastorall Philips on the Mall to day, & took a Turn with them; But they both looked terrible dry and cold; a Curse of Party; and do you know that I have taken more pains to recommend the Whig Witts to the Favor & mercy of the Ministers than any other People. Steel I have kept in his Place; Congreve I have got to be used kindly and secured. Row I have recommended, and got a Promise of a Place; Philips I shoud certainly have provided for if he had not run Party-mad and made me withdraw my Recommendation; and I sett Addison so right at first that he might have been

---

17 The government offered £500 for the apprehension of Maccartney. To this the Duchess of Hamilton offered a further reward of £300 (*The Post Boy*, 29 Nov.–2 Dec.; *London Gazette*, 2–6 Dec. 1712). The reading of Hawkesworth, Nichols, and Scott, 'a reward', misses the point. The Duchess at first intended to offer £500, but reduced the sum for fear of appearing to compete with the Queen's offer (*Portland MSS*. v. 258).

18 In the *History* he was composing.

employd; and have partly secured him the Place he has. Yet I am worse used by that Faction than any man. Well, go to Cards sollah, ppt, & dress the Wine & Olange sollah Md; and I'll go seep, tis rate—Nite Md.

28. My Cold is so bad that I could not go to Church to day, nor to Court but, I was engagd to Ld Orkney's with D. Ormd at dinner, and ventured; because I could cough & spitt there as I pleased: the Duke[19] and Ld Arran left us, and I have been sitting ever since with Ld & Ldy Orkney, till past 11, and my Cold is worse, & makes me giddy, I hope it is onely my Cold; oh, says ppt, every body is giddy with a Cold; I hope it is no more; but I'll go to bed, for the fellow has bawld past 12. Nite deels.

29. I got out early to day, & scaped all my Duns. I went to see Ld Bolinbroke about some Buisness, & truly he was gone out too; I dined in the City upon the boild leg of a Goose, & a bitt of Brawn, with my Printer.[20] did I tell you; that I forbeer printing what I have in hand, till the Court decides something about me: I will contract no more Enemyes, at least I will not imbitter worse those I have already, till I have got under Shelter; & the Ministers know my Resolutions; so that you may be disappointed in seeing this Thing as soon as you expected: I hear Ld Treasr is out of order. My Cold is very bad: Every[21] has one. ⌐Nite two dee logues.⌐

30. I suppose this will be full by Saterday; ⌐zen it sall go.⌐[22] D. Ormd, Ld Arran & I dined privatly to day at an old Servants house of his. the Council made us part at 6. one Mrs Ramsy[23] dined with us, an old Lady of about 55 that we are all very fond of.. I calld this Evening at Ld Treasrs, and sate with him 2 hours; he has been cupped for a cold, & has been very ill. He cannot dine

---

[19] Swift wrote 'left us' after 'Duke', and then struck it through.
[20] John Barber.   [21] 'body' or 'one' omitted.
[22] These words are scratched through. Forster reads 'iss' for 'zen', which is certainly wrong.
[23] This is the only mention of her in the *Journal.*

with Parnel & me att Ld Bol—'s to morrow; but says he will see Parnel some other time. I hoise[24] up Parnel partly to spight the envious Irish folks here, particularly Tom Lee; I saw the Bp Cloghrs Family to day. Miss[25] is mighty ill of a Cold coughs incessantly. Nite Md.

31. To day Parnel & I dined with Ld Bolinbrokle,[26] to correct Parnel's Poem, I madde him shew all the Places he disliked, and when Parnel has corrected it fully, he shall print it. I went this evening to sitt with Ld Treasur, he is better, & will be out in a day or two. I sate with him while the young Folks went to Supper; and then went down, & there were the young Folks merry togethr, having turnd Ldy Oxford up to my Ld: and I stayd with them till 12, There was the young Couple Ld & Lady Caermarthen, & Ld & Lady Dupplin,[27] & Ld Harley and I; & the old Folks were togethr above; It lookd like what I have formerly done so often, stealing togethr from the old Folks, thô indeed it was not from poor Ld Tr— who is as young a Fellow as any of us; but Lady Oxford[28] is a silly meer old Woman. My Cold is still so bad that I have not the least Smelling. I am just got home, & tis past 12; and I'll go to bed, & settld my head, heavy as Lead. Nite Md.

Janr. 1. ⌜a sousand melly new eels to deelest richar Md

---

24 Hoist. The nautical use was once common. Cf. 'Hoised up the mainsail', Acts xxvii. 40.

25 The Bishop's daughter.

26 The spelling of this name was a difficulty for Swift. Here he spelt it, at first, with two 'o's. He then wrote a 'k' crookedly over the second 'o', and transformed the original 'k' into an 'l'.

27 He had been Lord Hay for a year (pp. 45, 450 and notes).

28 Oxford's second wife, Sarah, daughter of Simon Middleton of Edmonton. A story related by Lady Strafford (*Wentworth Papers*, p. 263) is perhaps illustrative of her character. The Duchess of Shrewsbury, visiting Lady Oxford, said: '"Madam I and my Lord are so weary of talking Politicks, what are you and your Lord?" and Lady Oxford sighed and said she knew no Lord but the Lord Jehova, and the Duchess made answer again "Oh, dear! Madam, who is that? I believe 'tis won of the new Titles, for I never heard of him before."'

pray Gd almighty bless you and⌐ send ⌐you ever happy⌐[29]..
I forgot to tell you, tht Yesterday Ld Abercorn was here
teazing me about his French Dutchy; and suspectig my
Partiality to the Hamilton Family in such a whimsicall
Manner, tht Dr Prat who was by thought he was made.[30]
He was no soonr gone, but Ld Orkney sent to know
whethr he might come and sitt with me half an hour about
some Business. I returnd answer, that I would wait on
him; which I did, we discoursed a while, and he left me
with Lady Orkney: and in came the Earl of Selkirk whom
I had never seen before; he is anothr Brothr of D. Hamilton, and is going to France by a Power[31] from his Mother
the old Dutchess,[32] to negotiate their Pretensions to this
Dutchy of Chattellerault. He teazed me for 2 hours in
spight of my Teeth,[33] and held my hand when I offerd to
Stir, would have had me engage the Ministry to favor him
agst Ld Abercorn, & to convince them that Ld Abercorn
had nó Pretensions; and desired I would also convince
Ld Abercorn himself so, & concluded he was sorry I was
a greater Friend to Abercorn than Hamilton. I had no
Patience, & used him with some Plainness. Am not I
purely handled between a couple of Puppyes.. Ay says
⌐Ppt, y⌐ must be medling in other Folks Affairs. I appeal
to the Bp of Cl, whethr Abercorn did not complain that I
[would][34] not let him see me last year, and tht he swore he
would take no denyals from my Servant when he came
again. The Ministers gave me leave to tell the Hamilton

---

[29] 'A thousand merry new years'. The sentence as far as 'happy' is
scored through, save for one word, the first part heavily.
[30] Mad.   [31] An obliteration before 'a Power'.
[32] Anne, *suo jure* Duchess of Hamilton, second but first surviving
daughter of James, first Duke of Hamilton, and niece of William, the
second Duke, who was mortally wounded at the battle of Worcester, 1651,
succeeded to the title and dignities. She was born in 1631 or 1632.
In 1656 she married William, Earl of Selkirk, who was, on her petition,
created Duke of Hamilton for life, 1660. She died in 1716.
[33] Despite my opposition, or indifference.
[34] Or 'did'. The paper is torn.

Family it was their Opinion that they ought to agree with Abercorn. Ld Anglesea was then by; & told Abercorn, upon which he gravely tells me I was Commissiond by the Ministers, & ought to perform my Commission &c— But I'll have done with them. I have warned Ld Tr & Ld Bol— to beware of Selkirks teazing.—'x on him. Yet Abercorn vexes me more; The Whelp owes to me all the kind Receptions he has had from the Ministry.—I dined to day at Ld Treasurers with the young Folks; & sate with Ld Treasr till 9. and then was forced to Ldy Masham's and sate there till 12—talking of Affairs till I am out of humor, as every one must that knows them inwardly; A thousand things wrong, most of them easy to mend; yet our Scheams availing at best but little, & sometimes nothing at all. One evil[35] which I twice patchd up with the hazard of all the Credit I had, is now spread more than ever.—But burn Politicks. & send me from Courts & Ministers. ⌜Nite deelest richar Md.⌝

2. I sauntrd about this morning, and went with Dr Prat to a Picture Auction where I had like to be drawn in to buy a Picture that[36] was fond of, but it seems was good for nothing. Prat was there to buy some Pictures for the Bp Cl—[37] who resolves to lay out ten pound to furnish his House with curious Peeces. we dined with the Bp, I being by chance disengaged: & this Evening I sate with Bp Ossory, who is layd up with the Gout the French Ambasd Duke D'Aumont[38] came to Town to night; & the Rabble conducted him home with Shouts; I cannot smell yet thô my Cold begins to break; it continues

---

[35] The quarrel between Oxford and Bolingbroke.
[36] 'I' omitted.   [37] Clogher.
[38] Louis, 1667–1723, Duc d'Aumont, was sent to England, as French Ambassador, as soon as the Treaty of Utrecht was concluded. He busied himself in secret, with the understanding of Torcy, in working for a Jacobite restoration on the death of Anne (Trevelyan, *England under Q. Anne*, iii. 248, 336 ff.). He entered London in great state, scattering money out of his coach to the crowd; and constantly aimed at 'making himself acceptable to the nation' (Burnet, *Own Time*, vi. 131).

cruell hard frosty Weathr. Go and be ⌐melly & nite sollahs.⌐

3. Ld Dupplin & I went with Ld & Ldy Orkney this morning at ten to Wimbleton 6 miles off; to see Ld & Ldy Caermarthen, It is much the finest place about this Town;[39] did oo never see it. I was once there before about 5 years ago. You know Ldy Caermarthen is Ld Treasr Daughter, marryed about 3 weeks ago. I hope the young Fellow will be a good Husband.—I must send this away now. I came back just by night fall. cruell cold weathr. I have no smell yet. but my cold something better. ⌐. . . sollahs; I'll take my reave.⌐ I forgett how ⌐Md Accounts are; pray let me know allways timely before Md wants;⌐[40] & pray give the Bill on tothr side to Mrs Brent as usuall. I believe I have not payed her this great while. ⌐Go play Cards & be melly dee sollahs, & rove pdfr who roves Md bettle zan his Rife. Farewell deelest Md Md Md Md Md . . . Me Me Me FW FW FW FW Me Me

lele
lele lele lele⌐

The six odd Shillings tell Mrs B——[41] are for her New years gift.

I am just now told that poor dear Lady Ashburnham, the Duke of Ormd's daughter dyed yesterday at her Country House; the poor creature was with Child. She was my greatest Favorite, and I am in excessive Concern for her Loss. I hardly knew a more valuable Person on all Accounts: you must have heard me tell of her. I am afraid

[39] The manor-house of Wimbledon was rebuilt by Sir Thomas Cecil, eldest son of Lord Burghley, about 1588. The property was purchased by Thomas Osborne, Earl of Danby, afterwards Marquis of Caermarthen, and first Duke of Leeds. For an account of the manor and the vicissitudes of the mansion see Brayley, *History of Surrey*, iii. 499–503.

[40] The words are obliterated to 'reave', and again from 'MD' to 'wants'. Forster reads 'Nite dee' before 'sollahs', but this is certainly not apparent.

[41] Mrs. Brent.

to see the Duke and Dutchess; she was naturally very healthy; I am afraid she has been thrown away for want of care. Pray condole with me; tis extreamly moving, Her Lord's a Puppy, and I shall never think it worth my while to be troubled with him, now he has lost all that was valuable in his Possession. Yet I think he used her pretty well.—I hate Life, when I think it exposd to such Accidents. and to see so many thousand wretches burthening the Earth while such as her dye, makes me think God did never intend Life for a Blessing.—Farewell.[42]

Address: To Mrs Dingley, att her
         Lodgings over against St Mary's
         Church near Capel-street
         Ireland   Dublin

Postmark: $\dfrac{IA}{6}$

Endorsed by   57
Rebecca Dingley: Janr. 13.

LETTER LVIII

58. [SUNDAY]   London. Janr. 4. 1712–13

I ended my last with the melancholy news of poor Ldy Ashburnhams death.. The Bp Cl. & Dr Prat made me dine with them to day at Ld Mountjoys pursuant to an Engagemt wch I had forgot. Ldy Mountjoy told me that Maccartney was got safe out of our Clutches, for she had spoke with one who had a Lettr from him from Holland; others say the same thing. Tis hard such a dog should escape. As I left Ld Mountjoy's I saw the Duke d'Aumont the Fr. Ambassador going from Ld Bolingbrokes where he dined, to have a private Audience of the Qu— I followd & went up to Court, where there was a great Croud. I was talking with the Duke of Argyle by

---

[42] Swift's account book (Forster Collection, 509) notes the dispatch of this letter, 3 Jan. 1712–13.

the Fireside in the Bedchambr, when the Ambassador came out from the Qu— Argyle presented me to him, & Ld Bolingb & we talked togethr awhile. He is a fine Gentleman, something like the D. Ormd, and just such an expensive[1] man. After Church to day I shewd the Bp of Cl. at Court who was who.—ᴦNite my too dee logues & lastles.ᴾ[2]

5. Our Frost is broke, but it is bloody cold. Ld Treasr is recovred, & went out this evening to the Qu— I dined with Ldy Oxford[3] & then sate with Ld Tr while he went out. he gave me a Letter from an unknown Hand relating to Dr Brown Bp of Cork,[4] recommending him to a better Bishoprick as a Person who opposed Ld Wharton, and was made a Bp on that Account, celebrating him for a great Politician &c, in that all directly contrary to His Character; which I made bold to explain—What dogs there are in the World. I was to see the poor Duke & Dutchess of Ormd this morning, the Duke was in his publick Room with Mr Southwell, and two more Gentlemen, when Southwell and I was alone with them, he talked something of Ld Ashburnham, that he was afraid the Whigs would get him again, he bore up as well as he could, but something accidentally falling in discourse, the Tears were just falling out of his Eyes, and I looked off to give him an Opportunity (which he took) of wiping them

---

[1] Moorhead proposes 'expansive'. The letter, if anything, is more like an 'a' than an 'e'. But 'expensive' is probably right. The use of 'expansive' in our modern sense seems unlikely.

[2] The sentence is scribbled over and difficult to read. The last word stands for 'rascals'. Forster reads 'lastalls', and Aitken suggests 'ledles'.

[3] 'Oxford' is scrawled over another beginning.

[4] Dr. Peter Browne, who became Provost of Trinity College, Dublin, in 1699. In 1710 he was appointed Bishop of Cork and Ross. His learning won him general respect; and his *Letter in Answer* (1697) to Toland's *Christianity not Mysterious* was held in high esteem. Swift, however, as these remarks, and others (*Corresp.* i. 119–20; iii. 244), show, regarded him doubtfully. But he is mentioned particularly as one of Stella's friends (*Prose Works*, xi. 134). He died in 1735. See *D.N.B.*; *Fasti Eccl. Hib.* i. 231.

with his Hankerchief. I never saw any thing so moving, nor such a mixture of greatness of mind and Tenderness and Discretion. ⌜Nite Md⌝.

6. Ld Bolinbr— & Parnel & I dined by Invitation with my Friend Dartinuff, whom you have heard me talk of. Ld Bolinbr. likes Parnel mightily, and tis pleasant to see that one who hardly passt for any thing in Ireld makes his way here with a little friendly forwarding. It is scurvy rainy weathr, & I have hardly been abroad to day, nor know any thing that passes. Ld Treasr is quite recovered, and I hope will be carefull to keep himself well. Dutchess of Marlbrough is leaving Engld to go to her Duke, and makes Presents of Rings to severall Friends, they say worth 200ll a piece. I am sure she ought to give me one, Though the Duke pretended to think me his greatest Enemy, & got People to tell me so, and very mildly to let me know how gladly he would have me softned[5] towrds him. I bid[6] a Lady of his Acquaintance & mine let him know, that I had hindred many a bitter thing against him, not for his own sake, but because I thought it looked base; and I desired every thing should be left him except Power. ⌜Nite Md⌝.

7. I dined with Ld & Ldy Masham to day; & this Evenig playd at Ombre with Mrs Vanhom— mearely for Amusemt; the Ministers have got my Papers & will neithr read them nor give them to me, & I can hardly do any thing.—Very warm slabby weather; but I made a shift to get a walk, yet I lost half of it, by shaking of Ld Rochester, who is a good civil simple Man—Th Bp of Ossory[7] will not be Bp of Hereford, to the great grief of

5 An obliteration before 'softned'.

6 Swift began to write 'told', scratched this out, and wrote 'bid'.

7 John Hartstonge (p. 223 n.[1]). Humphrey Humphreys, Bishop of Hereford, died 20 Nov. 1712. The vacant bishopric was filled by the translation of Philip Bisse, Bishop of St. Davids since Oct. 1710 (Hearne, *Collections*, iii. 71, 81). Scott (*Memoirs of Swift*, 1814, p. 169) argues that Swift himself hoped for the see of Hereford. But there is no indication that Swift sought this bishopric. On 20 Jan. he refers casually to the

himself and his Wife.—And ⌐hat is Md doing now I wonder; playing at Cards⌐ with the Dean & Mrs Walls; —I think it is not certain yet that Macartney is escaped.— I am plagued with bad Authors, Verse and Prose, who send me their Books and Poems; the vilest Trash I ever saw. but I have given their names to my man, never to let them see me. I have got new Ink, & tis very white,[8] & I don't see that it turns black at all—I'll go to seep tis past 12. ⌐Nite Md.⌐

8. ⌐Oo⌐ must understad tht I am in my Geers[9] and have got a Chocolate pot a present from Mrs Ash of Clogher, and some Chocolate from my Brothr Ormd; & I treat Folks sometimes. I dined with Ld Treasr at 5 a Clock to day, & was by while He & Ld Bol— was at Business; for it is fit I should know all that passes new[10] because—&c. the D. of Ormd emplyd me to speak to Ld Treasr to day about an Affair, and I did so; & the Duke had spoke himself 2 hours before; which vext me, and I will chide the Duke about it. I tell you a good Thing: there is not one of the Ministry but what will employ me as gravely to[11] speak for them to Ld Tr—as if I were their Brother or his; and I do it as gravely: thô I know they do it onely[12] because they will not make themselves uneasy, or had rathr I should be denyed than they— I believe our Peace will not be finished these 2 Months; For I think we must have a return from Spain by a Messenger who will not go till Sunday next.[13] Ld Treasr

vacancy; and on the 24th he knew that it had been filled, over three weeks before Bisse was translated, 15 Feb. 1713. See further Sir Charles Firth in *The Review of English Studies*, ii. 5–6.

[8] The pale ink begins after the words 'this morning' on the 5th, and continues to the words 'his Office' on the 14th of January.

[9] p. 455 n.[13]   [10] Previous editors read 'now'.

[11] Small obliteration before 'to'.

[12] Small obliteration before 'onely'.

[13] It is probable that on this day, 8 Jan., Swift wrote to Archbishop King the letter filled with political news, first printed by Sheridan, which appears in the correspondence dated 3 Jan. (*Corresp.* ii. 1). King's reply

has invited me to dine with him again to morrow. Your Commissnr Keatly[14] is to be there. ⌐Nite dee richar Md⌐.

9. Dr Prat drunk Chocolate with me this morning & then we walkt. I was yestrday with him to see Ldy Betty Butler grieving for her Sister Ashburnham: the Jade was in bed in form; and she did so cant she made me sick. I meet Tom Lee every day in the Park to preserve his Health; he is as ruddy as a Rose, & tells me his Bp of Dromore recovers very much. that Bp has been very near dying. To day's Examiner talks of the Play of what is it like?[15] and you will think it to be mine, and be bit, for I have no hand in those Papers at all. I dined with Ld Treasr. & shall again to morrow, wch is his day when all the Ministers dine with him. He calls it whipping day; it is always on Saterday; and we do indeed usually railly him about his Faults on that day. I was of the Originall Clubb when onely poor Lord Rivers, Ld Keepr, & Ld Bolinbr—came, but now Ormd, Anglesea, Ld Steward,[16] Dartmouth, & other Rabble intrude, and I scold at it, but now they[17] pretend as good a Title as I, & indeed many Saterdays I am not there: the Company being too many I don't love it. Nite Md.

10. At 7 this Evening as we sate after dinnr at Ld Treasrs, a Servant sd Ld Peterborow was at the door. Ld Tr & Ld Bol— went out to meet him, and brought

---

(*Corresp*. ii. 6) refers to Swift's letter of 'the 8th instant'. Furthermore, on the 3rd Swift was otherwise occupied, and his mind distracted by the news of Lady Ashburnham's death.

14 The Right Hon. Thomas Keightly, a Commissioner of the Irish Revenue (*Corresp*. ii. 80 and n.[4]).

15 An account of the game of 'What is it like?', or Similitudes, is given in *The Examiner*, 5–9 Jan. 1712–13. One person thinks of a subject, and the others try to guess it by naming similitudes. In 'Bons mots de Stella' (*Prose Works*, xi. 141) an illustration is given of Stella's aptitude in playing the game. Mentioned also in *A Letter of Advice to a Young Poet* (*Prose Works*, xi. 102).

16 Earl Poulett (p. 239 n.[10]).

17 'thy p' struck through before 'they'.

him in. He was just returnd from abroad, where he has been above a year. Soon as he saw me, he left the D. Ormd, & othr Lds, and ran and kisst me before he spoke to them, but chid me terribly for not writing to him; which I never did this last time he was abroad, not knowing where he was; and he changed places so often, it was impossible a Lettr should overtake him. he left Engd with a Bruise by his Coach overturning, that made him spitt Blood, & was so ill we expected any Post to hear of his Death: But he outrode it, or outdrunk[18] it, or something: & is come home[19] lustyer than ever; he is at least 60, & has more Spirits than any young fellow I know in Engld: He has got the old Oxford Regimt of horse; & I believe will have a Garter, I love the hangdog dearly. ⌈Nite dee Md⌉.

11. The Court was crammd to day to say[20] the Fr Ambassdr; but he did not come. Did I never tell you tht I go to Court on Sundays as to a Coffee-house to see acquaintance, whom I should otherwise not see twice a year. The Provost & I dined with Ned Southwell by appointment; in order to settle your Kingdom, if my Scheam can be followed, but I doubt our Ministry will be too tedious; You must certainly have a new Parlmt, but they would have that a Secret yet. Our Parlmt here will be prorogued for 3 weeks. those Puppyes the Dutch will not yet come in, thô they pretend to submit to the Qu— in every thing: but they would fain try first how our Session begins, in hopes to embroyl us in the House of Lds. & if my advice had been taken, the Session should have begun, & we would have trusted the Parlmt to approve the Steps already made towards the Peace, & had an Address perhaps from them to conclude without the Dutch, if they would not agree. Others are of my mind; but[21] it is not reckoned so safe, it seems. Yet I doubt

[18] Not 'outdrank' as previously read.
[19] An obliteration before 'home'.
[20] i.e. 'see'.   [21] An obliteration after 'but'.

whethr the Peace will be ready so soon as 3 weeks. but
that's a Seret.[22] ⌐Nite Md⌐.

   12. Prat and I walkt into the City to one Bateman's a
famous Bookseller for old books; there I layd out 4ll like
a fool, and we dined at a hedge alehouse for 2sh and 2
pence like Emperors. Let me see: I bought Plutarch[23]
2 Vollumes for thirty shillings.[24] ⌐Well I'll tell y no⌐
more; ⌐oo don't understand Greek;⌐ We have no news,
and I have nothing more to say to day. I can't finish my
Work, these Ministers will not find time to do what I
would have them. ⌐So Nite nown dee dallars⌐.

   13. I was to have dined to day with Ld Keepr;[25] but
would not, because that Brute Sr John Walter was to be
one of the Company. You may remembr he raild at me
last Summer was twelvemonth at Windsor, and has never
beggd my pardon, thö he promisd to do it; and[26] Ld
Mansel who was one of the Company, would certainly
have sett us togethr by the Ears out of pure roguish
mischief. So I dined with Ld Treasr. where there was
none but Ld Bol— I stayd till 8, and then went to Lady
Orkney's who has been sick, and sate with her till 12,
from whence you may conclude it is late Sollahs. The
Parlmt was prorogued to day as I told you, for 3 weeks.—
Our weathr is very bad & slobbery; and I shall spoil my
new Hatt (I have bought a new Hat) or empty my Pockets.
Does Hawkshaw pay the Interest he owes?[27] Ld Abercorn plagues me to death I have now not above six People
to provide for, and about as many to do good offices to,

[22] Secret.
[23] The well-known Paris edition of Plutarch in two folio volumes,
1624, containing a long life of Plutarch by Ruault. This work appeared
as lot No. 243 in the sale catalogue. H. Williams, *Dean Swift's Library*,
pp. 5 n.¹, 46.
[24] An obliteration after 'thirty shillings' is read by previous editors,
except Moorhead, as '&c'; but without justification.
[25] Harcourt.
[26] A small obliteration before 'and'.
[27] An uncertain line may be intended for a mark of interrogation.

and thrice as many that I will do nothing for, nor can if I would. Nite dee Md.

14. To day I took the Circle of mourning[28] Visits I went to the Dutchess of Ormd; & there was she & Ldy Betty, & Ld Ashburnham together: this was the first time the Mothr & Daughtr saw each othr since Ldy Ashburnham's death; they were both in Tears, and I chid them for being together, & made Ldy Betty go to her own Chambr, then sate a while with the Dutchess, & went after Lady Betty, & all was well. there is something of Farce in all these Mournings let them be ever so serious. People will pretend to grieve more than they really do, & that takes off from their true Grief. I then went to Dutchess Hamilton, who never grieved but raged & stormed & railed. She is pretty quiet now, but has a diabolicall Temper,[29] Ld Keeper & his son, & their two Ladyes and I dined to day with Mr Cesar, Treasurer of the Navy at his House in the City where he keeps his Office—We happend to talk of Brutus, and I sd something in his Praise, when it struck me immediatly that I had made a Blunder in doing so, and therefore I recollectd[30] my self, & sd, Mr Cesar I beg your Pardon. So we laughd &c. ⌐Nite my own deelest richar logues Md⌐.

15. I forgot to tell you tht last Night I had a present sent me (I found it[31] when I came home. in my Chambr) of the finest wild fowl I ever saw, with the vilest Letter and from the vilest Poet in the World, who sent it me as a bribe to get him an Employmt; I knew not where the Scoundrel lived, so I could not send them back, & therefore I gave them away as freely as I got them, and have

---

[28] All previous editors read 'morning'; but the word is clearly 'mourning', and the context confirms it.

[29] His earlier description of the Duchess, 16 Nov. 1712, is markedly different.

[30] The word 'immediatly' is struck out before 'recollected'. He had already used it in the same sentence.

[31] The words 'at home' are struck out after 'it'.

ordered my man never to let up the Poet when he comes. the Rogue should have kept the Wings at least for his Muse. One of his foul was a large Capon Pheasant, as fat as a Pullet. I eat share of it to day with a friend. We have now a drawing room every Wednesday, Thursday and Saterday at one a Clock: the Qu— does not come out, but all her Ministers, Foreignrs & Persons of Quality are at it. I was there to day; & as Ld Treasr came towards me I avoyded him, & he hunted me thrice about the Room. I affect never to take notice of him at Church or Court. He knows it, for I have told him so; and to night at Ld Mashams he gave an Account of it to the Company, but my Reasons are, that People seeing me speak to him causes me a great deal of teazing—I tell you what comes into my head; that I never knew whether ⌐Md¬ were Whigs or Toryes; and I value our Conversation the more, that it never turnd on that Subject. I have a ⌐Fancy that ppt¬ is a Tory, and a violent one; I don't know why; but methinks she looks like one; and Dd a sort of a Trimmer. Am I right.—I gave the Examiner[32] a hint about this Prorogation, & to praise the Qu— for her tenderness to the Dutch in giving them still more time to submitt. It fitted the Occasions at present. ⌐Nite Md.¬

16. I was busy to day at the Sertys Office and stayd till past 3; the D. of Ormd & I were to dine at Ld Orkneys. the Duke was at the Committee: so I thought all was safe; when I went there they had almost dined; for the Duke had sent to excuse himself, which I never knew. I came home at 7, & began a little Whim wch just came into my Head, & will make a threepenny Pamphlet,[33] it shall be

---

[32] *The Examiner*, 12–16 Jan. 1712–13.

[33] *Mr. C[olli]ns's Discourse of Free-Thinking, Put into plain English, by way of Abstract for the Use of the Poor.* This fourpenny pamphlet was handed to the printer on the 21st, and was published on the 25th of January 1712–13. It was advertised in *The Examiner* for the 26th. One of Swift's most successful essays in the art of irony, it is not only a satire on Anthony Collins's *Discourse of Freethinking*, recently published; it goes further and represents atheistical views as typical of the Whig party.

finished and out in a Week, and if it succeds you shall know what it is, otherwise not. I cannot send this to morrow and will put it off till next Saterday cause I have much business; so my Journalls shall be short, & ⌐Md⌐ must have Patience; so ⌐Nite dee sollahs⌐.

17. This Rogue Parnel has not yet corrected his Poem, & I would fain have it out. I dined to day with Ld Treasr, and his Saterday company, nine of us in all. they went away at 7, and Ld Treasr & I sate talking an hour after. After dinner he was talking to the Lds about the Speech the Qu— must make when Parlmt meets. He asked me how I would make it. I was going to be serious; because[34] it was seriously put; but I turned it to a Jest, and because they had been speaking of the Dutchess of Marlbr going to Flanders after the Duke, I sd, the Speech should begin thus. My Lds & Gentlemen; In order to my own Quiet, and that of my Subjects I have thought fit to send the Dutchess of Marlbr abroad after the Duke—This took well, & turned of the Discourse. I must tell you, I do not at all like the present Situation of Affairs; and remembr I tell you so. Things must be on anothr foot, or we are all undone. I hate this driving always to an Inch. ⌐Nite Md⌐.

18. We had a mighty full Court to day. Dilly was with me at the French-church, and edifyed mightily. D. Ormd & I dined at Ld Orkney's, but I left them at 7, and came home[35] to my whim. I have made a great Progress. My large Treatise[36] stands stock still; some think it too dangerous to publish, and would have me print onely what relates to the Peace. I can't tell what I shall do. The Bp of Dromore is dying. they thought yesterday he could not live 2 hours, yet he is still alive, but is utterly past all hopes. Go to Cards ⌐sollahs, and Nite⌐.

19. I was this morning to see the D. & Dutchess of Ormd, the Duke[37] D. Aumont came in while I was with

---

[34] An obliteration before 'because'. [35] An obliteration before 'home'.
[36] *The History of the Four Last Years of the Queen.*
[37] 'Duke' is written above the line.

the Duke of Ormond, and we complimentd each other like Dragons. A poor Fellow calld at the door where I lodge, with a Parcil of Oranges for a Present for me; I bid my man know what his name was, & whence he came; he sent word his Name was Bun, and I knew him very well. I bid my Man tell him I was busy, & he could not speak to me, & not to let him leave his Oranges. I know no more of it But I am sure I never heard the Name, and I shall take no such Presents from Strangers; Perhaps he might be onely some Beggar who wanted a little Money; perhaps it might be something worse. Let them keep their Poison for their Rats. I dont love it. ⌐..........
..............⌐38 that blot is a Blundr. nite dee Md.

20. A Committee of our Society dined to day with the Chancllr of the Exchequr;39 Our Society does not meet now as usuall; for wch I am blamed, but till Ld Tr will agree to give us money & Employmts to bestow, I am averse to it; & he gives us nothing but promises. Bp of Dromore is still alive, & that is all; we expect every day he will dy, & then Tom Leigh40 must go back, which is one good thing to the Toun. I belive Prat will drive at one of these Bishopricks. Our English Bishoprick41 is not yet disposed of. I believe the Peace will not be ready by the Session. Nite Md.42

21. I was to day with my Printer, to give him a little Pamphlet I have written; but not Politicks; it will be out

38 Most of a line is here blotted out. Forster imagined that he read the first part as: 'Nite dear MD—drowsy, drowsy, dear.' Pons (op. cit., p. 19) explains the following words as an expression of regret for having effaced 'des mots les plus chers'.   39 Robert Benson.
40 Tom Leigh was related by marriage to the Bishop of Dromore, whose wife, Elizabeth Leigh, died in 1691.
41 That of Hereford (p. 597 n.7).
42 It may be noted that, on this day, Swift sent the Duke of Argyle a letter of remonstrance on the change in his behaviour, following upon a misunderstanding which had arisen between them. The coolness cannot have been of long duration, for on the 4th of January Argyle had introduced Swift to the French Ambassador. See *Corresp.* ii. 5–6, and notes.

by Monday: if it succeeds I will tell you of it, otherwise not. we had a prodigious Thaw to day, as bad as rain, yet I walked like a good Boy all the way: Bp of Dromore still draws Breath, but cannot live 2 days longer. My large Book lyes flat; some people think, a great part of it ought not to be now printed: I believe I tod you so before. This Lettr shll not go till Saterday which makes up the 3 weeks exactly, and I allow Md 6 weeks, which are now almost out, so, oo must now[43] I expect a Rettle vely soon; & tht Md is vely werr,[44] and so Nite dee Md.

22. This is one of our Court days; and I was there. I told you, there is a drawing room Wednesday, thursday & Saterday: the Hamiltons and Abercorns have done teising me; the latter I heer is actually going to France. Ld Tr quarrelld with me at Court for beig 4 days without dining with him, so I dined there to day. And he has at last fallen in with my Project (as he calls it) of coining Halfpence & Farthings, with devices like Medals, in honor of the Q, evry year changing the Device:[45] I wish it may be done. Nite Md.

23. D. Ormd & I appointd to dine with Ned Southwell to day, to talk of settling your Affairs of Parlmt in Ired; but there was a mixture of Company, & the D. Ormd was in hast, & nothing was done. If your Parlmt meets this Summer it must be a new one; but I find some are of opinion there should be none at all these 2 years. I will trouble my self no more about it. my design was to serve the D. Ormd. Dr Prat & I sate this Evenig with Bp Cl. & playd at Ombre for threepences. that I suppose is but low with you. I found at comig home a Lettr flom Md. N. 37;[46] I shall not answr it zis bout, but will the next. I

[43] Know.   [44] Very well.

[45] This same proposal is set out in detail in *The Guardian*, No. 96, 1 July 1713, which has been attributed to Swift. The paper was included by Nichols in his *Supplement*, 1779; in his edition of Swift's *Works*, 1801, v. 466; and by Scott, 1814, ix. 285.

[46] The receipt of Stella's letter, No. 37, on this day, is noted in Swift's account book (Forster Collection, 509).

am sorry for ⌜poo poo ppt;⌝ pray walk hen oo can. I have
got a terrible new Cold before my old one was quite gone;
and dont know how. ⌜Pay . . . .⌝47 I shll have
Dd's mony soon from the Exchequr—Bp Dromore is
dead now at last. ⌜Nite dee Md.⌝

24. I was at Court to day, & it was comicall to see Ld
Abercorn bowing to me, but not speaking, & Ld Selkirk
the same. I dined with Ld Treasr, & his Saterday Club,
& sate with him 2 hours after the rest were gone, & spoke
freer to him of affairs than I am afraid others do, who
might do more good. All his Friends repine, & shrug
their shoulders, but will not deel with him so freely as
they ought. Tis an odd Business. the Parlnt just going
to sit, and no Employnts given; they say they will give
them in a few days. There is a new Bishop made of Hereford;48 so Ossory is disappointed; I hinted so to his
Friends 2 Months ago, to make him leave of49 deluding
himself, and being indiscreet as he was.—I have just time
to send this without going to the Bellman. ⌜Nite deelest
richr Md, farewell dee Md Md Md FW FW
　　　　　　FW Me Me Me lele lele lele⌝—

My second cold is better now.
　　　　　　　　　　⌜lele lele lele　　lele⌝50

Address: To Mrs Dingley at
　　　　　her Lodgings over against St
　　　　　Mary's Church near Capel-street
　　　　　　Ireland　　　Dublin
Postmark cut through and illegible
Endorsed by　　　　58:
Rebecca Dingley: Febr. 4.

47 Forster reads, 'Pay, can oo walk oftener—oftener still?' Moorhead
suggests, 'Pay aah well of oo Helth?'—i.e. 'Pray are [you] well of your
health?' The latter reading, if doubtful, is the more probable.
48 p. 597 n.7
49 Off.
50 The dispatch of letter 58 is marked in Swift's account book (Forster,
509) as 23 Jan. '(about)'.

LETTER LIX

59. [SUNDAY]   London. Janry. 25th. 1712–13.

We had such a Terrible Storm to day, that going to Ld Bolinbrokes I saw a hundred Tiles fallen down, & one Swinger fell about 40 yards before me, that would have killd a Horse. So after Church & Court, I walked through the Park, & took a Chair to Ld Treasrs, next door to his House, a Tin Chimney top had fallen down, with a hundred Bricks. It is grown calm this Evening, I wonder had you¹ such a Wind to day. I hate it as much as any Hog does. Ld Treasr has engagd me to dine with him again to morrow. He has those Tricks sometimes, of inviting one from day to day, wch I am forced to break through; My little Pamphlet² is out, tis not Politicks; if it takes I say again, you shll hear of it. ⌐Nite dee logues⌐.

26. This morning I felt a little Touch of Giddyness, which has disorderd & weakend me with its ugly remains all this day, ⌐poo poo pdfr.⌐³ After dinner at Ld Treasr, the Fr Ambassdr Duke d'Aumont sent Ld Tr word that his House was burnt down to the Ground, it took fire in the upper rooms while he was at Dinner with Monteleon the Span. Ambassdr, & other Persons, & soon after Ld Bolinbroke came to us with the same story.⁴ We are full of Speculations upon it, but I believe it was the Carelessness of his French Rascally Servts. Tis odd that this very day Ld Sommers, Wharton, Sunderld Hallifax, and the whole Club of Whig Lords dined at Pontacks in the City, as I received private Notice; Thy have some damned

---

¹ 'should' scored through after 'you'.   ² p. 603 n.³³
³ Forster, Ryland, and Aitken read 'Pity Pdfr'.
⁴ An account of the fire and its possible causes appears in Boyer's *Political State*, v. 43–6. The total damage was estimated at not less than £20,000. The government offered a reward for the discovery of incendiaries, but without success. It is not unlikely that the fire was due to accident. The Queen provided rooms in Somerset House for the French Ambassador.

design. I tell you anothr odd thing: I was observig it to Ld Treasr: that he was stabbed on the day K. Willm dyed, and the day I saved his life with opening the Ban-box,[5] was K. Wms birth-day. My Friend Mr Lewis has had a Lye spread on him by the mistake of a Man who went to anothr of his name to give him thanks for passing his privy seal to come from France; that tother Lewis, spread about that the Man brought[6] him thanks from Ld Perth, & Ld Melfort, (two Lds with the Pretender) for his great Services &c.[7] the Lds will examine that tother Lewis to morrow in Council, and I believe you will hear of it in the Prints, for I will make Abel Roper give a Relation of it. Pray tell me if it be necessary to write a little plainer; for I lookt over a bit of my last Letter, & could hardly read it; I'll mend my Hand if oo please, but you are more used to it *Nor*[8] I; as Mr Raymd says. ⌜Nite Md.⌝

27. I dind to day with Ld Treasr, this is 4 days togethr, & he has invited me again to morrow, but I absolutely refused him. I was this evening at a Christnig with him of Ld Dupplins[9] Daughter,[10] he went away at 10, but

---

5 Swift first wrote 'Band', then obliterated the 'd' by writing 'b' over it.

6 A slight obliteration before 'brought'.

7 Charles Skelton, a Roman Catholic, and an officer in the service of France, called on Henry Levi, or Lewis, a Hamburg merchant, in mistake for Erasmus Lewis. In consequence a rumour spread abroad, and the Whigs made the most of it, that Erasmus Lewis was in correspondence with the Court of St. Germains. Swift, to clear his friend of the charge, composed a paper (*post*, 31 Jan., 1 Feb.), which appeared in *The Examiner* for 30 Jan.–2 Feb. 1712–13. The paper was reprinted in the works as 'A Complete Refutation of the Falsehoods alleged against Erasmus Lewis, Esq.' (*Prose Works*, v. 227–35). See further Boyer's *Political State*, v. 46–58. James Drummond, 1648–1716, fourth Earl of Perth, who had held high office in Scotland, followed the fortunes of the exiled king, and died at St. Germains. John Drummond, *c.* 1650–1715, second son of the third Earl of Perth, was created Earl of Melfort by James II in 1686, and Duke of Melfort at St. Germains.

8 Underlined.   9 Baron Hay (p. 450 n.[31]).

10 'young' struck out before 'Daughter'.

thy kept me & some others till past 12, so yr may be
sure tis late as they say; We have now stronger Suspicions
that the D. D'aumonts House was sett on fire by malice.
I was to day to see Ld Keeper, who has quite lost his Voice
with a Cold, there Dr Ratcliff told me, that it was the
Ambassdrs Confectionr sett the House on fire by boiling
Sugar, & going down & letting it boyl over; yet others
still think differently, so I know not what to judge. ⌈Nite
my own dearest Md. rove pdfr.⌉

28. I was to day at Court, where the Span. Ambassdr
talked to me as if he did not suspect any design[11] in burning D'Aumont's House, but the Abbè[12] Gautier, Secrty for
France here, sd quite otherwise: & that D'Aumont had a
Letter the very same day to let him know his[13] House
should be burnd and thy tell severall other Circumstances
too tedious to write: one is that a fellow mending the
Tiles just when the fire broke out, saw a Pot with wild
fire in the room. I dined with Ld Orkney; neithr Ld
Abercorn nor Selkirk will now speak with me I have dis-
obliged both sides. ⌈Nite dear Md.⌉

29. Our Society mett to day, 14 of us,, and at[14] a
Tavern, We now resolve to meet, but once a fortnight,
and have a Commttee every other week of 6 or 7, to consult about doing some good. I proposed anothr Message
to Ld Tr by 3 principall Membrs to give 100 Guinneas
to a certain Person, & they are to urge it as well as they
can; We also raised 60 Guinneas upon our own Society;
but I made them do it by Sessers,[15] and I was one of them,
& we fitted our Tax to the severall Estates; the D. Ormd
pays 10 Guinneas, & I the 3d part of a Guinnea; at that
Rate they may tax as often as they please. Well; but I
must answer ⌈oo Rettle ung oomens⌉ not yet; tis ⌈rate⌉
now, and I can't tind it. ⌈Nite deelest Md.⌉

---

[11] A small obliteration before 'design'.   [12] Wrongly accented.
[13] 'his' above the line. Swift first wrote 'te'.
[14] After 'at' Swift first wrote 'te', effaced this, and wrote 'a'.
[15] Assessors.

30. I have drank Spaw Waters this 2 or 3 days; but they do not pass, and mak me very giddy: I an't well ⌐fais,⌐ I'll take them no more; I sauntrd aftr Church with the Provost[16] to day to see a Library to be sold, and dined at 5 with Ld Orkney. We still think there was malice in burnig D'Aumonts house. I hear little Harrison is come over; it was he I sent to Utrecht; He is now Queens Secretary to the Ambassy; and[17] has brought with him the Barrier Treaty as it is now corrected by us; and yielded to by the Dutch; which was the greatest difficulty to retard the Peace. I hope he will bring over the Peace a month hence; for we will send him back as soon as possible; I long to see the little Brat; my own Creature; his pay is in all a thousand Pounds a Year, & they have never pd him a Groat, though[18] I have teazed their Hearts out. He must be 3 or 4 hundred Pounds in debt at least, the Brat. Let me go to ⌐bed sollahs; Nite dee richar Md.⌐

31. Harrison was with me this morning, we talked 3 hours, and then I carryed him to Court. When we went down to the door of my Lodging; I found a Coach waited for him, I chid him for it, but he whispered me, it was impossible to do otherwise; and in the Coach he told me[19] had not one farthing in his Pocket to pay it; and therefore took the Coach for the whole day, and intended to borrow money somewhere or other, So there was the Queens Minister, entrusted in Affairs of greatest Importance, without a Shilling in his Pocket to pay a Coach. I payd him while he was with me 7 Guinneas, in part of a dozen of Shirts he bought me in Holland. I presented him to the D. Ormd, & sevrall Lds at Court. And I contrivd it so, that Ld Treasr came to me & asked[20] (I had Parnel by

---

[16] Dr. Pratt.

[17] A small obliteration before 'and'.

[18] Swift wrote 'though' twice, once at the end of a line, and again at the beginning of the next. The former is struck out.

[19] 'he' omitted.

[20] 'whethr', before the words within parentheses, struck out.

me) whethr that was Dr Parnel, and came up and spoke to him with great kindness, & invited him to his House. I value my self upon making the Ministry desire to be acquainted with Parnel; & not Parnel with the Ministry; His Poem is almost fully corrected, and shall soon be out. Here's enough for to day, onely to tell you, that I was in the City with my Printer to alter an Examiner about my Friend Lewis's Story, which will be told with Remarks. ⌐Nite Md.¬

Febr. 1. I could do nothig till to day about the Examinr; but the Printer came this morning, and I dictated to him what was fitt to be sd, and then Mr Lewis came and correctd as he would have it. So I was neither at Church nor Court. D. Ormd & I dined at Ld Orkney's. I left them at 7, and sate with Sr. A. Fountain, who has a very bad sore Leg; for wch he designs to go to France. ⌐Fais¬ here's a Week gone, and one side of this Letter not finished. oh, but I write now but once in 3 weeks; ⌐iss fais¬, this shall go sooner. The Parlmt is to sitt on the 3d but will adjourn for 3 or 4 days: for the Qu— is layd up with the Gout. and both Speakers out of order, thô one of them the Ld Keepr is almost well. I spoke to D. Ormd a good deal about Ireld; we do not altogethr agree, nor am I judge enough of Irish Affairs; but I will speak to Ld Tr— to morrow, that we 3 may settle them some way or other. ⌐Nite sollahs both, rove pdfr.¬

2. I had a Lettr some days ago from Mol Geree, her name is now Wigmore,[21] & her Husbd is turned Parson, she desires nothing but that I would get Ld Keepr to give him a Living, but I will send her no answer, thô she desires it much, she still makes mantuas at Farnham. It raind all this day; & Dilly came to me, and was coaching

[21] Mary Geree, a sister of the Rev. John Geree (p. 533 n.[12]). The clergyman, Wigmore, whom she married, cannot be identified. The matriculation record of Trinity College, Dublin, reveals a William Wigmore, sizar 9 Jan. 1700–1, aged 20, who graduated B.A. in 1705. Whether he proceeded to ordination is in doubt.

it into the City, so I went with[22] him for a shaking, because
it would not cost me a Farthing; thus I mett my Friend
Stratford the Merchant, who is going abroad to gathr up
his Debts, & be clear in the World. he beggd me I would
dine with some Merchant friends of ours there, because
it was the last time I should see him, so I did, & thought
to have seen Ld Treasr in the Evening; but he happend
to go out at 5, so I visited some Friends, and came home.
and now I have the greatest part of your Lettr to answer;
& yet I will not to it to night, say what ⌜oo⌝ please. The
Parlmt meets to morrow, but will be prorogued for a fortnight,[23] which disappointmt will, I believe vex abundance
of them though they are not whigs; For they are forced
to be in Toun at Expence for nothing. But we want an
answer from Spain, before we are sure of every thing right
for the Peace; and God knows whethr we can have that
Answer this Month. It is a most ticklish juncture of
Affairs; We are always driving to an Inch. I am weary of
it. ⌜Nite Md.⌝

3. The Parlnt mett & was prorogued as I sd; and I
found some cloudy faces, & heard some grumbling. We
have got over all our Difficultyes with France, I think.
They have now settled all the Articles of Commerce
between us and them, wherein they were very much
disposed to play the Rogue if we had not held them to,
and this Business we wait from Spain is to prevent some
other Roguerys of the French, who are finding an Evasion
to trade to the Spanish West Indyes, but I hope, we shall
prevent it; I dined with Ld Treasr, and he was in good
humor enough. I gave him that Part of my Book in

22 'with' written twice. The first struck out.
23 The French ministers, trusting to dissensions among the allies, were
now attempting to obtain better terms than they had recently been prepared to accept. Furthermore, the Pretender, despite English insistence,
was still on French territory. The postponement of the meeting of Parliament was due to the uncertainty of the situation. See Stanhope's *Queen
Anne*, 1889, ii. 281 ff.

manuscript to read, where his Character was, and drawn pretty freely;[24] he was reading & correcting it with his Pencil, when the Bp of St Davids (now removing to Hereford) came in, & interrupted us; I left him at 8. & satt till 12 with the Provost, & Bp of Cl. at the Provost's ⌐Nite Md.⌐

4. I was to day at Court, but kept out of Ld Trr's way, because I was engagd to the D. Ormd, where I dined, and I think eat and drank too much. I sate this Evenig with Ldy Masham, & then with Ld Masham & Ld Treasr at Ld Mashams: it was last year, you may remembr, my constant evening Place. I saw Ldy Jersey[25] with Ldy Masham, who has been laying out for my Acquaintance, and has forced a Promise for me to drink Chocolate with her in a day or two, which I know not whether I shall perform, (I have just mended my Pen you see)[26] for I do not much like her Character, but she is very malicious, and therefore I think I must keep fair with her. I can not send this Letter till Saterday next I find. So I will answer oors now. I see no different days of the Month; yet it is dated Janr. 3d, so it was long a coming.—I did not write to Dr Coghill that I would have nothing in Ireld; but that I was solliciting nothing any where, & that is true: I have named Dr Stearn to Ld Tr, Ld Bolingbr and D. Ormd for a Bishoprick: and I did it heartily; I know not what will come of it; but I tell you as a great Secret, that I have made D. Ormd promise me to recommend nobody till he tells me; and this for some Reasons too long to mention. My head is still in no good Order, I am heartily sorry for ⌐pooppt⌐ I am sure; ⌐her⌐ head is good for ⌐sumsing.⌐[27] I'll answer more to mo⌐llow. Nite . . . . dee Sollahs Md.⌐[28]

[24] See Appendix IV.

[25] p. 618 n.[43] The dowager Lady Jersey. Swift was probably already acquainted with the wife of the second Earl, with whom Bolingbroke was on friendly terms.

[26] A change in the character of the writing is apparent.

[27] Forster reads 'something'. Either reading is doubtful.

[28] Badly obliterated. All readings are doubtful.

5. I must go on with ⌐oo⌐ Letter. I dined to day with
Sr A. Fountain, & Provost & I playd at Ombre with him
all the afternoon, I wone yet Sr Andrw is an admirable
Player. Ld Pembroke came in, & I gave him 3 or 4
scurvy Dilly-Puns, that begin with an *if*.[29] Well but oor
letter; well, ret me see. No, I believe I shall write no more
this good while; nor publish what I have done.—⌐Maram
ppt . . . oo . . . .⌐[30] I did not suspect ⌐oo⌐ would tell
Filby. ⌐oo⌐ are so ⌐. . . . .⌐[31] Turns and Visitations, what are those; Ill preach & visit as much for
Mr. Walls.—Pray God mend poopts Health, mine is but
very indifferent; I have left Spaw-water: it[32] makes my
leg swell. ⌐Nite deelest Md⌐.
   6. This is the Qu—'s birthday, and I never saw it
celebrated with so much Luxry, and fine Cloaths, I went
to Court to see them; & I dined with Ld Keeper, where
the Ldyes were fine to admiration; I passt the Evenig at[33]
Mrs Vanhomrighs, and came home pretty early; to
answer ⌐oo⌐ Rettle again. Pray Gd keep the Qu— she
was very ill about ten days ago, & had the Gout in her
Stomach; when I came from Ld Keeprs, I calld at Ld
Treasrs, because I heard he was very fine, and that was
a new Thing; & it was true, for his Coat & Wastcoat
were embroyderd. I have seen the Provost, often since,
& never spoke to him to speak to the Temples about
Daniel Corr[34], nor will; I don't care to do it. I have writt
lately to Parvisol. ⌐Oo⌐ did well to let him make up his
Accounts.. All things grow dear in Ireld but Corn to the
Paasons. For my Livings are fallen much this Year by
Parvisol's Account. ⌐Nite dee logues.⌐

[29] Underlined.
[30] Forster reads, 'Nauty Ppt, oo are vely tempegant'. But the first word
is certainly 'Maram'; and the word which Forster reads 'vely' looks more
like 'only'.
[31] Forster reads, 'recise; not to oor health'. The first word is most
unlikely. The last four may be 'How is oo health?', as Moorhead suggests;
but even this is doubtful.   [32] A small obliteration before 'it'.
[33] A small obliteration before 'at'.   [34] Unidentified.

7 [?8.]³⁵ I 'was at Court to day, but saw no Birthday Cloaths, the great Folks never wear them above once or twice I dined with Ld Orkney: and sate the Evening with Sr A. Fountain, whose Leg is in a very dubious Condition. Pray let me know when ⌐Dd's⌐ money is near due; allways let me know it before hand; this I believe will hardly go till Saturday; for I tell you what: being not very well, I dare not study much; so I let Company come in a morning; & the afternoon pass in dining & sitting some where. Ld Tr— is angry if I dont dine with him every 2d day; & I cannot part with him till late; he kept me last night till near 12. Our Weathr is constant rain above these 2 Months, which hinders walking, so that our Spring is not like yours. I have not seen Fanny Manly yet. I cannot find time. I am in rebellion with all my Acquaintance; but I will mend with my Health and the Weather:—Cloghr make a Figure! Cloghr make a —— Colds; why we have been all dying with Colds, but [now]³⁶ they are a little over, & my Second is almost off. I can do nothing for Swanton indeed. Tis a thing impossible, and wholly out of my way; if he buys he must buy. So now I have answrd oo Rettle, and there's an end of that now: and I'll say no more but bid ⌐oo Nite dee Md.⌐

8. [?9] It was terrible rainy to day from morning till night. I intendd to have dined with Ld Treasr; but went to see Sr A. Fountain, & he kept me at dinner, which saved Coachhire, &³⁷ stayd with him all the afternoon, & lost 13s-6d at Ombre, there was managmt, & Ld Tr will chide, but I'll dine with.him to morrow: Bp Cl's

³⁵ Between this date and the 12th (see entry for the latter date) a day was somewhere dropped. The 6th was correctly dated, for 6 Feb. was the Queen's birthday. The figures in square brackets are probably correct. Presumably Swift missed writing up the Journal on Saturday, the 7th. On 7 [?8] he speaks of being at Court, a Sunday habit; and, further, refers to the unlikelihood of sending away the letter 'till Saturday'. The letter was dispatched on Saturday the 14th.
³⁶ Former reading. The paper is torn and mended.
³⁷ 'I' omitted.

Daughtr has been ill some days, and it proves the Small Pox, she is very full, but it comes out well, & they apprehend no danger. Ldy Orkney has given me her Picture a very fine Originall of Sr Godfry Knellers it is now a mending. He has favored her squint admirably, & you know I love a Cast in the Eye; I was to see Ldy Worsley to day, who is just come to Toun, She is full of Rumatick pains, all my Acquaintance grow old & sickly. She lodges in the very house in Kingstreet³⁸ between St. James's Street & St. James square where Dd's Brothr³⁹ brought⁴⁰ the Sweetbread, when I lodged there, & ⌈Dd⌉ came to see me. Short ⌈sigh⁴¹ Nite Md.⌉

9. [?10.] I thought to have dined with Ld Tr to day, but he dined abroad at⁴² Tom Harley's. So I dined at Ld Masham's. and was winning all I had lost with playing with Ldy Masham at Crown Picket, when we went to Pools, & I lost it again. Ld Tr— came in to us, and chid me for not following him to Tom Harley's. Miss Ash is still the same, & they think her not in dangr: my man calls there daily; after I am gone out, and tells me at night.

---

³⁸ The word 'near' is scored out after 'Kingstreet'.

³⁹ Stella's brother, Edward, baptized 8 July 1688 (*Surrey Parish Register Society*, i. 85), 'died young abroad', according to a manuscript genealogy in a copy of Deane Swift's *Essay*, 1755, in the possession of Lord Rothschild. The reference is, therefore, to Rebecca Dingley's brother Robert, to whom in her will she left her watch and chain. Lady Louis Mountbatten has the original of letters (written on opposite sides of the same sheet of paper) from Stella and Rebecca Dingley, both dated 21 May 1723, addressed 'To Capt. Dingley in | Crown & Scepter Court | in St James's- | -Street. | London.' thanking him for money remittances. They both ask to be remembered to his wife. Lady Giffard left ten pounds to 'Mrs. Elizabeth Hamond (Dingley) who lived some time with me at Sheen.' She was 'the cousin who married her cousin Captain Dingley' (Julia Longe, *Martha Lady Giffard*, pp. 347, 351).

⁴⁰ Nichols, Scott, Ryland, and Aitken read 'bought'. Hawkesworth and Sheridan omit everything after 'sickly'. Forster and Moorhead correctly read 'brought'.

⁴¹ Forster reads 'Sighs', but the final 's' is questionable.

⁴² 'with' struck out before 'at'.

I was this morning to see Ldy Jersey,[43] & we have made twenty partyes about dining together, & I shall hardly keep one of them. She is reduced after all her greatness, to Seven Servants, and a small House; & no Coach: I like her tolerably as yet. ⌐Nite Md.⌐

10. [?11.] I made[44] visits this Morning, to the D. & Dutchess Ormd, & Ldy Betty,[45] & Dutchess Hamilton (when I was writing this near 12[46] a Clock the Dutchess Hamilton sent to have me dine with her to morrow, I am forced to give my answer thro the door, for my Man has got the Key, & is gone to bed; but I can not obey her, for our Society meets to morrow) I stole away from Ld Tr by 8, and intended to have passed the Evening with Sr Thomas Clarges[47] & his Ldy, but met them in anothr Place, & there have sate till now. my Head has not been ill to day; I was at Court, & made Ld Mansel walk with me in the Park before we went to dinner. yesterday & to day have been fair, but yet it rained all last night. I saw Stearne staring at Court to day; He has been often to see me he says; but my Man has not yet let him up; he is in deep mourning; I hope it is not for his Wife: I did not ask him. ⌐Nite Md.⌐

12.[48] I have reckond days wrong all this while for this is the 12, I don't know when I lost it I dined to day with our Society, the greatest dinner I have ever seen; it was at

---

[43] Swift refers to the Dowager Lady Jersey, widow of the first Earl (p. 345 n.[1]). He married, in 1681, Barbara, daughter of William Chiffinch, closet-keeper to Charles II. Upon his death she was left heavily in debt. (*Wentworth Papers*, p. 357). She was an active Jacobite, became a Roman Catholic, and died in Paris in 1735.

[44] A word is struck out before 'made' (? 'dined').

[45] Lady Betty Butler (p. 23 n.[46]), the Duchess of Ormonde's daughter.

[46] A small obliteration before '12'.

[47] Sir Thomas Clarges, 1688–1759, second Baronet of Aston, near Stevenage, married Barbara, youngest daughter of John Berkeley, fourth Viscount Fitzhardinge, by Barbara Villiers (p. 570 n.[12]), sister of Lady Orkney. He was M.P. for Lostwithiel 1713–15.

[48] The '12' is altered from '11'. See p. 616 n.[35]

Jack Hills the Governr of Dunkirk. I gave an Account of 60 Guineas I had collectd, & am to give them away to 2 Authors to morrow. and Ld Tr has promised us 100ll to reward some others. I found a Letter on my Table last night[49] to tell me that poor little Harrison the Queens Secrty that came lately from Utrecht with the Barrier Treaty was[50] ill & desired to [? see][51] me at Night but it was late & I could not go till to day.[52] I have often mentiond him in my Letters. you may remembr. ⌈. . . . . . .⌉[53] I went in the morning, & found him mighty ill, & got 30 Guineas for him from Ld Bolinbroke; & an order for a 100ll from the Treasury to be pd him to morrow. & I have got him removed to Knights bridge for Air. He has a Feavr & Inflammation on his Lungs; but I hope will do well. ⌈. . .⌉.

13. I was to see a poor Poet one Mr Diaper, in a nasty Garret, very sick; I gave him 20 Guineas from Ld Bolingbrok, &, disposed the othr 60 to 2 other Authors, & desird[54] a Friend to receive the 100ll for poor Harrison; and will carry it him to morrow morning. I sent to see how he did, & he is extreamly ill, & I very much afflicted for him, for he is my own Creature, & in a very honorable Post, and very worthy of it. I dined in the City. I am in much concern for this poor Lad. His Mothr & Sister attend him, & he wants nothing. ⌈Nite poo dee Md⌉[55]

14. I took Parnel this morning and we walkt to see poor Harrison, I had the 100ll in my Pocket. I told Parnel I was afraid to knock [at][56] the door; my mind misgave me.

---

49 'last night' is written between the lines above an obliteration.

50 Swift first wrote 'lyes', scrawled this over, and wrote 'was' above the line.

51 The sheet is worn.

52 Swift first wrote, 'but it is late & I can not go till to morrow', and corrected above the line.

53 Several words following 'remembr' are obliterated.

54 A small obliteration before 'desird'.

55 Forster reads: 'Nite Ppt, nite deelogues, Nite'.

56 The sheet is worn. The word may be 'at'.

I knockt, & his man in Tears told me his Master was dead an hour before. Think wht Grief th[is is]⁵⁷ to me; I went to his Mothr, & have been ordering things for his Funerall with as little Cost as possible, to morrow at ten at night. Ld Treasr was much concernd when I told him. I could not dine with Ld Tr nor any where, but got a bit of meat towards Evening. no loss ever grieved⁵⁸ me so much. poor Creature.—Pray Gd Almighty bless poor ⌈Md⌉—adieu—

> I send this away to night
> and am sorry it must go while
> I am in so much Grief.

Address: To Mrs Dingley, att her
Lodgings over against St Mary's
Church near Capel-street
Ireland   Dublin

Postmark: $\dfrac{\text{FE}}{17(?)}$

Endorsed by   59.
Rebecca Dingley: Febr. 26

LETTER LX

60. [SUNDAY]   London, Febr. 15¹

I dined to day with Mr Row and a Projector, who has been teazing me wit 20 Scheams, to get Grants, and I don't² like one of them. and besides I was out of humor for the Loss of poor Harrison. at ten this night³ I was at his Funerall, wch I orderd to be as private as possible, we

---

⁵⁷ The sheet is worn.

⁵⁸ A word or two obliterated before 'grieved'.

¹ The year '1712–13', is omitted.

² The word 'don't' is written twice, at the end of a line and the beginning of the next. The first is struck out.

³ At this time funerals commonly took place at night.

had but one Coach, with 4 of us, and when it was carrying us home after the Funerall the Braces broke, and we were forced to sitt in it and have it held up, till my Man went for chairs,[4] at 11 at night, in terrible rain. I am come home very melancholy;[5] and will go to bed. ⌐Nite my .... Md.⌐[6]

16. I dined to day with Ld Dupplin, & some company to divert me, but left them early, & have been reading a foolish book for amusement—I shall never have courage again to care for making any body's Fortune. The Parlnt meets to morrow, and will be prorogued anothr fortnight; at wch sevrall of both Partyes are angry; but it cannot be helped, though every thing about the Peace is past all danger I never saw such a Continuance of rainy weathr, we have not had 2 fair days together these 10 weeks. I have not dined with Ld Tr these 4 days, nor can till Saterday, for I have severall engagements till then, & he will chide me to some purpose.. I am perplexed with this 100ll of poor Harrisons, wht to do with it, I cannot pay his Relations till they administer, for he is much in debt; but I will have the Staff[7] in my own hands; and venture nothing. ⌐Nite poo dee Md⌐.

17. Lady Jersey & I dined by Appointmt to day with Ld Bolinbr— He is sending his Brothr[8] to succeed Mr. Harrison; It is the prettyest Post in Europe for a young Gentleman I lose my money at Ombre sadly; I make a

---

4 As Aitken points out, sedan chairs were still something of a novelty.

'Coaches and Chariots yet unfashion'd lay,
Nor late invented Chairs perplex'd the Way.'
(Gay's *Trivia*, i. 103–4).

5 See *Wentworth Papers*, p. 320: 'Poor Mr. Harrison is very much lamented; he died last Saturday. Dr. Swift told me . . . he owed about £300, and the Queen owed him £500.'

6 Forster reads: 'Nite MD, my own deelest MD Ppt.'

7 He is thinking of the Lord Treasurer's staff.

8 George St. John, half-brother of Bolingbroke, who was an only son by his father's first wife. George became secretary to the English plenipotentiaries at Utrecht. He died at Venice, Jan. 1715–16.

thousand Blunders, I play putt[9] threepenny Ombre, but it is wht you call running Ombre—Lady Clarges & a drab I hate, won a dozin shillings of me last night. The Parlnt was prorogud to day, and people grumble. & the good of it is, the Peace can not be finished by the Time they meet; there are so many fidlig things to do.—Is ⌐Ppt⌐ an Ombre Lady yet. you know all the Tricks of it now I suppose. I reckon you have all your Cards from France; for ours pay 6 pence a Pack taxes,[10] wch goes deep to the Box. I have given away all my Spaw water, and take some nasty steel drops, & may[11] head has been bettr this week past. I send every day to see how Miss Ash does; she is very full they say, but in no danger. I fear she will lose some of her Beauty; The son lyes out of the House. I wish he had them too, while he is so young. ⌐Nite Md.⌐

18. the Earl of Abingdon[12] had been teazing me these 3 Months to dine with him, & to day was appointd about a week ago; and I named my Company, Ld Stawell,[13] Coll Disney, & Dr Arbuthnott; but the 2 last slippt out their Necks & left Stawel and me to dine there. we did not dine till 7, because it is Ashwednesday, we had nothing

[9] Hawkesworth, Sheridan, Nichols, Scott, Aitken, print 'but, and Ryland takes the word in that sense. 'Putt', however, was the name of an old card game resembling nap. Swift uses the word as a pejorative, describing the standard of ombre he played.

[10] A duty was first levied on cards in England in 1615, at the rate of five shillings a gross of packs. In 1710, as one means of raising money for the war, the rate was raised to sixpence a pack.

[11] i.e. 'my'.

[12] Montagu Bertie, second Earl of Abingdon, who succeeded to the title in 1699. He held a number of important positions—Constable and Lord Lieutenant of the Tower of London, 1702-5; twice Lord Lieutenant of Oxfordshire, 1702-5, 1712-15; and, on the death of Queen Anne, was nominated one of the Lords Justices, Regents of the Realm. He died in 1743.

[13] William Stawel, c. 1683-1742, third Baron Stawel of Somerton. He had been Gentleman of the Bedchamber to George, Prince of Denmark. Cf. p. 136 n.[76]

but Fish, which Ld Stawel could not eat, and gott a broyld leg of a Turkey. Our wine was Poison; yet the Puppy has 12 thousd pd a year. His Carps were raw, & his Candles tallow. I[14] shall not catch me again in hast, and every body has laughd at me for dining with him. I was to day to let Harrisons mothr know I coud not pay her till she administers, wch she will do; I belive she is ⌐an old Bawd⌐ & her Daughter ⌐a —— ⌐.[15] There were more whigs to day at Court than Toryes; I believe they think the Peace must be made, and so come to please the Qu.—She is still lame with the Gout. ⌐Nite Md.⌐

19. I was at Court to day to speak to Ld Bolinbroke to look over Parnels Poem since it is correctd, & Parnel & I dined with him to day & he had shewn him 3 or 4 more Places to alter a little. Ldy Bolinbr— came down to us while we were at dinner, & Parnel stared at her as if she were a Goddess. I thought she was like Parnels wife; & he thought so too. Parnel is much pleased with Ld Bolinbrs favor to him, & I hope it may one day turn to his Advantage. His Poem will be printed in a few days. Our Weather continues as fresh raining as if it had not rained at all. I sate to night at Ldy Masham's where Ld Tr— came, and scolded me for not dining with him, I told him I could not till Saterday. I have staid there till past 12. So ⌐Nite dee sollahs Md.⌐

20. Ldy Jersey, Ldy Catherine Hide, the Spanish Ambasdr,[16] the Duke d'Atree[17] anothr Spaniard, & I, dined

[14] A slip for 'He'.

[15] Hawkesworth and Sheridan omit all words between 'do' and 'There'. Nichols, Scott, and Forster read the obliterated words descriptive of the mother as, 'an old devil'. Ryland has 'an old bitch'; but the scrawl seems to cover the words 'an old Bawd', the reading also of Aitken and Moorhead. Of the daughter Swift contented himself with writing that she was 'a ——'. Forster alone, but without the slightest justification, succeeds in deciphering, 'no better'.

[16] Monteleon.

[17] Victor Marie, 1660–1737, duc d'Estrées, served with distinction both by land and sea, and in 1703 he received a marshal's baton from

to day by appointment with Ld Bolinbrok, but thy fell a drinking so many Spanish Healths in Champagne, that I stole away to the Ladyes, and drank Tea, till 8, and then went and lost my money at Ombre with Sr A. Fountain, who has a very bad Leg: Miss Ash is past all danger, and her Eye which was lately bad (I suppose one Effect of her distemper) is now better. I do not let the Bishop see me, nor shll this good while. Good luck, when I came home I warrant I found a Letter from ⌜Md⌝ N. 38. and ⌜oo⌝ write so small now ⌜a days⌝ I hope ⌜oo poor eyes are better.⌝ Well, this shll go to morrow sennight, with a Bill for ⌜Md⌝.—I will speak to Mr Griffin to morrow about ⌜ppt⌝ Brothr, Filby, and desire, whethr he deserves or no, that his Employmt may be mended; that is to say if I can see Griffin, otherwise not. & I'll answr ⌜oo Rettle hen I Pdfr⌝ think fitt—⌜Nite Md⌝.

21. Mesinks I writt a little sawcy last night, I mean ⌜te last words God . . .⌝[18] I saw Griffin at Court, he says he knows nothing of a salt work at Recton,[19] but that he will give Filby a better Employmt, & desires Filby will write to him; If I knew how to write to Filby I would; but pray do you: bid him make no mention of you; but only let Mr. Griffin know, that he had had the honr to be recommended by Dr S— &c, that he will endeavr to deserve &c; and if you dictated a whole Letter for him it would be bettr; I hope he can write & Spell well. I'll enquire for a direction to Griffin before I finish this. I dined with Ld Treasr, & 7 Lords to day; you know Saturday is his great day; but I sat with them[20] alone till 8, & then came home,

Louis XIV. In his leisure he cultivated literature and science, and amassed a large library and a varied collection of statuary and objects of art. A comma should follow 'd'Atree'; the duc d'Estrées was a French nobleman.

[18] Hawkesworth and Sheridan begin the entry at 'I saw Griffin'. Nichols, Scott, Ryland, and Aitken decipher the first two of the obliterated words only—'te last'. The next two are, apparently, 'words (? word) God'. To these Forster adds ' 'give me''; but this is certainly wrong.

[19] The situation is doubtful.

[20] Apparently a slip for 'him'.

and have been writing a Lettr to Mrs Davis[21] at York, she took care to have a Lettr delivred for me at Ld Tr's, for I would not own one she sent by Postt: She reproaches me for not writing to her these 4 Years; & I have honestly told her, it was my way never to write to those whom I never am likely to see, unless I can serve them, wch I cannot her &c. Davis the Schoolmastrs Widow. ⌐Nite Md.⌐

22. I dined to day at Ld Orkneys with D. Ormd & Sr T. Hanmer; have you ever heard of the latter. He marryed the Dutchess of Grafton in his Youth (she dind with us too) he is the most considerabl Man in the H. of Commons, He went last Spring to Flanders with D. Ormd, from thence to France, & was going to Italy, but the Ministry sent for him, & he has been come over about ten days. He is much out of Humor with things, he thinks the Peace is kept off too long; & is full of Fears and doubts. It is thought he is designed for Secrty of State[22] instead of Ld Dartmouth. We have been acquainted these 2 years, and I intend in a day or two to have an Hours talk with him on Affairs. I saw Bp Cloghr at Court; Miss is recovering, I know not how much she will be marked. The Qu— is slowly mending of her Gout, & intends to be brought in a Chair to Parlnt when it meets. wch will be Mar. 3, for I suppose they will prorogue no more; yet the Peace will not be signed then; & we apprehend the Toryes themselves will many of them be discontented. ⌐Nite dee Md⌐.

23. It was ill weath to day, & I dind with Sr A.

21 The widow of the Rev. Peter Davys, master of the school attached to St. Patrick's Cathedral, who died in 1698. She was an occasional correspondent of Swift's, but no letter has been preserved. Her death took place at Cambridge (where for some time she kept a coffee-house) in 1732 (*Corresp.* i. 382–3; iv. 361 n., 383–4). She was the author of various plays and novels. See *D.N.B.*, which, however, requires correction. It is possible that Swift may have visited Mrs. Davys at York in May 1709. See *Prose Works of Swift*, ed. Herbert Davis, ii, p. xxix and note.

22 Hanmer was not made Secretary of State. In 1714 he was, for a short time, Speaker of the House of Commons.

Fountain, & in the Evenig playd at Ombre with him & the Provost, & won 25 shillings, so I have recovered my self pretty well. Dilly has been dunning me to see Fanny Manley, but I have not yet been able to do it. Miss Ash is now quite out of danger, and they hope will not be much marked. I can not tell how to direct to Griffin, I think he lives in Bury Street near St James's Street, hard by me; but I suppose your Brothr may direct to him to the Salt Office and as I remembr he knows his Christian name because you sent it me in the list of the Commissioners. ⌈Nite dee Md.⌉23

24. I walkd this morning to Chelsea to see Dr. Atterbury Dean of Christ-church. I had business with him about entering Mr Fitsmorris24 My Ld Kerry's son into his Colledge, & Lady Kerry is a great Favorite of mine. Ld Harley, Ld Dupplin Young Bromly the Speakers son,25 and I dined with Dr Stratford and some othr Clergymen, but I left them at 7, to go to Ldy Jersey to see Monteleon the Span. Ambassdr play at Ombr. Ldy Jersey was abroad, & I chid the Servants, and made a Rattle, but since I came home, she sent me a Message, that I was mistaken, & that the meeting is to be to morrow. I have a worse memory than when I left you, and every day forget Appointments, but here my memory was by chance too good. But I'll go to morrow, for Ldy Kath. Hide & Ldy Bolinbroke are to be there by my Appointmt, and I tifted26 up my Perewig

---

23 Obliterated, and (lower right-hand corner of the leaf) paper thumbed. Reading of previous editors followed.

24 William Fitzmaurice (p. 122 n.24), Lord Kerry's eldest son, entered Christ Church, Oxford, matriculating on 10 Mar. 1712-13.

25 William Bromley, 1699?-1737, second son of Bromley, Speaker of the House of Commons. In 1727 he was elected M.P. for the borough of Warwick, and in 1737, shortly before his death, for the University of Oxford.

26 Hawkesworth and Sheridan close the entry for the day at 'appointment'. Nichols, Scott, Forster, and Aitken read 'listed'; and Aitken has a note attempting to explain the meaning of the word in this context. Ryland hesitates between 'listed' and 'lifted'. But the word is, as Moorhead reads

and all, to make a Figure; Well. who ⌐tan help it. not I. vow˥ to ⌐. . . . Nite Md.˥[27]

25. Ld Tr met me last night at Ld Mashams, & thanked me for my company in a Jear because I had not dind with him in 3 days; He chides if I stay but two days away togethr. what will this come to——nothing. My Grandmothr usd to say, More of your Lining, and less of your dining. Howevr I dind with him, & could hardly leave him at 8 to go[28] Ldy Jerseys, wher 5 or 6 foreign Ministers were, & as many Ldys. Monteleon playd like the English, & cryed gacco,[29] and knocked his Knuckles for Jump;[30] and playd at smell-Games[31] like ⌐Ppt.˥ Ldy Jersey whisperd me to stay & sup with the Ldys when the Fellows were gone, but thy playd till 11, and I would not stay;—I think this Lettr must go on Saterday thts certain, & it is not half full yet. Ldy Katherine Hide had a mighty mind I shoud be acquainted with Ldy Dalkeith her Sister, the D. of Monmouths eldest son's Widow;[32]

it, 'tifted'. 'Tiff' or 'tift', a dialectical word, meant to brush up, smarten, 'tittivate'.

[27] Obliterated, except for the word 'to', but not difficult to decipher save for one word, which Nichols, Scott, and Ryland read 'Heaven'. The obliteration does not, however, support this too obvious guess.

[28] 'to' omitted.

[29] The word, as editors read, certainly looks like 'gacco', whatever that may mean. Moorhead conjectures that it may merely be 'game' badly written.

[30] All editors, before Moorhead, read 'trump'; but the word is certainly 'Jump', and may possibly have been used in the sense of 'Pass'.

[31] Editors before Moorhead read 'small games'; but the first word looks more like 'smell', and there is a distinct hyphen between the two. It is possible also that in the advice 'don't play small games when you lose' (*ante*, 13 Dec. 1710), the word 'small' should have been read 'smell'. The original is there lacking. The meaning, lost to us, was, presumably, clear to Stella and Rebecca Dingley.

[32] Lady Henrietta Hyde, *c.* 1677–1730, second daughter of Laurence Hyde, first Earl of Rochester (p. 84 n.[25]), was married in 1694 to James Scott, Earl of Dalkeith, son of the Duke of Monmouth. Lord Dalkeith died in 1705. Lady Catherine Hyde (p. 476 n.[8]) was younger sister of Lady Dalkeith, who is described by Evelyn as 'one of the wittiest and craftiest of her sex'.

who[33] was of the Company to night; but I did not like her, she paints too much. ⌈Nite Md.⌉

26. This day our Society met at the D. Ormnd's but I had Business tht calld me anothr way, so I sent my Excuses, and dind privately with a Friend. Besides Sr T. Hanmer whisprd me last night at Ldy Jersey's that I must attend Ld Tr and D. Ormd at Supper at his House to night, which I did at 11 and stayd till 1. so ⌈oo⌉ may be sure tis late enough there was the Dutchess of Grafton, & the Duke her son,[34] nine of us in all. D. Ormd chid me for not[35] beig at Society to day, & sd 16 was there; I sd I never knew 16 People good Company in my Life; no ⌈fais⌉ nor 8 neither.—We have no news in this Town at all; I wonder why I don't write you news: I know less of what passes than any body; because I go to[36] no Coffee House, nor see any but Ministers and such People, and Ministers never talk Politicks in Conversation; the Whigs are forming great Schemes against the meeting of Parlmt, wch will be next Tuesday I still think, without fail. and we hope to hear by then, tht the Peace is ready to sign; the Qu—'s Gout mends daily. ⌈Nite Md⌉—

27. I passed a very insipid day, and dined privately with a Friend in the Neighborhood, did I tell you, tht I have a very fine Picture of Ldy Orkney,[37] an Originall by Sr Godfry Kneller, 3 quarters length. I have it now at home with a fine Frame. Ld Bolingbr— & Ldy Masham have promised to sit for me, but I despair of Ld Tr, onely

[33] A slight obliteration before 'who'.

[34] Charles Fitzroy, 1683–1757, second Duke.

[35] A slight obliteration before 'not'.

[36] Swift first wrote 'frequent', struck this through, and wrote 'go to' above the line.

[37] This portrait, described in Swift's will as 'the half-length picture of the late Countess of Orkney in the drawing-room' (*Prose Works*, xi. 414), was bequeathed to John, fifth Earl of Orrery, author of the famous *Remarks on the Life and Writings of Dr. Jonathan Swift*, 1752. Orrery married in 1728, as his first wife, Henrietta, third and youngest daughter of Lady Orkney.

I hope he will give me a Copy, and then I shall have all the Pictures of those I really love here; just half a dozen. onely I'll make Ld Keepr give me his Print in a frame: this Lettr must go to morrow, because of sending Me a Bill, else it shuld not till next week, I assure ⌐oo⌐. I have little to do now with my Pen; for my grand Business[38] stops[39] till they are more pressing, and till something or othr happens, and I belive I shall return with disgust to finish it, it is so very laborious. Sr T. Hanmer has my Papers now.—And ⌐hat⌐[40] is ⌐Md⌐ doing now; oh, at Ombr with the Dean always on Friday night, with Mrs Walls, pray don't play at smell[41] Games. I stood by tothr night while the Duke d'Atree lost 6 times with malilio,[42] basto, and 3 small Trumps. and Ldy Jersey won above 2oll. ⌐Nite dee richr Md⌐.

28. I was at Court to day when the Abbè Gautier whisperd me that a Courier was just come with an Account tht the F. King had consentd to all the Qu—'s demands, and His Consent was carryed to Utrecht, and the Peace will be signed in a few days; I suppose the Genrll Peace cannot be so soon ready but that is no matter. The News presently ran about the Court. I saw the Qu carryed out in her Chair to take the Air in the Garden. I met Griffin at Court, & he told me, that Orders were sent to examine Filby, and if he be fitt, to make him (I think he calld it) an Assistant; I don't know what, Supervisor, I think; but it was some Emplymt a good deal bettr than his own. The Parlmt will have anothr short Prorogation, thô it is not known yet. I dined with Ld Treasr and his Saterday company, and left him at 8 to putt this into the Post Office

---

38 *The History of the Four Last Years of the Queen.*

39 The reading of all editors, although the word is doubtful. It may be 'stayes'.

40 i.e. 'what'.

41 The third letter is not so distinct here, and there is no hyphen; but the reading of 25 Feb. is followed.

42 Should be Manilio. For this term and Basto see p. 43 n.[35]

time enough. And now I must bid oo farewell ⌐deelest richr Md God bless ever ever, & rove pdfr¬—farewell ⌐Md Md Md FW FW FW FW Me Me—lele—lele—¬

Address: To Mrs Dingley, att her
    Lodgings over against St Mary's
    Church, near Capel-street
    Ireland   Dublin
Postmarks: Two. One imperfect. The other:
      MR
      ―――
      3
Endorsed by   60.
Rebecca Dingley: Mar. 7.

LETTER LXI

61. [SUNDAY]   Lond. Mar. 1. 1712–13

Tis out of my head whether I answerd all your Lettr in my last yesterday or no. I think I was in hast and could not but now I see I answerd a good deal of it, no, onely about your Brothr, and Me Bill. I dined with Ldy Orkney, and we talkt Politicks till 11 at night—and as usuall, found every thing wrong, & put our selves out of humor.—Yes I have Ldy G's[1] Picture, sent me by your Mothr; It is Boxed up at a Place where my other things are; I have goods in 2 or 3 Places; & when I leave a Lodging, I box up the Books I get (for I always get some) and come naked into a new Lodging; and so on—Talk not to me of Deanry's I know less of that than ever by much ⌐Nite Md¬.

2. I went to day into the City to see Pat Rolt, who lodges with a City Cozen, a daughter of Coz Cleve[2] (you are much the wiser) I had never been at her House before. My He Coz Tompson[3] the Butchr is dead or dying. I dined with my Printer, and walked home, and went to

---

[1] Giffard's.   [2] See p. 72 n.[30]   [3] See p. 72 n.[30]

sitt with Ldy Clarges, I found 4 of them at whist, Ldy
Godolphin⁴ was one. I sat by her, & talked of her Cards
&c, but she would not give one Look, nor say a word to
me. She refused some time ago to be acquainted with me.
You know, she is Ld Marlbroughs eldest Daughter. She
is a fool for her Pains, & I'll pull her down.——What
can⁵ I do for Dr Smiths daughters husband:⁶ I have no
personall Credit with any of the Commissnrs. I'll speak
to Keightly, but I believe it will signify nothing. in the
Customs people must rise by degrees; and he must at first
take what is very low, if he be qualifyed for that. ⌜Ppt⌝
mistakes me; I am not angry at your recommending any
one to me, provided you will take my Answer. Some things
are in my way; & then I serve those I can: But People will
not distinguish, but take things ill when I have no Power. .
but Ppt is wiser. And Employmts in genrll are very hard
to be got. ⌜Nite Md.⌝

3. I dined to day with Ld Tr; who chid me for my
absence, wch was onely from Saterday last. The Parlmt
was again prorogued for a week; and I suppose the Peace
will be ready by then, & the Qu— will be able to be
brought to the House, and make her Speech.—I saw Dr.
Griffith 2 or three Months ago at a Latin Play at Westminstr; but did not speak to him: I hope he will not dye.
I should be sorry for ⌜ppt's⌝ sake, He is very tender of
her. I have long lost all my Colds; and the weathr mends
a little—I take some steel drops; & my Head is pretty
well, & I walk when I can, but am grown very idle, and
not finishing my thing, I gamble⁷ abroad, & play at
Ombre. I shall be more carefull in my Physick than Mrs
Price;⁸ tis not a farthing matter her death, I think; and

---

4 Formerly Lady Rialton (p. 434 n.¹⁸).

5 A small obliteration before 'can'.

6 For Dr. Smith see p. 539 n.¹⁰ He had two daughters, Elinor De Butts
and Catherine Hawkins.

7 Apparently not merely a spelling, but intended as a pun on 'gambol'.

8 Perhaps the wife of 'Price of Galway', p. 288 n.²⁷

so I say no more to night, but will read a dull book and go sleep. ⌈Nite dee Md⌉.

4. Mr Ford has been this half year inviting me to dine at his Lodgings, so I did it to day & brought the Provost and Dr Parnel with me, & my Friend Lewis was their, Parnel went away, & the othr 3 playd at Ombre, & I lookt on;[9] wch I love; & would not play. Tisdal is a pretty fellow as you say; & when I come back to Ireld with nothing, he will condole with me with abundance of secret Pleasure. I believe I told you wht he writ to me, that I[10] have saved Engld, & he Ireld.[11] but I can bear that: I have learnt to hear and see and say nothing. I was to see Dutchess Hamilton to day. and met Blyth of Ireld just going out of her House into his Coach; I asked her how she come to receive young Fellows; It seems he had a Ball in D. Hamilton's House where[12] the D. dyed; and the Dutchess got an Advertismt put in the Post-boy reflecting on the Ball, because the Marlbrow daughtrs were there. and Blith came to beg the Dutchess's pardon, & clear himself; He's a sad dog. ⌈Nite poo dearest Md⌉.[13]

5. Ldy Masham has miscarryed but is well almost again. I have pd many Visits to day. . I met Blith at the D. of Ormd's & he beggd me to carry him to Dutchess Hamilton to beg her Pardon again. I did, on purpose to see how the Blunderbuss behaved himself; but I beggd the Dutchess to use him mercifully, for she is the devil of a Teazer. the good of it is; she ought to beg his Pardon, for he meant no Harm, yet she woud not allow him to put in an[14] Advertismt to clear himself from hers, thô hers was all A Lye.. he appealed to me & I gravely gave

---

9 A small obliteration before 'on'.

10 A small obliteration before 'I'.

11 With his pamphlet on the *Conduct of the Dissenters* (p. 584 n.⁷).

12 All editors before Moorhead read 'when', but the word is almost certainly 'where'.

13 The word 'dearest' is, apparently, correctly spelt.

14 'ad' obliterated before 'an'.

it against him. I was at Court to day; & the Forein
Ministers have got a Trick of employing me to speak for
them to Ld Tr & Ld Bolingbrok; which I do when the
Case is reasonable. the College need not fear, I will not
be their Governr.[15] I dined with Sr T. Hanmer & his
Dutchess; D. Ormd was there; but we parted soon, & I
went to visit Ld Pembroke for the first time; but it was
to see some curious Books. Ld Chomley came in; but I
would not talk to him tho he made many advances. I hate
the Scoundrel, for all he is your Griffiths friend.—Yes
yes, I am abused enough, if that be all. ⌐Nite sollahs⌐.

6.[16] I was to day at an auction of Pictures with Pratt,
& layd out 2ll 5s for a Picture of Titian, & if it were a
Titian it would be worth twice as many Pounds; if I am
cheatd I'll part with it to Ld Masham, if it be a bargain
I'll keep it my self; that's my Conscience. but I made
Prat[17] buy severall Pictures for Ld Masham; Prat is a
great Virtuoso that way. I dind with Ld Tr; but made him
go to Court, at 8, I allways teaze him to be gone. I thought
to have made Parnel dine with him but he was ill, his
Head is out of order like mine, but more constant, poor
boy. I was at Ld Tr's Levee, with the Provost, to ask a
Book for the Colledge: I[18] never go to his Levee unless
to present somebody:—for all oor Raillying ⌐Mrs Ppt⌐,
as hope ⌐savd⌐ I expected they would have decided about
me long ago; & as hope ⌐saved⌐, as soon as ever things
are given away, & I not provided for, I will be gone with
the very first Opportunity, & put up bag and Baggage.
But People are slower than can be thought. ⌐Nite Md.⌐

7. Yes I hope Leigh will soon be gone a P— on him.
I met him once, & he talked gravely to me of not seeing
the Irish Bps here & the Irish Gentlemen; but I believe

---

[15] Provost of Trinity College, Dublin.

[16] A letter of this date, 6 March, to Sir Andrew Fountaine, is preserved
(*Corresp.* ii. 12).

[17] Little more than a blurred symbol, but intended for 'Prat'.

[18] A slight obliteration before 'I'; and 'I' is written over another letter.

my Answers fretted him enough; I would not dine with
Ld Tr to day though it was Saterday, (for he has engaged
me for to morrow) but went and dine with Ld Masham;
& playd at Ombre 6 penny running Ombre for 3 hours,
there were 3 Voles[19] against me, & I was once a great
Loser, but came off for 3s-6d. one may easily lose 5
Guinneas at it. Ldy Orkney is gone out of Town to day:
and I could not see her for Lazyness; but writ to her.
She has left me some Physick.. ⌜Fais⌝ I never knew
⌜Md's⌝ Politicks before, and I think it pretty extrdy, &
a great Complment to you; & I believe never 3 People
conversed so much with so little Politicks. I avoid all
Conversation with the othr Party. it is not to be born, &
I am sorry for it, Oh yes things very dear. ⌜ppt⌝[20] must
come in at last with ⌜. .⌝[21] 2 Eggs a Penny, there the
Proverb was well applyed; Parvisol has sent me a Bill of
5oll. as I orderd him; wch I hope will serve me & bring
me over, pray Gd ⌜. . . .⌝[22] does not be delayd for it; but
I have had very little from him this long time. I was not
at Court to day. a Wonder ⌜Nite sollahs b . . . & . . .
Pdfr.⌝[23]

8. ⌜Oo⌝ must know, I give Chocolate almost every day,
to 2 or 3 People tht I suffr to come to see me in a morning.
My Man begins to lye pretty well. tis nothing for people
to be denyed ten times. My Man knows all I will see, and
denyes me to every body else. This is the day of the
Qu—'s coming to the Crown, & the day Ld Tr was

---

[19] A term used both in quadrille and ombre for the winning of all the
tricks.
[20] Obliterated; but 'ppt' decipherable. 'DD', the reading of Nichols,
Scott, Forster, Ryland, and Aitken is wrong.
[21] Obliterated, and undecipherable. Nichols, Scott, Forster, Ryland
(and Moorhead with hesitation) read 'her'; but if this were the word
there was no reason for its obliteration. Aitken ventures 'DD's'.
[22] Quite undecipherable, although Nichols, Scott, Ryland, Aitken read
'MD'.
[23] Obliterated and partly undecipherable. Forster hazards: 'Nite
Sollahs. Rove poo Pdfr'.

stabbd by Guiscard. I was at Court, where every body had their Birth-day Cloaths on, & I dined with Ld Treasr, who was very fine; He shewd me some of the Qu—'s Speech, wch I corrected in sevrall Places and penned the vote of Address of thanks for the Speech;[24] but I was of opinion the House should not sit on Tuesday next, unless they hear the Peace is signed. that is, provided they are sure it will be signed the Week after, and so have one Scolding for all. Nite Md.

9. Ld Tr would have had me dine with him to day, he desired me last night, but I refused; because he would not keep the day of his Stabbing, with al the Cabinet, as he intended. so I dined with my friend Lewis, & the Provost, & Parnel & Ford was with us; I lost 16s at Ombre,—I dont like it, as &c at Night Lewis brought me word that the Parlnt does not sit to morrow: I hope they are sure of the Peace by next week, and then they are right in my opinion, otherwise I think they have done wrong &[25] might have sate 3 weeks ago. People will grumble, but Ld Tr cares not a rush. Ld Keepr is suddenly taken ill of a Quinzy and some Lds are commission, I think Ld Trevor,[26] to prorogue the Parlmt in his Stead. You never saw a Town so full of Ferment & Expectation. Mr Pope[27] has publishd a fine Poem calld Windsor Forrest; read it. ⌈Nite.⌉

24 Swift makes further mention of the address of the House of Lords to the Queen under 15, 17 Mar. and 7 Apr. For the address see *Journals of the House of Lords*, xix. 515. For two drafts in Swift's hand among the Portland MSS., Welbeck Abbey, see Appendix V.

25 'wrong to' obliterated after '&'.

26 Editors prior to Aitken and Moorhead misread 'Trevor' as 'Treasurer'. Sir Thomas Trevor, Chief Justice of the Common Pleas, was one of the Queen's creation of twelve peers (p. 450 n.31). By commission of 9 Mar. 1712–13 he occupied the woolsack during the illness of Lord Keeper Harcourt. Bolingbroke (*Letter to Sir William Windham*, 1753, p. 63) described Trevor as 'one of the honestest men in Britain'.

27 This is the only mention of Pope in the *Journal*. *Windsor-Forest*, dedicated to Lord Lansdown, was published on 7 Mar. 1713. Its praise of the Tory peace adapted it to the political situation.

10. I was early this morning to see Ld Bolinbr— I find he was of Opinion the Parlnt should sitt; and says they are not sure the Peace will be signed next Week. the Prorogation is to this day Sennight. I went to look on a Library, I am going to buy, if we can agree; I have offerd 12oll., and will give ten more; Ld Boling— will lend me the money; I was two hours poring on the Books, I[28] will sell some of them & keep the rest; but I doubt thy won't take the money. I dined in the City, and sate an hour in the Evening with Ld Tr, who was in very good humor, but reproached me for not dining with him yesterday and to day. What will all this come to.—Ld Keepr had a pretty good night and is better, I was in pain for him. ⌐How do oo do sollahs, ... Md.⌐[29]

11. I was this morning to visit D. & Dutchess of Ormd; & Dutchess Hamilton; & went with the Provost to an Auction of Pictures, & Layd out fourteen shillings; I am in for it, if I had money, but I doubt I shall be undone; for Sr Andr Fountain invited the Provost and me to dine with him, & play at Ombre; where I fairly lost 14 Shillings; ⌐fais⌐ it won't do; and I shall be out of conceit with Play this good while; I am come home, & tis late, & my Puppy let out my Fire; & I am gone to bed; & writing there, & it is past twelve a good while. went out 4 Matidores[30] and a Trump in black, & was beasted, ⌐vely bad fais. Nite ny two dee logues Md.⌐[31]

12. I was at anothr Auction of Pictures to day, and a great Auction it was: I made Ld Masham lay out 4oll, there were Pictures sold of twice as much value a piece. Our Society met to day at the D. of Beauforts; a prodigious

---

[28] 'I' written twice, at the end of a line and the beginning of the next.

[29] Obliterated, and only decipherable in part. Forster reads: 'How do oo do, Sollahs? Rove Pdfr, poopdfr. Nite MD MD MD'. This is more than the space would contain, and much of it guesswork.

[30] p. 43 n.[35]

[31] Obliterated. Ryland and Aitken read 'deelest' for 'two dee'. Forster's reading is impossibly long.

fine dinner, which I hate; but we did some Business; our
Printer was to attend us as usuall, & the Chancellr of the
Exchequr sent the Authr of the Examiner[32] 20 Guinneas.
He is an ingenious fellow, but the most confounded vain
Coxcomb in the World; so that I dare not let him see me,
nor am acquainted with him. I had much discourse with
D. Ormd this morning, and am driving some Points to
⌐secure us all in case of Accidents &c⌐[33] I left the Society
at 7, I can't drink now at all with any Pleasure; I love
white Portugall wine better than Claret Champain or Burgundy: I have a sad vulgar appetite. I remembr ⌐Ppt⌐
used to maunder when I came from a great dinner, and
⌐Md⌐[34] had but a bit of Mutton: I cannot endure above
one dish; nor ever could since I was a Boy and loved
Stuffing. It was a fine day; wch is a rarity with us I assure,
never fair 2 days together. ⌐Nite Md.⌐

1 3. I had a Rabble of Irish Parsons this morning drinking my Chocolate. I cannot rememb Appointments: I
was to have suppd last night with the[35] Swedish Envoy at
his House, & some othr Company; but forgot it: & He
raillyd me to day at Ld Bolingbr's; who excused me by
saying the Envoy ought not to be angry, because[36] I serve
Ld Tr, and him the same way: for that reason I very
seldom promise to go any where; I dined with Ld Tr; who
chid me for being absent so long, as he always does if I
miss a day: I sate 3 hours this evening with Ldy Jersey
but the two first hours she was at Ombre with some Company: I left Ld Treasr at 8, I fancyed he was a little
thoughtfull, for he was playing with an Orange by fits,
wch I told him among common men looked like the Spleen.

32 William Oldisworth.

33 Forster's reading, which seems to be correct, save that he has 'Ppt'
for '&c,' and introduces 'the' before 'accidents'.

34 Editors prior to Moorhead read 'DD'.

35 Swift first wrote 'at te' at the end of the previous line, and then
struck it through.

36 Swift began to write 'for', scrawled the word through, and wrote
'because'.

This Letter shall not go to morrow; no hast ⌐ung oomens¬; nothing that presses. I promised but once in 3 weeks, & I am better than my word. I wish the Peace may be ready I mean, that we have notice it is signed before Tuesday; otherwise the grumbling will much encrease. ⌐Nite logues.¬

14.[37] It was a lovely day this, and I took the Advantage of walking a good deal in the Park: before I went to Court. Coll Disney one of our Society is ill of a Feaver; and we fear, in great Danger: We all love him mightily, and he woud be a great Loss. I doubt I shall not buy the Library,[38] for a Roguy Bookseller has offered 60ll more than I designed to give; so you see I meant to have a good Bargain. I dined with Ld Tr and his Saterday company; but there were but 7 at Table. Ld Peterborow is ill, and spits blood with a Bruise he got before hè left Engld; but I believe, an Italian Lady he has brought over, is the Cause that his Illness returns. You know old Ldy Bellesis[39] is dead at last. She has left Ld Berkeley of Stratton one of her Executors, and it will be of great Advantage to him, they say above ten thousd Pounds. I stayd with Ld Tr upon Business after the Company was gone; but I dare not tell you upon wht. My Letters would be good Memoirs, if I durst venture to say a thousd things that pass; but I hear so much of Letters opening at your Post Office, that I am fearfull &c. and so ⌐good nite sollahs & rove pdfr Md¬.

15. Ld Tr engaged me to dine with him again to day;

[37] Hawkesworth divides this letter into two, beginning afresh with the 14th. See Introduction, p. xlix.

[38] First written 'Librarty', or possibly 'Liberty', and struck through.

[39] Susan, elder daughter of Sir William Armyne, Bart., of Osgodby, Lincolnshire, married firstly, in 1662, the Hon. Sir Henry Belasyse, son and heir of John, Baron Belasyse of Worlaby. He was killed in a duel, 1667, and she was created a life peeress in 1674, as Baroness Belasyse of Osgodby. She married secondly, before 1684, James Fortrey of Chequers. She died on the 6th of March, and was buried on the 13th at Twickenham. According to Burnet (*Own Time*, ii. 15–16) the Duke of York, in 1673, paid his addresses to her.

& I had ready what he wanted,[40] but he would not see it, but put me off till to morrow, The Qu goes to Chappell now: She is carryed in an open Chair, and will be well enough to go to Parlmt on Tuesday if the Houses meet, wch is not yet certain, neither indeed can the Ministers themselves tell, for it depends on Winds and Weather, and Circumstances of Negotiation; however we go on as if it was certainly to meet, and I am to be at Ld Tr's to-morrow upon that Supposition, to settle some things relating that way ⌐Now ppt may⌐[41] understand me, the Doctors tell me, that if poor Coll Disney does not get some sleep to night he must dye. What care you; ah but I do care; he is one of our Society, a fellow of abundance of humor, an old battered Rake, but very honest, not an old man but an old Rake. It was he that sd of Jinny Kingdom[42] the maid of honor, who is a little old, that since[43] she could not get a Husband the Qu— should give her a Brevet to act as a married woman: I[44] don't understand this. they give Brevets to Majors & Captains to act as Collonells in the Army; Brevets are Commissions, ask Soldiers ⌐dull sollahs, Nite Md.⌐

16. I was at Ld Tr's before he came, and as he entered he told me the Parlmt was prorogued till thursday sen-

---

[40] The address to the Queen (p. 635 n.[24]).

[41] The reading is doubtful, save for 'ppt'. Editors from Hawkesworth to Aitken read 'Ppt may', ignoring the first word. Forster reads, 'Yes, ppt, oo may'; but the first word cannot be 'Yes', nor is there any sign of 'oo'. Moorhead reads 'Now ppt y'. The first word may be 'Now'; the last certainly seems to be 'may'—there is too much space for 'y' only.

[42] In Nov. 1711 a report was abroad that Miss Kingdom was privately married to Lord Conway (*Wentworth Papers*, p. 207); but this is difficult to explain, for the second wife of Francis Seymour Conway, Lord Conway, was at the time alive.

[43] A small obliteration before 'since'.

[44] The symbol which Hawkesworth takes for 'Y', and renders as 'You', in which he is followed by later editors, looks more like 'I'. The word 'ask', before 'Soldiers', has been written over, and looks like editorial tampering; and 'dull' may also have been touched by another pen.

night. They have had some Expresses by wch they count that the Peace may be signed by that time, or at least, that France, Holland & we will sign some Articles by which we shall engage to sign the Peace when it is ready; but Spain has no Minister there, for Monteleon, who is to be their Ambassdr at Utrecht is not yet gone from hence, and till he is there the Spaniards can sign no Peace: and one thing take notice, that a generall Peace can hardly be finished these two Months, so as to be proclaimed here. for after signing it must be ratifyed, that is, confirmed by the Severall Princes at their Courts, which to Spain will cost a Month, for we must have notice that it is ratifyed in all Courts before we can proclaim it. So be not in too much hast. ⌐Nite Md.⌐

17. The Irish Folks were disappointed that the Parlmt did not meet to day, because it was St Patricks day, and the Mall was so full of Crosses, that I thought all the world was Irish. Miss Ash is almost quite well. and I see the Bishop, but shall not yet go to his House. I dined again with Ld Tr, but the Parlmt being prorogued I must keep what I have till next week, for I believe he will not see it till just the Evening before the Session. He has engaged me to dine with him again to morrow, thô I did all I could to put it off; but I don't care to disoblige him. ⌐Nite dee sollahs, tis rate. Nite Md.⌐

18. I have now dined 6 days successively with Ld Tr; but to night I stole away, while he was talking with some body else, and so am at liberty to morrow. there was a flying report of a geneall Cessation of Arms, every body had it at Court, but I believe there is nothing in it. I asked a certain French Minister, how thinks[45] went, and he whispered me in French, Your Plenipotentys and ours play the fool. None of us indeed approve the Conduct of either at this time. but Ld Tr was in full good humor for all that. He had invited a good many of his Relations, and of a dozen at table, they were all of the Harley family

45 i.e. 'things'.

but my self. Disney is recovering, tho you don't care a straw. Dilly murders us with his If-Puns. you know them. ⌈Nite my own dee . . . . Md.⌉[46]

19. Bp Cl. has made an If-Pun that he is mighty Proud of, and designs to send it over to his Brothr Tom, but Sr A. Fountain, has writ to Tom Ash last post, and told him the Pun, & desired him to send it over to the Bp as his own, and if it succeeds will be a pure bite, the Bp will tell it us as a Wonder, that he & his Brothr should jump so exactly. I'll tell you the Pun. If there was a Hackney Coach at Mr Pooley's door, what Town in Ægypt would it be; why it would be *Hecatompolis, Hack at Tom Poley's*[47] —Silly, says ppt.[48] I dined with a private Friend to day, for our Society, I told you meet but once a fortnight. I have not seen Fanny Manley yet, I can't help it. Ldy Orkney is come to Town, why, she was at her Country house, hot[49] care you. ⌈Nite darling dee Md.⌉[50]

20. Dilly read[51] me a Letter to day from ppt; she seems to have scratched her head when she writt it; tis a sad thing to write to People without tast:[52] There ⌈y say⌉ you hear I was going to the Bath, no such thing. I am pretty well, I thank God; the Town is now sending me to Savoy.[53]

---

[46] Forster fills the blank with 'sollahs. Pdfr roves', but the words do not seem to be there.

[47] Underlined. Thomas Pooley, 1646–1723, a painter in Dublin, was brother of the Bishop of Raphoe (p. 354 n.[30]). See W. G. Strickland's *Dictionary of Irish Artists*, ii. 251. In a letter to the Rev. Thomas Wallis, 12 Feb. 1722–3, Swift refers to the death of 'old Pooley, the painter' (*Corresp.* iii. 158).

[48] Probably what Swift meant to write, but it looks more like 'tpt'.

[49] i.e. 'what'.

[50] Forster and Aitken, the latter with a doubt, read 'darling'. The word seems probable, but by no means certain. Moorhead adopts it.

[51] A slight obliteration before 'read'.

[52] A frequent spelling; and editors from Hawkesworth to Scott correctly read 'taste'. Ryland and Aitken read 'tact'; but this word in the sense of discrimination, delicacy, was not in use till the latter end of the eighteenth century. See *O.E.D.*

[53] As Master of the Savoy.

fourty People have given me joy of it; yet there is not the least Truth that I know in it. I was at an Auction of Pictures but bought none. I was so glad of my Liberty, that I would dine no where; but the weathr being fine, I sauntred into the City, and eat a Bitt about 5, and then supped at Mr. Burk's⁵⁴ your Accountant generall, how⁵⁵ had been engaging me this month, Bp Cl. was to have been there. but was hindred by Ld Paget's⁵⁶ Funerall. the Provost & I sate till one a Clock, and if that be not late, I don't know what is late. Parnels Poem will be published on Monday, & to morrow I design he shall present it to Ld Tr & Ld Boling— at Court. the poor Lad is almost always out of order with his head. Burk's Wife is his Sister,⁵⁷ she has a little of the pert Irish way. ⌐Nite Md.⌐

21. Morning.—I will now finish my Letter; for Company will come, and a Stir and Clutters, and Ill keep the Letter in my P⌐ottic⌐k⁵⁸ & give it into the Post my self— I must go to Court, & you know on Saterdays, I dine with L. Tr of course. Farewell ⌐deelest Md Md Md FW FW FW Md Me Me Me lele sollahs⌐—⁵⁹

Address: To Mrs. Dingley, att her
      Lodgings over against St Mary's
      Church near Capel street
      Ireland   Dublin

Postmark (imperfect): $\frac{—}{21}$

Endorsed by Rebecca ˉ61.
  Dingley: Mar 27.

⁵⁴ William Burgh, son of Ulysses Burgh, Bishop of Ardagh, was Comptroller and Accountant-General for Ireland from 1694 to 1717.

⁵⁵ 'who'.

⁵⁶ William Paget, b. 1637, seventh Baron Paget, was Ambassador at Vienna, 1689–93; and at Constantinople 1693–1702. He was buried at St. Giles in the Fields.

⁵⁷ Parnell's sister, Margaret, married William Burgh. She died in 1744.

⁵⁸ i.e. 'Pocket'.

⁵⁹ The most probable reading of this obliteration.

LETTER LXII

62. [SATURDAY]   London. Mar. 21. 1712–13

I gave your Lettr in this night. I dind with Ld Tr to day; and find he has been at a meeting at¹ Ld Hallifax's House with 4 principall whigs. But he is resolvd to begin a Speech agst them when the Parlmt sitts, and I have beggd that the Ministrs may have a meeting on purpose to settle that matter, and let us be the Attackers; and I believe it will come to something; for the Whigs intend to attack the Ministers, & if instead of that, the Ministers attack the Whigs, it will be bettr; and further I believe we shall attack them on those very Points they intend to attack us. the Parlmt will be again prorogued for a fortnight, because of Passion week. I forgot to tell you that Mr Griffin has given ⌐Ppts⌐ Brothr a new² Employmt about 10ll a year better than his former, but more remote, and consequently cheaper; I wish I could have done bettr; and hope ⌐oo⌐ will take what can be done in good part. and that ⌐oo⌐ Brothr will not dislike it. ⌐Nite own dear . . . Md.⌐³

22. I dined to day with Ld Steward⁴ . . there Frank Annesly⁵ (a Parlnt man) told me, he had heard that I had writt to my Friends in Ireld to keep firm to the Whig Interest, for tht Ld Tr would certainly declare for it after the Peace: Annesly sd 20 People had told him this, You

---

¹ 'at' written above 'with' struck through.

² 'anothr Empl' struck out before 'a new'.

³ Forster reads, 'Nite, own·dear MD, Ppt.'

⁴ Earl Poulett.

⁵ Francis Annesley, 1663–1750, was a grandson of the first Viscount Valentia of that family. He was M.P. for the borough of Westbury in the English Parliament, and a prominent member of the October Club. In the reign of William III he sat for the borough of Downpatrick in the Irish Parliament. He and Archbishop King were close friends; and Swift, in a letter to King (28 Mar. 1713; *Corresp.* ii. 15), repeats this story about Annesley. See also *Letters of Swift to Ford*, ed. Nichol Smith, p. 28, and note.

must know this is what they endeavor to report of L.T. that he designs to declare for the Whigs, and a Scotch Fellow has writt the same to Scotland, and his meeting with those Lds gives occasion to such Reports. let me henceforth call Ld Tr, *eltee*,[6] because possibly my Letters may be opened; pray remember Eltee; you know the Reason, LT and Eltee p⌐l o⌐[7] onounced the same way— Stay, tis 5 weeks since I had a Lettr flom Md; I allow oo[8] Six. You see why I cannot come over the beginning of April, whoever has to do with this Ministry can fix no time; but has[9] hope ⌐saved⌐ it is not ⌐poopdfrs fault, pay dont blame poopdfr. Nite deelest logues Md.⌐

23. I dined to day at Sr T. Hanmer's by an old Appointmt, there was D. Ormd, & Ld & Ldy Orkney; I left them at 6, Every body is as sower as vinegar. I endeavor to keep[10] a firm friendship between D. Ormd & Eltee. ⌐oo⌐ know who Eltee is have ⌐oo flodot[11] it⌐already? I have great designs if I can compass them. But delay is rooted in Eltee's heart. yet the Fault is not altogether there that things are no better. Here is the cursedest Libel in Verse come out, that ever was seen, called the Ambassadress;[12] it is very dull too. It has been printed in 3 or 4 different[13] ways, & is handed about, but not sold: it abuses the Qu— horribly. The Examiner has cleard me to day of being Author of his Paper, and done it with great Civilityes to me.[14] I hope it will stop peoples mouths,

---

6 Underlined.

7 The first three letters are spaced out, and 'l o' has been scrawled over.

8 Afterwards altered to 'you'.   9 i.e. 'as'.

10 'keep' written twice. The first struck out.   11 i.e. 'forgot'.

12 *The Br[iti]sh Embassadress's Speech to the French King*, a folio broadside. The printer, William Hart, or Hurt, printer of *The Flying-Post*, 1711, was tried in the court of the Queen's Bench, 27 June 1713, and sentenced to stand twice in the pillory, to pay a fine of £50, and to be imprisoned for two years till he should pay the fine.

13 A word following 'different' has been obliterated.

14 *The Examiner* informed those who attributed the authorship of the paper to Swift, that he was 'a gentleman of the first character for learning,

if not, they must go on, and be hangd, I care not. Tis
terrible rainy weather. I'll go seep.[15] ⌐Nite deelest Md⌐.
24. It rained all this day, & ruind me in Coach-hire. I
went to see Coll Disney, who is past danger; then I visited
Ld Keepr, who was at dinner; but I would not dine with
him, but drove to Ld Tr— (Eltee I mean) payd the Coachman, & went in, but he dined abroad, so I was forced to
call the Coachman again, & went to Ld Bol— he dined
abroad to;[16] and at Ld Dupplins I lighted, and by good
Luck got a dinner there, & then went to the Latin play
at Westminster School, acted by the Boys & Ld Tr—
(Eltee I mean again) honored them with his Presence.
Ldy Masham's eldest boy, about 2 years old is ill, and I
am afraid will not live; she is full of grief, and I pity and
am angry with her. 4 shillings to day in Coachhire; ⌐fais⌐
it won't do. Our Peace will certainly be ready by Thursday fortnight. but Our Pleniptyes were to blame that it
was not done already; they thought their Powers were not
full enough to sign the Peace, unless every Prince was
ready; wch can not yet be, for Spain has no Minister yet
at Utrecht. but now ours[17] have new Orders. ⌐Nite Md⌐.
25. Weather worse than ever, terrible rain all day. but
I was resolved I would spend no more money. I went to
an Auction of Pictures with Dr Prat, & there met the D.
of Beaufort, who promised to come with me to Court, but
did not, so a Coach I got, & went to Court, and did some
little Business there; but was forced to go home; for ⌐oo⌐
must understand; I take a little Physick over night, wch
works me next day: Ldy Orkney is my Physician. Tis
Hiera picra[18] 2 spoonfull, devilish Stuff. I thought to have

good sense, wit, and more virtues, than even they can set off and illustrate
by all the opposition and extremes of vice, which are the compounds of
their party'; but 'they needed not to charge him with writing the *Examiner*'.

[15] Afterwards altered to 'sleep'.

[16] i.e. 'too'.

[17] 'ours' is written above 'they', which is struck through.

[18] A purgative electuary made of aloes, saffron, honey, and other
ingredients.

dind with Eltee but would not, merely to save a Shilling: but I dined privatly with a Friend, and playd at Ombre, & won Six Shillings. Here are severall people of Quality lately dead of the Small Pox. I have not yet seen Miss Ash; but hear she is well. The Bp. Cl. has bought abundance of Pictures; & Dr Prat has got him very good Penny-worths.[19] I can get no Walks, the Weathr is so bad. Is it so with ⌈oo Sollahs . . . . Md.⌉[20]

26. Tho it was shaving day head & beard, yet I was out early to see Ld Bol— and talk over Affairs with him. & then I went to the D. Ormds, & so to Court, where the Ministers did not come, because the Parlnt was this day prorogued till this day fortnight. We had terrible Rain and Hail to day. Our Society mett this day; but I left them before 7, and went to Sr A. F; & playd at Ombre with him and Sr T. Clarges till ten, & then went to Sr T. Hanmer, His Wife the Dutchess of Grafton left us after a little while, and I stayd with him about an Hour upon some Affairs &c. Ld Bol— left us at the Society before I went, for there is an Express from Utrecht, but I know not yet what it contains. onely I know the Ministers expect the Peace will be signed in a week; which is a week before the Session. ⌈Nite Md.⌉

27. Parnels Poem is mightily esteemed, but Poetry sells ill, I am plagued with that ⌈Nasty Bawd⌉,[21] poor Harrison's mother, You would laugh to see how cautious I am of paying her the 100ll I received for her son from the Treasury; I have asked every Creature I know, whethr I may do it safely; yet durst not venture, till my Ld Keeper assured me there was no danger. yet I have not payd her;

---

[19] Bargains. A common usage in the eighteenth century.

[20] Heavily obliterated. Forster conjectures 'Nite, nite, own'; Moorhead, 'Nite', and possibly 'deelest', for the missing words.

[21] This is Moorhead's reading and almost certainly right. Cf. under 18 Feb. The only reading previously attempted, that of Forster, 'devil's brood', is not borne out by traceable remnants of the script. Aitken surmised 'bawd' for the second word.

but will in a day or two. tho I have a great mind to stay till ⌈Ppt⌉ sends me ⌈her⌉ Opinion, because ⌈ppt⌉ is a great Lawyer. I dined to day with a mixture of People at a Scotchmans,[22] who made the Invitation to Mr Lewis & me, and has some design upon us wch we know very well. I went afterwards to see a famous moving Picture,[23] & I never saw any thing so pretty. You see a Sea ten miles wide, a Town on tothr end, & Ships sailing in the Sea, & discharging their Canon. You see a great Sky with Moon & Stars &c. I'm a fool. ⌈Nite dee Md.⌉—

28. I had a mighty Levee to day, I deny my self to every body except about half a dozen, & they were all here, & Mr Addison was one, & I had Chocolate twice, wch I don't like. Our rainy weather continues, Coach hire goes deep, I dined with Eltee, & his Saterday company as usuall, & could not get away till 9. Ld Peterborow was making long Harangues, & Eltee kept me in spight; then I went to see Bp Ossory, who had engagd me in the morning, he is going to Ireld. Bp of Killaloo & T. Leigh was with us, the Latter had wholly changd his Stile,[24] by seeing how the Bps behaved themselves; & he seemed to think me one of more Importance than I really am. I put the ill conduct of the Bps about First fruits with relation to Eltee and me, strongly upon Killaloo; & shewd how it had hindred me from getting a better thing for them calld the Crown rents, wch the Qu— had promised. He had nothing to say, but was humble, & desired my

22 Probably Arbuthnot.
23 There are many references to moving pictures in early-eighteenth-century newspapers. See A. H. Scouten on 'Swift at the Moving Pictures', *Notes and Queries*, clxxxviii, 38. A notice in *The Daily Courant*, 20 Apr. 1715, frequently repeated thereafter, advertises a representation which seems to be that which Swift saw. The elder Christopher Pinchbeck invented a clockwork machine producing motion pictures accompanied by sounds. In *The Spectator*, No. 31, Addison speaks of 'a moving picture' as a known London entertainment; and in No. 414 describes moving pictures as experiments 'very common in optics'.
24 See p. 587.

Interest in that & some othr things. This Letter is half done in a week; I believe ⌜oo⌝ will have it next. ⌜Nite Md.⌝25

29. I have been employd in endeavoring to save one of your Junior fellows,26 who comes over here for a dispensation from taking Orders, and in solliciting it, has run out his time, and now his Fellowship is void if the College pleases, unless the Qu— suspends the Execution, and gives him time to take Orders. I spoke to all the Ministers yesterday about it; but thy say the Qu— is angry, & thought it was a Trick to deceive her, & she is positive, & so the Man must be ruined, for I can not help him. I never saw him in my Life, but the Case was so hard, I could not forbear interposing; Your Governmt recommended him to D. Ormd, & he thought they would grant it, and by the time it was refused, the Fellowship by rigor is forfeited. I dined with Dr Arbuthnot (one of my Brothers) at his Lodgings in Chelsea, and was there at Chappel, and the Altar put me in mind of Tisdal's outlandish would27 at your Hospital for the Soldiers. I was not at Court to day; and I hear the Qu was not at Church; perhaps the Gout has seised her again. Terrible rain all day, have oo such Weathr. ⌜Nite Md.⌝

30. Morning.28 I was naming some time ago to a certain Person, another certain Person, that was very deserving, and poor and sickly; and tother, that first certain Person gave me a hundred Pounds to give the

<hr />

25 On this day, 28 Mar., Swift wrote a long letter to Archbishop King about the peace negotiations and the posture of affairs at home (*Corresp.* ii. 14–17).

26 Charles Grattan, seventh son of the Rev. Patrick Grattan of Belcamp, a Senior Fellow of Trinity College, Dublin. Swift's intervention on his behalf was unsuccessful (*Corresp.* ii. 19, and note). Later Charles Grattan became master of Portora School. In after years a warm friendship between Swift and the Grattan family developed.

27 *Sic.* The word cannot be read as 'world'. Swift possibly intended to write 'one'. Forster suggests a mistake for 'wood'.

28 'Morning' is written above the line.

other;[29] which I have not yet done. The Person who is to have it, never saw the Giver, nor expects one farthing, or has the least Knoledge or Imagination of it; so I believe it will be a very agreeable Surprise. For I think it a handsom present enough.—At Night[30] I dined in the City at Pontacks, with Ld Dupplin & some others, we were treated by one Coll Cleland,[31] who has a Mind to be governr of Barbadoes, and is laying these long Trapps for me and others to engage our Interests for him. He's a true Scotchman.[32] I paid the 100ll this evening, and it was an agreeble surprise to the Receiver. we reckon the Peace is now signed, and that we shall have it in 3 days—I believe it is pretty sure. ⌐Nite Md.⌐

31. I thought to day on ⌐Ppt⌐ when she told me she suppose[33] I was acquainted with the Steward, when I was giving my self Airs of being at some Lds House. Sr. A. Fountain invited Bp Cl. & me & some othrs to dine where he did, & he carryed us to the D. of Kents,[34] who was gone out of Town; but the Steward treated us nobly; &

29 Perhaps the hundred guineas referred to 29 Jan. 1712–13.

30 A full-stop omitted.

31 Probably William Cleland, 1674?–1741, the friend of Pope, who signed the 'Letter to the Publisher', prefixed to *The Dunciad, Variorum*, 1729. The letter was actually composed by Pope himself. Cleland served in Spain under Lord Rivers; after the peace he became a commissioner of customs in Scotland; and, after 1723, a commissioner of the land tax and house duties in England (Elwin and Courthope, *Pope*, iv. 48; vii. 214 n.¹; *Corresp.* iv. 196 and note; James Sutherland, *The Dunciad*, p. 434). Scott (*Works of Swift*, 1814, iii. 194) describes him as the son of William Cleland, the covenanting colonel. But this is impossible, for Colonel Cleland was born about 1661.

32 'Scto' struck out before 'Scotchman'.

33 'd' omitted.

34 Henry Grey, grandson of the ninth Earl of Kent, succeeded to the title as twelfth Earl in 1702, and was created Duke of Kent in 1710. On the death of the Queen he was appointed one of the Lords Justices of the Realm. He held various offices under George I. In a note to Macky's *Characters* Swift described him as 'a good natured man, but of very little consequence' (*Prose Works*, x. 279). See also *Wentworth Papers*, p. 134; *Hervey's Memoirs*, p. 226.

shewed us the fine Pictures &c. I have not yet seen Miss
Ash; I wait till she has been abroad & taken the Air. This
Evening Ldy Masham, Dr Arbuthnott & I were contriving a Lye for to morrow; that Mr Noble, who was
hangd last Saterday,[35] was recovered by His Friends, and
then seised again by the Sheriff, & is now in a Messenger's
hands at the black Swan in Holborn; We are all to send
to our Friends to know whethr they have heard any thing
of it, and so we hope it will spread. However we shall do
our Endeavors, nothing shall be wanting on our Parts &
leave the rest to Fortune. ⌈Nite Md.⌉

Apr. 1. We had no Success in our Story, thô I sent my
Man to sevrll Houses to enquire among the Footmen,
without letting him into the Secret, but I doubt my Col-
leagues did not contribute as they ought. Parnel & I dined
with Dartenuff to day; you have heard of Dartenuff, I have
told you of Dartenuff. after dinner we all went to Ld Bol—
who had desired me to dine with him, but I would not,
because I heard it was to look over a dull Poem of one
Parson Trap,[36] upon the Peace. The Swedish Envoy told
me to day at Court, that he was in great Apprehensions

[35] Richard Noble, an attorney, formed an intimacy with Mary, daughter
of Admiral John Nevell, and wife of John Sayer, a gentleman of fortune,
and persuaded her to elope with him. The husband tracked the seducer
down, but was killed by him. Noble was hanged at Kingston (Howell,
State Trials, xv. 731–62). Hogarth had the story in mind in the fifth
scene of 'Marriage à la Mode'. Forster discovered at Narford, the seat of
the Fountaine family, a paper on which was written, in Swift's hand, the
'Lye' contrived by Swift and his friends: 'Do you know, that Mr. Noble
was but half hanged, and was brought to life by His Friends, but was since
seised again, and is now in a Messenger's hands at the Black Swan in
Holborn, this was talked all over the Court last Night'. The paper is now
in the Pierpont Morgan Library, New York.

[36] 'Trap' is written twice; the first writing struck out. The poem, which
Swift, the following day, was prevailed on to read and correct, appeared in
folio, title+pp. 22. The title reads: *Peace. A Poem: Inscribed to the
Right Honourable the Lord Viscount Bolingbroke. . . . London: Printed for
John Barber, . . . and Henry Clements, . . . MDCCXIII.* The author's
name does not appear.

about his Master; and indeed we are afraid that Prince[37] is dead[38] among those Turkish Dogs. I prevaild on Ld Bol— to invite Mr Addison to dine with him on good Friday; I suppose we shall be mighty mannerly. Addison is to have a play of his acted on Friday in Easter week; tis a Tragedy called Cato. I saw it unfinished some Years ago:[39] did I tell you, tht Steel has begun a new daily Paper calld the Guardian,[40] they say good for nothing; I have not seen it. ⌈Nite dee Md.⌉

2. I was this morning with Ld Boling— and he tells me a Spanish Courier is just come with the News that the K. of Spain has agreed to every thing the Qu— desires, and the Duke d'Ossuna has left Paris in order to His Journy to Utrecht.[41] I was prevaild on to come home with Trap, and read his Poem, & correct it, but it was good for nothing; while I was thus employd, Sr T. Hanmer[42] came up to my Chamber, and baukt me of a Journy he & I intended this week to Ld Orkney's at Cliffden: But he is not well & his Physicians will not let him undertake such a Journey. I intended to dine with Ld Tr— but going to see Coll Disney, who lives with Genrll Withers,[43] I liked the Genrll's little dinner so well,

37 After his defeat at Pultowa, in 1709, Charles XII fled across the Turkish frontier.

38 The word might be read 'died'.

39 Steele and Cibber saw the first four acts of *Cato* as early as 1703 (Cibber, *Apology*, chap. xiv). The fifth act, according to Steele, was written in less than a week (Aitken, *Life of Steele*, i. 371–2). The first public performance was on 14 Apr. 1713.

40 *The Guardian* ran to 175 numbers, 12 Mar. to 1 Oct. 1713. Steele wrote 82 numbers. Prior, also, could 'make but little of the English wit, the Guardian' (*Corresp.* ii. 19).

41 Swift says that the Duke d'Ossuna, the King of Spain's representative, was delayed because the Dutch made difficulties about his passports (*Corresp.* ii. 14).

42 'Hanmer' written twice. The first struck out.

43 Cf. Gay, 'Mr. Pope's Welcome from Greece', ll. 29–30:
'*Withers* the good, and (with him ever join'd)
Facetious *Disney*'.

that I staid & took share of it, & did not go to Ld Tr—
till 6, where I found Dr Sacheverell, who told us that the
Bookseller had given him 100ll for his Sermon preached
last Sunday,[44] & intended to print thirty thousd: I believe
he will be confoundedly bit; & will hardly sell above half.
I have fires still though April is begun, agst my old
maxim, but the Weathr is wett & Cold, I never saw such a
long[45] run of ill weather in my Life. ⌈Nite dee logues Md.⌉
   3. I was at the Qu—'s Chappel to day, but she was not
there. Mr St John Ld Bol—'s Brother, came this day at
noon with an Express from Utrecht that the Peace is
signed by all the Ministers there but those of the Empr,
who will likewise sign in a few days: so that now the great
Work[46] is in effect done, and I believe it will appear a most
excellent Peace for Europe, particularly for Engld. Addison & I & some others dined with Ld Bol— and sate with
him till 12; we were very Civil, but yet when we grew
warm, we talkt in a friendly manner of Party, Addison
raised his Objections, & Ld Bol— answered them with
great Complaisance. Addison began Ld Sommers Health,
wch went about; but I bid him not name Ld Wh—'s[47]
for I would not pledge it, and I tod Ld Bol— frankly that
Addison loved Ld Wh— as little as I did. so we laughd
&c—Well, but you are glad of the Peace, you ⌈Ppt⌉ the
Trimmer, are not you? as for Dd I don't doubt ⌈her⌉.
Why now, if I did not think ⌈Ppt⌉ had been a violent
Tory, & ⌈DD⌉ the greater Whig of the two: tis late.
⌈Nite Md.⌉

---

[44] Sacheverell's first sermon, after the three years' silence imposed upon
him by the House of Lords, was delivered at St. Saviour's Church, Southwark. He chose as his text Luke xxiii. 34; and the published title of the
sermon was *The Christian's Triumph, or the Duty of Praying for our
Enemies.* Forty thousand copies are said to have been sold. In this same
month, April, he was presented by the Queen to the rectory of St. Andrew's,
Holborn.

[45] An obliteration between 'a' and 'long'.

[46] The first line of Trapp's poem describes the peace as 'The wondrous
Work'.   [47] Wharton's.

4. This Passion week People are so demure, especially this last day, that I told Dilly who calld here, that I would dine with him, and so I did ⌐fais⌐ & had a small shouldr of Mutton of my own bespeaking. It rained all day; I came home at 7, and have never stirrd out, but have been reading Sacheverell's long dull Sermon wch he sent me, It is [h]is first sermon since his Suspension is expired; but not a word in it upon the Occasion, except two or three remote Hints. Bp Cl has been sadly bit by Tom Ash, who sent him a Pun, wch the Bp had made & designd to send to him, but delayd it, and Ld Pembr & I made Sr A. Fountain write it to Tom. I believe I told you of it in my last.[48] It succeeded right, & the Bp was wondring to Ld Pembr how he and his Brothr coud hit on the same thing. Ill go to bed soon, for I must be at Church by 8 to morrow morning, Easter day. ⌐Nite dee Md.⌐

5. Warburton writt to me 2 Lettrs[49] about a Living of one Foulks[50] who is lately dead in the County of Meath: my Answer is, that before I received the first Genrll Gorge[51] had recommended a friend of his to the D. Ormd, wch was the first time I heard of it's vacancy, & it was the Provost told me of it. I believe verily that Foulks was not dead when Gorge recommended the other; for[52] Warburtons last Letter sd that Foulks was dead the day before the date; this has preventd me from serving Warburton as I woud have done, if I had received early notice enough;

---

48 See p. 641.

49 The letters have not been preserved.

50 The Rev. Francis Foulke, educated at Trinity College, Dublin, and at Cambridge (M.A. 1694). He was rector of Kilbrew from 1699 to 1712, the year of his death at the age of forty-four. Resided at Ratoath, co. Meath. He was a nephew of John Bolton, Dean of Derry.

51 Cf. p. 498 n.[11] Richard Gorges was the eldest son and heir of Dr. Robert Gorges of Kilbrew, co. Meath. He was appointed Adjutant-General of the Forces in Ireland in 1697, Major-General of the Forces in 1707, and Lieutenant-General in 1710 (Dalton's Army Lists, iii. 75). He died in 1728.

52 A short obliteration before 'for'.

pray say or write this to Warburton to justify me to him. —I was at Church at 8 this morning; and dresst & shaved after I come back, but was too late at Court, & Ld Abingdon was like to have snappt me for dinner, & I believe will fall out with me for refusing him; but I hate dining with them, &[53] I dined with a private friend, & took 2 or 3 good walks, for it was a very fine day, the first we have had a great while. Remembr was Easter day a fine day with you. I have sate with Ldy Worsley till now. ⌈Nite dee Md.⌉

6. I was this morning at 10 at the Rehearsall of Mr Addisons Play called Cato, which is to be acted on Friday, there were not above half a score of us, to see it; we stood on the Stage & it was foolish enough to see the Actors promptd every moment, & the Poet directing them, & the drab that Acts Catos daughter[54] out in the midst of a passionate Part, & then calling out, What's next? Bp of Cl was there too, but he stood privatly in a Gallery. I went to dine with Ld Tr, but he was gone. to Wimbleton his Daughter Caermarthen's Country Seat, 7 miles off, so I went back and dined privatly with Mr. Addison, whom I had left to go to Ld Tr. I keep fires yet; I'm very extravagant. I sate this Evening with Sr A. Fountain, & we amused our selves with making If's for Dilly. It is rainy weather again. nevle saw ⌈ze rike⌉.[55] This Lettr shall go to morrow. remembr ⌈ung oomens⌉ it is 7 weeks since oor last, and I allow ⌈oo⌉ but 5 weeks; but ⌈oo⌉ have been galloping into the Country to Swantons; o, Pray tell Swanton I had his Letter, but can not contrive how to serve him. If a Govrnr[56] were to go over: I would recommend him as far as lay in my Power, but I can do no more; & you know all Employmts in Ireld[57] at least almost all, are engaged in reversions. If I were on the Spot, & had Credit with

---

[53] An obliteration, apparently 'and', after '&'.
[54] Mrs. Oldfield.
[55] the like.   [56] Lord Lieutenant.
[57] 'are en', i.e. the beginning of 'are engaged', struck out after 'Ireld'.

a Ld Lt I would very heartily recommend him, but Emplymts here are no more in my Powr than the Monarchy it self. ⌐Nite dee Md.⌐

7. Morning. I have had a Visiter here that has taken up my time. I have not been abroad ⌐oo⌐ may be sure, so I can say nothing to day but tht I ⌐rove MD, bettle zan⌐ ever if possibur.⁵⁸ I will put this in the Post office, so I say no more. I write by this Post to the Dean, but is is not above 2 Lines, & one inclosed to you, but that enclosed to you is not above 3 Lines, & then one inclosed to the Dean,⁵⁹ which He must not have but under Conditions of burning it immediatly after reading, & that before your Eyes; for there are some things in it, I would not have lyable to Accident. You shall onely know in generall, that it is an Account of what I have done to serve him¯in his Pretensions on these Vacancyes &c—but he must not know, that you know so much. ⌐Does this perplex y, hat care I, but rove pdfr, sawcy pdfr. Farewell deelest Md Md Md FW FW FW Me Me Me lele⌐—

Address: To Mrs Dingley, att her
               Lodgings over against St Mary's
               Church, near Capel-street
               Ireland   Dublin
Postmark: $\frac{AP}{7}$
Endorsed by   62.
Rebecca Dingley: Apr. 13.

⁵⁸ Or 'possibere'.
⁵⁹ Dean Stearne. Swift had realized that English preferment was improbable, and that even an Irish bishopric, involving the consent of the Crown, was unlikely. He was now prepared to contemplate the Deanery of St. Patrick's, which was in the gift of the Lord Lieutenant, if Stearne was promoted to one of the two vacant Irish bishoprics, Raphoe or Dromore. See pp. 567, 605, 660-4.

LETTER LXIII

63. [TUESDAY]   London. Apr. 7. 1713

I fancy I marked my last which I sent this day, wrong, onely 61 & it ought to be 62 I dined with Ld Tr. and thô the Business[1] I had with him is something agst Thursday when the Parlmt is to meet, & this is Tuesday yet he put it off till to morrow, I dare not till[2] you what it is, lest this Lettr should miscarry or be opend; but I never saw his Fellow for Delays. the Parlnt will now certainly sitt, and every body's Expectations are ready to burst. At a Council to night, the Ld Ch Justice Parker, a Whig, spoke agst the Peace, so did Ld Chomley, anothr Whig, who is Treasur of the Houshold. My Ld Keeper was this night made Ld Chancellr We hope there will soon be some Removes. ⌐Nite dee sollahs both[3] rove Pdfr.⌐

8. Ld Chomley the right name is Cholmondeley, is this day removed from his Employmt for his last nights Speech, & Sr Richd Templ Lt Genrll, the greatest Whig in the Army is turned out, & Lt Genrll Palmes[4] will be obliged to sell his Regimt, This is the first fruits of a Friendship I have established between two great men. I dined with Ld Tr, and did the Business I had for him to his Satisfaction, I won't tell ⌐Md⌐ what is was. ⌐. . . .[5] for zat.⌐ the Palnt sitts to morrow for certain. Here is a Letter printed in Macartneys name vindicating himself from the murder of D. Hamilton. I must give some hints

---

[1] The address of the House of Lords to the Queen (p. 635 n.24).

[2] i.e. 'tell'.

[3] Forster and Aitken read 'Late', instead of 'both', but the latter seems to be the right word, and it better suits the context.

[4] Francis Palmes, who fought at Blenheim, became a Lieutenant-General in 1709. In 1708 he was sent as Envoy Extraordinary to the Duke of Savoy, and in 1710 on a similar mission to Vienna.

[5] Forster reads 'So much', which Ryland thinks probable. Aitken conjectures 'so heed'. Moorhead reads 'Sankee', i.e. 'thank you'. But any reading can hardly be more than a guess.

to have it answred; tis full of Lyes and will give an Opportunity of exposing that Party. To morrow will be a very important day; all the World will be at Westminster; Ld. Tr is as easy as a Lamb; They are mustring up the Proxyes of the absent Lds;[6] but they are not in any fear, of wanting a Majority, wch Death & Accidents have increased this year. ⌐Nite Md.⌐

9. I was this morning with Ld Tr to present to him a young son of the late E. of Jersey[7] at the desire of the Widow. there I saw the Mace & great Coach ready for Ld Tr who was going to Parlmt. Our Society met to day, but I expected the Houses would sitt longer than I cared to fast; so I dined with a Friend, and never enquired how matters went till 8 this evening, when I went to Ld Orkneys where I found Sr T. Hanmer, The Qu. delivered her Speech very well, but a little weaker in her Voice; the Crowd was vast. The Order for an Address was moved; & opposed by Ld Notingham, Halifax & Cowper[8]—Ld Tr spoke with great spirit and Resolution; Ld Peterborow flirted agst D. Marlbrow, (who is in Germany you know) but it was in answer to one of Halifax's Impertinences. The Order for an Address passd by a Majority of 33, &

---

[6] Members of the House of Lords, by ancient privilege, were entitled to vote by proxy. Each peer present could vote for himself and for two absentees who had authorized him. For the purpose of proxies the temporal lords and the bishops were separately grouped. The privilege was voluntarily abandoned in 1868. See further Stubbs, *Constitutional History of England*, 1880, iii. 527–8.

[7] Henry Villiers, second son of the first Earl of Jersey. He died without issue in 1743 (Collins, *Peerage of England*, 1812, iii. 793).

[8] William Cowper, the son of Sir William Cowper, of Ratling Court, Nonington, Kent, whom he succeeded as second baronet in 1706. In November of the same year he was created Baron Cowper. He was called to the Bar in 1688; and had a distinguished legal career. He was Crown Prosecutor, 1694–9; Lord Keeper, 1705; first Lord Chancellor of Great Britain, May 1707 to Sept. 1710; and again Lord Chancellor, 1714–18. In 1718 he was created Earl Cowper. In politics he was a Whig, although in later life, 1718 to the year of his death, 1723, he frequently voted with the Tory peers.

the Houses rise before 6⁹ This is the account I heard at
Ld Orkneys. the Bp of Chester[10] a high Tory was agst
the Court; the Dutchess of Marlbrow sent for him some
Months ago to justify her self to him in relation to the
Qu.— and shewd him Letters, & told him Storyes, which
the weak man believed, & was perverted. ⌐Nite Md.⌐

10. I dined with a Cousin[11] in the City, & poor Pat
Rolt was there; I have got her Rogue of a Husband leave
to come to Engld from Port-mahòn; the Whigs are much
down; but I reckon they have some Scheam in agitation.
This Parlmt time hinders our Court meetings on Wednes-
days, Thursdays, & Saterdays. I had a great deal of
Business to night, which gave me a Temptation to be idle,
& I lost a dozen Shillings at Ombr with Dr Prat &
anothr. I have been to see tothr day the Bp Cl. & Lady,
but did not see Miss. It rains every day, & yet we are all
over dust. Ldy Mashams eldest boy is very ill, I doubt he
will not live; & she stays at Kensington to nurse him,
which vexes us all. She is so excessively fond it makes me
mad; she should never leave the Qu, but leave every thing
to stick to what is so much the Interest of the Publick
as well as her own. This I tell her, but talk to the Winds.
⌐Nite Md.⌐

11. I dined at Ld Tr with his Saterdays company; we
had ten at Table, all Lds but my self & the Chancellr of
the Exchequer. Argyle went off at 6, & was in very indifferent humor, as usuall. D. Ormd & Ld Bolingbr—
were absent. I stayd till near ten, Ld·Tr shewd us a small

⁹ *Journals of the House of Lords*, xix. 511–13; *Journals of the House of
Commons*, xvii. 277–9, 280–1.

10 Previous editors state the bishop to have been Francis Gastrell. But
at this time Sir William Dawes was Bishop of Chester. Upon the death of
John Sharp, 2 Feb. 1714, Dawes was translated to the Archbishopric of
York, and Gastrell, then a Canon of Christ Church, was appointed to
Chester. He was consecrated at Somerset House Chapel on 4 Apr. 1714
(Hearne's *Collections*, iv. 313, 316, 321, 328; Nichols, *Lit. Anec.*, i.
138–40).

11 Presumably Dryden Leach.

Picture enamelld work, & sett in gold, worth about 20ll, a Picture I mean of the Qu; which sh gave to Dutchess Marlbrough sett in Diamonds. When the Dutchess was leaving Engld, she took of[12] all the Diamonds, & gave the Picture to one Mrs Higgins, (an old intriguing woman whom every body knows) bidding her to make the best of it she could. Ld Tr sent to Mrs Higgins for this Picture, & gave her a hundred Pounds for it. was ever such an ungratefull Beast as that Dutchess? or did you ever hear such a Story. I suppose the Whigs will not believe it, pray try them: takes off the diamonds & gives away the Picture to an insignificant woman as a thing of no consequences, & gives it her to sell, like a piece of old fashiond plate. Is she not a detestable Slut. ⌐Nite deelest Md.⌐

12. I went to Court to day on purpose to present Mr Berkeley[13] one of Your Fellows of Dublin Colledge, to Ld Berkeley of Stratton. that Mr Berkeley is a very ingenious man, & great Philosophr; & I have mentiond him to all the Ministers, & given them some of his writings, & I will favor him as much as I can. This I think I am bound to in honor & Conscience, to use all my little Credit towards helping forward Men of Worth in the world. The Qu was at Chappell to day, & looks well. I dined at Ld Orkneys with D. Ormd, Ld Arran & Sr T. Hanmer. Mr St John, Secrty at Utrecht expects every

---

[12] i.e. 'off'.

[13] George Berkeley, 1685–1735, at this time a young fellow of Trinity College, Dublin, who had already made a name for himself as an original philosophical thinker with *A New Theory of Vision*, 1709, and *Treatise concerning the Principles of Human Knowledge*, 1710, now brought with him his *Dialogues between Hylas and Philonous*, published in 1713. Swift always regarded Berkeley with the greatest friendliness and esteem, although he found his writings 'too speculative' (*Corresp.* iv. 295). In Nov. 1713 he obtained for Berkeley the office of Chaplain and Secretary to Peterborough, while envoy to Sicily. George Berkeley's father, William Berkeley, had some family relationship to Lord Berkeley of Stratton, Lord Lieutenant of Ireland, 1670–72.

moment to return there with the Ratification of the Peace. Did I tell you in my last, of Addison's Play called Cato, & that I was at the Rehearsall of it.[14] ⌈Nite Md⌉.

13. This Morning My Friend Mr Lewis came to me, and shewed me an Order for a Warrant for the 3 vacant Deanryes,[15] but none of them to me; this was what I always foresaw., and receive the notice of it better I believe than he expected. I bid Mr Lewis tell Ld Tr that I took nothing ill of him, but his not giving me timely notice, as he promised to do, if he found the Qu would do nothing for me. at Noon Ld Tr hearing, I was in Mr Lewis's Office, came to me, & sd many things too long to repeat. I told him I had nothing to do but go to Ireld immediatly, for I could not with any Reputation stay longer here, unless I had somethink honorabl immediatly given to me; we dined togethr at D. Ormds, he there told me, he had stopt the Warrants for the Deans, that what was done for me, might be at the same time, & he hoped to compass it to night; but I believe him not. I told the D. Ormd my Intentions; He is content Stearn should be a Bp, & I have St Patricks; but I believe nothing will come of it; for stay I will not; and so I believe for all ⌈oo . . . .[16] oo⌉ may see me in Dublin before April ends. I am less out of humor than you would imagine, & if it were not that impertinent People will condole with me, as they used to give me Joy, I would

---

[14] See under 6 Apr.

[15] The three vacant deaneries were Wells, Ely, and Lichfield. Wells, vacant by the death of William Graham, was given to Dr. Brailsford (p. 508 n. 4). Charles Roderick, Provost of King's and Dean of Ely, died on 25 Mar. 1712. He was succeeded by Robert Mosse, chaplain in ordinary to William III and Anne, and afterwards to George I. Lichfield became vacant by the death, 19 June 1712, of William Binckes, a high Tory, Dean since 1703. His place was given to Jonathan Kimberley, Chaplain to the Speaker. See Sir Charles Firth's paper 'Dean Swift and Ecclesiastical Preferment' in *The Review of English Studies*, ii. 6–10.

[16] Forster fills in with 'sawcy ppt can say', but not a stroke of the pen justifies this fiction.

value it less: but I will avoid company, & muster up my Baggages & send them next Monday by the·Carrier to Chester, and come & see my Willows, agst the Expectation of all the World. hat ⌐care I. Nite deelest logues Md⌐.

14. I dined in the City to day, and ordered a Lodging to be got ready for me agst I come to pack up my things; for I will leave this end of the Town as soon as ever the warrants for the Deanryes are out, wch are yet stopt: Ld Tr told Mr Lewis, that it should be determined to night; & so he will for a hundred nights, so he said yesterday; but I value it not. my daily journall[17] shall be but short, till I gett into the City, & then I will send away this; and follow it my self, and design to walk it all the way to Chester my man & I by 10 miles a day; it will do my Health a great deal of good; I shll do it in 14 days. ⌐Nite dee Md⌐.

15. Ld Bol— made me dine with him to day, I[18] was as good company as ever; & told me the Qu would determine something for me to night, the dispute is Windsor or St Patricks: I told him I would not stay for their disputes, & he thought I was in the right. Ld Masham told me that Ldy Masham is angry I have not been to see her since this Business: & desires I will come to morrow. ⌐Nite deelest Md.⌐

16. I was this noon at Ldy Mashams, who was just come from Kensington where her eldest son is sick; she said much to me of what she had talkt to Qu— & Ld Tr. the poor Ldy fell a ⌐crying⌐[19] shedding tears openly: She coud not bear to think of my having St Patricks &c. I was never more moved than to see so much Friendship: I woud not stay with her, but went and dined with Dr

---

[17] Swift first wrote 'daily writing', struck these two words through, and substituted 'daily journall'.

[18] Aitken substitutes 'he'. But Hawkesworth and Sheridan, enclosing the words 'I was as good company as ever' within round brackets, correctly interpret the phrase as parenthetical. Swift means that he was good company despite his disappointments.

[19] 'crying' scrawled over before 'shedding'.

Arbuthnot, with Mr Berkeley one of your Fellows, whom I have recommended to the Dr, & to Ld Berkeley of Stratton Mr Lewis tells me, that D. Ormd has been to day with Qu— & she was content that Dr Stearn should be Bp of Dromore and I Dean of St Patricks, but then out came Ld Tr, & sd he would not be satisfied, but that I must be Prebend of Windsor, thus he perplexes things— I expect neither: but I confess, as much as I love Engld, I am so angry at this Treatmt, that if I had my Choice I would rather have St Patricks. Ldy Masham says she will speak to purpose to Qu— tomorrow. ⌐Nite . . . . . . Md.¬20

17. I went to dine at Ldy Mashams to day, & she was taken ill of a sore throat, & Aguish; She spoke to Qu last night, but had not much time. Qu— says she will determine to morrow with Ld Tr. The warrants for the Deanry's are still stopt, for fear I should be gone. Do you think any thing will be done: I don't care whethr it is or no, In the mean time I prepare for my Journy; and see no great People; nor will see Ld Tr any more, if I go. Ld Tr. tod Mr Lewis it should be done to night, so he sd 5 nights ago. ⌐Nite Md.¬

18. This morning Mr Lewis sent me word that Ld Tr21 told him, Qu would determine at noon. at 3 Ld Tr sent to me to come to his Lodgings at St James's, and tod me the Qu was at last resolved, that Dr Stearn should be Bp Dromore, and I Dean of St Patrick: and tht Stearns warrant should be drawn immediatly. You know the Deanry is in the D. Ormonds gift, but this is concerted between the Qu— Ld Tr, & D. Ormd, to make room for me. I do not know whethr it will yet be done, some unlucky Accident may yet come; neither can I feel Joy at passing my days in Ireld: and I confess I thought the Ministry would not let me go; but perhaps thy cant help it. ⌐Nite Md.¬

---

20 What appear to be two words are here undecipherable. They may be 'dee dee', or, as Forster reads 'own dee'.

21 'Qu— would' struck out before 'Ld Tr'.

19. I forgot to tell you that Ld Tr forced me to dine with him yesterday as usuall with his Saterday company, wch I did after frequent refusals; to day I dined with a private Friend, & was not at Court. after dinner Mr Lewis sent me a note, that Qu— staid till she knew whether duke Ormd approved of Stearn for Bp: I went this Evening and found D. Ormd. at the Cockpit, & told him, and desired he would go to Qu, and approve of Stearn. He made Objections, desired I would name any other Deanry, for he did not like Stearn, that Stearn never went to see him, that he was influenced by Ar. B. Dublin[22] &c; so all is now broken again. I sent out for Ld Tr, and told him this. He says all will do well, but I value not what he says. This Suspense vexes me worse than any thing else. ⌐Nite Md.⌐

20. I went to day by appointmt to the Cockpit, to talk with D. Ormd; he repeated the same Proposall of any othr Deanry &c. I desired, he would put me out of the Case, & do as he pleased; then with great kindness he said he would consent, but woud do it for no man alive but me &c, and he will speak to the Qu— to day or to morrow. So perhaps something will come of it. I can't tell. ⌐Nite dee dee logues Md⌐.[23]

21. D. Ormd has told Qu— he is satisfied that Stearn should be Bp, & she consents I shall be Dean, and I suppose the Warrants will be drawn in a day or two. I dined at an Ale-house with Parnel & Berkeley; for I am not in humor to go among the Ministers, thô Ld Dartmouth invited me to dine with him to day, & Ld Tr was to be there. I sd I would if I were out of suspense. ⌐Nite sollahs Md⌐.[24, 25]

[22] Archbishop of Dublin.
[23] The reading is fairly clear, though Moorhead leaves a blank for one 'dee', and Forster reads 'Nite, dear de Rogues. Nite MD.'
[24] This reading also seems clear, though Ryland and Aitken read 'Nite deelest MD.'
[25] On this day, 21 Apr., Atterbury wrote to Swift congratulating him

22.[26] Qu says Warrant shall be drawn, but she will dispose of all in Engld & Ireld at once, to be teazed no more, this will delay it sometime; & while it is delayd[27] I am not sure of the Qu— my Enemyes being busy; I hate their Suspense—⌐Nite sollahs.¬[28]

23.[29] I dined yesterday with Genll Hamilton[30] I forgot to tell oo: I write short Journals now, I have Eggs on the Spit. This Night the Qu— has signed all the Warrants, among which Stearn is Bp of Dromore, & D. Ormd is to send over an Order for making me Dean of St Patricks. I have no doubt of him at all; I think tis now past: and I suppose Md is malicious enough to be glad & rathr have it than Wells. But you see what[31] a Condition I am in. I thought I was to pay but 600ll for the House but Bp Cl. says 800ll. First Fruits 150ll and so with Patent, a thousand Pounds in all, so that I shall not be the better for this Deanery these 3 years. I hope in some time they will be persuaded here to give me some money to pay off these debts. I must finish the Book I am writing,[32] before I can come over; & thy expect I shall pass next winter here, and then I will dun[33] them to give me a Summ of

on his preferment, which 'my Lord Bolingbroke yesterday confirmed . . . to me' (*Corresp.* ii. 22).

[26] '21' corrected to '22'; and '20' previously corrected to '21'.

[27] 'deala', before 'delayd', struck through.

[28] This appears to be the correct reading. Ryland has 'Nite dee MD' and Aitken 'Nite deelest MD', both almost certainly wrong. Forster's 'Nite, dee logues. Poo pdfr' is absurd. There is no room for it.

[29] '22' corrected to '23'.

[30] Most probably Gustavus Hamilton, 1639–1723, who commanded a regiment at the Boyne. He became a Brigadier-General in 1696, and a Major-General in 1703. He was at the siege of Vigo in 1707. He was created an Irish baron in 1715, and Viscount Boyne in the peerage of Ireland in 1717. There was also a George Hamilton, who became a Lieut.-General in 1709, but it is unlikely that Swift refers to him.

[31] 'I' written after 'what', and then scrawled over.

[32] *The History of the Four Last Years of the Queen.*

[33] Hawkesworth, Sheridan, Nichols, Scott read 'drive'; Ryland, Aitken, Moorhead have the correct reading, 'dun'.

money: however I hope to pass 4 or five months ⌜with Md, and whatever comes on it, Md's Allowance must be encreased, & shall be too fais, . . .⌝[34]. I received ⌜oo rettle N. 39⌝[35] to night, just 10 weeks since I had your last. I shall write next Post to Bp Stearn;[36] never man had so many Enemyes of Ireld as he.[37] I carryed it with the Strongest hand possible: If he does not use me well and gently in what dealings I shall have with him, he will be the most ungratefull of Mankind. A.Bp York,[38] my mortall Enemy, has sent by a third hand that he would be glad to see me; Shall I see him or not?—I hope to be over in a Month; & that ⌜Md⌝ with their Raillery, will be mistaken tht I shall make it 3 years. I will answr oor Rettle soon; but no more Journals: I shall be very busy. Short letters from henceforward. I shall not part with Laracor: that is all I have to live on; except the Deanry be worth more than 400ll a year;[39] is it? if it be, the overplus shall be divided ⌜. . . . . besides te usuall . . . .⌝[40] Pray write to me a good humored Lettr immediatly, let it be ever so short. This Affair was

---

34 This is Forster's reading, and probably correct. Part is easily legible, part almost effaced. The last word, for which Forster reads 'iss truly', is completely blotted out. See Pons, *Du nouveau sur le 'Journal à Stella'*, pp. 13–14.

35 In Swift's account book (Forster Collection, 509) this letter is noted as received 24 Apr.

36 This letter has not been preserved.

37 'as he' is written above the line. Swift means that Stearne had more Irish enemies than any man.

38 Swift attributed to the influence of Sharp, Archbishop of York (p. 474 n. ¹) the Queen's refusal of any English preferment for him. William King (*Political and Literary Anecdotes*, pp. 60–1) records Bolingbroke's assurance that the suspicion was unjustified, and that Oxford had invented the story 'to deceive Swift, and make him contented with his Deanery in *Ireland*'. See also *Poems*, p. 193 and note.

39 Sheridan, *Life of Swift*, 1784, p. 156 n.: 'This Deanery was worth more than seven hundred'.

40 Only three words seem certain. Forster supplies 'between MD and FW, beside usual allowance of MD dee rogues'. The two final words are almost certainly wrong; and, save for 'beside usual', the rest is a guess.

carryed with great difficulty, wch vexes me, but they say here tis much to my Reputation, that I have made a Bp in spight of all the Wor[l]d, to get the best Deanry in Ireld.[41] ⌐Nite dee sollahs.⌐

24.[42] I forgot to tell you, I had Stearns Lettr[43] yesterday in answr to mine. ⌐oo performd oor Commission well, dood Dallars both.⌐ I made mistakes the 3 last days and am forced to alter the Numbr. I dined in the City to day[44] with my Printer, and came home early; & am going to[45] busy with my Work. I will send this to morrow, & I suppose the warrants will go then. I wrote[46] to Dr Coghill to take care of passing my Patent, & to Parvisol to attend him with money, if he has any; or to borrow some where he can. ⌐Nite Md⌐—

25. Morn. I know not whethr my Warrant be yet ready from the D. Ormd; I suppose it will by to night; I am going abroad, & will keep this unsealed till I know whethr all be finisht: ⌐mollow Sollahs.⌐[47]——I had this Letter all day in my Pocket, waiting till I heard the Warrants were gone over. Mr Lewis[48] sent to Southwells Clerk at 10, & he sd the Bp Killaloo had desired they shoud be stoppt till next post, he sent again that Bp Killaloo's Business had nothing to do with ours; then I went my self; but it was past 11, & asked the Reason. Killaloo is removed to Rapho, and he has a mind to have an Order for the Rents of Rapho that have

[41] Not in money value, but in standing.

[42] '23' corrected to '24'.

[43] The letter is not preserved.

[44] 'to day' above the line. Below is an obliteration.

[45] 'be' omitted.

[46] The 'o', if it be meant for 'o', looks like an undotted 'i'. If the word is 'wrote', this is the only time, as Moorhead notes, that it occurs in the *Journal*. Swift preferred 'writt', a form of the verb which died out before the end of the eighteenth century.

[47] Forster reads 'Morng. dee Sollahs.'

[48] 'Mr Lewis' is written above the line. Below, the beginning of a word is struck out.

fallen[49] since the Vacancy, & he would have all stop till he has got that. a pretty Request; but the Clerk at Mr Lewis's message sent the Warrants for Stearn & me. but it was then too late to send this, wch fretts me heartily, ⌐tht Md shoud not have Intelligence first from Pdfr¬. I think to take a hundred Pound a year out of the Deanry, & divide it ⌐between Md & Pr. & so be one year longer be paying te Debt, but we'll talk of zis hen I come over, so Nite dee sollahs lele¬[50]—

26. I was at Court to day; & a thousand People gave me joy, so I ran out. I dined with Ldy Orkney—Yesterday I dined with Ld Treasur & his Saterday People as usuall, & was bedean'd—A.B. York says he will never more speak agst me—Pray see that Parvisol stirs about getting my Patent. I have given Took Dd's note to prove she is alive. I'⌐ll answer Md Rettle anoddle time—Nite.¬[51]

27. Nothing new to day. I dined with Tom Harley &c. I'll seal up this to night. pray write soon.—
⌐................ Md Md FW FW FW Me Me
                                                    Me Lele lele¬

Address: To Mrs Dingley at her
                 Lodgings over against St. Mary's
                 Church near Capel-street
                 Ireland   Dublin
Postmark: AP
Endorsed by   63.
Rebecca Dingley: May. 4.

---

49 Previous editors, except Moorhead, silently supply 'due' after 'fallen'. But the word, doubtless intended, is not there.

50 'Pr.', which seems to be right, is presumably a contraction of 'Pdfr'. The last word is, apparently 'lele'. Forster reads 'Lo Pdfr'. The debt is explained under the entry for 23 Apr.

51 This is Moorhead's reading, and seems to be well justified. Forster has 'I'll answer oor Rattle and addle soon'. Ryland and Aitken are hesitant to complete.

LETTER LXIV

64 [SATURDAY]   Lond. May. 16[1]

I had yours N. 40 yesterday. Your new Bp acts very ungratefully, I cannot say so bad of it as he deservd. I beggd at the same Post his warrant & mine went over, that he would leave those Livings to my disposal—I shall write this post to him, to let him know how ill I take it.[2] I have Letters to tell me, that I ought to think of employing ⌐Parvisol⌐ somebody to sett the Tyths of the Deanry. I know not what to do at this distance: I can not be in Irld under a Month; I will write two Orders one to Parvisol & tother to Parvisol & a Blank for whatever Fellow it is whom the last Dean employd, and I would desire you to advise with Frends which to make use of & if the latter, let the Fellow's name be inserted, and both act by Commission. If the former, then speak to Parvisol, & know whether he can undertake it. I doubt it is hardly to be done by a perfect Stranger alone, as Parvisol is. He may perhaps venture at all, to keep up his Interest with me, but that is needless, for I am willing to do him any good that will do me no harm. Pray advise with Walls & Raymd, & a little with Bp Stearne for form. Tell Raymd I cannot succeed for him to get that Living of Moymed;[3] It is represented here as a great Sine-cure, sevrll Chaplns have sollicited for it, & it has vexed me so, that if I live, I will make it my Business to serve him bettr in something else: I am heartily sorry for his Illness, and that of the other two. If it be not necessary to let the Tyths till a

---

[1] '1713' omitted.

[2] Cf. p. 71 n. 21 In addition to the Deanery of St. Patrick's Stearne held the two livings into which the parish of St. Nicholas Without, Dublin, had been divided. On his appointment to the Bishopric of Dromore Stearne and the Chapter hastened to nominate incumbents to the two livings lest the Crown should claim presentation to them as well as to the deanery. Swift was much incensed, for he hoped to present Parnell to one of the livings (*Corresp*. ii. 51 n.). Swift's letter to Stearne has not been preserved.

[3] See p. 671 n.[3]

month hence, You may keep the 2 Papers, and[4] advise well in the mean time, and when evr it is absolutely necessary, then give that Paper wch you are most advised to. I thank Mr Walls for his Lettr, tell him that must serve for an Answr, with my Service to him & her. I shall buy[5] Bp Stearns Hair as soon as his Houshold goods. I shll be ruined or at least sadly crampt unless the Qu— will give me 1000ll I am sure she owes me a great deal more. Ld Tr raillyes me upon it, and I believe intends it; but, quando? I am advised to hasten over as soon as possible; & so I will, & hope to sett out the beginning of June. Take no Lodging for me. What at your old Tricks again? I can ly somewhere after I land, & I care not where nor how, I will buy your Eggs & Bacon, ⌐yr whadeecallit⌐[6], your Cups[7] & Bible, & pray think immediatly, & give me some Commissions, & I will perform them ⌐as far as a poopdfr can⌐. The[8] Lettr I sent before this was to have gone a Post before, but an accident hindred it, & I assure ee I wam vely ⌐. . . . .⌐ Md[9] did not write to Dean ⌐pdfr⌐. & I think oo might have had a Dean under your Girdle for the Superscription. I have just finisht my Treatise[10] & must be ten days correcting it. ⌐Farewell deelest Md Md FW FW FW Me Me Me lele⌐

You'll seal the 2 Papers, after my name

London: May. 16. 1713.
I appoint Mr Isaiah Parvisol and Mr   to Sett and let the Tyths of the Deanry of St Patricks for this present

---

[4] An obliteration before 'and'.

[5] 'by' scrawled out before 'buy'.

[6] Brilliantly deciphered by Moorhead. Almost certainly correct. Forster reads, 'DD, and, dee deelest Ppt'. Ryland and Aitken give 'DD' and leave the rest blank.

[7] Nichols, Scott, Ryland, and Aitken read 'caps'. Hawkesworth and Sheridan omit.   [8] 'yr' before 'Th' scrawled over.

[9] Forster, Ryland, and Aitken read 'akree', 'akklee', or 'akkree', i.e. 'angry'; but the word does not look like any of these.

[10] *The History of the Four Last Years of the Queen.*

year, in witness whereof I have hereunto sett my Hand and Seal the day and year above written.[11]

London. May. 16. 1713
I do hereby appoint Mr Isaiah Parvisol my Proctor to sett and let the Tyths of the Deanry of St Patricks. In witness whereof I have hereunto sett my Hand and Seal, the Day and Year above written.

Jonat: Swift.

Address: To Mrs Dingley, at her
    Lodgings over against St Mary's
    Church near Capel-street.
     Ireland   Dublin

Postmark: $\dfrac{\text{MA}}{16}$

Endorsed by   64
Rebecca Dingley: May. 22.

LETTER LXV

[SATURDAY]   Chester. Jun. 6. 1713.[1]
I am come here after 6 days, I sett out on Monday last, and gott here to day about 11 in the morning. A Noble Rider ⌐fais¬; and all the Ships and People went off yesterday with a rare wind. This was told me to my Comfort upon my Arrivall. Having not used riding these 3 years, made me terrible weary; yet I resolve on Monday to sett out for Holyhead, as weary as I am. Tis good for my Health mun. When I came here I found ⌐Md's¬ Letter of the 26th of May sent down to me,—had you writt a Post sooner, I might have brought some Pins; but you were lazy, & would not write your orders immediatly as I desired you— I will come when God Pleases, perhaps I may be with you in a week; I will be 3 days going to

[11] The signature has been cut off.

[1] Above the place-name and date some one, possibly Rebecca Dingley or Stella, has written '64'. The correct number was '65'. Swift omitted to number his letter in the top left-hand corner of the first page. This letter covers one page only.

Holyhead; I cannot ride faster; say ⌐hat oo⌐ will. I am
upon Stay-behind's mare. I have the whole Inn to my self,
I would fain scape this Holy-head Journy, but I have no
Prospect of Ships, and it will be almost necessary I should
be in Dublin before the 25th instant, to take the others;[2]
otherwise I must wait to a quarter Sessions. I will lodge
as I can; therefore take no lodgings for me, to pay in my
absence, the poor Dean can't afford it. I spoke again to
D. Ormd about Moimed for Raymd & hope he may yet
have it.[3] for I laid it strongly to the Duke, & gave him the
Bp of Meath's Memoriall: I am sorry for Raymd's Fistula,
tell him so. I will speak to Ld Tr— about Mrs South to
morrow—Odso, I forgot; I thought I had been in London.
Mrs Tisdal is very big, ready to ly down. Her Husband
is a puppy. Do his feet stink still:—The Letters to Ireld
go at so uncertain an Hour, that I am forced to conclude
—farewell ⌐Md Md Md FW
FW FW Me Me Me Me
lele lele
lele Logues ad
Ladies bose fais
and . . . . . .⌐4

---

[2] A slip for 'oaths'.

[3] A draft memorial, in Swift's autograph, on a small piece of folded
paper, 18·3 × 15·7 cm., has been preserved; and is now in Lord Rothschild's
library. It is endorsed, 'Memoriall about | Dr Raymond. | May. 5. 1713 |
Dr Prat & | Dr Swift. |', and reads: 'The Rectory of Moimed within two
Miles of Trim in the County of Meath, value about 40ll per Annum in the
Gift of Ldy Roscommon, but now on Dr Stearn's Promotion, in the Gift
of the Governmt. It hath been usually given to the Minister of Trim, and
is no Sinecure, but the Bishop will oblige whoever has it to keep a Curate.
It is onely convenient for the Minister of Trim, being hardly worth while
for any Body else to pass Patent for it. Therefore his Grace is desired to
bestow it to Dr Raymond Minister of Trim, ⌐if none of His Grace's
Chaplains⌐ unless any body whom His Grace hath a mind to oblige, think
it worth their Acceptance.

The Cure of Trim is very great, and Profits small.'
The words in brackets are scrawled over.

[4] Forster, Ryland, and Aitken read the last three words, 'fair and

[On the inside of the cover.]
I mightily approve ppt's Project of hanging the blind
Parson—when I read that Passage upon Chester walls, as
I was coming into Town, & just receivd the Lettr: I sd
aloud—Agreable B—tch—5

Address: To Mrs Dingley, at her
       Lodgings over against St Mary's
       Church, near Capel-street
        Ireland   Dublin
No Postmark
Endorsed by   6. 5.
Rebecca Dingley: Chester-Letter.

slender'. But, as Moorhead notes, the last letter of the first word is not 'r',
and the last word is not 'slender'. It looks like 'slainte', Irish for 'health'.
But it is questionable whether Swift would have used this word.
  5 The key to the meaning of this is lost.

APPENDIXES

APPENDIX I

SWIFT'S COMMISSION FROM THE ARCHBISHOPS AND BISHOPS OF IRELAND

IN the hand of a scribe on a folded sheet, four quarto pages (British Museum, Add. MS. 4804, folios 32, 33), the commission on the first page, the second and third pages blank, Swift's endorsement on the fourth page. See p. 2, n.9

Our very good Lords

Whereas severall Applications have been made to her Majestie about the first Fruits and Twentieth parts payable to her Majestie by the Clergy of this Kingdome, beseeching her Majestie that she wou'd be gratiously pleased to Extend her bounty to the Clergy here in such manner as the Convocation have humbly laid before her Majestie, or as her Majestie shall in her Goodnes and Wisdome think fitt, and the Said Applications lye still before her Majestie and We do hope from her Royal Bounty a favourable answer.

We do therefore Entreat your Lordships to take on you the Solicitation of that affair, and to use such proper Methods, and Applications as you in your prudence shall Judge most like to be effectual. We have likewise desired the Bearer Doctor Swift to Concern himself with you being persuaded of his Diligence and good affection, And We desire that if your Lordships occasions require your leaving London before you have brought the business to effect, that you wou'd leave with him the papers relateing to it, with your Directions for his Management in it if you think it advisable so to do

We are your Lordships most

Dublin August the ⎫
   Thirty first 1710–⎰.

humble Servants and Brethren
Narcissus Armath
Will. Dubliniensis
W. Cassel
W. Meath
W. Kildare
Wm. Killala

To the Right Revd fathers in God
John Lord Bishop of Ossory and Thomas
Lord Bishop of Killalo

[*Endorsed
   by Swift:*]

Commission from
the Bps of Ireld to me
about the first Fruits
Aug. 31st. 1710

675

Appendix II

APPENDIX II
SWIFT'S COMMISSION FROM PRIMATE MARSH AND ARCHBISHOP KING

IN the hand of a scribe on a folded sheet, four quarto pages (British Museum, Add. MS. 4804, folios 40, 41), the commission on the first two pages, the third blank, address and endorsements on the fourth page. See p. 80, n.[11]

We directed a Letter to the Bishops of Ossory and Killaloe last August, desiring and empowering Them to Solicite the Affair of our First Fruits and Twentyeth Parts, with Her Majesty, which has depended so long, notwithstanding Her Majesty's Good Inclinations & several Promises of the Chief Governours how to lay our Addresses before Her Majesty in the best Manner; We now then apprehensive that These Bishops might return from England before the Busyness could be effected, and therefore We desired Them to concern You in it: having so good Assurance of your Ability, prudence and fitness to prosecute such a Matter; We find the Bishops returned before you came to London, for which We are very much concerned, and judging this the most proper Time to prosecute it with Success, We intreat you to take the full Management of it into your Hands, and do commit the care of solliciting It to your Diligence and Prudence; desiring You to let us know from Time to Time, what progress is made in it; and if any Thing further be necessary on our Part, [*p. 2*] On your Intimation We shall be ready to do what shall be judged reasonable, This with our Prayers for You and the Good Success of your Endeavours, is all from

Dublin. October   Sr. Your affectionate, Humble
ye 24th: 1710.   Servants and Brothers
                      Narcissus Armath
                      Will. Dublin

[*Address:*]   To
          The Revd Dr. Jonathan Swift
                              these
[*Endorsed by*   Power from the Ld
  Swift:]   Primate and Ar Bp Dubln
                 Octbr. 24th. 1710.
                 First fruits
  [*and again*] Primate & AB, Dublin

676

APPENDIX III

SWIFT'S MEMORIALS TO ROBERT HARLEY CONCERNING THE FIRST-FRUITS

FOR a note on the earlier draft of Swift's memorial to Harley (British Museum, Add. MS. 4804, folios 36, 37), and the later copy, see p. 45. Both are here printed from Swift's autographs. The British Museum draft is written in a small hand on the first two pages of a sheet folded to four pages, small quarto. The memorial occupies the first and second pages, the third page is blank, and an endorsement by Swift is on the fourth page. The later copy, among the manuscripts of the Duke of Portland, at Welbeck Abbey, is written on four quarto pages, the text occupying two pages with two lines on the third page. On the fourth page are endorsements by Swift and Harley.

From the draft in the British Museum

In Ireland hardly one Parish in ten hath any Glebe, and the rest very small, and scattered, except a very few, & then have seldom any Houses.

There are in Proportion more Impropriations in Ireland than in England, which added to the Poverty of the Country make the Livings of very small and uncertain Value, so that five or six are often joyned to make a Revenue of 50ll per a ann̄. but these have seldom above one Church in repair, the rest being destroyed by frequent Wars &c.

The Clergy for want of Glebes are forced in their own or neighboring Parish to take Farms to live on at Rack Rents.

The Queen having some years since remitted the First Fruits to the Clergy of England, the Bishop of Cloyn being then in London did petition Her Majesty for the same Favor in behalf of the Clergy of Ireland and received a Gracious Answer, But this Affair, for want of solliciting, was not brought to an Issue during the Governmts of the Duke of Ormond and Earl of Pembroke.

Upon the Earl of Wharton's succeeding, Dr Swift (who had sollicited this matter in the preceding Governmt) desired[1] by the Bishops of Ireland to apply to His Excy., who thought fitt to receive the Motion as wholly new, and what he could not consider till he were fixt in the Governmt. and till the same Application were made to Him as had been to his Predecessors. Accordingly an Address

---

[1] Written above 'directed', which is struck through.

was delivered to his Ldship with a Petition to te Queen and a Memoriall annexed, from both Houses of Convocation; But a dispute happening in the Lower House, wherein His Chaplain concerned and which was represented by the sd Chaplain as an affront designed to His Excy; who was pleased to understand and report it to Court, the Convocation was suddenly prorogued, and all further thoughts about the first Fruits, lett fall as desperate

The Subject of te Petition was to desire that the 20th Parts might be [*p. 2*] remitted to te Clergy, and the First fruits made a Fund for purchasing Glebes and Impropriations, and rebuilding of Churches.

The Twentyth Parts, are twelpe pence in the Pound paid annually out of all Eccliasticall Benificy, as they were valued at the Reformation. they amount to about 500ll pr ann. but of little or no value to the Queen, after the Officers and other Charges are paid, tho of much trouble and Vexation to the Clergy

The first Fruits paid by Incumbents upon their Promotion amount to about 450 p añ so that Her Majesty in remitting about 1000ll p añ to the Clergy will really lose not above 500ll.

Upon Aug. 31. 1710. The two Houses of Convocation being met to be further prorogued; te Arch-Bishops and Bishops conceiving there was now a favorable Juncture to resume their Applications, did in their private Capacityes sign a Power to te sd Dr Swift to sollicite the Remitting the First Fruits and Twentyth Parts.

But there is a greater Burthen than this and almost intollerable upon severall of the Clergy in Ireland, the easing of which, the Clergy only lookt on as a Thing to be wisht, without making it part of their Petn.

The Queen is Impropriater of severall Parishes, and the Incumbent pays her half-yearly a rent generally to the third Part of the reall Value of the Living, and sometimes half; some of their Parishes by the encrease of Graziers are seised on by the Crown, and cannot pay the required Rent. The Value of all their Impropriations are about two Thousand Pounds p añ to Her Majesty.

If the Queen would graciously please to bestow likewise these Impropriations to the Church; part to be remitted to the Incumbent, where the Rent is large, & the Living small; and the rest to be layd out in buying Glebes and Impropriations, & building of Churches It would be a most pious and seasonable Bounty

The Utmost value of the 20th Parts, First Fruits and Crown rents, is 3000ll per ann. of which about 500ll per añ is sunk among Officers; so that her Majesty by this great Benefaction would lose but 2500ll per añn.

[*p. 4*] [*Endorsed*   Copy of Memorial to
  by Swift:]   Mr Harley – about 1st Fruits

From the Portland Manuscript

There are in Proportion more Impropriations in Ireland than England, which added to the Poverty of the Country, makes the Livings of very small and uncertain Value, so that five or six united do often hardly amount to 50ll p añn; but these have seldom above one Church in repair, the rest being destroyd by the Wars. &c.

Hardly one Parish in ten hath any Glebe, and the rest, very small ones, and scattered, except very few; and even these have seldom any Houses; For want of which, the Clergy are forced to take Farms at Rack-rents in their own or some neighboring Parish.

The Queen having some years since remitted the First-fruits to the Clergy of England, the Bishop of Cloyn being some time after in London, petitioned her Majesty to grant the same Favor for Ireland, and received a gracious Answer; But this Affair for want of solliciting, was not brought to an Issue during the Government of the Duke of Ormond or Earl of Pembroke.

Upon the Earl of Wharton being nominated Lord Lieutenant, Dr Swift (having sollicited the Matter in the preceding Government) was desired by the Bishops of Ireland to apply to His Excellency; who thought fit to receive the Motion as wholly new, and what He could not consider (as He said) till He were fixed in the Governmt, and till the same Application were made to Him, as had been to His Predecessors. Accordingly, soon after His Arrivall in Ireland, an Address was delivered to His Lordship, from both Houses of Convocation, with a Memoriall, and Petition to the Queen annexed to it. But a dispute happening in the lower House, wherein His Chaplain was concerned, and which was represented by the sd Chaplain as an Affront designed to His Excellency; He was pleased to understand and report it so to the Court: Upon which the Convocation was suddenly prorogued, and all further Thoughts about the First-fruits, let fall as desperate.

The Subject of the sd Petition was to desire, that the Twentyth Parts might be remitted to the Clergy, and the First-fruits made a Fund [*p. 2*] for purchasing Glebes and Impropriations, and rebuilding Churches.

The Twentyth Parts, are twelvepence in the Pound payd yearly out of all Eclesiasticall Benefices, as they were valued at the Reformation; they amount to about 500ll p añn, but of little or no value to the Queen, after the Officers and other Charges are payd; though of much Trouble and Vexation to the Clergy.

The First-fruits payd by Incumbents upon their Promotion, amount to about 450ll p añn; so that Her Majesty in remitting near 1000ll p añn to the Clergy, will realy lose onely 500ll p añn.

But there is a greater Burthen than this, and almost intolerable upon severall of the Clergy in Ireland; the easing of which, the Convocation for some Reasons, of weight at that Time, did not make a Part of their Petition.

In certain Dioceses the Queen is Impropriator of many Parishes, and the Incumbent pays Her Majesty a yearly Rent, generally to the third Part of the reall Value of the Living; and often, a full half. Nay, some of these Parishes are sunk so low by the Increase of Graziers, that they are seised on by the Crown, which out of the whole Profits cannot make the reserved Rent. The Value of all these Impropriations is about 2000ll p añn to Her Majesty.

If the Queen would graciously please to bestow likewise these Impropriations to the Church; part to be remitted to the Incumbent, where the Rent is large and the Living small, and the rest to be layd out in purchasing Glebes, &c; it would be a most pious and seasonable Bounty.

The utmost Value of the Twentyth Parts, First-fruits and Impropriations together, is 3000ll p añn; of which above 500ll is sunk by Salaryes, and other Charges of collecting; so that Her Majesty by this great Benefaction to the Church would lose but 2000ll p añn.

Upon August 3d, 1710, the two Houses of Convocation being met onely to be further prorogued, the Arch-Bishops and Bishops conceiving there was now a favorable Juncture to resume their Applications, did in their [*p. 3*] private Capacities sign a Power to the sd Dr Swift, to sollicite the remitting the First-fruits and Twentyth Parts.

[*p. 4*] [*Endorsed   Dr Swift's Memoriall
   by Swift:*]   about the First-fruits of Ireland.
                 Octbr. 7. 1710

[*Endorsed   ℞ octo: 16: 1710
   by Harley:*]

APPENDIX IV
SWIFT'S CHARACTER OF ROBERT HARLEY, LORD OXFORD

SEE p. 614. On 3 Feb. 1712–13, while he was engaged upon the composition of his *History of the Four Last Years of the Queen*, Swift dined with Lord Oxford, and 'gave him that Part of my Book in Manuscript to read, where his Character was, and drawn pretty freely'. While Oxford was 'correcting it with his Pencil' the Bishop of St. David's came in and interrupted them. A fair copy of this character, in Swift's hand, is preserved among the manuscripts of the Marquess of Bath, at Longleat (*Portland Papers*, vol. xiii, folios 47, 48). Presumably, as it is carefully written throughout, without markings, the Longleat manuscript was a revision submitted to Oxford a few days after the earlier draft had been returned with pencil corrections, for, on the verso of the second leaf, there is an endorsement in his hand: 'Ry Febr: 11: $17\frac{12}{13}$.' The text of this revision, with some insignificant verbal variants, was adopted in the printed work, save for the addition of the following criticism of Oxford, which does not appear in the Longleat manuscript: 'There is one thing peculiar in his temper, which I altogether disapprove, and do not remember to have heard or met with in any other man's character: I mean, an easiness and indifference under any imputation, although he be never so innocent, and although the strongest probabilities and appearance are against him; so that I have known him often suspected by his nearest friends, for some months, in points of the highest importance, to a degree, that they were ready to break with him, and only undeceived by time and accident.'

The complete character appears at pp. 170–6 of the original edition of *The History of the Four Last Years of the Queen; Prose Works*, x. 93–6. Swift's manuscript, here printed as written, covers nearly three folio pages, the text written to the right hand, leaving the left of the page for additions and corrections.

'In this oppressed and entangled State was the Kingdom with relation to its Debts, when the Queen removed the Earl of Godolphin from his Office, and putt it into Commission, of which the present Treasurer was one. This Person had been chosen Speaker successively to three Parliamts, was afterwards Secretary of State, and allways in great Esteem with the Queen for His Wisdom and

Fidelity. The late Ministry about two Years before their Fall, had prevailed with Her Majesty much against her Inclination to dimiss him from her Service, for which they cannot be justly blamed, since he had endeavored the same thing against them, and very narrowly failed; which makes it the more extraordinary that he should succeed in the same Attempt a second time, against those very Adversaryes who had such fair warning by the first. He is firm and steddy in his Resolutions, not easily diverted from them after he has once possessed himself of an Opinion that they are right: Nor very communicative where he can act by himself, being taught by Experience that a Secret is seldom safe in more than one Breast. That which occurs to other Men after mature Deliberation, offers to him as his first Thought, so that he decides immediatly what is best to be done, and is therefore never at a loss upon sudden Exigencyes. He thinks it a more easy and safe Rule in Politicks, to watch Incidents as they come, and then turn them to the Advantage of what he pursues, than pretend to foresee them at a great Distance. Fear, Avarice, Cruelty, and Pride are wholly Strangers to his Nature; but he is not without Ambition. His Detractors who charge him with Cunning, are but ill acquainted with his Character: For, in the Sense they take the Word, and as it is usually understood, I know no Man to whom that mean Talent could be with less Justice applyed, as the Conduct of Affairs while he hath been at the Helm, doth clearly demonstrate: Very [*p. 2*] contrary to the Nature and Principles of Cunning: which is always employd in serving little Turns, proposing little Ends, and supplying daily Exigencyes by little Shifts and Expedients. But, to rescue a Prince out of the Hands of insolent Subjects, bent upon such Designs as must probably end in the Ruin of the Governmt; to find out Means for paying such immense Debts as this Nation is involved in, and reduce it to better Managemt: to make a potent Enemy offer advantageous Terms of Peace, and deliver up the most important Fortress of his Kingdom as a Pledge; and this against all the Oppositions mutually raised and enflamed by Partyes and Allyes: Such Performances can only be called Cunning by those whose Want of Understanding or of Candor puts them upon finding ill Names for great Qualityes of the Mind which themselves do neither possess nor can form any just Conception of. However, it must be allowed, that an obstinate Love of Secrecy in this Minister, seems at Distance to have some Resemblance of Cunning, for he is not only very retentive of Secrets, but *Appears* to be so too; which I number among his Defects. He hath been blamed by his Friends for refusing to discover his Intentions, even in those Points where the wisest Man may have need of Advice and Assistance: and some have censured him upon that Account, as if he were jealous of Power; to which he hath been heard to answer that he seldom did otherwise without Cause to repent. However, so undistinguished a Caution cannot in my Opinion be altogether justifyed; by which the Owner loses many Advantages, and whereof all men who are really honest may with some Reason complain. His Love of Procrastination (wherein doubtless Nature has her share) may probably be encreased by the same means; but this is an Imputation layd upon many other great Ministers, who like Men under too heavy a Load, let fall that which is of least Consequence, and go back to fetch it when their Shoulders are free. For Time is often gained as well as [*p. 3*] lost by Delay, which at worst is a Fault on the securer Side. Neither probably[1] is this Minister answerable for half the Clamor raised against Him upon this Article. His Endeavors are wholly turned upon the generall welfare of His Country, but perhaps with too little regard to that of particular Persons, which renders him less amiable than he would otherwise have been from the goodness of his Nature, and his agreeable Conversation in a private Capacity, and with few Dependers. Yet some Allowance may be given to this Failing, which is one of the greatest he has, since he cannot be more careless of other Mens Fortunes than he is of his own. He is Master of a very great and faithfull Memory, which is of mighty use in the management of publick Affairs: And I believe there are few Examples to be produced in any Age of the World, of a Person who hath passed through so many Employments in the State, endowed with so great a Share both of divine and human Learning.

'I am persuaded that Foreigners, as well as those at home who live too remote from the Scene of Business to be rightly informed, will not be displeased with this Account of a Person who in the space of . . . . . . Years hath been so highly instrumentall in changing the face of Affairs in Europe, and hath deserved so well of his own Prince and Country.

'In that perplexed Condition of the publick Debts which I have above described, this Minister was brought into the Treasury and Exchequer &c—'

1 'probably' is written above 'perhaps', which is scored out.

683

APPENDIX V

SWIFT'S DRAFTS FOR THE ADDRESS OF THE HOUSE OF LORDS TO THE QUEEN

SEE p. 635 n.²⁴ The first draft, [A], is written on the recto and verso of two quarto leaves. On the verso of the second leaf is written, also in Swift's hand, 'Address. &c.'

The second draft, [B], is written on a torn and much mended piece of paper, endorsed on the verso, 'Vote. &c'

[A] We Your Majesty's most dutifull and loyall subjects the Lords spirituall and Temporall in Parlmt assembled, do with the greatest Joy and Satisfaction return out humblest Thanks to Your Majesty for Your most gracious Speech from the Throne, and for communicating to this House, that a Peace is concluded, *so honorable to Your Majesty and safe and advantageous to Your Kingdoms*; by which we hope with the Blessing of God, that your People will in a few Years recover themselves after so long and expensive a War, *We likewise beg leave to congratulate with Your Majesty upon the generall Peace you have procured for all Your Allyes, wherein the true Interests and just Pretensions of each are so fully provided for that the Tranquillity and Welfare of Europe will be owing (next to the Divine Providence) to Your Majesty's Wisdom and Goodness.* We never had the last [*sic*] doubt, but that Your Majesty who is the greatest Ornament and Protector of the Protestant Religion, would continue to take the wisest Measures for securing the Protestant success . . . [blot]: towards which [*p. 2*] nothing can be more necessary than the perfect *Harmony*¹ there is between Your Majesty and the House of Hanover. And we do humbly assure Your Majesty, that as you are pleased to express Your Dependance (next under God) upon the Duty and Affection of Your People; we think our selves bound by the strictest Tyes of Religion, Loyalty, and Gratitude, to make all Returns that can be due from the most obedient Subjects to the most indulgent Soverain.

[B] Ordered that an humble Address be made to Her Majesty to return the Most humble thanks of this House to her Majesty, for Her most gracious Speech from the Throne., and for Her

¹ The word 'friendshipp', roughly scribbled in the left margin, is apparently in Oxford's hand.

Majesty's communicating to this House that a Peace is agreed on, and to congratulate Her Majesty upon the success of her Endeavors for a generall Peace, and for what Her Majesty has done to secure
_{& the Harmony between her & the House of Hanover[1]}
th[e] Protestant Succession; and to assure Her Majesty, that as she is pleased to express her Dependence next under God upon the Duty and Affection of her People, this House will make all Returns that are due from obedient Subjects to the most indulgent Soverain

[1] The interlineation is in another and very angular hand.

APPENDIX VI

IN four account books (Forster Collection, 506, 507, 508, 509) Swift gives lists of letters written to and received from correspondents, together with the dates of dispatch and receipt. Entry dates from 507, 508, and 509, so far as they relate to letters contained in the *Journal*, or received from MD, are extracted below.

To MD				*From MD*	
			1710	Sept. 21	
				25	
1711	Nov. 3	No. 33			
	17	34	1711	Nov. 21	No. 23
	Dec. 1	35			
	14	36		Dec. 27	24
	29	37	1712	Jan. 11	25
1712	Jan. 12	38			
	26	39		29	26
	Feb. 9	40			
	23	41			
	Mar. 8	42		Mar. 19	27
	22	43			
	Apr. 10	44		Apr. 21	28
	25	45 (short)		May 9	29

	To MD			From MD	
1712	May 10	46 (short)			
	29	47			
	June 17	48	1712	June 13	30
	July 3	49			
	19	50		July 4	31
	Aug. 7	51		29	32
	Sept. 20	52			
	Oct. 9	53		Sept. 23	33
				Oct. 22	34
	31	54			
	Nov. 18	55			
				Dec. 2	35
	Dec. 13	56		11	36
1713	Jan. 3	57			
	23 (about)	58	1713	Jan. 23	37
	Feb. 14	59			
	28	60		Feb. 18 (about)	38
	Mar. 2	61			
	Apr. 7	62			
	28	63		Apr. 24	39
	May 16	64			

APPENDIX VII

PORTRAITS OF STELLA AND VANESSA

by

HENRY MANGAN

THERE appears to be no contemporary reference to a portrait of Stella or of Vanessa, but several paintings exist which are said to represent their features, and these may as well be considered in the order of their appearance.

I (*see plate facing p.* 160)

First comes the Stella seen as frontispiece to vol. xvii of George Faulkner's edition of Swift's works, published in Dublin in 1768, and described as 'From an Original Drawing by the Revd. George Parnel, Archdeacon of Clogher, in the Possession of G. Faulkner'. The artist, whose name is given incorrectly, was Dr. Thomas Parnell, the poet, a friend of Swift's, who died in Oct. 1718. Faulkner, too, was intimate with Swift, who refers to him as 'the prince of Dublin printers';[1] and, as he appears to have been known to Swift in 1726,[2] he was probably familiar with Stella's appearance.

The portrait, however, is a poor and lifeless reproduction, some 4 in. by 3 in., which one may hope is not a faithful rendering of the 'Original Drawing', not now forthcoming. The fact that it was published as Stella, with the artist's name, in the lifetime of some of her contemporaries, and by one of them, invests it with a measure of authenticity, so far as it goes. While it evokes no vivid personality, it shows crudely certain characteristics resembling those in other portraits, and may be found useful for comparative purposes. Faulkner's reason for selecting this portrait for publication was probably that it was in his own 'Possession'.

II (*see plate facing p.* 288)

There is, so far as I am aware, no printed reference to any other portrait of Stella until 1814, when Sir Walter Scott in the Memoir prefixed to his edition of Swift's works, stated that 'the only por-

---

[1] *The Correspondence of Jonathan Swift,* ed. F. Elrington Ball, iv. 389.
[2] Ibid. iii. 343.

trait of Stella known to exist, is in the possession of my kind and respected friend, the Rev. Mr. Berwick'.[1]

The Rev. Edward Berwick has a memorial column in the *D.N.B.*, which tells us that he was born in 1750, took orders, and in 1795 was preferred from his native Co. Down to the vicarage of Leixlip, Co. Kildare, by the Earl of Moira, who made him his domestic chaplain. It was the Earl's sister, Lady Charlotte Rawdon, who first advised Sir Walter Scott to consult Berwick as the best authority on Swiftiana at the time.

His interest had probably been aroused when he came to live at Esker, near Leixlip, and only a few miles from Marlay Abbey, Celbridge (then called Kildrought), the former home of Vanessa. Indeed, Sir Walter tells us that 'Mr. Berwick has a picture of one of the Miss Vanhomrighs, but whether Vanessa or her sister is, I believe, doubted'.[2] Curiously enough, beyond this tantalizing peep, we see and hear no more of this portrait.

Mr. Berwick had been noted for his humanity during the insurrection of 1798, and was a close friend of Henry Grattan, who, in 1805, congratulated him on having been presented with a portrait of Swift, though he added 'he was a Tory, and everything that was said of him'.[3] Mr. Berwick had also another portrait of the Dean. As Scott said, he was 'well known to the literary world', having published in 1810 a *Life of Apollonius of Tyana*, from the Greek, with notes and illustrations, and in 1811 *A Treatise on the Government of the Church*.

It was from him that Scott got, with other manuscripts, the transcript of 'the suppressed correspondence between Swift and Miss Vanhomrigh', which he was the first to publish. Berwick had transcribed a copy made by Robert (afterwards Judge) Marshall, one of Vanessa's executors, and although the originals were acquired by the British Museum in 1919 and are said to 'differ considerably from the printed versions',[4] they appear to confirm the substantial authenticity of Berwick's copy of a copy. Though Mr. Berwick had no direct connexion with Swift, he had probably become aware of a tradition regarding his portrait of Stella extending back into the eighteenth century, but we have not been told when or where he

---

[1] *Works of Swift*, 1814, i. 241 n.   [2] Ibid. 228 n.

[3] *Life of Grattan*, by his son, v. 278.

[4] *Vanessa and her Correspondence with Jonathan Swift*, ed. A. Martin Freeman (1921), p. 47.

got it, and its history up to the beginning of the nineteenth century is a blank. Moreover, his dubious Vanessa remains unaccounted for.

The portrait of Stella passed to Berwick's son, Judge Berwick, from him to his brother Edward Berwick, President of Queen's College, Galway, whose widow died in 1894, leaving the Stella and one of the Swifts to two relatives and Sir Frederick Falkiner, Recorder of Dublin, in trust for a health retreat for young girls, to be founded out of her fortune. 'It was', Sir Frederick tells us, 'the trustees' duty of appraising the value of the bequest which induced an inquiry into their pedigrees, leading to a quest after all authentic likenesses, painted, engraved, or sculptured.'

The results of the investigation, which extended over several years, are set out in Sir Frederick's essay on the portraits of Swift and Stella (and, incidentally, a Vanessa) in vol. xii of the Temple Scott edition of Swift's *Prose Works* (pp. 1–82). Sir Frederick died as that volume was passing through the press, and in the same year, 1908, the portrait of Stella was acquired, with the Swift by Bindon, by the Board of Governors and Guardians of the National Gallery of Ireland, where it now is.

The latest catalogue of the National Portrait Gallery of Ireland (1928) thus describes this Stella: 'Oil picture—Artist unknown. Half-length, nearly full face; in low-cut, blue dress, with red mantle falling from her shoulders—Dark hair, with curl falling over her left shoulder.'

The portrait was reproduced in 1897 as frontispiece to vol. ii of Swift's *Prose Works*, and has appeared later, e.g. in Sir Shane Leslie's *The Skull of Swift* (1928) and in Carl Van Doren's *Swift* (1931).

III (*see plate facing p. 432*)

In 1848 Sir William Wilde published *The Closing Years of Dean Swift's Life*, revised and enlarged in 1849, in which he discussed the personal appearance of Stella and her portraits (pp. 118–25). He had, he said, 'opportunities of examining several portraits and miniatures said to have been painted for her. There are two oil paintings in this city which tradition asserts to be originals of Esther Johnson. They are both of females about twenty years of age. One of them was lately, along with a very good original of the Dean, in the possession of Mrs. Hillis. These were purchased several years ago in the Liberty of Dublin, and are said to have been the property of Swift's butler. The other likeness of Stella is that which Sir Walter Scott alluded to as the only portrait known to exist; it is in the possession of Walter Berwick, Esq., who has kindly lent it to us for the purposes of this inquiry.'

It is remarkable that Wilde makes no further reference to the portrait 'lately' owned by 'Mrs Hillis', although it was apparently one of the three portraits of Stella which he states (p. 123) 'are now before us'; the other two being the Berwick and another from Bellinter, Co. Meath.

'Wilde,' says Falkiner, 'who regarded the Bellinter portrait as a discovery of his own, disparages this Berwick Stella because the black tresses show some shades of brown, as those of most dark beauties do when the light is full upon them.' Wilde alleged that the Berwick Stella was 'unknown beyond the last thirty years; and even Mr. Berwick's father himself had some doubts about its authenticity at the time'. He said, 'There certainly is a likeness; the hair, however, is brown, not black, which would be a fatal objection to any picture supposed to be that of Stella.' He quoted from the 'character' of Stella which Swift wrote on the night of her death. 'She was sickly from her childhood until about the age of 15, but then grew into perfect health, and was looked upon as one of the most beautiful, graceful, and agreeable young women in London, only a little too fat. Her hair was blacker than a raven, and every feature of her face in perfection. She had a gracefulness somewhat more than human in every motion, word, and action.'

Here I may add that in other references by Swift to Stella 'black' cannot, of course, be taken literally, but indicates that she was of dark complexion, or a brunette. Thus, writing from London, 26 Nov. 1713, to Archdeacon Walls, he says, 'I think if the black lady does not find amendment in her health they had better come where company is stirring.'[1] Writing to the Archdeacon again from Gaulstown on 18 June 1716, he says, 'I leave the rest to your black Privy Counsellor—be not frightened, I mean only Mrs. Johnson.'[2]

Wilde quoted also the glowing description of her beauty given by an anonymous writer in *The Gentleman's Magazine*, Nov. 1757 (xxvii. 487 ff.); but this article was considered of doubtful authenticity by Dr. F. Elrington Ball.[3] He mentioned, too, Scott's quotation

[1] *Corresp.* ii. 94. [2] Ibid. 324. [3] Ibid. iv. 450.

of Mrs. Delany's recollection of Stella, as given to him by a friend of hers. Long before her marriage to the Doctor, Mrs. Delany 'once saw her by accident, and was struck by the beauty of her countenance, and particularly with her fine dark eyes. She was very pale, and looked pensive, but not melancholy, and had hair black as a raven'.[1] The last phrase is but an echo of Swift's, and the description is merely the product of an old lady's imagination, for the first visit of Mrs. Pendarves (later Mrs. Delany) to Ireland was in Sept. 1731,[2] three years after Stella's death, and Stella and Mrs. Dingley in 1707 and 1708 'paid the only visit [to England] they are known to have made during their residence in Ireland',[3] when Mrs. Delany was only eight years old.

During repairs to St. Patrick's Cathedral, which became necessary in 1835 owing to damp from the adjoining underground river Poddle, the skulls of Swift and Stella were exhumed, and were examined by the British Association, then meeting in Dublin. Wilde gives a sketch of a cast of the skull of Stella, which he describes as 'a perfect model of symmetry and beauty' which it required 'no great stretch of the imagination to clothe' with its former beauty. 'Most of the biographers of Swift', he said, 'describe Stella as "a dumpy woman", but this idea has evidently arisen from the expression of the Dean's already alluded to.'

The Bellinter Stella is not of that type, and Wilde pointed out that in later life Stella lost much of her plumpness and also some of her beauty, as is mentioned by Swift himself in the later odes upon her birthday. In 1721 (when Stella was forty) he said that this was

> Stella's Case in Fact;
> An Angel's Face, a little crack't.[4]

In her poem for Swift's birthday, 30 Nov. 1721, Stella herself (then nearing forty-one) alludes to the fact.

> Behold that beauty just decay'd,
> Invoking art to nature's aid.[5]

'In 1725', Wilde goes on, 'Swift wrote the "Receipt to restore Stella's Youth", and in that poem her thinness and want of flesh form the burden of the Dean's song.'

In Wilde's opinion there was but one portrait, 'the history of

[1] *Works of Swift*, i. 241.
[2] *Life and Correspondence of Mrs. Delany*, i. 286.
[3] *Corresp.* iv. 454.   [4] *Poems*, p. 734.   [5] Ibid. 737.

which is undoubtedly authentic, and which perfectly answers both to the foregoing description and to the characteristics of the skull'. It was originally in the possession of Charles Ford, the most intimate friend of Swift, Stella, and Vanessa, all of whom had visited him at his home, Woodpark, Co. Meath, where, as Wilde points out, Stella 'spent several months in 1723, when probably it was painted', Stella being then about forty-two. Between the Dean and Stella, Ford was 'Don Carlos'; between the Dean and Vanessa, he was 'Glassheel'. Mrs. Pilkington says[1] he was 'one of the oddest little Mortals I ever met with', who could sup with the Dean and dictate and contradict with impunity!

Charles Ford was son of Edward Ford, or Forth, Co. Cavan. Born in Dublin, 1682, he spent most of his later years out of Ireland, left Wood Park, 1731, and died, unmarried, in London, 1743.[2] His property passed to Mr. Preston of Bellinter in the same county, near historic Tara, from whom it was later inherited by Mr. G. Villiers Briscoe, and the picture is still in Bellinter House, in the possession of Mr. Cecil H. Villiers Briscoe.

Wilde's description runs, 'The hair is jet black, the eyes dark to match, the forehead fair, high, and expansive, the nose rather prominent, and the features generally regular and well-marked. Notwithstanding that it has not been highly worked by the artist, there is a "pale cast of thought" and an indescribable expression about this picture, which heighten the interest its historic recollections awaken. She is attired in a plain white dress, with a blue scarf; and around her bust hangs a blue ribbon, to which a locket appears to be appended, and she wears attached to the lower part of her dress a white and red rose.' A note explains that there was a tradition that Stella wore a locket with a miniature of the Dean.

The engraving which forms the frontispiece to Wilde's book shows a young and lovely woman, and he tells us (p. 125 n.) that Mr. James Forde 'copied the painting of Stella at Bellinter', which forms the frontispiece to his book, and that it was engraved by Mr. Engleheart. Between them, as by touches of fairy wands, they transformed the Bellinter Stella into a younger and more beautiful woman.

The reproduction of the Bellinter portrait which appears in

[1] *Memoirs,* i. 65.

[2] *The Letters of Jonathan Swift to Charles Ford,* ed. D. Nichol Smith (1935), Introduction, *passim.*

vol. ii of the Temple Scott edition of Swift's prose works (facing p. 266) is more faithful than Wilde's engraving, but appears somewhat idealized as compared with the picture as it is at present.

In his essay, already referred to, Sir Frederick Falkiner says, 'The premier portrait of Stella is certainly that . . . at Bellinter. . . . It is a splendid likeness of a splendid woman . . . her snowy, pillared neck beneath her jet black hair. In the valley of her full bosom are two roses, red and white . . . rising from her pearly dress with a background of blue-green poplin.'

Sir Frederick said 'it must have been painted some time about 1717–18' (p. 64) but later contradicted this (p. 67) by agreeing with Wilde that it was probably during Stella's six months' stay at Woodpark in 1723 'that Ford had Stella painted'. The likelihood of her having been painted when away from Dublin, especially after Vanessa's death and during Swift's absence in the country, is far from clear.

Wilde, as has been seen, not only insisted upon jet-black hair for Stella, but stated it was to be found only in the Bellinter portrait; and Falkiner, while generously allowing a measure of authenticity to brown-haired maidens, agreed that 'the premier portrait' was the Bellinter one and had jet-black hair. It is almost incredible that this is not so. The Bellinter Stella, like the others, has dark-brown hair. More astonishing still, there is at Bellinter House a fine portrait of a lady of the period *with black hair*, but neither Wilde nor Falkiner made any reference to it. It is dealt with later on (IX).

Another surprising, but minor, inaccuracy of Wilde's regarding the Bellinter Stella is the statement that 'around her bust hangs a blue ribbon, to which a locket appears to be appended'. There is no blue ribbon and no locket (with legend) attached. Falkiner does not repeat Wilde's mis-statement, but both of them omitted to mention a red ribbon running round the frill of the bodice and down the front.

IV

Wilde referred briefly to a 'medallion bust painted in oils', in a little temple in the grounds of Delville, Glasnevin, Dublin, the old home of Swift's friend, Dr. Delany. There was a tradition that it was Stella, by Mrs. Delany, but as Wilde points out, the Doctor did not marry her until long after Stella's death, and more conclusive evidence against the story has already been given (III).

Although the evidence was only traditional and the medallion was 'evidently the work of an amateur', still, as it had never been engraved, had been greatly defaced, and must soon be obliterated, Wilde gave a woodcut of it from a sketch by Mr. James Forde. It was of no significance and has long since disappeared.

V

Falkiner stated, 'it is probable that the premier portrait was not finished till some time after from an original study, for in the same room at Bellinter is another Stella traditionally said to have been the first sent there from Woodpark. It is in pose and outline nearly identical with the finished portrait, but as a painting wholly inferior.'

Wilde did not mention this second Stella, which is not young or beautiful, but has a rather determined expression. However, he does not record a visit to Bellinter as Falkiner does; and it is apparent from his remarks that the first Stella was lent to him for the purpose of his inquiry, as the Berwick Stella was.

VI *(see plate facing p.* 576)

Sir Frederick Falkiner referred to a portrait which had been in the National Portrait Gallery of Ireland since 1893. The catalogue description is, 'Half length in painted oval, turned towards the left; in amber coloured, low-cut dress, lined with blue.' Falkiner gave more details. 'The face', he said, is 'slightly turned so as to show three-quarters: the black tresses are of the strong and wiry texture which causes them to curl in irregular coils, and they show still more brown lights than the Berwick, and are not the raven blue-black which Wilde deemed essential. The eyes are very beautiful, dark brown. As a likeness it is not perhaps equal to the Bellinter or the Berwick, for there is something of smallness in the contour of the mouth which takes from the dignity seen in these two portraits. But it is manifestly the same lady and of similar date and mould: similar in the pose of the erect neck and the swelling bosom, which almost escapes from the confinement of the close-fitting pearl bodice, identical with that of Bellinter, the sleeves lined similarly with Swift's green poplin. And yet this portrait has a very doubtful pedigree. It was purchased for the Gallery from a Dublin dealer in 1893, who only knew of it that he bought it about 1891 at the sale of a Mr. Harvey, who had been a wealthy merchant in Dublin for over fifty years.'

While Falkiner's description of the portrait may be accepted, his comparison of it with the Bellinter portrait is open to question. I do not think 'it is manifestly the same lady and of similar date and mould'.

The Registrar of the National Gallery of Ireland informed me that this portrait 'was purchased from Mr. J. G. Nairn, Denzille Street, Dublin, in 1893. It originally belonged (with a portrait of Swift) to — Harvey of Wellington Quay, Dublin. Its first ascription, as a "Female Portrait", was to William Hogarth. This was changed later to Charles Jervas and so it stands.' Sir Walter Armstrong, Director of the Gallery, 1892–1914, recorded his opinion that it was 'more probably Jervas', and Strickland included it in his list of Jervas's works. It is hereinafter short-titled as the Jervas Stella.

Now Mr. Harvey of Wellington Quay was not a wealthy merchant, but first appears in the Dublin Directory of 1849 as Reuben T. Harvey, Solicitor, 59 Gardiner Street, Lower, at which address he remained until 1859. From 1860 to 1891 his office address was 13 Wellington Quay, his private residence in the latter year and previously being 6 Alphonsus Road, Drumcondra. He died at Howth on 9 July 1894.

Mr. Harvey evidently became a solicitor in 1848, the year in which Wilde's book on Swift appeared and all Dublin was talking about it. It is possible that he heard of, or read in the book itself or in reviews of it, Wilde's statement that 'there are two oil paintings in this city which tradition asserts to be originals of Esther Johnson. . . . One of them was lately, along with a very good original of the Dean, in the possession of Mrs. Hillis. These were purchased several years ago in the Liberty of Dublin, and are said to have been the property of Swift's butler.'[1]

As Wilde effectively disparaged the 'Hillis' portrait by saying nothing more about it, I give some further information about his mysterious 'Mrs. Hillis', gleaned from old Dublin directories and other sources. In the first place there was apparently no such person; but on 10 July 1787 one Annesley Hillas entered Trinity College, Dublin, aged nineteen.[2] On 2 Apr. 1819 'Ansley' Hillas was elected master to the school attached to St. Patrick's Cathedral, then 'in a room in the South Close'. He was awaiting the Arch-

---

[1] *Supra*, pp. 689–90.
[2] *Alumni Dublinenses* (1924).

bishop's licence but was superannuated with pension on 7 Feb. 1821.[1]

From 1829 to 1834 the name of Rev. A. Hillas appears at the address 1 South Patrick's Close, in the Liberty of St. Patrick's, beside the school and in the shadow of the Cathedral. He probably died in the latter year, for in 1835 Mrs. Hillas emerges as the occupier of 1 Patrick's Close South, for that year only, having, no doubt, been permitted to stay there for some little time after her husband's death.

I can find no trace of Mrs. Hillas's pictures of the Dean and Stella until Wilde's cryptic reference to them in 1848, but the statement that they were purchased in the Liberties of Dublin, near St. Patrick's, and the tradition.that they were 'the property of Swift's butler' cannot be so airily dismissed when a Mrs. Hillas's connexion with St. Patrick's (undisclosed by Wilde) is proved. As it is recorded that when he retired in 1891 Mr. Harvey had portraits of both Swift and Stella, there is some ground for the presumption that these were the very portraits formerly owned by Mrs. Hillas, especially as they have not been otherwise accounted for.

The Jervas portrait is not signed, but we know that Jervas was in Dublin from June to December 1716[2] and again in the summer of 1717.[3] Swift's accounts tell us that Jervas was dining with Stella and himself at the Deanery on 17 May and 5 Sept. 1718,[4] and he was still in Ireland in December.[5] He was there also in the summer of 1721.[6] During his visits Swift sat to him at least once, for, writing to the Earl of Oxford in August 1725, the Dean refers to the picture 'which Mr. Jervas drew in Ireland, and carried over'.[7] It seems likely that Jervas took the opportunity of painting one or more portraits of Stella while he was in Dublin, for he seems to have liked painting his friends' portraits as souvenirs. Strickland[8] mentions that in his will, 2 Sept. 1738, he left his wife a collection of 'his portraits of relations and friends done by him' and desired his many other pictures to be sold, which was done partly in Mar. 1740, and the remainder in Apr. 1747, after his widow's death, the sales occupying many days. Perhaps a Stella was among those at the latter sale?

---

[1] *The Fasti of St. Patrick's*, by H. J. Lawlor, D.D., p. 255.
[2] *Corresp.* ii. 325 n., 333, 347.   [3] Ibid. iii. 18 n.
[4] Ibid. iv. 458.   [5] Ibid. iii. 18 n.   [6] Ibid. iii. 97.
[7] Ibid. iii. 262.   [8] *Dictionary of Irish Artists* (1913).

Appendix VII

Charles Jervas was an Irishman, a son of John Jervas of Clon-liske,[1] Shinrone, Offaly. He was born about 1675, and was for some time a pupil of Kneller, whom he succeeded in 1723 as principal painter to George I, a position which he retained under George II. He died in 1739. In the D.N.B. Mr. Lionel Cust, a former Director of the National Portrait Gallery, London, alludes to his 'facile style of portrait painting' and taste in costume which gained him fashionable patronage. Strickland says, 'Extravagantly praised in his own day, Jervas's art was afterwards as unduly depreciated. . . . His drawing, indeed, is indifferent . . . but he was a good colourist, with clearness and brilliancy in his flesh tints; and often . . . redeemed his faulty drawing by a certain grace and style.'

The Jervas portrait has been reproduced at least twice in recent years, viz., in *Vanessa and the Dean*, by Lewis Gibbs (1938), and in *Jonathan Swift, Dean and Pastor*, by R. Wyse Jackson, LL.D. (1939).

VII

Sir Frederick Falkiner also dealt with three portraits of Swift, Stella, and Vanessa, then at Coolmore, Co. Kilkenny, the residence of Major Connellan, D.L. Although long in the family, he said, the pedigrees of these pictures were obscure. 'The Stella, however, at once declares itself a replica or copy of the Bellinter picture. The pose, the figure, and the dress are identical, save that a green silk tie at the bosom takes the place of the red and white roses, whilst the silk bodice is saffron instead of pearl colour, and the green poplin overshawl is less developed than at Bellinter. But it is noteworthy that the black tresses are not the raven or blue-black, on which Sir W. Wilde set such store as essential to Stella, but in the full light show a brown tinge as in the Berwick portrait.'

Falkiner may have been making his comparison with the Bellinter portrait from memory, but the statement that 'the pose, the figure and the dress are identical' is certainly inexact. The pose is quite different—the faces are looking in opposite directions. In the Coolmore portrait the face appears thinner, the chin narrower, and the shoulders more sloping; and as to the dress, the lace frill of the bodice is more elaborate, and an ornamental chain, unnoticed by Falkiner, is clasped under the tie at the bosom and curves downwards to the right side of the waist.

This picture has been reproduced—but as Vanessa (see VIII).

[1] Strickland, op. cit.

697

VIII

As already mentioned, Sir Frederick Falkiner brought Vanessa on the stage for the first time from Coolmore and complications followed. 'Vanessa's portrait', he said, 'is apparently of the same date and artistic style [as the Stella] in the fashion of the costume and pose of the figure', and he admits, 'Her face is certainly not beautiful, rather what we might name of the pansy type, pale, sentimental and weakish, although intellectual; the mouth plaintive and inquiring, but not lovely, yet characteristic as of a blue-stocking who died of love.'

The three pictures at Coolmore afterwards came into the possession of the late Dr. R. R. Leeper of St. Patrick's (Swift's) Hospital, Dublin, where they still are. Dr. Leeper, however, reversed Falkiner's decision and maintained that Falkiner's Vanessa was Stella and his Stella was Vanessa, and as Vanessa the portrait distinguished by the lace and the ornamental chain, i.e. Falkiner's Stella (VII), has been reproduced in Mr. Stephen Gwynn's *The Life and Friendships of Dean Swift* (1939), p. 246.

IX

It is strange that neither Wilde nor Falkiner mentioned a fine portrait, reputed to be of Vanessa by an unknown artist, which has been long at Bellinter House. No doubt they were primarily interested in Stella.

This portrait is half-length, of the same dimensions as the 'Premier' Stella there, 30 in. by 25 in.; the hair is black and the eyes dark brown. The bodice is light blue, not so low-cut as Stella's, with a daintier lace frill; the folds of a cloak are in the background and at the bosom is a pinkish-grey silk bow. The bust is turned to the spectator's right, but the nearly full face is looking to the front, with an alert, intelligent expression and a firm mouth.

The arguments in favour of the authenticity of the Bellinter Stella apply also to the Vanessa, as Charles Ford was an intimate friend of the Vanhomrigh family as well as of herself. Although not recorded by Falkiner, this picture has become well known in recent years, having been reproduced (as Vanessa), for instance, in Sir Shane Leslie's *The Skull of Swift* (1928), in Carl van Doren's *Swift* (1931), and in Lewis Gibbs's *Vanessa and the Dean* (1938).

X

Another portrait of Stella was in the possession of the late Dr. Leeper and was left to his daughter, Mrs. McClelland, Palmerston Park, Dublin, where it now is. It came from a sale at Charleville House, near Enniskerry, Co. Wicklow, which had been the principal residence of Lord Monck's family, but it does not appear as a Stella in the auction catalogue.

It represents an older lady than the Jervas Stella (VI), but the pose is identical. The three-quarter face is turned to the left, the dark-brown hair gathered behind the ear; the bodice is not pearl-grey but orange, and a dull-red cloak shows at the left.

A good reproduction appeared in 1931 in Mr. Stephen Gwynn's *The Life and Friendships of Dean Swift*, but no information regarding its earlier history has been given. A definite link with Swift can, however, be established. One of his intimate friends was Sir John Stanley, and several allusions to dining with him occur in the *Journal to Stella* in 1710 and 1711: for instance, 9 Oct. 1710, 'I dined to-day at Sir John Stanley's; my Lady Stanley is one of my favourites.'

Sir John owned considerable property in Dublin and is known to readers of Mrs. Delany's Correspondence as her uncle by marriage.[1] When writing to Swift, 9 Sept. 1734, she (then Mrs. Pendarves) alludes to 'a few weeks I spent at Sir John Stanley's, at Northend, the Delville of this part of the world'.[2] Swift's friendship was a lasting one, for, so late as 30 Oct. 1736, he writes pleasantly to Sir John on behalf of one of his Irish tenants and tells him, 'as to this country, I am only a favourite of my old friends the rabble, and I return their love because I know none else who deserve it.'[3]

This Sir John Stanley, who came to Dublin as Secretary to the Duke of Shrewsbury when Lord Lieutenant, was an ancestor[4] of Charles Stanley Monck of Charleville, Co. Wicklow, and Grange Gorman, Co. Dublin, who was born in Dublin about 1754, created Baron Monck in 1797, and Viscount in 1801.[5] In an early letter Mrs. Delany says, 'I dined at Sir John Stanley's to meet the whole blood of the Moncks'.[6] A Stella from such a source is, therefore, entitled to respect.

[1] *Corresp.* ii. 67 n.　　　[2] Ibid. v. 89.　　　[3] Ibid. 387.
[4] Ibid. ii. 67 n.　　　[5] *The Complete Peerage* ix (1936).
[6] *Life and Correspondence*, i. 281.

XI

The late Dr. R. R. Leeper had yet another portrait of Stella which he had picked up at a Dublin auction in a dirty condition, with a hole in the forehead. He had it cleaned and restored, and it hung in St. Patrick's Hospital until his death, when it came with the Monck Stella to his daughter, Mrs. McClelland, with whom it remains. It appears to be a fine idealized copy or replica of the Bellinter Stella, and if Wilde and Falkiner had been referring to it, one could understand their superlatives. Dr. Leeper was 'for many years an enthusiastic collector of Swift relics, and Mrs. McClelland has also, in addition to two portraits of Swift in youth and in old age, minatures of Swift and Stella. A pastel of Stella remains in St. Patrick's Hospital.

XII

Although Sir Frederick Falkiner devoted a special section of his essay on the portraits of Swift and Stella (pp. 57–63) to an account of the family portraits at Swifte's Heath, which he visited in the course of his inquiries, he made no reference to the existence of a portrait of Stella there. However, an inquiry addressed to Major E. G. M. Swifte, the present owner (whose family preserves the old spelling of the name), brought a courteous invitation to inspect the pictures.

Swifte's Heath, a fine old mansion in a wooded demesne some seven miles from the city of Kilkenny, is the ancestral home of the Irish branch of the Swifte family. Here came Jonathan's uncle Godwin, its first owner, who was called to the bar, married a relative of the Marchioness of Ormond, and after the Restoration was made by the First Duke Attorney-General of his County Palatine of Tipperary. Here came, as the third of Godwin's four wives, Hannah Deane, daughter of Admiral Deane who, as Jonathan wrote to Pope, 'having been one of the regicides, had the good fortune to save his neck by dying a year or two before the Restoration'.[1] It was her grandson, Deane Swift, who became friendly with Jonathan in his old age, and later his biographer. Here Jonathan himself, as a boy, came on holidays from Kilkenny College and here now, among numerous family portraits in the dining-room, hangs his portrait—in old age—with red skull-cap and flowing white locks, similar to the Moore Abbey picture.[2]

[1] *Corresp.* vi. 126.   [2] *Prose Works*, xii. Frontispiece.

Though Jonathan's uncle Godwin was the eldest son of the Rev.
Thomas Swift, the family portraits were not at Swifte's Heath in
his time, and when he died, in 1695, Stella was not yet fifteen years
of age. Swift's uncle William, who 'appears to have been the first
of his family to settle in Ireland',[1] was the owner of the collection.
He died in 1706 and his widow (who was his fourth wife) by her
will, dated 21 Nov. 1716 and proved 18 Jan. 1717,[2] left to her
step-daughter Elizabeth—her husband's only surviving child—the
Swift family portraits as well as a painting of the Swift coat of
arms, to which Swift refers in writing to Stella.[3] Elizabeth Swift
had married her first cousin Godwin, son of the Dean's uncle Godwin, and so the family portraits came to Swifte's Heath, probably
about 1717.

Stella herself saw this collection, for she was on familiar terms
with the owner, Swift's aunt, Mrs. William Swift of Dublin, for
several years before that lady's death. Writing to Stella from
London, 24 Feb. 1712, Swift says, 'Is my aunt alive yet? O, pray,
now I think of it, be so kind to step to my aunt, and take notice of
my great-grandfather's picture. You know he has a ring on his
finger, with a seal of an anchor and dolphin about it. . . . My reason
is, because I would ask some herald here whether I should choose
that coat, or one in Guillim's large folio of heraldry, where my
uncle Godwin is named with another coat of arms of three stags.'
That picture, which Stella was asked to inspect, can be seen at
Swifte's Heath to-day.

There has been some rearrangement of the pictures since
Falkiner's visit in 1908, and there are now two portraits of Stella
with the others in the old dining-room. One declared itself a
modern copy of the Berwick Stella, the other recalled the Jervas.
The pose, the dress, the outlines, the distinctive arrangement of
the hair indicated identity of subject and period, but certain differ-
ences in detail, a mellow tone harmonizing with the old pictures,
and traces of nail marks at the margins of the canvas, showing that
it had been previously on a smaller stretcher, raised the possibility
of its being an original. It had been at Swifte's Heath before
Major Swifte came into occupation, and he readily consented to the
taking of a photograph.

Later, the question was definitely settled by a visit to Mrs.
Elizabeth Natalie Swifte, of Eversham, Stillorgan, Co. Dublin,

[1] *Corresp.* i. 9 n.   [2] Ibid. vi. 216.   [3] *Journal*, pp. 496–7

widow of the late Godwin B. M. Swifte, the previous owner of Swifte's Heath, who died in 1923. Although an invalid, Mrs. Swifte most kindly granted me an interview and at once identified the photograph as that of a copy of the Jervas portrait in the National Gallery of Ireland, which she had got a Belgian artist, now dead, to paint for her husband, after the war of 1914–18. This artist had also painted the copy of the Berwick Stella as well as a portrait of the late Godwin Swifte, and a fine view of Swifte's Heath, now at Eversham. Mrs. Swifte said she could not explain the nail marks on the picture, but added that she had, herself, bought the frame for it. This was, of course, the simple explanation: the artist's original stretcher had not been large enough for the frame.

Mr. H. M. Hake, the Director of the National Portrait Gallery, London, has been good enough to examine the photographs of all the portraits referred to above, and to give me the benefit of his views. Of them, he says, 'Two only can be accepted as certainly portraying the costumes and hairdressing habits of Stella's own time. These are the drawing engraved for Faulkner, and the painting in the National Portrait Gallery in Dublin, which in 1814 belonged to the Rev. Edward Berwick.' As to the Jervas in the National Portrait Gallery of Ireland and the Bellinter portrait, Mr. Hake thinks 'they show a style of costume and hairdressing more generally associated with the two decades following Stella's death', in 1728. 'The test of features', he adds, 'is negative, in the sense that no two seem clearly identical.'

So ends the long quest for Stella (and Vanessa) by the uncertain light of tradition, and we are left in doubt before the presentments of these ladies, so long dead. Bereft of colour by the camera, marmoreal, they remind one of the fifteenth-century sarcophagus, in the Louvre, of that Seneschal of Burgundy whose effigy is borne on a bier on the shoulders of cowled mourners—large as life—their features hidden by their hoods, so that imagination deepens the sorrow which is unseen. Here, indeed, are faces, but the serious eyes keep their secrets, the closed lips tell no tales; their identities we may but guess.

Sincere thanks are due: to Mr. Cecil H. Villiers Briscoe, Bellinter House, Co. Meath; to the late Dr. R. R. Leeper, St. Patrick's (Swift's) Hospital, Dublin; and to Major E. G. M. Swifte, Swifte's Heath, Co. Kilkenny, for information regarding portraits in their possession and for permission to photograph them; to the Governors and Guardians of the National Gallery of Ireland for permission to photograph two portraits, and to Dr. George J. Furlong, Director, and Mr. Brinsley MacNamara, Registrar, of that institution, for information concerning them; to Mrs. Elizabeth Natalie Swifte, Eversham, Stillorgan, Co. Dublin, for identification of a portrait at Swifte's Heath; to Dr. Francis S. Bourke, 14 Fitzwilliam Square E., Dublin, for friendly liaison services; and to Mr. Sparks of the College Studios, Westmoreland Street, Dublin, for his great care and skill in taking photographs of eleven portraits used in preparing this iconography.

I have, especially, to thank Mr. H. M. Hake, Director of the National Portrait Gallery, London, for his examination and valuable criticism of the photographs.

HENRY MANGAN

DUBLIN
19 October 1945

INDEX

S. indicates Swift (Jonathan). Italic numerals indicate footnote references.

Index

Somerset, 206, 446, 467, 471 (*see also* Somerset); her physicians, surgeons, and oculist, *219*, 240, *315*, 370, *513*; orders the body of Guiscard to be buried, *224*; and Charles III of Spain, *247*; S. fears she will not live long, *255*; touches for the King's Evil, 264 & n.; going to, or at, Windsor, 319, 322, 540, 547, 560, 562, 568; horse-racing and hunting, 324, 328, 329 & n.; S.'s descriptions of her, 324, 328, 356, 361; and cards and dancing, 363; and a jest about the Maids of Honour, 363-4; in council, 366; and Bernage's promotion, 372; secret audience w. French ministers, *372*; at Hampton Court, 384, 394; and Prior, 384, 575; transfers Peterborough, 386; and the dismissal of Count Gallas, 396; and a pension for Frowde, 410; coming to, or in, Town, 416, 419, 579, 580, 584-5; at Court, 428; and the political crisis, 433-6, 439-41, 443, 450; creates new peers, 450 & n., 454; and Prince Eugene, 456, 479, 481; and the Peace, 489, 629, 631; procrastinations of, 496; discourages libels, 499; lessening of her power, 501; anniversary of her accession, 507, 634; her servants ill, 553; her death, *568*; and the Duchess of Hamilton, 573, 575; and a daily Drawing Room, 588; and the French Ambassador, 595; and the Dutch, 603; libellous poem on, 644; her animosity to Grattan, 648; will be 'teased no more' over the Deaneries, 664; petitioned in S.'s *Commission*, 675, 676, 681; *Address of House of Lords* to, 684-5.

Annesley, Francis, M.P., 643 & n.

Answers to the *Conduct of the Allies*, *523*.

Apocalypse, The, *544*.

Apoplexy, 337, 345, 381.

Appleby, *284*, *374*.

Apprentices, in procession, 415.

Apprenticeship, 559.

April Fools, 228, 229.

Apron, an, for Stella, 234, 250, 390, 395, 397, 402, 420, 458, 462, 472, 487, 519; cost of, 398; Italian silk, 398.

Apronia, 182.

Arbuthnot, Captain George, brother of Dr. A., *370*; his promotion, 370, 371-2.

Arbuthnot, John, physician to the Queen and author, 20, *219-20*, 327, 361, *382*, *438*, *460*, *489*, 514, 515, 517, 622, 650; friendship w. Erasmus Lewis and Peterborough, 35, 60; shaving habits of, 47; his *Lewis Baboon*, *137*; letter to S. about Gay, *214*; date of S.'s meeting w., *219*; length of their friendship, *219*; his degree, *219*; S.'s praise of, *220*; S. rides and sups w., 329, 356, 362, 376; visits Mrs. Masham, 363, 494; his *History of the Maids of Honour*, 363-5; plays picquet, 364; his power w. the Queen, 370; attempts to get his brother promoted and S.'s to dissuade him, 370-1; resigns his claim in order to please S., 371; a 'handsome letter' to S. from, 372; S.'s gratitude, 373; his and his family's illness, 377, 505; and the political crisis, 433-4, 439; and a ballad on Marlborough, 454 & n.; S. dines w., 461, 525, 647, 648, 662; and the Society, 461, 525; his *Law is a Bottomless Pit*, 510 & n., 516 & n., 554; his *History of John Bull*, 510, 516, 532, 554 & n.; S.'s affection for, 513; *John Bull* attributed to S., 532; and the Queen's health, 561; his *Treatise of the Art of Political Lying*, 562 & n., 579; S. introduces Berkeley to, 662.

Arbuthnot, Margaret, wife of above, 362; dines w. S. at Windsor, 362.

Ardglass, Earl of, 40.

Index

Index

Bathurst, Allen Bathurst, Baron and 1st Earl, M.P. and friend of S. and Pope, *423*; S. and the Society dine w., 423, 447; provides the wine, 447; S. visits the Duke of Ormonde w., 448, 451; made Baron, *450*.

Battersea, 313.

Baudrier, M., S.'s character in *A New Journey*, 381; the name used by Harley for Prior, 381.

Bawdowin, Elizabeth, m. Sir William Frankland, 27.

Beaufort, Henry Somerset, 1st Duke of, *204*.

Beaufort, Henry Somerset, 2nd Duke of, nephew of the Duchess of Ormonde, *467*, 645; and the Society, 467, 473, 488, 493, 636; S. opposes, 481; gives S. a poem, *523*.

Beaufort, Mary (Osborne), Duchess of, wife of 2nd Duke and dau. of Duke of Leeds, 505.

Beaumont, Sir George, Bt., of Stoughton Grange, Leicestershire, M.P. for Leicester, Lord of the Admiralty, *241*; S. calls him out from the October Club dinner, 241; discusses mutual illnesses w. S., 263.

Beaumont, Joseph ('Joe'), linen draper of Trim, *1*, *21*, 22, 26, 27, 31, 33, 34, 35, *41*, 537, 540, 581; S. supports his claims to a government award, *11*, 14, *15*, 27, 40; letter from, to S., 108, 265; Stella rides with, 197; S. commends him to Duke of Ormonde, 263, 288; asks S. to get him a collector's place, 266; asks S. to write about his father's position, 292; full of complaints, 309; his £200, 406, 425; his sneers and S.'s good wishes, 447; a foolish request, 508, 519; and a parliamentary vote, 581-2.

Beaumont, Mrs., 178.

Bed: S. keeps the curtains shut in cold weather, 171; S.'s, in Chelsea, 262; custom of sitting up in, in Ireland and England, 353.

Bedchamber, the Queen's, 328.

Bedlam, *see* Bethlehem.

Bedroom, S.'s, and its washing, 411.

Beef-eaters, the, 112.

Beer, small, 260.

Beggar's Opera, The, by John Gay, 485.

Behn, Mrs. Aphra, her novel *Oroonoko, or The Royal Slave, 168*.

Belasyse, Sir Henry, M.P., 306 & n., 307.

Belasyse, Hon. Sir Henry, son of John, *638*; his wife, 638 & n.

Belasyse, John, Baron Belasyse of Worlaby, *638*.

Belasyse, Sir Richard, of Ludworth, *306*.

Balasyse, Thomas, Viscount, later Earl, Fauconberg, 94.

Belcamp, *648*.

Belfast, 67, 392.

Belgian artist, 702.

Bell, a grocer, his son has The King's Evil, 264.

Bell metal, 117.

Bellamont (or Bellomont), Lucia Anna, Countess of, dau. of Count Henry of Nassau, rails at S., 250 & n.

Bellamont, Nanfan Coote, 3rd Earl of, *250*.

Bellesis, *see* Belasyse.

Bellinter, co. Meath, and the 'Bellinter Stella', 690, 692, 693, 694, 695, 697, 698, 700, 702.

Bellinter Vanessa, the, 698.

Bellman, the, letters sent by, 11, 35, 343, 467, 472, 537, 607; S. imitates, 453.

Belturbet, *12*.

Benefices, ecclesiastical, 678, 680.

Benson, Robert, Chancellor of the Exchequer, *60*; shows S. a ballad, 395; S. dines w., 461, 587; and S.'s *Representation*, 494, 496; and the Society, 532, 605, 637; and inner cabinet dinners, 658.

Bentley, Richard, 99, *514*.

Cakehouse, or Cheesecake House, *511* & n.

Cakes and Cake Shop, Twelfth Day, *157* & n.

Calendar, the, New Style and Old, *489*.

Calves Head Club, *544*.

Cambrai, *373*.

Cambridge, *359*, *625*.

Cambridge University, *115*, *527*, *653*; colleges—Downing, *329*; Emmanuel, *423*; King's, *331*; Magdalene, *115*; St. John's, *59*; Trinity, *191*.

Cambridgeshire, *329*.

Camisards, insurrection of, *211*.

Camocke (or Cammock), Capt. George, *268* & n.; Rear-Admiral in the Spanish navy, *268*; in command of the *Speedwell* and *Monck*, *268*.

Camomile, *207* & n.

Campaign of Valencia, The, by John Freind, *91*.

Campden, Baptist Noel, 3rd Viscount (father of Elizabeth, Countess of Berkeley), *23*.

Campion, Henry, M.P., *240* & n.

Canada, expedition to, *196*, *257* & n.

Canal, The, St. James's Park, *178* & n., *181*.

Candlemas Day, *478*.

Canterbury, Archbishop of (John Tillotson), *384*; Cathedral, *497*; Dean of (George Stanhope), *17*; St. Andrew's, *497*.

Cardinals, effigies of, *415*; S. sees, *421*.

Cardonnel, Adam de, Secretary to Marlborough, *240*.

Cards (*see also* Ombre, Picquet), *51*, *580*; Stella and, xxxi, *12*, *13*, *109*, *125*, *488*, *515*, *519*, *525*, *622*, *627*, *629*; at Windsor, *363*; tax on, *375*, *622* & n.; Mrs. Masham invites S. to, *447*, *480*; Harley plays with S., *561*; one and thirty, *561* & n.; S.'s losses at, *570*; S. leaves off playing, *589*; pools, *617*; putt, *622* & n.; from France, *622*; whist, *631*.

Carey, Henry, satirizes style of Ambrose Philips, *129*.

Carleton of Carleton, 1st Baron, *see* Boyle, Henry.

Carlingford, *254*.

Carlisle, Dean of, *see* Atterbury, Francis.

Carmarthen, *80*.

Carnarvon, 3rd Earl of, *see* Brydges, James.

Caroline Wilhelmina, Queen of George II, *91*.

Carteret, Lady Frances, dau. of Sir Robert Worsley and wife of 2nd Baron Carteret, *170*, *287* & n.; a tale of small-pox, *217*; and S.'s hat, *287*.

Carteret, John, 2nd Baron, afterw. Earl Granville and Viscount Carteret, *71*, *287*; puns w. S. and Prior, *153* & n.; S. chooses him for a guest, *200*, *484*; his mother's lawsuit, *568* & n.

Casaubon, Isaac, *179*.

Case of Ireland's being bound by Acts of Parliament in England, The, by William Molyneux, *567*.

Case of the Present Convocation Consider'd, The, by William Wotton, *169*.

Cashel, Archbishop of, William Palliser, *2*, *109* & n., *675*.

Cass, John, *55*.

Castle, The, *see* Dublin Castle.

Castlebar, *77*.

Castleknock, S.'s poem on vestry of church of, *10*.

Castlehaven, Mervyn Tucket, 4th Earl of, *376*; his three daughters, *376*.

Cataline, The English, *431* & n.

Catalonia and the Catalans, *272*.

Catholics, Roman, *272*; *see also* Papacy.

Cato, Addison's play, *651* & n., *654*, *660*; S. attends rehearsal, *654*.

Cattle Houghers, or Slaughterers, *525* & n.

Caudres, de, Mr., *209*.

718

Index

Codille, *see* Ombre.

Coffee, *see* Food and Drink.

Coffee Houses, 107, 113, 130, 135, 141, 154, 165, 180, 221, 225, 406, 413, 416, 419, 507; St. James's, 3, *11, 25, 57, 72, 92, 167 (see also* Elliot, Mr. and Mrs.); Garraway's, *24, 157* & n.; Jonathan's, *24*; Robin's, *24*; Smyrna, *60, 61*, 98, 196; S. sends for or calls for Stella's letters at, 72, 100, 167, 168, 222, 225, 248, 260, 263; S. visits, w. Addison, 97, 142; Christmas boxes at, 140; Harley comments on Stella's writing in window of, 183; S. does not visit, 207, 210, 248, 282, 580, 628; S. dines at, 219; S. does not call for Stella's letters at, 246; Harley sets S. down at, 279; the soldiers', 371; S. describes end of political crisis from, 450; gossip of the Mohocks in, 511; at Cambridge, 625.

Coghill, Marmaduke, Judge of the Prerogative Court in Ireland, lii, 304 & n.; in town, 514; dines w. S., 523; letter to S., 567; and S.'s recommendations, 614; and S.'s patent, 666.

Coinage, S.'s proposal concerning, 606 & n.

Coke, Thomas, M.P., Teller of the Exchequer, Vice-Chamberlain to the Queen, 327 & n.; invites S. to dine, 328, 330; lends his horses to S. at Windsor, 329; tells S. Court gossip, 475; alleged sale of his office, 522.

Coke, Mrs., 2nd wife of Thomas, maid of honour and celebrated beauty, 328 & n.; goes to the races, 332.

Colchester, 52.

Cole, Mr., father-in-law of Mr. Reading, 341 & n.

Cole, Sir Mark, 516; one of the Mohocks, 511, 516.

Collection of Poems by Several Hands, Dodsley's, *54.*

Colledge, Mrs., Seamstress to King William, 272; lodges at Whitehall, 272; S. visits, 382.

Colledge, Stephen, fanatical carpenter, 272, 382; inventor of the Protestant flail, *272*; accused of treason and executed, *272*; father of S.'s friend Mrs. C., 272.

College of Advocates, 52.

Colley, Richard, afterw. Baron Mornington, *3.*

Collins, Anthony, his *Discourse of Free Thinking, 603.*

Colt, Sir Henry Dutton, Whig candidate for Westminster, *42.*

Combes, Daniel, marries Addison's sister, widow of Rev. James Sartre, 69.

Commissioners of Revenue, 116 & n.; Irish, 281, 299, 369, 631.

Commissioners of Salt, 626.

Committee of Council, 416, 575, 603.

Companion for the Festivals and Fasts of the Church of England, by Robert Nelson, 192.

Compton, Henry, Bishop of London, his death in Wexford rumoured, 341–2; dies at Fulham, *341*; his generosity, *341*; cracks his skull, 562.

Compton, James Compton, 6th Baron, afterw. 5th Earl of Northampton, 242 & n., *448.*

Condoning Letter to the Tatler, A, pamphlet concerning Steele in debt, *127.*

Conduct of the Dissenters of Ireland w. Respect to the Church and State, by William Tisdall, *584.*

Conduitt, John, m. Catherine Barton, *17.*

Confectioner, a French, sets a house on fire, 610.

Conformity Bill, **444.**

Congress of Utrecht, 406, 466.

Congreve, William, *16, 75*, 113; failing eyesight, 69, *305, 455*; afflicted w. gout, 69, 191; S. at

720

Index

school with, 70; works published by Tonson, 70; celebrates Sir Richard Temple, 75; and *The Tatler*, 111; S. spends evening w., 83; S. dines w., 111, 191, 193; writes a *Tatler* for Harrison, 191; prevails on Kneller to paint S., 114; Stella jests about his eyesight, 127; S. advances him w. Harley, 295, 304, 589; his other sinecure offices, 295; lives by himself, 305; an agreeable companion, 310; to dine w. Harley, 311; and the Duchess of Queensberry, 317; S. visits, 384; Patrick and S. read his plays, 396.

Connaught, 370.

Connellan, Major, D.L., 697.

Connor, Charles, 578; his wife, 578.

Conolly, William, 31, 191; going to Hanover, 458.

Constantine, Alderman, 277.

Constantinople, 642.

Contes des Fées, by Comtesse d'Aulnoy, S. reads, 475.

Convocation, Houses of, 678–80.

Convocation, Irish, 66, 67.

Conway, Francis Seymour Conway, 1st Baron, 639; his wife, 639.

Conyngham, Maj.-Gen. Henry, of Slane, co. Meath, 132.

Cook, Mr., threatens Harley, 412, 413.

Cookshops, 380.

Coolmore, 697, 698.

Coote, Charles, *see* Mountrath, Earl of.

Coote, Henry, brother of Earl of Mountrath, 51; S. dines w., 345, 394, 397; fails to ask S. to dine, 360.

Coote, Hon. Thomas, 3rd son of Lord Coote of Coloony, M.P., Justice of the King's Bench, Recorder of Dublin, 391; letter to S., 391; wishes to justify his principles to S., 448.

Cope, Robert, of Loughgall, co. Armagh, 189 & n.

Cope, Mrs. Robert, 2nd wife of above (dau. of Sir William Fownes), 189.

Cork, Brodrick, Whig M.P. for, 130; Deanery of, 132; Sir John Perceval, M.P. for, 222.

Corn, condition and price of, in Ireland, 560, 565, 615.

Cornwall, 169.

Coroner's inquest, 574, 575.

Corr, Daniel, 615.

Cosmetics, paint, 443.

Cotesworth, or Coatesworth, Caleb, physician to St. Thomas's Hospital, 384.

Cotterill, Anne, wife of Adam Swift, 274.

Counterpane, a, 353.

Couriers, 629.

Court, the, 489, 642, 654, 678–9; S. at, 84, 85, 112, 118, 121, 130, 137–9, 158, 218, 257, 267, 421, 428, 440, 451, 456, 479, 507, 633, 635; dismayed at losses in Spain, 139; Collar Day at, 139; and the Queen's birthday, 181, 480–1, 485, 615; crowded in anticipation of seeing Harley, 267; Harley never appears at, 268; Harley goes to, 283; S. attends at Windsor, 322, 326, 328, 350; S.'s remarks repeated at, 323; thin until Saturday night, 364; very full, 366; and those who voted against, 433–4; and a ballad of S.'s, 442; and the Duke of Marlborough, 451; no secrets at, 452; Prince Eugene at, 463, 473; S. wishes to be done w., 487; S.'s views on, 489, and the passing of a Parliamentary Bill, 501; Sir W. Wyndham absent from, 503; a scoundrel who sells places at, 522; S. uses, as a coffee house, 522, 580, 585, 600; S. too ill to attend, 528; at Kensington, 538; dismissals from, 544; S. stays away from, in order to write to Stella, 547; S.'s behaviour at, 580; and the French ambassador, 595, 600; S. avoids Harley at, 603; S. receives secret news at, 629; S. talks w. French minister at, 640; S. forced to leave, 645; ministers fail to

Index

Derry, Bishops of, *see* Ashe, St. George; Hartstonge, John.
Derry, Deanery of, S.'s hopes of, *56*.
Desertcreat, *189*.
D'Estrées, Victor Marie, duc, *623–4*; S. dines w., *623*; at cards, *629*.
Dettingen, *120*.
De Veres, *see* Veres.
Devil, the, *412*; effigy of, *404*, *415*, *416*; made to resemble Harley, *417*; S. sees, *421*; not like Harley, *426*.
Devil Tavern, *51* & n.
Devonshire, *171*, *291*.
Devonshire, William Cavendish, 2nd Duke of, Lord Steward, *22*: turned out of office, *24*; examination of Gregg, *340*.
Dialogues of the Dead, Fontenelle's, *404*; William King's, *442*.
Diamonds, *659*.
Diaper, Joseph, of Bridgewater, father of the poet, *512*.
Diaper, Rev. William, poet, *512*; and the Society, *512*, *513*, *519*; his *Nereides: or Sea Eclogues*, *512* & n.; his *Dryades: or the Nymph's Prophecy*, *512*, *586*; S. introduces to St. John and gets him made a Parson, *586*.
'Dilly', *see* Ashe, Dillon.
Dingley, Sir John, Rebecca's grandfather, xxvii.
Dingley, Rebecca, *21*, *33*, *40*, *59*, *66*, *71*, *72*, *85*, *87*, *90*, *111*, *290*, *291*, *299*, *301*, *353*, *563*, *566*, *569*, *577*, *581*, *582*, *585*, *691*; early letters from S. to, xvii, xlvii, xlviii; her age, xxvii; related to Sir William Temple, xxvii, *9*; her last visit to England, xxviii; her change of lodgings, xxxi, xxxvi, *4*; S. asks Jack Temple for assistance for, *9*; living with the Walls, *10*; her tobacco, *31*, *56*, *61*, *112*, *126*; annuity held by Lady Giffard, *74*; play on her name, *88*; spectacles for, *95*, *97*, *134*, *187* (*see also* Spectacles); her letter to S., *100*; her share in Stella's letters, *107*; S.'s message to, for Mr. Walls, *110*; S. reproves,

125; and S.'s prolonged absence, *126*, *233*; her reading-glass, *134*; her chocolate, *134*; and her petticoats, *134*, *409*; S.'s allowance to, *137*; errand through Raymond, *149*; S. chaffs her about 'shorter journals', *151*, *153*; Patrick buys a linnet for, *156*, *181* (*see* Linnet); S. urges her to visit Bishop of Clogher, *173*, *175*; S. asks her for her opinion of Stella's appearance, *185*; and the candle-ends, *187*; handles letter for Bernage, *196*; her handwriting, *209* & n., *234*; 'as fair and fresh as a lass in May', *210*; her exchequer business, *226*, *386*, *387*, *391*; her money transactions w. Mrs. Vedeau, *231* & n., *233*, *241*, *284*, *292*; S. corrects her spelling and English, *234*, *459*, *471*; her money affairs w. Tooke, *241*, *284*, *418*, *449*, *530–1*, *607*, *616*, *667*; her pocket books, *250*; Stella to dictate to, *276*; reads S.'s letters to Stella, *278*, *296*; S. inquires for, *285*, *296*; 'full of carking and caring', *298*; her fondness for ale, *298*, *322*; her 'millions of businesses', *314*; S.'s imagined picture of, *319*; weary of Wexford, *367*; advises S. about his health, *401*; Mrs. St. John sends her a snuff-rasp, *402*, *458*, *471*; S. asks for his accounts from, *449*; her interest in politics, *477*, *603*, *652*.
Dingley, Capt. Robert; brother of Rebecca, *209*, *617*; his wife Elizabeth, *617*; Stella's and Dingley's letters to, *617*.
Dining, time of, *311*, *321*.
Dining-room, S. refers to, as if it were a new word, *156*,
Dining-tables of the great on Sundays, *323*.
Discourse of Free Thinking, A, by Anthony Collins, *603*.
Diseases, *see* Illnesses.
Dismal, see Nottingham, Daniel Finch, 2nd Earl of.

724

Index

Disney (or Desney), Col. Henry, 'Duke', *196*, *471*, *622*, *651*; recommends Bernage, *196*, *213*; elected to the Society, *424*, *505*; has a fever, *638*; likely to die, *639*, *641*; his character, *639*; out of danger, *645*.

Dissenters, *438*; S.'s advice to, *240*.

Ditton, Humphry, *527*.

Dobbins, Mrs. Mary, wife of Rev. James, *233* & n.

Dobbins, Rev. James, Chancellor of Armagh, *233*.

Doblane, Lord, *see* Dupplin.

Dockwra, William, establishes penny post, *26*.

Doctor's Commons, *52*, *442*.

Dodsley, Robert, his *Collection of Poems by Several Hands*, *54*.

Dodson, Thomas, involved in a duel with John Manley, *37*.

Doiley (or Doyley), linen draper, S.'s pun on his napkins, *249* & n.

Dollardstown, co. Meath, *581*.

Domville, Bridget, dau. of Sir Thomas, m. 3rd Baron Barry of Santry, *268*.

Domville, Sir Thomas, Bt., *268*.

Domville, Sir William, Attorney-General for Ireland, *100*.

Domville, William, grandson of Sir William, letter to S., *100*, *109*, *268*; returns from his travels, *421*; S.'s character of, *422*; S. sups w., *461–2*; S. dines w., *463*, *470*, *517*, *523*; leaving for Ireland, *523*, *526–7*.

Donegal, *581*.

Donnybrook, *79*, *216*, *270*, *284*, *349*, *537*; a mile from Dublin, *174*; Dingley at, *174*; Mrs. Stoyte at, *174*, *199* & n.; Mrs. Walls at, *175*; Stella should go to, *258*, *264*, *364*.

Dopping, Anthony, Bishop of Meath, *79*; his son Anthony, Bishop of Ossory, *79*.

Dopping, Samuel, M.P. for Armagh, *79*, *90*, *126*; S. drinks bad claret w., *131*; S. gives him Prior's verses, *231*.

Dorchester, Evelyn Pierrepont, Mar-

quis of, later 1st Duke of Kingston-upon-Hull, father of Lady Mary Wortley Montagu, *286*.

'Dorinda', *see* Giffard, Lady.

D'Ossuna, duc, Spanish representative, *651* & n.

Dothill, Salop, *329*.

Douai, capture by Marlborough, *76*.

Douglas, Archibald Douglas, 3rd Marquis and 1st Duke of, also called Earl of Angus, *461*; S. dines w., *461*.

Douglas, Charles, Marquess of Beverley, later 3rd Duke of Queensberry, *54*.

Douglas, George, 4th son of 2nd Duke of Queensberry, *54*.

Dover, *358*, *568*.

Dowgate Hill, *96*.

Down, co., *688*.

Down, Dean of, *see* Pratt, Benjamin.

Down, Deanery of, *127*.

Downing, Sir George, Bt., *329*.

Downing, George, son of above, child marriage of, *329*; foundation of College at Cambridge, *329*.

Downpatrick, *643*.

Doyne, Robert, Chief Baron of the Exchequer and Chief Justice of the Common Pleas in Ireland, *130* & n.

Drapier's Letters, *26*.

Drawing-room, at Court, *328*, *331*, *379*; a daily one, *588*; three times a week, *603*, *606*.

Draycot, Wilts., *446*.

Drayton, Germain property in Northamptonshire, *27*.

Drink, *see* Food and Drink.

Drogheda, Henry Moore, 3rd Earl of, *224*.

Dromore, Bishops of, *see* Pullein, Tobias; Stearne, Dean; Lambert, Ralph.

Drumcondra, *695*.

Drumcree, *392*.

Dryden, Elizabeth, wife of Rev. Thos. Swift, *73*.

Dryden, Sir Erasmus, grandfather of the poet, *73*.

Index

403, 410, 484; S. spends evening w., 83; turns away his butler, 119; S. speaks for him to the Ministry, 226; a 'violent Whig', 226; likely to be dismissed, 226, 312, 410, 466; S. warns him, 312, 387; S. attempts to aid, 317; dismissed, 484.

Duels, 264, *265*, 337; Hamilton *v.* Mohun, *570–2* & notes.

Duguay-Trouin, René, *474*.

Duke, Richard, chaplain to the Queen, 191 & n.

Dun Laoghaire (Dunlary), ancient name of Kingstown, *2*.

Dunboyne, *400*.

Dunciad, The, see Pope, Alexander.

Duncombe, Sir Charles, banker and alderman, Lord Mayor of London, 238 & n.; his niece, Duchess of Argyle, 238.

Dundalk, *9*, *310*.

Dunkirk, *104*; 522, 543, 548, 544, *554*, *559*, French Governor of, 546 (English Governor of, *see* Hill, John); a head-dress from, 550.

Dunmore, co. Galway, *458*, *519*.

Dunton, John, 73; his *Dublin Scuffle*, *223*; and Thomas Proby, *223*.

Dupplin, George Hay, Viscount, afterw. 8th Earl of Kinnoull (Harley's son-in-law), *45*, 125, 591, 594, 649; travels to Windsor w. S., 335; attends christening of Mr. Masham's son, 352; detains S. at Windsor, 361; S. to dine w., 391, 393, 491, 661, 626, 645; created Baron Hay, 450 & n.; president of the Society, 453, *505*; and a pamphlet of S.'s, *470*; S. walks w., *505*; christening of his daughter, 609.

Dupplin, Robert, Archbishop of York, Harley's grandson, *408*.

Dupplin, Lady, *see* Harley, Abigail.

Durham, *307*.

Durham, Bishop of (Lord Crewe), report of his death, *23*.

Dutch, the (*see also* Holland), xiv, 379; and the Hanoverian succession, 478 & n.; 'Those scoundrels the', 478;

a Dutch mail, 479, 487; playing the English false, 487, 496; and the Peace negotiations, 487, 563, 566, 581, 582, 600, 603, 611; English rail against, 544–5; and rumour of S.'s arrest, 490; 3,000 taken prisoner, 551 & n., 554; and the Spanish representative, 651 & n.

Dutchman, a, 477; a learned, 569.

D—y, 28 & n., 148.

Dyer, John, Jacobite newsmonger, 473 & n.

Dyot, Richard, Commissioner of the Stamped Paper, charged w. felony, *39*, *40*, *52*.

Earl, Mr., his sister has Stella's box, 185.

Ears, S. threatens to crop Patrick's, 322; S. cuffs Patrick's, 376.

East Grinstead, Prior M.P. for, *59*.

East India Company, 76.

East India House, a thief at, 399.

Eastcourt, *see* Estcourt.

Easter Sunday, 229, 236, 653, 654.

Easter Week, 651.

Easton, Suffolk, *376*.

Eaton, Rev. Richard, *xxxiii*.

Echlin, James, 392.

Eckershall, James, Clerk of the Kitchen, 202 & n., 587; S. dines w., 202, 375.

Edenhall, *258*.

Edgar, The, admiral's ship of the fleet, blows up in the Thames, *385*.

Edgeworth, Col. Ambrose (son of Sir John), *62*.

Edgeworth, Mrs. (widow of Col. Ambrose), leaving for Ireland and will take charge of Stella's box, 185, 197, 198, 208, 233, 276; married on the way, 271.

Edgeworth, Sir John, *62*.

Edinburgh, *415*, *422*.

Edinburgh Castle, *348*.

Effigies, processional, in wax, 404, 415; their number and worth, 426.

Index

Filby, Mr., a baker, Stella's brother-in-law, *39*, *576* & n., *579*, *615*, *624*, *626*, *629*, *643*.

Filby, Mrs. Anne, Stella's sister, xxiv, *39* & n., *564*, *576*.

Filby, Nancy, a dau. of above, *39*.

Finch, Anne, wife of Heneage Finch, later 4th Earl of Winchelsea, poetess, known as the Countess of Winchelsea, *282* & n., *555*.

Finch, Anne, wife of 2nd Earl of Nottingham, *397*.

Finch, Heneage, 1st Earl of Aylesford, *242* & n.

Finch, Heneage, 2nd Earl of Aylesford, *242* & n.

Finch, Heneage, 2nd Earl of Winchelsea, *138*, *282*, *287*.

Finch, Heneage, 4th Earl of Winchelsea, *282*, *555* & n.

Finch, William, 2nd son of the Earl of Nottingham, *397*; S. dines w., *397*.

Finglas, *28*, *360*; Stella should go to, *258*; Stella walks from, *388*.

Fires, disastrous, in S.'s chimney, *139*; Sir William Wyndham's, *502*; in Drury Lane, *524*; French Ambassador's, *608*.

First-fruits of England, xiv, *307*, *677*.

First Fruits of Ireland: remission of, xv, xx, xxii, *2*, *15*, *22*, *34*, *43–6*, *50*, *66*, *72*, *78*, *80*, *89*, *102–4*, *136*, *206*, *307*; S.'s memorials to Harley, *45* & n., *50*, *59*, *61*, *677–80*; 'business will soon be over', *108*; 'nothing remains but the forms' for, *125*; St. John promises letter from the Queen, *145*; St. John assures S. warrant is drawn, *150*, *155*; the patent, *185*; the Queen's letter and the warrant, *185* & n.; and the Duke of Ormonde, *205*, *247*; S.'s use of them as excuse for not returning to Ireland, *254*; finished, *291*; message from Stella about, *291*; the Queen and Harley lose a paper on, *311*; S. refuses to advertise his part in, *347*; Harley's recognition of S.'s part in, *348*; S.'s bitterness over,

387–8, *546*; S. attacks Bishop of Killaloe over, *647–8*; cost of, to S., *664*; S.'s Commissions and Memorial concerning, *675–80*.

Fisher, Edward, of Fulham, father of Mary Thornhill, *264*.

Fishes, the six, S.'s imaginary Bill of Exchange, *177*.

Fishmonger, S.'s pun about, *400*, *402–3*.

Fitzhardinge, Barbara (Berkeley), Viscountess (dau. of Sir Edward Villiers), *570*, *618*; her wise saying, *570*.

Fitzhardinge, John Berkeley, 4th Viscount, *570*, *618*.

Fitzjames, Henry, Grand Prior of France, illegitimate son of James II, *364*.

Fitzmaurice, William, 2nd Earl of Kerry, *122* & n.

— his son, William, *122*; S. visits at Eton, *324*; and his entrance to Christ Church, *626* & n.

Flanders, *119*, *83*, *147*, *257*, *332*, *485*; the Army in, *471*; Captain-Gen. of the Forces in, *483*; Ormonde in, *522*, *524*, *535–7*, *551*; Sir Thomas Hanmer in, *625*.

Flodden Field, *326*.

Florence wines, *see* Wines.

Floyd, 'Biddy', a noted beauty, *217* & n., *223*, *382*; companion and friend of Lady Betty Germain, has the small-pox, *217*, *221*; out of danger, *223*; much marked, *263*, *380*, *386*.

Floyd, Mrs., a beauty of Chester, *382*.

Flying-Post, The, the Whig paper, *396*, *554*, *568*, *572–3*, *579*; William Hart, printer of, *644*.

Foley, Thomas, of Whitley Court, Worcestershire (father of Thomas and of Elizabeth, 1st wife of Robert Harley), *135*, *253*; his 2nd dau. m. Harley's brother, *162*.

Foley, Thomas, Baron Foley of Kidderminster, *253* & n., *450*; his sister 1st wife of Harley, *253*.

Index

Dudley, 226; passes S. in the Park, 498; and Lord Wharton, 541; eulogies of, 557; death of, 557, 562; a Knight of the Garter, 562; to be buried in the Abbey, 562.

Gold-beaters' skin, a remedy for broken shins, 215.

'Golden Farmer', nr. Frimley, an inn named after a highwayman, 285 & n.

Goldsmith, Oliver, his *Life of Parnell*, 365.

Good Friday, 227, 236.

Goodrich, Herefordshire, 497.

Gore, Lady, and a jest of S.'s, 388.

Gore, Mr., S. dines w., 98.

Gore, Sir William, Lord Mayor of London, 98.

Gorge, Brigadier, 62.

Gorges, Lt.-Gen., Richard, of Kilbrew, co. Meath, 498, 653 & n.

Gorges, Dr. Robert, father of Richard, 653.

Gospel, S. quotes from, 400.

Gout, Queen Anne and, 255, 335, 350, 356, 373, 399, 402, 405, 466, 467, 562, 612; S. fears, 323, 377; Lord Jersey dies of, 345; Dean of Carlisle and, 346; The Lord Treasurer and, 399; S.'s printer has the, 477; Bishop of Ossory and, 593.

Government, the, 677, 679; the late, 677, 679.

Governors, Chief, 676.

Grafton, Charles Fitzroy, 2nd Duke of, 628 & n.

Grafton, Henry Fitzroy, 1st Duke of, 418; his widow, *see* Hanmer, Lady Isabella.

Graham, Col. James, brother of Viscount Preston, a Jacobite, M.P., 284 & n.; S. dines w., 284.

Graham, Sir Richard, 1st Viscount Preston, 284.

Graham, William, Dean of Wells, 552, 660.

Granard, 429.

Grange, The, Anthony Henley's seat, 337.

Grange Gorman, co. Dublin, 37, 699.

Granville, George (afterw. Baron Lansdown), Secretary of War, 37, 245, 353; author, 168; S. asks him to make Bernage a Captain, 169; a patron of Pope, 169; M.P. for Fowey, and for Cornwall, 169; S. chosen as a guest, 201; S. dines w., 238, 247, 348, 357, 359; S. threatens to expel him from the Society, 308; informs S. of Bernage's promotion, 371; and the Queen's wishes, 372; his illness, 381; made Baron Lansdown, 450; marries Mary Thynne, 454; tells S. Whig rumours, 469; and the Society, 473, 505; and a passage in *The Examiner*, 512, 525; and a quarrel w. S., 525; and a lawsuit w. Carteret's mother, 568; and Pope's poem, 635.

Granville, Jane, dau. of John, Earl of Bath, 37.

Granville, John, 1st Earl of Bath, 37.

Granville, Mary (afterw. Mrs. Delany), 37.

Grattan, Charles, S. intervenes on his behalf, 648 & n.

Grattan, Henry, 688.

Grattan, Rev. Patrick, father of Charles, 648.

Gravel Pits, *see* Kensington.

Gray's Inn, 157, 497.

Graziers in Ireland, increase of, 678, 680.

Great Britain, S.'s dislike of the term, 420 & n.

Great Fire, The, 122.

Green, Mr., surgeon to Dr. Radcliffe, sits up w. Harley, 212 & n.; cares for Harley, 225; an 'ill surgeon', 239; dresses Harley's wound, 315.

Greencastle, co. Down, 274.

Green Cloth, The Committee of Management of the Royal Household, 329, 330, 364; cost of, to the Crown, 328; purpose of, 328; S. invited to, 363, 364, 374; S. dines

735

w., 373; *see also* Foster, Sir William, Scarborow, Charles.

Greenwich, 313, *417*.

Gregg, William, clerk in Harley's office, treasonable actions of, *340*; examination of, by lords, 340; S.'s part in controversy over, *340*.

Gresham College, 122 & n.

Gresham, Sir Thomas, founder of the college (1579), *122*.

Griffith, Mr., or Dr., 128 & n., *633*; and playing chess w. Stella, 236; and a difference w. S. 490; fondness for Stella, 631.

Griffith, Edward, Commissioner of the Salt office, *576*.

Griffith, Humphrey, son of Edward, Commissioner of the Salt office, 576 & n., 624, 626, 629, 643.

Grimsby, *204*.

Groat, a, 445.

Gronovius, *501*.

Grub Street, 178, 337, 416, 426, 430, 431, 441; the Queen's wish to limit libels of, 466, 499, 539; paper alleging arrest of S., 468-9; and the Mohocks, 511; fruitful, 548; S.'s contributions, 548, 551, 553; taxation on pamphlets, 553; persecution of S., Harley, and St. John by writers of, 568; system of punishment of writers of, 568-9; screamers, 572; and the Bandbox Plot, 579.

Grub Street Ballads, *see* Ballads and Broadsides.

Guardian, The, 13; character of Will Pate in, *20*; Pope's ironical paper in, *129*; No. 96, *606*; 'a new daily paper' begun by Steele, 651 & n.

Guards, The Queen's, 324.

Guernsey, Baron (Heneage Finch), *242*.

Guildford, *410*.

Guildhall, the, drawing of lottery in, 19.

Guilds and the guild system, *559*.

Guillim, John, *Display of Heraldrie*, 497 & n., 701.

Guinea, the, value of, in Ireland, *189*.

Guiscard, Antoine de, formerly Abbé de la Bourlie, *211*, 221, 223, 225, *339*, 402; attempts to assassinate Harley, xxii, 211, 255, 262; taken up for treason, 212; likely to die of his wounds, 212, 217; designs on the Queen's life, 217; his death and coroner's verdict, 218; his body pickled in a trough for 14 days, and exhibited, 224; his burial, 224 & n.; poems following the attempt on Harley, 228 & n., 244, 254; Harley would have had him live, 241; a portrait of, 491.

Gulliveriana, xxx.

Gum-Dragon, 500 & n.

Guy Fawkes Day, 404.

H——, a 'worthless Irish fellow', 192 & n.

Hackney Coaches, *see* Coaches.

Hagley, nr. Slough, *190*.

Hague, The, *54*, *59*, *121*, *417*; Envoys to, *121*, *216*, 217, 485, 512; Sir William Temple's letter from, *244*.

Hake, Sir H. M., 702, 703.

Hale, Miss, m. Thomas Coke, *328*.

Hales, a lodging-house keeper, *576*.

Halifax, Charles Montagu, Earl of, xiii, xvii, xxiii, *36*, 38, 41, 282, *340*, 536, 608; relations w. S., xviii, 6, *36*; relations w. Catherine Barton, *17*; his character drawn in S.'s *Contests and Dissensions*, *36*; S. dines w., *36*, 55, 106; Ranger of Bushy Park and Hampton Court, *37*, 55; his politics, 106; S. seldom sees, 173; provides for Congreve, *295*; S. talks w., at Court, 378; forces his bow on S., 440; Harley dines w., 643; opposes the address, 657.

Hamburg, wine and books from, 312, 334-5 & n.; a merchant of, 609.

Hamilton, Anne (Douglas), Duchess of (dau. of 1st Duke of), 'the old dutchess', 517, 588, 592 & n.

Hamilton, Lord Claud, 517.

Hamilton, Elizabeth, Duchess of (dau. of Lord Gerard), 378, *419*, 580, 636; arranges a visit to S., 473; not yet up, 523; visits S. in his illness, 533; sews for S., *559*; her husband's duel, 571–2; S. cares for her in her grief, 571–2, 573; her nature, 574, 602; S. tries to reconcile her w. Lady Orkney, 574; S. informs her of results of the Duke's murder, 575; S. fears he is in disgrace w., 582; and Lord Abercorn's claim, 583, 588, 592, 606; and a reward for Maccartney, 589; asks S. to dine, 618; offended by Bligh, 632.

Hamilton, Lord George, son of 3rd Duke, *see* Orkney, Earl of.

Hamilton, Lt.-Gen. George, *664*.

Hamilton, Gen. Gustavus, Viscount Boyne, *664*; S. dines w., *664*.

Hamilton, James Douglas, 4th Duke of, Lord Lt. of Lancashire, *323*, *419*, 517; plays a prank on S., 323; S.'s character of, *323*; angry w. the House, 464 & n.; his patent, 477, 479; gives S. snuff, 569; his quarrel and duel w. Mohun, 570–2 & nn., 579; inquest on, 574; trial of his second, 579; 'never dreamt of a chaplain', 579; his house, 632.

Hamilton, Col. John, 571 & n., 578 & n.

Hamilton, Hon. John, 2nd surviving son of Earl of Abercorn, *347*; his share in a lottery, 347.

Hamilton, William, 2nd Duke of, *592*.

Hamilton, William, 3rd Duke of, *557*, *592*.

Hammersmith, Lord Berkeley's steward lives at, 133; S. walks from, to Kensington, 538.

Hammond, Jane and Mary, xxvii.

Hampstead, S. at, 17; S. dines at, 26.

Hampton Court, the Queen, Court, and Ministers at, 35, 36, 37, 38, 41, *55*, 63, 328, 337, 379, 384, 385, 390, 394, 399, 400, 402, 404, 406, 412, *419*; description of the town, 400;

no room for S. at, 400; Marlborough w. the Queen at, 417.

Handkerchiefs, S. buys, for Stella, 63; Indian, 260; snuff ones, 260; S. loses his in the Mall, 342.

Handwriting, Rebecca Dingley's, 209 & n., 234; Stella's, 183 & n., 209, 234, 353, 355, 364, 418, 459.

Hangings, 319–20, 325, 650.

Hanmer, Isabella (1st wife of Sir Thomas), widow of Duke of Grafton, Countess of Arlington, *418*, 646; her head-dress, 418; dines w. S., 625, 628, 633.

Hanmer, Sir Thomas, Speaker of the House of Commons, 96, *418*, 646, 657; S. composes *Representation to the Queen* w., xlvi, 493 & n., 494, 496, 499; leader of Hanoverian Tories, 96; his edition of Shakespeare, 96; S. dines w., 114, 142, 240, 418, 625, 633, 644, 659; Chairman of a Committee, 492; his activities and reputation, 625; and S., 625, 628; and S.'s *History of the Four Last Years*, 629; unwell, 651.

Hanover, 297, 374; Envoys to, *119*, *138* (Winchelsea), 281; Elector of, 430; Envoy from (Bothmar), 430 & n., 479; votes about, 444; Tom Harley goes to, 455; Conolly going to, 458; House of, 684.

Hanoverian succession, the, *478*, 488, *526*; guarantee of, 479.

Harcourt, Sir Simon, Baron and 1st Viscount Harcourt, Lord Keeper, 84, 96, 308, 317, 331, 342, 350, 364, 365, 431, 567, 645; S. calls 'triming Harcourt', *18*; defends Sacheverell, *18*; Attorney General, *18*, 22; Lord Keeper, *19*, 135; sworn of Privy Council, *19*; follows Harley out of office, 46; S. introduced to, 50, 135; S. visits, 189; and inner cabinet dinners, 193, 205, 261, 356, 599; S. speaks of Addison and Steele to, 218; S. intends to inform him of the treatment he expects,

Index

Harley, Robert (*cont.*)

239, 244, 247, 249, 263; to be made a peer, 249, 265, 267, 271, 273, 274, 278; dislikes being called 'My Lord', 279; to have the garter, 282; his Staff of office, 282–4; carries a 'dead warrant', 285; petitions to, 285; at the top of power and favour, 285; blamed for slowness in dismissing others, 298; exonerated by a clerk, *340*; bad verses on, 430–1; quotes scriptures, 434, 544; and a jest about his death, 435; helps too many in office, 516; his daughter's marriage, 584; easy in mind, 657; endorsement by, 677, 680; his handwriting, *684*; his Arab horses, 498.

— attempt on his life by Guiscard: xxii, 211, 255, 262; illness from, 212–16, 218, 220, 222–4, 228, 229, 236, 249, 488; fate of penknife w. which he was stabbed, 215 & n.; Stella and his stabbing, 220; Irish report of, 237; complains to S. of neglect of Guiscard's cure, 241; shows S. his wound, 261, 262, 315; his thoughts after the attempt, 262; anniversary of the attempt, 492, 507–8; warned about the Mohocks, 509, 515; other attempts and threats, 412, 413, 609, 635.

— character: 206, 275, 365, 378, 613–14, 681–3; forgetfulness, 298; melancholy, 504; moderation, 44; procrastinations, xlv, 318, 400, 486–7, 496, 644, 656.

— effigies of, *415*, 417, 426.

— health: unwell, 205, 207, 385–7, 390–1, 393, 395, 398, 400, 405, 408, 506–10; deafness, 353; lameness, 424.

— and the Bandbox Plot, 572, 579.
— and Benson, 60.
— and Dalrymple, 60.
— and the Dublin aldermen, 113.
— and Lord Dupplin, 45.
— and the Dutch envoy, 419, 422.
— and Flanders: the orders not to fight in, 537 & n.

Harley, Robert, and Grub Street editor, 568.

— and Guiscard: claims a painting of him, 491 (*and see above*—attempt on his life).
— and inn signs, 382.
— and the 'inner cabinet dinners', 193, 205, 356, 599, 624, 629, 638, 647, 658, 663, 667.
— and Irish affairs, 612.
— and Kensington, 535 (moves to).
— and Archbishop King, 251, 253, 261.
— and Marlborough, hatred of, 452, 454.
— and Mrs. Masham, *34*, *190*, 333, 335, 352, 412, 480, 494; she backs S. to, 661.
— and the Master of the Rolls, 476.
— Moore against, *204*.
— and the national finances, 76, 91.
— and the new Privy Seal, 347, 348.
— and Ormonde, 644.
— and Parliament: held up without him, 215, 221, 223, 224; carelessness over parliamentary matters, 432–4; and the political crisis, 433–7, 439, 442, 447, 450, 451, 536; and the Conformity Bill, 443–4; a Whig vote against, 490; rumour of his turning Whig, 643–4; speaks in the House w. spirit, 657.
— and William Penn, 45.
— arrival of Lord Peterborough at his house, 599, 600.
— and Prince Eugene, 440.
— and the Quebec expedition, 257.
— and the Queen, 126, 185, 247, 388, 447; S. and he corrects her speech, 635, 639, 640, 656; and a painting of her, 659.
— and Lord Rivers, executor for, 563.
— and St. John, *see* St. John, Henry.
— and the Society: S. refuses to admit him, 306.
— and the South Sea Company, 351, 395.
— and Spain, argues against losses in, 140.
— and S.: S. introduced to, xxii,

739

Index

Illnesses (*see also* Gout, King's Evil, Plague, Small-pox, Swift (Health)): the stone, 377; the gravel, 385, 390, 408; rheumatism, 400, 422, 430, 526–8, 558, 561, 617; consumption, 442; asthma and dropsy, 445; dropsy, 474, 561; King's Evil, 264, 488, 532; the shingles, 528 et seq.; Herpes 531; palsy, 544; St. Anthony's fire, 547, 554; a fever at Windsor, 553, 563, in London, 638; a fit of the ague, 557, 310; common in England, 348; diabetes, 558; fever in Dublin, 565; epidemic of colds, 615; laryngitis and quinsy, 610, 635; inflammation of the lungs, 619; sore throat and ague, 662; a fistula, 671.

Impropriations, 66.

Inchiquin, William O'Brien, 3rd Earl of, 475; his letter to Harley, 475.

Indian, an (imaginary), 254; and his travels in England, S.'s idea, 254; S. intended to write a book on it, 255.

Ingoldsby, Lt.-Gen. Richard, Commander of the Forces in Ireland, 130 & n., 476; abuses the Archbishop of Dublin, 254; impertinent discourse w. S., 350; to be made a peer, 405.

Inner Cabinet Dinners, *see under* Harley, Robert.

Inner Temple, 421.

Inns (London) (*see also* Taverns, Coffee Houses): Globe, 151 & n.; Three Crowns, 151; Bell, 194, 241; Bell and Dragon, 382; Star and Garter, 518 & n.; Black Swan, Holborn, 650.

Inn-signs, Harley and S. note, 382 & n.

Insurrection of 1798, 688.

Ireland, xxviii, xxix, xxxv, xxxix, xliv, xlviii, 49, 53, 60, 64, 65, 66, 67, 74, 86, 87, 92, 94, 95, 677–80, 691, 696, 701; S.'s anticipation of an early return to, 24, (*and see below*);

Lord Anglesey and, *115*; Sir Constantine Phipps and, 158 & n.; S. advocates use of household coal in, 166; Mr. Smyth leaves for, 172; S. longs to be in, 205; English interest in, *207*; S. dreams he is in, 221; S. leaves, 268; privateers cruising off the coast of, *268*; Trapp's MS. in, 269; Richardson going to, 271; Mrs. Pratt going to, 271 (*see also* Ormonde, Duke of; Kerry, Lady; Ford, etc.); Commissioners of Revenue in, *281*, 299, 369, 631; S.'s feeling of neglect from, 282; lack of public paths for walking in, 310 & n.; S. on his way to, *319*; S. hopes to return to, 373, 391, 462, 472, 481–2, 500, 525, 534, 557; never discussed in England, 405; society in, compared w. London, 413; Godwin Swift emigrates to, 497; Domville leaving for, 523; the Ladies of, 523; S. will be over in the spring, 575, 634; in a month, 665; neglect of Parnell, 597; S.'s scheme for improving, 600, 606, 612; employments in, 654; and Lords Lt. of, 654, 655 & n.; S. protests he must return to, at once, 660; S. joyless at passing his days in, 662; irregularity of post to, 671.

Ireland, Accountant General of, 479.

— Admiralty Court, 442.

— former Commissary Generals of, *see* Robinson, Sir William; Vanhomrigh, Bartholomew.

— Lords Lieutenant of, *see* Wharton, Thomas; Ormonde, 2nd Duke of; Shrewsbury, 1st Duke of; Bolton, 2nd Duke of.

— Prerogative Court in, *304*.

Irish, in London, 640; feminine character, 642.

— Archbishops and Bishops, 678–80 (*and see under their names*); 'fools', 336; and the First Fruits, 102 & n., 103, 105, 106, *185*, 311,

of hot weather, 314; of rare food, 387; of riding, *see* exercise, *supra*; of water, 322; dislike of fruit, 331.

Johnson, Esther, message from Lord Rivers for, 222.

— monetary affairs, xxviii, 73, 74, 87, 99, 246.

— movements: at Ballygall, *482*, 518; at Donnybrook, 174; returns to Dublin, 336, 340; last visit to England, xxviii, 691; goes to Ireland, xxviii; at Portrain, 579; to go to Templeogue, 540, 546; to go to Trim, 555; at Wexford, 305–6.

— obstinacy, 475.

— pet names for, 58, 166, 214, 225, 242.

— poem to S., 691.

— politics, 144, 160, 603, 634, 652; S. talks politics easily with her, 159, 160.

— portraits of: 687–703; Jervas portraits, 696, 699; miniature, 700; pastel, 700.

— property: *21*; legacy from Sir William Temple, xxvii, *74*; annuity of, in Lady Giffard's hands, xxviii, *74*.

— reading: and S.'s comments on, 150, 296, 313, 315, 324, 403, 406, 479, 510, 519, 537, 543, 554, 562, 568, 578, 582; S. sends her books and pamphlets, 395, 399, 402; surmises S.'s authorship of the *Short Character*, 148.

— relations w. other men: Lt. Bernage, 372; Dr. Griffiths, 631; James Leigh, *9*; William Lloyd, xxxi, 63; Isaac Manley, xxxi, *12*, 290; Dean Stearne, xxxi, 13; Enoch Sterne, 204, 383; Rev. W. Tisdall, xxxi–xxxv; Rev. and Mrs. Walls, xxxi.

— skull of, 691.

— social attitude towards, xxix.

— spelling and English, S. corrects and instructs her in, *33*, 85, 123, 234, 354, 388, 392–3, 418, 426, 459, 512, 639.

— stranger inquires for, at Court, 138.

Johnson, Esther, writings, 340, 391, 420, 457, 482, 691.

— and S.'s family portraits, 496–7, 701.

— and S.'s snuff-box, *31*, 254, 559.

— alleged change in tone of S.'s letters to, xxxvii–xli.

— alleged marriage to S., xxxv, xxxvi, *2*.

— allowance from S., *see* Swift financial affairs, &c.

— commissions for S., 42, 63, 81, 97, 112, 126, 134, 234, 255, 389, 390, 395, 398, 402, 549, 561, 669–70.

— dines with S. and Jervas, 696.

— first meeting, xxiv.

— letters, early, xvii, xlvii; she writes w. her eyes shut, 109.

— loves only him, 153.

— petitions S. w. many apologies, 564.

— poem to S., 691.

— reproaches S., 314, 665; fails to reproach, 233.

— S. calls her a *virtuoso*, 97.

— S. calls her malicious, 664; lazy, 670.

— S. complains of her puns, *33*, 250.

— S. imagines her peeping from the windows of her expensive lodgings, 224.

— S. praises or criticizes her beauty, 210, 382, 402, 410, 520; carriage, and walk, 409; docility, 459; opinion, 127; tact, 168, 333, 487, 631, 666; wisdom, 472, 520, 647; wit, 385.

— S. refers to, as male, 387, 449, 450, 475; wishes she were a young man, 245.

— S. talks politics easily with her, 159, 160.

— S. urges her to be a careful housewife, 186, 266 et seq.

— S. visualizes her, 410–11.

— S.'s early education of, xxvi.

— S.'s fear of losing credit w., 525, 534.

Index

Kilmainham, *408*.

Kilmore, Bishop of, *see* Wettenhall, Edward.

Kilmore, Prebendary of, *see* Price, Rev. John.

Kilmoylan, co. Galway, *288*.

Kilroot, xxxi.

Kimberley, Jonathan, Dean of Lichfield, and Chaplain to the Speaker, *660*.

King, William, Archbishop of Dublin, xv, xvii, xxix, 7, *105*, 106, 108, 219, 233, *695–6*; S.'s commissions signed by, xx, *2*, *68*, *69*, *80*, *676*, *695*; S.'s letters to, *5* & n., 6, 7, 8, *45*, *49*, *50*, *66*, 80, 81, 90, 103, 114, 144, 145, 151, 155, *211*, *235*, *261*, 293, 297, 312, *332*, *334*, *336*, *345*, *359*, *363*, *372*, *374*, 401, *432*, 449, 457, *525*, *526*, *527*, *599*, *648*; his letters to S., 102 & n., 141, 180 & n., 225, 277, 288, 293, *332–3*, 359, *407–8*, 414, *452*, *526*, *599*, *643*; his *De Origine Mali*, 7; Whig principles, 7; correspondent of Southwell's, *40*; and the First Fruits, 114, 151, 155, 307; his reference to S.'s *Short Character of Wharton*, *115*; his friend Richardson, 229; and Guiscard's attack, 236 & n., 237, 238, 277; a tale about his indiscretion, 236, 251; S. defends him, 251, 253, 261; but fears he is guilty, 253; his letter of 'a squabble', *282*; advises S. to be mentioned in Harley's letter to the Irish bishops, 347; advises S. to seek preferment and to write on Divinity, 359 & n.; sends Walls as a messenger to S., 368; S. accused of being his agent, 387; Stella's parody of his letter to S., 391; recalls Dillon Ashe, 413; complaints against, 449, 488; S.'s distrust of, 457; S. praises to the Duchess of Shrewsbury, 518; and S.'s advancement, 663.

King, William, Judge of the Admiralty Court in Ireland, *442*; his satirical pieces, *442*; death of his footman, 442; S. gets him the *Gazette*, 452 & n., 543; to dine w. St. John, 452.

King, William, Principal of St. Mary Hall, Oxford, satirizes John Pratt, *14*; author of *The Toast*, *14*; and of *Political and Literary Anecdotes*, *665*; and the Queen's refusal to prefer S., *665*.

Kingdom, state of, 681.

Kingdom, Jane, Maid of Honour, 639 & n.

King's Bench, *see* Prisons.

King's Evil (scrofula), Queen Anne and touching for, *264*; S. recommends a lad to be touched by the Queen, 264; Dr. Johnson and, *264*; Lord Masham's child and, 488, 517.

King's Lynn, Anne Long retires to, xlii, *17*, 119, 445; Sir Robert Walpole, M.P. for, *442*.

Kingsmill, Sir William, of Sidmonton, *282*; his dau. Anne, m. Heneage Finch, *282*.

Kingston, *650*.

Kingstown, *2*.

Kinnoull, Thomas Hay, 7th Earl of, and the rising of 1715, *348*; S. dines w., 348; his dau. m. Earl of Mar, *348*.

Kinsale, *40*, *95*, 246.

Kit-Cat Club, *75*, *320*.

Kitchens, the Royal, the Society's dinner prepared in, *525*; *see also* Eckershall, James; Green Cloth.

Kneller, Sir Godfrey, portrait painter, 42, *697*; persuaded to paint S., 114; to copy a painting of Guiscard 491; his portrait of Lady Orkney, 617, 628.

Knight, an unknown, solicits £2,000 per annum, 341.

Knights of the Garter, 139, 562, 600.

Knightsbridge, 619.

Knightsbrook, *429*.

Königsmark, Count, suitor to Baroness Percy, 206.

Index

Index

Index

Middleton, Simon, of Edmonton, father of 2nd Mrs. Harley, *135, 591*.

Midhurst, *120*.

Midsummer Day, 379.

Midwinter, Edward, printer, *572*.

Mildmay, Benjamin, later Earl Fitzwalter, *298*.

Military power, S.'s views on, *133*.

Militia, the, 415.

Milles, Thomas, Bishop of Waterford and Lismore, 316 & n.; dislikes S. and S. dislikes him, 316.

Millington, Francis, Commissioner of Customs, father of Lady Mansell, *228*.

Millington, Sir Thomas, 1st Physician, *513*.

Milnes, Richard Monckton, later Lord Houghton, said to have possessed a leaf of the *Journal, l*.

Milton, John, *40, 86*.

Miniature of the Queen, a, *659*.

Miniatures of S. and Stella, 692, 700.

Ministry, The, inquiry into corruptions of, 152; no good puns from, 153; nothing thrives under, 159; hear S. with regard, 159; character of members, 159, 160, *178, 179*; Marlborough's go-between and, 176; S.'s opinion that ministries neglect companions of pleasure, 194; and the October Club, *194, 195*; beg S. to stay in England, 205; S.'s description of their dilemma, 206; and the keeping open of places, 226; S. used barbarously by late, 233; S.'s credit w. the, 241, 303; character of late, 249, 492; ill management of the Treasury by late, 253; S. expects no reward from, 343; and the detention of Prior, 349; come to Windsor, 365; unsteady, 429; S. regards, as ruined, 439; the Queen intends to change, 440; 'desperate', 452; Ormonde a staunch supporter of, 472; delay in providing materials for S., 556; and the Hamilton–Abercorn dispute, 588; and Sir Thomas

Hanmer, 625; S.'s surprise that they let him go, 662; the late, 682.

Mint, The, 506.

Miscellanies, by Dryden, *191*.

Miscellanies, by Pope and S. (1727), *510*.

Miscellanies, by S., *see* Swift: Works of.

Miscellany, by Charles Gildon, *282*.

Miscellany, by Jacob Tomson (1709), includes works by Pope, Philips, &c., *129*.

Miscellany Poems, by Anne Finch, *282*.

Mohocks, the, 508 & n., 509 & n., 511, 515, 516, 524, 525; S. fears, 516; vanished, 522.

Mohun, Charles Mohun, 4th Baron, Maccartney, his second, *120*; his second wife, *513*; killed in a duel w. Duke of Hamilton, 570–2; a notorious rake, *571*.

Moimed, *see* Moymet.

Moira, Earl of, 688.

Molesworth, John, afterw. 2nd Viscount Molesworth, 26, 29; S. dines w., 26, 36, 68; fifth *Drapier's Letter* addressed to, 26; Envoy to Turin, 26.

Molesworth, Richard, afterw. 3rd Viscount, 29.

Molesworth, Robert, 1st Viscount, 26, 526 & n.

Molière, J.-B., 422.

Molt, Mr., Dublin chemist, 541.

Molyneux, Samuel, Secretary to the Prince of Wales and M.P., *567*; wishes S. to present him to Harley, 567; friend of Locke, 567.

Molyneux, William, M.P. and Irish patriot, father of Samuel, *567*; his *Case of Ireland, &c.*, 567 & n.

Monaghan, 227, 289.

Monck, Charles Stanley, Viscount, 699; the Monck Stella, 699, 700.

Monck, the, a frigate, *268*.

Monmouth, Duke of, 627 & n.

Montagu, Edward Wortley, M.P., 65, *314*; S. dines w., 65.

Index

Old Bailey, *264*, *578*.

'Old club', *see* Saturday Club.

Oldfield, Mrs., actress, *654* & n.

Oldisworth, William, revives *The Examiner*, *254*; and a payment of 20 gns., *637*.

Oldmixon, John, editor, *254*; and *The Medley*, *254*; and S.'s *Proposal*, *535*.

Ombre, a card game, *43*, *51*, *53*, *78*, *111*, *121*, *247*, *298–9*, *336*, *349*, *360*, *374*, *382*, *384*, *386*, *397*, *414*, *516*, *519*, *522*, *537*, *551*, *555*, *606*, *632*, *637*, *646*; Stella's spelling of, *354*; Mrs. Manley forswears, *388*; S. loses at, *570*, *616*, *621–2*, *624*, *631*, *634*, *635*, *658*; S. plays, w. Mrs. Vanhomrigh, *597*; S. wins at, *615*, *626*, *646*; running, *622*, *634*; and the Spanish Envoy, *636*; and the duc d'Estrées, *626*.

One Hundred Pounds, S. dispenses, *648–9*.

Onslow, Sir Richard, M.P. for Surrey, later Baron Onslow, *55*; Chancellor of the Exchequer, *55*.

Opera, the, *439*, *481*; Charles Ford and, *ix*, *144*, *162*, *171*, *188*, *197*, *200*, *207*; German musician's scheme for, *482*.

Oppy, *336*.

Orange, Prince of, *see* William III.

Oranges, a suspicious present of, for S., *605*; Harley toys w., *637*; *see also* Fruit.

Order for an Address, moved, opposed, and passed, *657*; for a Warrant for the 3 vacant Deaneries, *660*.

Ordnance, Master of, *see* Rivers, Lord, and Marlborough.

Ordnance, Stationers to, *455*, *464*, *465*.

Orford, Edward Russell, Earl of, *xiii*.

Orkney, Elizabeth (Villiers), Countess of, sister to Earl of Jersey, *345*, *580*, *619*, *644*; mistress of William III, *345*, *537*; assists S.'s writing, *557*; the wisest woman S. knows, *558*;

Harley and, *558*; S. sits w., *565*, and dines w., *581*, *584*, *667*; her gifts to S., *569*; her squint and her motherliness, *570*; S. reconciles her to her sister-in-law, *574*; S. goes to Wimbledon w., *594*; ill, *601*; gives her portrait to S., *617*, *628* & n.; her daughter, Henrietta, *628*; out of town, *634*; comes to town, *641*; doses S., *634*, *645*.

Orkney, George Hamilton, 6th Earl of, son of 3rd Duke of Hamilton, *557*, *570*, *574*, *590*, *592*, *594*, *603*, *604*, *610*, *611*, *612*, *616*, *625*, *644*, *657*, *659*.

Ormonde, James Butler, 1st Duke of, Lord Lt. of Ireland, *546*, *700*.

Ormonde, James Butler, 2nd Duke of, *8*, *9*, *11*, *34*, *65*, *69*, *78*, *88*, *96*, *282*, *285*, *332*, *425*, *474*, *503*, *507*, *508*, *515*, *523*, *544*, *559*, *582*, *590*, *595*, *603*, *604*, *606*, *618*, *636*, *644*, *646*, *648*, *653*, *658*, *677*, *679*; Lord Lt. of Ireland, *xiii*, *xv*, *8*, *50*, *53*, *63*; Deanery of St. Patrick in his gift, *xlvii*, *662*, *664*, *666*; befriends Capt. John Pratt, *14*; S. presents Charles Ford to, *15*; Irish bishops address, *102*; connexion w. First Fruits, *102*, *103*, *106*, *205*, *254*, *291*, *333*, *334*, *336*, *368*, *388*; against Bishop of Clogher's promotion, *130* & n.; letters from, *132*; going to Ireland, *204*, *254*, *263*; his exile, *204*; his second wife, *204*; S. presents Richardson to, *207*; breaks an appointment, *221*, *460*; sends for S., *235*; at the House of Commons, *235*; S. commends Beaumont to, *263*, *266*, *288*; S. suggests Price apply as his chaplain, *288*; his speech in Parliament to include mention of the First Fruits, *291*; at Chester, *299*; Stella and, *301*; censured, *364*; his character, *364*; brings away Irish society, *413*; returning to England, *414*, *431*; present at debate in the House, *432*;

Index

Index

Pewter plate, 378.

Philip, Duke of Anjou, King of Spain, *489, 575, 585,* 651.

Philip V, King of Spain, *489.*

Philips, Ambrose, poet, and secretary to Archbishop Boulter, xvii, 129 & n.; his *Pastorals, 129;* called 'Namby-Pamby', 129; S. solicits for a place at Geneva for, 129; S. never saw, 209; S. dines w., 297; tutor to Simon Harcourt, *297;* asks S. to support him, 304, 589; goes to Bath w. Addison, 342; dines w. S. and Addison, 360; walks in The Mall w. S., 589.

Phipps, Sir Constantine, Lord Chancellor of Ireland, 118 & n., 157, *157–8;* Raymond to be recommended to, 162; and the First Fruits, *185.*

Physicians to the Queen: S. designs to turn them all out, 311; summoned to Windsor, 557; Sir Thomas Lawrence, 513 & n.; *and see* Arbuthnot, John; Freind, John; and Radcliffe, John.

— to former sovereigns: Sir Thomas Lawrence, 513 & n.; Sir Thomas Millington, *513.*

Picquet, 364, *429,* 521, 549; Twelvepenny, 375; S. wins at, 417, 508; pools, 508, 617; S. loses at, in Windsor, 556; Stella and, 556; Crown, 617.

Picture auction, 593, 633, 636, 642, 645; S. buys an alleged Titian at, 633; Lord Masham and, 633, 636; S. spends 14*s.* at, 636.

Pierrepont, Lady Mary (Lady Mary Wortley Montagu), 65, *286.*

Pilkington, Laetitia, 692.

Pillory, the, *644.*

Pinchback, Christopher, father and son, *647.*

Pins, Stella's, 670.

Pipe Office, *295.*

Pistole, a, 160 & n.; value of, *160, 321;* S. gives one to Patty Rolt, *321.*

Pitsligo, *318.*

Plague, the, S.'s fear of, 115; at Newcastle, 115, 118, 184, *185;* and Stella's fears, 459; at Hamburg, 564.

Plantations, nr. Windsor, 363.

Plautus, *422.*

Plays, 302; Patrick goes to see, 301; Dillon Ashe goes to see, 318, 341, 348; Addison's *Cato,* rehearsal of, 654.

Plot upon Plot, a ballad, *573.*

Plumer, Anne, dau. of Col. John, m. Lord Paisley, 205 & n.

Plumer, Col. John, of Blakesware, Herts., *205.*

Plutarch, 601.

Poddle, river, 691.

Poetical Miscellanies, by Sir R. Steele, *54.*

Poetical Miscellanies: The Sixth Part, published by J. Tonson, xiv, *54.*

Poetry sells ill, 646.

Poets, Whig, S. solicits for, 304.

Polignac, Abbé Melchior de, diplomat and politician, 373 & n.

Political State of Great Britain, by A. Boyer, *271, 384, 573, 608, 609.*

Pomfret, *see* Pontefract.

Pompey, black servant of Col. Hill, 104.

Pontac, Arnaud de, and his son, *334.*

Pontack, Mr., innkeeper, 334 & n.

Pontack's, *see* Taverns.

Pontchartrain, Comte de, Secretary of State in France, 404 & n.

Pontefract, Baron, 545 & n.

Pontefract Castle, 545 & n., 550 & n.

Pooley, John, Bishop of Raphoe, *354;* S.'s character of, 354; his career, *354;* his death, 567; his successor, 567 & n.

Pooley, Tom, brother of above, a painter, 641 & n.

Pools, 508, 617.

Pope, the, effigy in Guy Fawkes procession, 404; effigy in Queen Elizabeth's birthday procession, 415, 416, 417; S. sees, 421; Savage kneels to, 423.

Index

Index

Index

Index

Index

Index

PRINTED IN GREAT BRITAIN
AT THE UNIVERSITY PRESS, OXFORD
BY VIVIAN RIDLER
PRINTER TO THE UNIVERSITY